MOSQUES & MIRACLES

Revealing Islam and God's Grace

By Stuart Robinson

PRAISE FOR
MOSQUES & MIRACLES

There is little doubt that the principalities and powers behind Islam have set in place formidable obstacles to the spread of the Gospel. The first step toward binding this strongman is to understand its foundations and operating principles. No one has helped us see Islam for what it really is more than Stuart Robinson in his revealing book, *Mosques & Miracles*.

C. Peter Wagner, *Chancellor*
Wagner Leadership Institute
Colorado Springs, USA

Here at last with encyclopaedic scope, profound biblical insight and scholarly intellectual balance is the indispensable landmark handbook on Islam, for which all concerned Christians have been waiting. Stuart Robinson has done the worldwide church a signal favour by alerting us all not only to the perils and challenges presented by militant Islam today, but also to the missionary opportunities this sets before all Christians everywhere.

Michael Cassidy
African Enterprise
KwaZulu-Natal, South Africa

Stuart Robinson has done our homework for us - he has researched and documented the most pertinent information relating to the current moment in Islam. *Mosques & Miracles* is a fact-filled book, but also a page-turner. It is a valuable tool for anyone ministering to, praying for, or thinking about Muslims all over the world.

Ted Haggard, *Senior Pastor*
New Life Church and President of
The National Association of Evangelicals USA
Colorado Springs, USA

Mosques & Miracles is a remarkable and revealing compendium on the whole issue of Islam that is facing the global church today. Stuart Robinson provides the reader with a virtual library of vital insights on this critical subject that no thinking pastor, Christian leader or lay person can afford to ignore.

Dr. Dick Eastman, *International President*
Every Home for Christ
Colorado Springs, USA

PRAISE FOR
MOSQUES & MIRACLES

Mosques & Miracles is one of the most important books any of us could read today. Stuart Robinson has done a brilliant job of making an incredibly complex subject easily read and stirringly inspirational. It is a shrill trumpet blast to the church to awaken to our enormous calling to reach the world. I'm recommending *Mosques & Miracles* to leaders everywhere. We cannot afford to be ignorant of the realities presented in this book.

Pastor Phil Pringle OAM, *Senior Minister*
Christian City Church Oxford Falls
Founder and President, Christian City Church International
Sydney, Australia

Islam is a great challenge to Global Harvest and Christian Missions. Understanding this religion's strategy, psyche and phenomenon will help gird us in a more valuable way to be effective witnesses for Christ. God's heart breaks for Muslim people everywhere. We must show His love to Muslims and Dr Stuart Robinson's outstanding book, *Mosque & Miracles* is a unique resource that will draw us closer to a world-wide understanding concerning Islam's foundational belief's, values and life-style.

Pastor Jack Hanes, *President*
AOG World Missions
Sydney, *Australia*

Now more than ever it is vital for Christians to pray, think and minister with discernment and spiritual understanding toward Muslims. Stuart Robinson has invested many years doing just that. His landmark book, *Mosques & Miracles* combines compassion with biblical fidelity. Any Christian who wants to see the Great Commission fulfilled will quickly see that this book is an important milestone. *Mosques & Miracles* will help you understand the Islamic world and respond with biblical insight and sensitivity to this paramount challenge to the Church.

David Shibley, *President*
Global Advance
Dallas, Texas, USA

PRAISE FOR
MOSQUES & MIRACLES

The tension between Christianity and Islam is emerging as one of the most crucial concerns of the 21st Century. I cannot think of a better way to enlighten your understanding on this significant issue than through reading this outstanding book by Stuart Robinson whose years of experience and research make him a world class authority on this subject.

Mark Conner, *Senior Pastor*
Waverley Christian Fellowship
Melbourne, Australia.

I commend Dr Stuart Robinson's latest book, *Mosques & Miracles*. Robinson has spent years as a practitioner among Muslims in southern Asia. He is an intelligent and accomplished participant-researcher. His years as a pastor of a large church in Australia have added an enhanced perspective to his writings.

Mosques & Miracles is an excellent overview of Islam. There are startling revelations as Robinson documents Muslim strategy to reach out and convert the world. A concise explanation of Islamic doctrine and practice follows. The relevant issues relating to a contextualised witness to Muslims are also explored.

There are many documented cases where Muslims have come to Christ through the medium of dreams, visions, healings and other miraculous happenings. Robinson has widely researched these occurrences and presents them with available documentation.

There is an abundance of footnotes which indicates the author has sought to go beyond just his personal experience. The glossary is extremely helpful. Robinson's bibliography is extensive and current.

Informed laypeople who are interested in Great Commission Christianity along with missionaries who are ministering among Muslims will welcome this excellent book. It will also be appreciated by mission professors who now have a contemporary tool to aid them in teaching on the subject of Islam.

Dr. Phil Parshall, *Islamic Specialist*
SIM International
Philippines

M
&
M

PRAISE FOR
MOSQUES & MIRACLES

Having worked among Muslims for the last 30 years and having personally experienced the terror of jihad and miraculous conversions, I welcome Stuart Robinson's excellently researched work *Mosques & Miracles*.

Three of my staff were slain by jihad terrorists. My wife, daughter and I were detained by jihad soldiers while headless bodies were stretched out across the road. A church in which I was preaching was attacked by jihad soldiers and a gunbattle ensued only 30 metres from the building. A mortar came through the roof but failed to explode. We helped rescue 1700 Christian villagers attacked by an Islamic army and force-converted. All were force-circumsized, men, women and children.

On the other hand we have seen many Muslims come to know Christ through healings, visions and angelic visits. Currently we are conducting mass meetings with hungry Islamic clerics of up to 350 at a time who are seeking for answers, seeking for the Saviour. That's why *Mosques & Miracles* is very timely. It provides a tool both to better equip Christians to deal with the rise of Islam as well as a wake-up call to the church. It is not all gloom, it is also a message of hope and faith that Christ died for Muslims and many are responding to His amazing grace. Reading, understanding and acting upon *Mosques & Miracles* is a must for all Christians who care about the type of community and nation that we will bequeath to our children. Let us respond to this challenge through faith and help set the Islamic world free to know the love and saving power of our Lord Jesus Christ.

Dr. Raymond Schultz, *Front line Missionary*
Indonesia.

Mosques & Miracles is a masterly honest account of Islam in today's world. It is based on sound research, a love for Muslim people and a lifetime of involvement with them. This book will alarm and challenge you. Hopefully, it will also encourage you to genuinely love Muslim people and pray earnestly for them.

Dr. Ian Hawley, *General Director*
Global InterAction Inc.
Melbourne, Australia.

MOSQUES & MIRACLES

Revealing Islam and God's Grace

By Stuart Robinson

CityHarvest®
Publications

Published by

CityHarvest Publications
PO Box 6462
Upper Mt Gravatt Qld 4122 Australia

www.cityharvest.org.au
chp@cityharvest.org.au

SECOND EDITION
FIFTH PRINTING

Mosques and Miracles
Copyright © 2004 by Stuart Robinson
ISBN 0-957-79055-4

Scripture quotations in this publication are from the *Holy Bible*, *New International Version* (NIV). Copyright 1973, 1978, 1984 International Bible Society, Zondervan Bible Publishers. All rights reserved.

Quranic quotations and references unless otherwise indicated are from *The Holy Qur-an* English translation of the meanings and Commentary, Revised and Edited by The Presidency of Islamic Researchers, IFTA, Call and Guidance, Mushaf Al-Madinah Al-Munawarah, The Kingdom of Saudi Arabia 1411 H (1991 CE).

Interior design by Ben F. Gray.

Cover design by David Gray. Christian World Media, Brisbane, Australia.

WITH GRATITUDE

I dedicate this second edition:

To Ben, Dave and Jenny of CityHarvest
who never wavered, lost hope or gave up.
They persevered in spite of extraordinary personal and
professional difficulties to produce not one but hopefully
two best selling editions of Mosques & Miracles.

To my grandchildren Hadassah, Obed and Kalani,
with the prayer that they will enjoy the same freedoms
in their time as I have in mine.

By the same author:

– *Praying the Price* (1994) Sovereign World & Regal Renew
– *Positioning for Power* (1998) Sovereign World & Regal Renew

CONTENTS

M&M

FOREWORD *By J. David Pawson*

Stuart Robinson and I have a great deal in common. We are both Baptist pastors, with an evangelical theology and a charismatic experience. Our preaching, rooted in the Bible, has a clear prophetic dimension.

And we are convinced that Islam presents a far greater challenge to Christianity than communism ever did, not least because we see it as a supernatural power and not just a religious or political phenomena. Therefore we are involved in spiritual warfare, in which carnal weapons (military, legal, etc.) are totally inappropriate.

We share a common shame and embarrassment over the state of the Church, both in Arabia in Mohammed's day and in the Western world today, effectively replenishing Muslim ammunition.

We are willing to speak out, whatever the cost or consequence, to a Church that seems unaware of and unprepared for an encounter with the fastest growing and second largest religion in the world. We are frustrated by the disparity between what Christians *need* to know and what they *want* to know.

But there the similarity ends. Stuart has ministered in a Muslim country; I have not. He has done far more research than I, packing this book with quotes and facts, which make his case unanswerable.

Above all, he is far more able to advise on mission to Muslims, having more knowledge and experience at a personal and practical level.

But, I share his ultimate optimism, knowing that the power of the Holy Spirit is greater than any other and that our Lord Jesus Christ, who is the Word, will have the last word in human history.

I have read many books on this vital subject, but this was the best.

J. David Pawson, M.A., B. Sc.
Basingstoke, England.

I

FOREWORD *By Brother Andrew*

Yet another book on Islam? Yes! We are hundreds of years behind in our research and study of this great subject, not to mention our outreach to the hundreds of millions of adherents of that religion. Admittedly, any analysis is incomplete. The subject is simply too big, our experience too little, our insight too one-sided, their culture too complicated, their zeal too radical for us to be fully understood and, maybe, the prospect of their expansion and future too frightening to us. Certainly their dedication is!!!

So why am I so happy with this new book? Simply put – because there is a great need for it and the author speaks from a deep experience, a profound understanding and a love for people. The latter is absolutely essential if we want to make an impact on the world of Islam, a name we have to start spelling as: '**I S**incerely **L**ove **A**ll **M**uslims'. That alone will help us to earn the right to their attention.

My prayer is that this book will do exactly that. It is not too late. All of us can play a role in it, all of us can be witnesses. And that begins with understanding.

As I write this, I happen to open one of my old notebooks from the 1960s, where I made the following entry:

'The vice president of the International World Court, Muhammed Safrullah Khan, is called "the greatest Muslim missionary to Europe". It is already established that Sir Muhammed Safrullah Khan performs the same role for the Islamisation of Europe, which Boniface accomplished for Christianity'. (quoted from the 'Islam')

Have we been sleeping those 40 years? Wake up, read this book, pray and ask what God wants you to do.

Brother Andrew
President Emeritus Open Doors
Netherlands

THE UNIQUENESS OF
'MOSQUES & MIRACLES'

There is no published attempt known to the author and publisher that seeks to piece together the international mosaic of Islam's contemporary progress in hitherto non-Muslim countries. This is the object of Part One – What's Happening?

Similarly, there is no known published attempt to date, to summarise comprehensively what God has been supernaturally initiating within Islam. Nor is there any recently published, well-tested, 'successful', practical guide on how to minister effectively to Muslims. This is the province of Part Three – Response – God and Us.

Part Two – Why It's Happening, is foundational to understanding and unravelling the spiritual and intellectual strands of Parts One and Three.

The text of *Mosques & Miracles* is deliberately written in an easy to read journalistic style. Each chapter has been meticulously documented in Endnotes at the conclusion of the book.

In addition to the main text, the Appendix outlines one simple, well-tested and effective approach for witnessing to Muslims.

Another compelling reason for publishing this book, is the decline in publishing definitive work on Islam since the surge of the 1980s. The author sees a great need to educate the upcoming generation on what is happening and how to respond.

As one well-placed British source who read the original manuscript stated, 'I would like to see a copy of this book in the hands of every British Member of Parliament'.

The final uniqueness of this book is in its ultimate optimism that Jesus Christ, God's Son, will have the last word on the affairs of man and all of human history.

PREFACE

Seldom does an author have the privilege of writing a second edition of any book. The first edition represented three decades of research, observation and experience compressed into four years of writing, rewriting, updating, field testing and almost endless correction of the text. Not surprisingly, in spite of the best efforts of many, there were still innumerable mistakes in the first edition.

When the publisher notified me of the necessity of a reprint, I requested permission to do all the corrections and to add new material throughout the text to account for much which had happened in the twelve months since the first manuscript was completed. He not only agreed to my request but generously allowed more pages for the new material. This is every author's dream.

The great challenge in addressing a subject such as Islam, in its historical development and the vast array of its many contemporary forms, is how does one avoid generalisations. Not all Muslims think and act the same. Some critics have rightly pointed this out. I readily agree. But all Muslims must agree to certain fundamentals of faith and practice or else they cannot be Muslim. It is in the call to conformity offered universally by religious leaders where individual differences blur or disappear – even if reluctantly. As one Muslim professor advised me, within the Muslim community survival depends more upon belonging than believing. That reality is a powerful factor for inducing conformity whenever needed, irrespective of individual opinion.

The second major challenge was how to achieve a positive change in attitude toward Muslims at a time of heightened international religious tension, caused by so many well documented international events, as well as a host of misunderstandings at local levels. Certainly this could not be achieved through a head in the sand (or the clouds) denial of what has happened and what is likely to continue to happen. Facts must be faced, no matter how brutal, unnerving or unpleasant. Christianity itself hardly has a history of unblemished innocence. But that is not the subject of this book. Although the content of this book is not 'feel good' to massage our egos or boost self esteem, it seeks to move more readers from ignorance or antipathy to an appreciation of what has happened and is happening on a vast scale, why this is so, and especially to encourage by recording what God is doing. In the process I had hoped that readers, in spite of my own mistakes, misinterpretations or other failings would end up by sharing my love and concern for Muslims and see them as God sees them, not as contemporary antagonists may wish to caricature them.

I am delighted with every letter I have received telling me of each reader's increase in understanding, love and prayer for all Muslims. May this in the end be your outcome as well.

Perhaps the first edition sold so well because on the day of its release war broke out again in the Middle East. What does one call that remarkable coincidence of events - supernatural marketing management?

May God enlighten you and sharpen your discernment for challenges and opportunities ahead – as you read.

Stuart Robinson
August 2003

INTRODUCTION

'In the next fifty years we will capture the Western world for Islam. We have the men to do it, we have the money to do it and above all we are already doing it.'[1]

So said a Muslim religious leader at the opening of yet another Islamic centre – this time in Stockholm, Sweden. An estimated 300 000 Muslims live in Sweden, making them the second largest religious group in the country after Protestant Christianity.[2]

According to Muslim strategists winning the West to Islam is already underway. The struggle is keenly anticipated and well defined.

Akbar S. Ahmed expressed it thus:

Two global civilisations appear to be poised in a complex confrontation on various levels of human activity. One is based in Muslim countries and the other in the West...Commentators are already seeing the confrontation in apocalyptic terms and calling it the Last Crusade.[3]

Islam is as determined to win this 'crusade' as it did those earlier military skirmishes of the Middle Ages that bore that title. Christian leaders are also at last starting to take note of what is happening in their midst.

In 1995, Don Richardson, best known as the author of *Peace Child* and other widely read Christian books, went on record as saying, 'Anyone in the world who does not become a Christian in the next two decades...will probably become a Muslim or at least will have been urged to join Islam ten, fifteen or twenty times.' This is becoming a reality.

Events within the already established Muslim world increasingly daily dominate our news headlines. 'Open any newspaper on any day of the week and you will find that much of the most troubling news comes from the Middle East and elsewhere in the Islamic world.'.[4]

We are informed of:

- ongoing repercussions from the Gulf Wars of 1991 and 2003;
- tensions of Middle East diplomacy;
- the vast oil wealth and influence of the OPEC nations;
- Muslim militancy in Somalia and Sudan;
- prolonged warfare in Afghanistan;
- Iraq or Chechnya;
- the long anticipated 'Islamic bomb' first unveiled in the form of a series of six nuclear explosions in Pakistan during May 28–30 1998;
- burning of churches and social upheaval in Indonesia;
- simmering tensions in the southern Philippines.

In October 1999 the United States Department of State made its legally mandated biennial declaration of 'Foreign Terrorist Organisations' (FTOs). Secretary of State Madeleine Albright designated 28 organisations. Of these 15 were identifiably Islamic.[5]

When the USA declared 'War on Terror' in 2001 again topping the hit list were Islamic organisations. Wherever one looks from Morocco to Mindanao, vast stirring movements are underway which could change the face of international relationships, political and religious alliances well into this millennium.

Allahu Akbar, God is Greater, is the familiar shout which is on the lips of teeming crowds processioning through the streets of many of the world's cities even beyond the traditional heartland of Islam. Instead of a calm statement of faith, a voiced hope for a better future, that shout heard almost daily on TV newscasts, has come to sound more like a war cry, a threat thundered against any who might hold other opinions. Allah is God. Muhammad is his prophet. The Quran is the holy book, the contents of which are meant to guide the whole of life.

At the beginning of the twentieth century it was estimated that the number of Muslims was slightly fewer than 12% of the world's population. By 1970 their percentage of world population had increased to 15.3%. By the year 2000 it was 19.6%.[6]

During the same period Christianity as a proportion of world population remained static at 33%[7], although some researchers calculate it may have declined to 28%.

This means that today, there are now over 1.2 billion people in the world living in over 165 countries whose 'irreversible' primary allegiance is to the faith and practice of Islam. From a Christian perspective they represent 70% of the world's unevangelised people.[8]

In over 40 nation states Muslims form a majority of the population. Of the 25 top super cities in the world (ie. those with populations of more than 10 million each) six are predominantly Muslim: Cairo, Dhaka, Istanbul, Jakarta, Karachi and Teheran. It has been estimated that by the year 2020, at current growth rates, the number of Muslims in the world will be 1.9 billion or more significantly, an increase to 25% of humanity. This represents one of the most dramatic shifts in global religious adherence that the world has ever seen. One of the reasons for this was summed up in 1996 by a Kuwaiti jurist who said, 'We always remind those who convert to Islam that they enter through a door but that there is no way out.'[9]

It is estimated (approximately) that there could be up to 17 million Muslims living in Europe. Islam has also become North America's fastest growing religion. In the United States there are now approximately 6 million Muslims, 44% of whom were born there. At the current rate of change some estimate that many major American cities may be predominantly Muslim within two decades.[10] Others go even further projecting that 'if the present trends continue, Islam could become the predominant religion in the US by the year 2020.'.[11]

In Africa mosques are being built from Cairo to the Cape. In London mosques have increased from two to over 400 in the last 25 years and Islamic shops display signs saying, 'Muhammad came to rule'. Fareed Zakaria said, 'Islamic expansion has been accelerated by "oil money from Saudi Arabia and the gulf states (which) has funded puritanical schools, mosques and foundations...This has been a state sponsored export."'[12]

The single-minded commitment of some Islamic leaders is almost unknown and unmatched in Western democracies. In June 1997 Al Mansour, an Algerian leader said, 'The army can't enter here – they don't like to die. We want to die every day.'.[13] He and his cadres have practised daily what Christians believe in theory. His colleagues push their theology and practice even further. On September 22 1997 after yet another massacre in Algeria, the armed wing of the Filisteen al-Muslima (FIS), declared a ceasefire. But Gama'at al-Islamiya (GIA) issued a declaration on September 26 which clearly spelled out where they intended to head. They faxed the Arab daily, Al-Hayat in London and said:

We are the group that kills and murders with Allah's permission. We will continue to do this until the word of religion has won and the word of Allah prevails. Let everyone know that what we are doing (killing, murdering and pillaging) is very close to Allah...Therefore we let you know that according to our faith and ways there will be no dialogue, no truce and no reconciliation.[14]

After the bombing of the US Marines' Battalion Headquarters in Lebanon Sheikh Muhammad Yazbeck speaking at a rally in nearby Baalbeck said, 'Let America, Israel and the world know that we have a lust for martyrdom and our motto is being translated into reality.'.[15]

That dangerous desire remains constant. Years later a suicide bomber destroyed himself and a bus in Tel Aviv, Israel. A leader of Hamas, the group who claimed responsibility for the destruction declared, 'Our love for death is greater than our love for life.'.[16]

Relationships between Muslim leaders and those of other religions and/or political entities have seldom been uniformly harmonious in the long-term. From the time of the Iranian revolution in 1979 which toppled the Shah and transformed Iran, the degree of tension and the intensity of denigration seem to have increased.

Under pressure from the spread of affluent Western consumer culture some Muslim leaders claim that Westerners want to 'transform the entire world into an entertainment house where they are free to perpetuate their evil deeds.'.[17] Furthermore Western leaders are 'Satan inspired, out to create havoc everywhere especially among Muslim states like Iraq, Algeria, Afghanistan...'.[18] This conclusion was summed up in a sermon delivered in Mecca's Grand Mosque to pilgrims on the annual Hajj to Mecca, on the first day of Eid al Adha (2000 CE). In his sermon Sheikh Abdul Rahman al Saud urged Muslims to 'shun Western traditions and materialism'. He added 'globalisation would lead to Western domination of Islamic nation(s).'.[19]

With the threat of having all nations becoming Islamic states and governed by Islamic law *(shariah)* the 'Christian' world is becoming somewhat uneasy, and with some cause. Open Doors, an organisation monitoring persecution, has noted that of the 25 states throughout the world in which Christians are most persecuted, 21 are Muslim.[20] This hardly builds confidence for peaceful Muslim–Christian relationships in the immediate future, irrespective of how many declarations of peacefulness are made by minority Muslim leaders in the West after the New York September 11 events.

The Islamic challenge to the church if not Western society, is no longer something in the far distance that can be ignored. Increasingly it is in all of our cities and neighbourhoods – now! Islam and Christianity are on a pathway of confrontation. Both take their message to the peoples of the world. Both are sure that they represent ultimate truth. However if history is any guide coexistence between these two great missionary faiths will be uneasy at best or something more akin to open warfare at worst – if we allow it to develop into that.

Islam is also the only religion in the world that has conquered peoples and lands that once belonged to the kingdom of Jesus Christ.[21] Its existence and expansion certainly ought not to be ignored.

To exacerbate tensions further, 'Islam is the only world religion which makes specific statements denying Christian doctrines such as the Trinity and the deity of Christ.'.[22] Long ago Dr. Samuel Zwemer described Islam as 'at once the most Christian and most anti-Christian of all non-Christian religions.'.[23]

Frequently, whenever representatives of these two religions talk, it usually ends in a standoff. There is considerable confusion because they often use exactly the same terms without asking each other to explain what those terms mean. Their worldviews are also quite different.

When Christians attempt to analyse what is happening they are often confused. On the one hand there is Islam which is represented by the Quran. But within the Quran itself there would seem to be contradictory statements (unless one understands the Islamic theological concept of abrogation whereby later statements cancel former ones). Western observers 'imbued with the assumptions of secular humanism, don't know how to respond to a religious force that refuses to be patronised or privatised out of the mainstream of life.'.[24]

Under the influence of secular humanism in the West, Christianity has been individualised and privatised. To some extent it has largely abandoned setting a moral and religious agenda for its own society. The church has been marginalised. 'Muslims on the other hand, whose world view does not separate religion from society, hold that the corrupt religion at its core, Christianity is responsible for producing a corrupt, amoral society.'.[25]

Islam encompasses the whole spectrum of life – political, public, economic, legal, and social. It will not be relegated to the domain of religious isolation. For Muslims the whole of life is seamlessly, interconnectedly religious.

Many Islamic scholars see nothing abnormal in the current upsurge of Islamic activity. Nor would they seek to categorise leaders in the current movement as 'fundamentalists'. They see the resurgence as revival *(tajdid)* or renewal *(ihya)*. They frequently cite historic precedents associated with Umar ibn Abd al-Aziz, Abul Hasan al-Ashari, al-Ghazali, Ibn Taymiyya Shaykh Ahmad and Shah Wali Allah. 'In other words to Muslims in general and the Muslim scholars in particular the phenomenon of Islamic resurgence far from being utterly strange and wholly inexplicable, is very much a natural process that is inherent in Islam.'[26] 'The resurgence is mainstream not extremist, pervasive not isolated.'[27] It involves the reintroduction of *shariah* law, the proliferation of Islamic curricula and schools' increased religious observance, opposition to secularism and increased cohesion and cooperation among Islamic states. Hassan Al-Turabi sees it as a 'comprehensive reconstruction of society from top to bottom'.[28]

How does one reach logical, rational (Western) conclusions concerning some of the events in say, Egypt in recent times? For example on February 12 1997 the Mar Girgis Church in southern Egypt was attacked. On that day 15 Christians were shot. As a result of this event Egypt's most prominent Muslim leader Sheikh Dr. Muhammad Tantawi, Grand Sheikh of Al-Azhar Mosque, Dr Ahmed Omar Hashim, President of the Islamic world's most prestigious university, Al-Azhar in Cairo and Sheikh Dr. Wasel, Mufti of Egypt, publicly stated that such acts are not in accordance with the teaching of Islam.

Egypt's President Hosni Mubarak also publicly spoke out against the assault. The government in an extraordinary gesture of generosity decided to pay US$900 to relatives of each person killed and US$100 for each person who was wounded. The Ministry of Religious Affairs paid approximately US$13 000 to the victims. To the Western observer that makes some sense. The government and its religious leaders were genuinely seeking to make amends for what was claimed to be a behavioural aberration which neither officials of the state religion nor the state itself could condone.

However the context of the event puts everything in a different light. The conflict in southern Egypt was said to be related to the Islamic practice of obliging non-Muslims to pay a special religious tax *(jizya)*. In practice this amount has usually been set according to the whim of local overlords. When the tax cannot be paid, property and even life may be forfeited. A local religious leader Sheikh Omar had been preaching attacking 'infidel' Christians in the area for the preceding 15 years. In similar situations in Egypt in 1992, 12 Christian farmers were killed at Sanabu and Dairud. In 1994 an attack on the monastery of el-Muharaq resulted in five deaths. In February 1996 at Ezbet el-Aqbat, eight Christians were killed.

While government ministries and their representatives were prepared to say appropriate words and give token financial response for the latest in a series of killings, this can hardly be reconciled with an attack by the Egyptian army in December 1996. This attack destroyed a Christian centre for the mentally handicapped with no compensation and a resulting court case that was interminably postponed. Not only that, at the instigation of the Ministry of Defence, the Ministry of Agriculture cancelled the contract by which land for the centre had been sold to its new Christian owners.[29]

It would seem that Islam, rather than being uniformly applied as based on the Quran and the practices and sayings of Muhammad, is in fact, whatever is practised at the local level. While for apologetic reasons some may protest that this is not true Islam, one might justifiably conclude that it is real Islam. 'We are learning that there is no norm about Islam. The norm is the local expression.'.[30] This is reflected in what they believe and do as compared with the difference between what they should believe and do.[31]

Real Islam changes according to the location and the culture of the people amongst whom it is embedded. For example when Saudi Arabia built the modern diplomatic city of Riyadh to accommodate foreign embassies, it installed computerised underground irrigation for its parks, superb supermarkets, leisure centres and sports stadiums, yet it allowed no Christian churches.

All Christian religious services are strictly banned within the kingdom. Anyone found by the special religious police practising any religion other than Islam is severely penalised. For Christians singing Christmas carols at home is not allowed. Christians are not permitted to come within several kilometres of the holy city of Mecca. The wearing of crucifixes is not allowed. 'The Saudi customs officers (even) confiscate Bibles as if they were pornographic literature.'[32] On and on the regulations go. But such severe restrictions are not equally applied in other Muslim countries.

In Teheran women may be punished for allowing the hair on their head to show in public. But in Cairo seductively attractive belly dancers may lead wedding processions down crowded streets. As the Christian looks at the Muslim not only is he confused. The reverse is also true.

A Western aid worker was standing under a baobab tree in northern Senegal along with about 30 inhabitants of the local village. They were all watching as a Western soil scientist took samples and a hydrologist discussed what he saw in his survey. The aid worker then asked the villagers what they thought was happening.

'Oh, that's simple,' they replied. 'They are witch doctors. That one down there is asking the spirit of the earth where the spirit of the water is. That one over there is consulting sacred texts written in a secret language just like our religious leaders do.'

'Are they any good?' asked the aid worker.

'Oh yes, they are better than our witch doctors. They always find water.'[33]

The capacity to misinterpret is not confined to illiterate, superstitious, uneducated, rural, African Muslims. Even scholars, Muslim and Christian, explaining the same passages of sacred texts arrive at quite different conclusions that confuse students of both faiths.

Commenting on chapter *(surah)* 33:36–38 in the Quran that relates to one of the marriages which Muhammad entered into, Raza F. Safa a former devout Muslim wrote:

Muhammad's adopted son, Zaid, was one of the first to accept the faith of Islam. He was married to Muhammad's cousin, Zainab. She was a beautiful woman to whom Muhammad was attracted. A revelation came to Muhammad from Allah to ask Zaid to divorce his wife 'after he had accomplished what he would of her' so that Muhammad could marry her. Fearing Allah, Zaid had no choice but to obey the command of the prophet, divorce his wife and allow her to marry Muhammad.[34]

It could be interpreted that this explanation of the text hardly puts Muhammad in the most honourable light (if the grid of interpretative values is twentieth-first century Western evangelical Christianity). But another commentary on the event of the unhappy marriage of Zaid is as follows:

The Prophet's freedman and adopted son married Zainab, the Prophet's cousin, a proud lady of Qureysh. The Prophet had arranged the marriage with the idea of breaking down the old barrier of pride and caste, and had shown but little consideration to Zainab's feelings. Tradition says that both she and her brother were averse to the match, and that she had always wished to marry the Prophet. For Zaid the marriage was nothing but a cause of embarrassment and humiliation. When the Prophet's attention was first called to their unhappiness he urged Zaid to keep his wife and not divorce her being apprehensive of the talk that would arise if it became known that a marriage arranged by him had proved unhappy. At last, Zaid did actually divorce Zainab and the Prophet was commanded to marry her in order, by his example, to disown the superstitious custom of the pagan Arabs, in such matters, of treating their adopted sons as their real sons, which was against the laws of God (that is, the laws of nature); whereas in arranging a marriage the woman's inclination ought to be considered. Unhappy marriage was no part of Allah's ordinance and was not to be held sacred in Islam.[35]

The first writer is Christian. The second is Muslim. Each brings his own bias to his commentary. A similar divergence of opinion often results when Christian and Muslim scholars seek to explain and interpret key passages in the Holy Bible. And as for political interpretations!

Dr Abdallah Al-Naggar commenting on the infamous events of September 11 2001 wrote in an Egyptian government daily newspaper, 'The Jews were behind these ugly acts, while we, the Arabs were innocent.'.[36] Sheikh Muyhammad Al-Gamei'a, Al-Azhar University Representative in the US and Imam of New York's Islamic centre, three days earlier went online and stated, 'The American attack against Afghanistan is terrorism...This war will be the end of America...If the Americans knew that the Jews carried out the September 11 attacks they would do to them what Hitler did.'.[37]

Such comments could be explained as expressions of the perennial hostility between two religious communities, if they were made immediately after the events. But they were made weeks later when it was widely known that the majority of the suicide squads were Muslim Saudi citizens. Similarly sometime after the Bali bombings Abu Bakar Bashir, as leader of Jemaah Islamiah, asserted that "...Americans and Jews did it to justify the claims that have been made so far that Indonesia is a terrorist haven...to prove their theory they created the incident in Bali".[38] The conclusions defy (Western) logic and beggar the imagination as objective truth is abandoned for 'total subjectivism' and becomes less important than religious correctness.[39]

To the Western observer a cursory glance at the world of Islam could leave one somewhat confused, bewildered or even alarmed, yet this is hardly so with God. While the church might have been remiss in its responsibilities, God has certainly been on the move. While Islam has been expanding around the world in recent decades and after centuries of seeming impregnability to the message of Jesus Christ, individual Muslims suddenly seem to be open to that Gospel which was hitherto rejected as fabrication by the movement of which they are members. This exemplifies the need to try to distinguish individual Muslims from the movement of Islam in general, a challenge which is difficult even for the most erudite of Christian scholars of Islamics, such as Kenneth Cragg.[40]

The 'Islamic world' is not a monolithic block any more than was the 'communist world'.[41] Nationalism, ethnicity, theological interpretations and political power plays sow seeds of disunity among Muslims as they have always done among all peoples. Nor can it be demonstrated that there is an established international conspiracy on behalf of all Islamic nations to take over the rest of the world through an Armageddon style cataclysmic holy war. Some leaders might wish it were so and for domestic political purposes might even say as much from time to time. But as in any country in any era there are often vast differences of opinion and practice between leaders and those whom they claim to lead. Non-Muslims must be careful not to misread extremist statements of a few leaders as being an accurate reflection of the sentiments of the majority in a religious movement which some seek to use or abuse to further their own ends. We must remember that 'not everything Muslims do is Islamic just as not everything Christians do is Christian'.[42]

For years I have lived among Muslim peoples and can personally testify to their wonderful sense of community, their legendary hospitality, their love for and generous acceptance of me as a stranger in their midst. Some became and remain true friends for life. Above all, one cannot help but be challenged and touched by their religious dedication, discipline and devotion in trying to please God about whom they long to know more. There is no reason we cannot respect people of other faiths even though they might deny essential tenets of our own. We need to be able to disagree with dignity.[43]

These are people whom God loves and longs to reach. Our attitudes must be the same. Of anything less than this we need to repent. As ministers of the love of God who presumably have something precious to share with all Muslims, we cannot afford to succumb to fear and ignorance. Rather than react to the threat of darkness we need to live as proactive children of the Light. As ambassadors for the Prince of Peace we cannot engage in war or even its rhetoric. Ishmael was rejected in his day. To continue to have a negative attitude toward his descendants will only perpetuate the sad inter-religious history of threat, conflict, bloodshed and death. If that path is followed skirmishes may be won, but at the expense of winning the victory of faith.

With the safer distance of lapsed time, history may one day show that during these last couple of decades, never have so many Muslims turned to Jesus Christ in such vast numbers while at the same time, have Christians been under such pressure to become Muslims in Islamic states.

Not a day goes by without some testimony of God sovereignly revealing himself to individuals or groups of Muslims, sometimes through dreams and visions or through acts of mercy. Other times it is through a bold proclamation of the Gospel under the direction of the Holy Spirit. Jesus Christ is reaching the hearts of Muslim people and breaking down the barriers to the good news.[44]

From my own experience over the last three decades of observing what is happening in Muslim countries I would confirm the above.

However there is much yet to be done. In many countries an excellent start has been made to meet the challenge of Islam. The stakes are indeed high, not just in terms of national control but for the destiny of millions of individuals in the future. For 'Christianity and Islam (both) have claims on truth. The consequence of rejecting one at the acceptance of the other is eternal punishment in the next life.'[45] Both cannot be right. Islam is the only religious movement which historically has threatened the survival of the West. Fifty percent of wars involving states of different religions were between Muslims and Christians in the period 1820 and 1929. In the mid-1990s 19 of 28 conflicts were between Muslims and Christians. Prominent Western politicians and Christian leaders have argued that the West does not have a problem with Islam. It is only with 'extremism'. But history clearly demonstrates that this is not so. Samuel Huntington's brilliant analysis concludes that the problem for the West is not 'fundamentalism' but Islam itself, 'a different civilisation whose people is convinced of the superiority of their culture and is obsessed with the inferiority of their power.'[46]

If it be thought that what is reported in this book may be dismissed as only the exaggerations and distortions of 'extremists', 'fundamentalists' or by whatever name one may wish to demonise others, this could turn out to be a grave mistake. History is replete with examples of otherwise competent people ignoring accumulated evidence because at the time it was unpalatable or unpopular. For example in November 1992, a few months after the global Earth Summit, a document was released which was signed by more than 1600 senior scientists, including more than half of all living winners of the Nobel Prize. It warned 'human beings and the natural world are on a collision course...'.[47] Mainstream media virtually ignored the document, its release and its contents. Just a decade further on the folly of such ignorance was better understood.

Dr Hassan Turabi, an internationally renowned Islamic thinker, provided the theological framework for President Umar Hassan Ahmad al-Bashir's 'programme' of Islamisation in Sudan. He gives a timely reminder to challenge Western analysts to redefine their understanding of much which is happening within international Islam when he says:

All Muslims are fundamentalists. We have to be fundamentalists because it is obligatory that we believe in the fundamentals of Islam. Those who do not believe in those fundamentals...are not Muslims. Thus it is irrelevant to call a Muslim a fundamentalist.[48]

Ibn Warraq concludes that to do so legitimises barbaric behaviour and shifts moral responsibility from Muslims onto the West. [49] Anisa Buckley, a convert to Islam is of the opinion that, 'The whole term fundamentalism essentially is something that has been coined and attached to Muslims, to a particular religious group. It is not something that comes out of the religious groups themselves.'.[50] Palestinian Khaldoun Hajaj drives the point further: 'Hezbollah, are they fundamentalists? The West sees them as fundamentalists. In my opinion, no, they are not at all fundamentalists.'.[51]

Islamic commentator, Ibn Warraq makes the point that 'there are moderate Muslims, but Islam itself is not moderate…There is no difference between Islam and Islamic fundamentalism.'.[52] Abu Bakar Bashir agrees. He says, 'There is no such thing as fundamentalists. There is only one Islam.'[53]

Amine Oygur Attaly kept questioning herself as to whether or not she had become a fanatic. 'But what is a fanatic? I looked at what I was doing and it was (only) the Prophet's example.' All Muslims are obliged to implement the teachings of the Quran which are for them eternally valid, absolutely true and beyond criticism.[54]

What makes non-Muslim commentators regard Afghan leader Mullah Omar as a radical or extremist while former Afghanistan President Rabbani was not also labelled as one? Khalid Duran who has studied that scene intensely says, 'The only difference between Rabbani and the Taliban's Mullah Omar is the length of their beards.'.[55]

If we can look through Islamic eyes at those whom non-Muslims label as fundamentalists or extremists, we will see that within the context of their own societies, they are mostly regarded as warrior heroes of the faith on behalf of the Faithful. Suicide bombers are glorified as martyrs whose deaths are celebrated more than mourned. Saudi Arabia used to pay US$4000 to each (Palestinian) martyr's family. By March 2002 Saddam Hussein of Iraq had increased the sum to US$25 000 per family 'as an enticement for others to volunteer for martyrdom'.[56] Seventy percent of Palestinians approved of suicide attacks against Israel, which is far more than those who approved peace negotiations.[57] A Saudi intelligence survey of educated Saudis between the ages of 25 and 41 concluded that 95% of them supported Osama bin Laden's cause.[58]

Even after September 11 2001 and the World Trade Centre event, still no Muslim nation would send men and material to attack the Taliban, al Qaeda and Osama bin Laden in Afghanistan. Middle Eastern press reports exhibited a not so hidden admiration for bin Laden. A Pakistani daily, *The Nation*, regarded the September 11 event as not one of mindless terrorism but of revenge or retribution and presumably therefore justified.[59]

Millions would seem to agree. Immediately after the September 11 events, reports of spontaneous jubilation (before authorities clamped down) came in from various Muslim communities. What surprises non-Muslims is the extent to which these attitudes are common in Islamic societies. Muslims can even surprise themselves. Egyptian politician Rifaat Said said, 'The sheer depth of it came as a shock to me...ordinary people handing out sweets when news of the Trade Towers first came in.'.[60]

Are all these people 'terrorists' or 'extremists'? Are the groups who nightly process through our comfortable lounge rooms via TV just 'fringe' operators? Such descriptions may seem true from Western, non-Muslim or victims' perspectives. It reassures us that the problem or challenge is not ours – yet. But if examined from an Islamic standpoint, things are interpreted differently. For example, in 2002 when Malaysian Prime Minister Dr Mahatir Mohammad urged representatives from 56 Islamic Conference nations to condemn all attacks directed at civilians as terrorism, not a single representative would agree with him. At the conference in Malaysia they insisted 'that the Palestinian suicide bombers and anyone else they approved of were not terrorists.'.[61]

Afghanistan born Hawa Ayra expresses it thus, 'The problem is that when you apply outside standards, Western standards to an Islamic country, it is totally out of context. The important thing is to judge Islam by Islam's own standards...and not one of the Western world.'.[62] Only then do some things make sense and those whom non-Muslims may regard as terrorists, extremists or fringe groups drift toward the centre of acceptable Islamic practice. When an Afghani was asked his opinion of Osama bin Laden, with a smile he replied, 'He was good to us and he was a Muslim.'.[63] 'And he was a Muslim' explains so much to which non-Muslims otherwise object.

To be a Muslim involves submission to Allah, his Word and frequently to his earthly representatives. It is difficult for the individualised West to understand the power which clerics wield in a religion which stresses collective cohesion. For example, a Karachi mob stoned to death an abandoned infant on a mullah's presumption it was illegitimate. Another mob of otherwise normal people was fired up by a mullah to amputate a man's hand because it was simply alleged that he was a thief.[64] Contemporary history shows that clerical power has an ability to topple regimes and therefore is mostly accommodated and appeased within Islamic states.[65]

As a counter to the recent rush for political correctness and conformity, Reza Safa disturbingly asks, 'If Islam is a peaceful religion why did Muhammad engage in 47 battles? Why are there so many contemporary Islamic dictators? Why is there so little freedom of religion or speech in Islamic countries? From whence comes the awful violence which kills innocent people in so many countries in the name of Allah?'[66]

In the spheres of human activity, social, political, religious, scientific or cultural, the inexorable flow of 'progress' demonstrates so frequently that today's leaders were also once regarded as yesterday's radicals and will mostly become tomorrow's conservatives. How seriously we evaluate and respond to today's 'fundamentalists' will certainly shape for good or ill the environment of our next generation.

With the hope of sharpening the focus on present and future challenges, clarifying confusion and dispelling doubts, this book is written:

- to present an overview of what is happening as Islam reaches out beyond its traditional territories,
- to give background as to why it is happening (in terms of basic Islamic history, belief and practice),
- to outline a response, God's and ours, with special attention to just one way that has proven effective in assisting Muslims to choose the freedom of a relationship with the living Lord – Jesus Christ,
- To awaken a deep love and concern for all Muslim peoples.

Because of the sensitive nature of work that continues in many countries some names, places and times have been generalised or withheld where necessary.

PART 1

WHAT'S HAPPENING

For the last half of the twentieth century Islam has been growing and expanding at a rate far greater than that of Christianity. It is now well resourced in terms of funding, organisation and staff. It claims the next century as 'theirs'.

In this section we patch together pieces of an international jigsaw puzzle to present an overview of what Islam is doing on each continent and how this is being achieved. Already Western countries that were Judeo–Christian are becoming Islamic–Christian. Christian leadership especially needs to grasp the big picture to prepare the Church for the challenge ahead.

CHAPTER 1

WHAT S HAPPENING

Back in the 1960s a musical called *Jesus Christ Superstar* was staged in many Western countries. Regardless of what is thought of the music and lyrics of Tim Rice and Andrew Lloyd Weber and their interpretation of the life of Jesus Christ, their storyline was a mere caricature of the man for whom the musical was named. Christians did react, often picketing theatres where the show was staged but with little effect. Had anything even remotely similar been done in a Muslim country or in just about any country, referring to the Prophet Muhammad in such distorted terms, there would have been violence in the streets with those responsible for such 'insult' required to forfeit their lives. This is but one of the many differences between Muslim and nominal 'Christian' societies.

In *Superstar,* one of the refrains which pounded out repetitiously was the line 'What's the buzz? Tell me what's a-happening?' While the musical, unlike its namesake, may not even rate a footnote in history, the question remains valid.

An analysis of change within Islam in the twentieth century shows that the worldwide community of believers has been increasing in religious cohesion. The term used for the whole community of Muslim believers is *ummah.* The background to the term is instructive to understand the mindset of the movement.

Refugees from Mecca who fled from there to Medina with the Prophet Muhammad in the seventh century of the Common Era, formed the original Islamic community. They were known as the *muhajirun.* To these were added *ansars* (helpers) from Medina. These two groups severed their previous relationships with their families, friends and tribes and became united in the original brotherhood of Islam. Such social realignment was quite unprecedented in Arabian tribal history and had world changing ramifications. Membership within the community took precedence over all other relationships or activities and became irrevocable.

On the surface *ummah* simply means the totality of all Muslim communities. But there is a second, more dynamic meaning within the term.

In the etymology of the term *ummah* we find the verb *amma* which means 'to proceed towards a given objective'. Thus unity and interdependence are the continuous dynamic objectives of the brotherhood of Islam...Furthermore the *ummah* is continuously proceeding towards the state of Islam. The Muslim communities are therefore united in their final goal as well as in the paths that should be followed to attain this goal.[1]

Although the desire to be a single people of the world, united in piety, politics and culture has never been realised, it remains a longed-for objective. Consciousness of the longed-for ideal without the momentum provided by essentially core states remains a frustration for Islamic peoples. In Pakistan the Interior ministry reports that there are nearly 3 million students studying in the country's many thousands of madrassas. That country's Human Rights commission says that a third of these religious schools provide military training. Abu Huraira believes that in the clash of civilisation religious war will continue until Islam becomes the dominant religion and that the *ummah* will usher in an Islamic world without frontiers.[2]

In south east Asia the Jemaah Islamiah network strives to see an Islamic republic which includes Malaysia, Indonesia, southern Thailand and the southern Philippines to which others add Singapore or even the possibility of northern Australia.[3]

The call for unity and coordinated action has been expressed in a succession of major international conferences throughout the twentieth century:

- the Islamic Caliphate Congress of Cairo in 1926;
- the Muslim Congress of Mecca in 1926;
- the Aqsa Islamic Conference of Jerusalem in 1931;
- the Islamic Conference of Jerusalem in 1953;
- the Afro Asian Muslim Peoples' Conference of Jakarta in 1965;
- the Arab Summit of Khartoum in 1968; and
- the Islamic Summit of Rabat in 1969.

Finally in 1972 this resulted in the creation of the Organisation of the Islamic Conference with its own permanent secretariat in Jeddah.[4]

Since the World Muslim League meeting of Mecca in 1974, Islam has become much more active in *Dawah* – its missionary enterprise.[5,]

As Islam examines the West which from its perspective is wholly Christian, its evaluation is far from complimentary. A former prime minister of the Sudan summed up the opinion of many of his colleagues when he concluded, 'Western civilisation riding in its blaze of glory in the Renaissance and its religious corollary, the Reformation, is now collapsing in a spiritual crisis, lost amid corruption and a sea of alcohol.'.[6]

With this some Western analysts agree. Peter Coleman says, *'We have adopted a culture of repudiation, a commitment to political correctness, a "down with us" mentality. We no longer believe in truth or even free inquiry. We are all relativists, feminists and multi-culturalists. We reject the old prohibitions on abortions, homosexuality or sex outside of marriage. There is little place if any for God in our lifestyle. If theology is still studied at all in the academies it is a godless variety, and if you reject it you will flunk your course.'*[7]

Islam commonly regards Christianity as having failed with the Church in particular having lost its way. The rise of secularism is itself regarded as a symptom of Christianity's failure.

> Islam commonly regards Christianity as having failed with the Church in particular, having lost its way. The rise of secularism is itself regarded as a symptom of Christianity's failure.

When Islam considers the way in which the Christian West now celebrates its weekly 'holy day' ie. Sunday or its most significant religious events Christmas and Easter, it observes that these times are now given over to sport, entertainment and fun. Muslims regard this as a travesty of the truths that these times and events were once purported to proclaim. Even worse they note that the name of Jesus Christ who is also one of their most honoured prophets, is seldom used with reverence but is more commonly used and abused as a mindless expletive, a 'swear' word in ordinary conversation and throughout the infotainment and entertainment industries. They are incredulous that no one seems to care, let alone object to such 'blasphemy'.

It is concluded that as the West has sunk under a deluge of 'drunkenness, sexual licence, political corruption, violence, blasphemy and corrupt lifestyles'[8], change is necessary if human civilisation is to be preserved from self-destruction. Jalal Al-e Ahmed called this deluge 'Occidentosis'. He applied it to such corrupt urban phenomena as Pepsi Cola, McDonald's and Brigette Bardot films.[9]

Following through on Iranian Ayatollah Ruhollah Mussavi Khomeini's desire 'to purge the "Satan" in the West', Amien Rais leader of Indonesia's 28 million member Mohammadiyah movement said, 'Islamic societies...must end Western toxification.'.[10]

Ustaz Ashaari Muhammad believes he has the solution:

We have something most invaluable and a priceless commodity to offer the West, Islam... What the world needs is a truly new leadership... This can only be found in Islam, a complete way of life that has emerged through the sacred struggle of the Prophet Muhammad and his companions... Only Islam can lead the way.[11]

Furthermore seldom seen or even understood in the West, Muslim leaders have a worldview and a long-term common commitment to realise their ideals. In television interviews screened in January 1991 just prior to the onset of what became known as the Gulf War, the difference in attitude was most telling when combatants on both sides were interviewed. When an Australian naval person was asked what concerned him about the war he replied, 'I may get sunburned'. This was classic laconic Aussie humour.

When a US marine was asked what he thought of the likely outcome his reply was, 'Petrol will be put up by $1 per gallon and then we'll all go home.' A somewhat shallow, trivial consumer response perhaps?

But when an Iraqi high school girl was interviewed she responded from her understanding that historically Kuwait was a part of Iraq until the colonial powers of Britain and France drew their artificial lines on maps. She replied that she saw war as inevitable between pure Islam and the 'decadent Christian West'. She went on to say, 'Our hero is not Madonna or Michael Jackson but Saddam Hussein. We follow him. We love death more than they love life.'

The memory of Saddam Hussein is still revered by many in his part of the world while many in the West appear to have found little to live for and even less worth dying for. Taking a longer term view, another Iraqi youth responded on television by saying, 'Our fate is in God's hands. Ultimately we must win come what may.' In other words this battle could be lost but never the ultimate war.

Even in so massive an undertaking as the 1991 Gulf War, Islamic leaders were never distracted from their ultimate long-term (religious) objectives. Prior to that war, Iraq's Saddam Hussein was urging all Muslims to unite in calling on the world to address the question of Israel. To the West he said 'If oil is important for you, Jerusalem is more important for us.'.[12]

When P.L.O. leader Yasser Arafat committed his resources to the conflict on Iraq's side he said, 'Iraq and Palestine will be together side by side and after the great battle we will pray together in Jerusalem.' The question as to who has political oversight over Kuwait is nowhere near as important as the claiming of the entire Middle East for Islam and in particular, the holy city of Jerusalem. No Muslim authority can ever permanently accept that greater Palestine and Jerusalem should be under the governance of any power other than a Muslim power. This territory is regarded as an Islamic trust.[13]

But if Islam is stalemated temporarily regarding Israel, how goes it in the rest of the world? Malaysian Muslim leader Ashaari, in common with many of his co-religionists, defines his approach to the West in terms of a two-pronged strategy '…by waging psychological warfare, while…exhibiting the Islamic approach to life.'.[14]

He encourages the preparation of books, speeches, magazines, newspapers, journals, cassettes, videos, electronic print media etc. aimed especially at youth and the educated. He advocates that Muslim students should stay as long as possible in the West and that they should try to obtain permanent residential status and employment so that they can carry on Islamic missionary activities. He encourages mixed marriages thereby to create an Islamic society that becomes a microcosmic superior example which Westerners may be persuaded to join. He urges also the use of existing Islamic communities as models with which to target and attract Western tourists. In already established Muslim societies, he wants to see tourist centres staffed by well-mannered Muslims who become attractive living advertisements for the virtues of Islam.

It hardly requires the vast resources of the world's leading intelligence agencies to conclude that what Ashaari is promoting is already being carried out. The *ummah* is increasingly well connected, coordinated and united to reach its objectives.

In June 1997 when Tatiana Susskind, a young Israeli woman, drew a cartoon which caricatured the Prophet Muhammad in the form of a pig standing on the Holy Quran and then stuck copies on shop walls in Hebron, protest was predictably swift. That was to be expected. No one should ever so crassly and grossly offend another's sensibilities.

Coincidentally within a few days of the Susskind cartoon, the Israeli science magazine *Galileo*, published a photo montage which had the head of a cow superimposed on a picture of Mary with the infant Jesus. In this case also there was reaction. Local Christians protested and the Israeli prime minister Benyamin Nettanyahu apologised to the Christians as he had also similarly done previously to the Muslims. There the Christian issue was dropped. But the reaction within the Islamic community was vastly different.

Muslims across the world protested about the Hebron poster event. A number of Arab countries denounced the posters. Strikes were held in various cities of Bangladesh. In South Africa Muslims marched on the Israeli embassy in Capetown. Kenyan Muslims marched through Mombasa. The head of the Iranian judiciary, Ayatollah Mohammad Yazdi called for Israel to be eliminated.[15]

In the meantime Muslim websites came into existence. They contained material that could only be described as abusive of Christianity. They are also harshly anti-Jewish. The Council for American–Islamic Relations coordinated a website which invited information on any incident from any place Muslims may deem offensive to themselves and has coordinated a response by putting the alleged offenders under pressure to withdraw. Islam presents a face that appears to be tough at home and well coordinated and united abroad. It will brook no criticism of itself. On the other hand both at home and abroad, it reserves the right to be publicly critical of anything not of the House of Islam.

So what effect is this united, committed, coordinated movement having beyond its current borders?

CHAPTER 2

THE UNITED (?) KINGDOM

On Sunday September 8 1996 the Muslim political organisation called Al-Muhajiroun held a large meeting in Hyde Park, London. About 800 people were present. The principal speakers were Syrian Omar Bakri Mohammad, who was Al-Muhajiroun's official spokesperson and Dr Muhammad Al-Mas'ari, a prominent Saudi Arabian. The aim was 'to initiate a valid Islamic leadership in every country of the world where Muslims live so that all Muslims can live under the *shariah*.'.[1] The speakers suggested this be done through the establishment of *khilafah* (the concept of a centralised world-wide Muslim government which administers totally through Islamic law – the *shariah*). Literature handed out by official stewards at the meeting explicitly advocated killing Jews in Israel as a means of 'sincere *jihad*'. The closing official declaration of the meeting was 'Islam must dominate the world'.

The only voice of objection raised at the public open air meeting was that of two groups known as Lesbian Avengers and Outrage. They had good reason to feel threatened because they had been labelled as 'filthy' by some Muslim leaders who would brook no compromise with practices of homosexuality represented by the groups.

On another occasion an overseas visitor to the same location, Speakers Corner in Hyde Park, observed:

Speaker after speaker proclaimed the decline of Western Christianity and of Western civilisation...the speaker who grabbed my attention was English born and bred. Bearded, robed and devoted to Islam, he claimed to be a former Christian. As I moved from speaker to speaker I was challenged that at the heart of a nation that once spearheaded the proclamation of the Gospel around the world, Islam was boldly proclaimed, not by immigrants but by a former Christian.[2]

When Hyde Park Christian, Jay Smith asked Muslims around him, 'Do you want Islam to take over Britain?' the Muslim crowd yelled, 'Yes, yes!'[3]

The Hyde Park scene is somewhat a picture in microcosm of what has happened during the last couple of decades in the United Kingdom and how it is occurring.

Today in Britain some Muslims claim there are 3 million of their co-religionists within the country. Based on projections from a government census, more conservative estimates range from 1.6 million to 2 million.[4] It is therefore reasonable to conclude that more than 3% of the population of Britain is now Muslim.

In Britain throughout the 1980s a new mosque was being opened every two weeks. About 300 of these were recycled Christian church buildings. One of them was previously the home church of a 'father of modern missions', William Carey. It is estimated that there are approximately 1800 mosques and from 3000 to 5000 other Islamic centres and Quranic schools.

Muslims are concentrated in the cities of London, Birmingham, Manchester, Liverpool, Glasgow, Sheffield, Leeds and in 14 other major cities, mostly in inner city areas.[5] In an edition of the Muslim News, one British Muslim succinctly stated the goal of his society. He said that they must seek 'the transformation of the UK from *Dar Al-Kufr* to *Dar Al-Islam* (ie. from being a country of non-believers to being a Muslim country). That must be our goal, or we have no business being here, and may Allah grant us success.'.[6]

For some decades the United Kingdom has been a prime target of Islamic missionary activity. They believe that if they can win Britain then in effect, they will be able to win much of the English speaking world. Today there are now more Arab papers published in London than anywhere else in the world. There are also more Muslim books published in English than in Arabic. Religious change is underway.

London, as the home of the dominant international language of English, is also seen as a critical political and economic centre for the rest of Europe. Forty-eight percent of all Muslims in Britain now live in London. Forty percent of all mosques are also situated in this city. According to Al-Muhajiroun's own publicity, London is 'the capital of world-wide Islamic movements.'.[7] Omar Bakri Muhammad has stated that his ambition and therefore presumably that of the group which he leads is 'to see the Islamic flag over Downing Street'.[8] In 2001 Cardinal Cormac Murphy O'Connor concluded that Christianity was close to being 'vanquished' in Britain.[9] On July 25 2002 Baptist preacher, David Pawson announced that he believed England would become Islamic. Many Christians begged to differ but Muslim spokesmen agreed and concluded that this would not happen for '5–10 years yet'.[10]

How is this all coming about?

On July 11 1989 the Aga Khan (the spiritual leader of Ismaili Muslims) was speaking at the inauguration of the John Addis Islamic Gallery in the British Museum. He said: 'Europe has become an important meeting point for Islamic culture and the West...barriers between the Islamic world and the West are beginning to break down everywhere...Change will happen.' Elsewhere he expanded by saying he believed the change would be 'evolutionary'.[11]

The process of change is effected through the tried and tested political means of initially being quiet and accepting of the status quo whatever that is for as long as numbers of the group are few. As numbers increase so does confidence and demands upon the society at the local and national level. Along the way the group seeking change paints itself as being victimised. This gains sympathy. Anyone who disagrees or is critical of the group's objectives is quickly and forcefully confronted.

> For some decades the United Kingdom has been a prime target of Islamic missionary activity. They believe that if they can win Britain then in effect, they will be able to win much of the English speaking world.

The Western world has seen the gay rights movement use this process with great effect over the last couple of decades. That movement generalises its opponents as 'homophobic'. Muslims label their critics –'Islamophobic'.

Immigration

The main means by which the number of Muslims in Britain has increased in recent times has been immigration. In the 1950s and 1960s this was principally from southern Asia especially Pakistan, India and Bangladesh. By 2001 the major groups by linguistic identity were:

Tamil 90 000;

Kashmiri 117 000;

Bengali 400 000;

Urdu 400 000;

Punjabi 471 000.[11]

These immigrants moved into inner city areas and formed discrete, identifiable communities based on their ethnic origins.

Then in the early 1970s as a result of unrest in a number of eastern African nations (Uganda, Rwanda, Burundi etc), an additional influx of peoples of southern Asian origins also moved into Britain. By the turn of the century it was from central and southern Asia. Placing emphasis upon strong cohesion within the extended family and education they became within a generation, sufficiently affluent to provide their own centres of religious activities (with the addition of significant outside finance).

Muslims in Europe are usually harder to reach from a Christian perspective than when they are in their countries of origin. Outside of their original context they perceive themselves as under threat from Western society in general and Christianity in particular. Mosques and Islamic centres provide a strong sense of identity in what is perceived as a hostile environment.

Organisation

Another way in which Islam has consolidated its position is through increasingly complex national organisational structures. In September 1989 the Islamic Party of Britain was formed as an alternative to both Labor and Conservative political parties. Its mandate was to lobby for and to represent Muslim interests.

Later a separate manifesto was drawn up which proposed a structure of a council for a lower house of 200 devout Muslims who would influence the Muslim community and an upper house of wealthy Muslims who would pay annually for their membership. The press interpreted this as being a separate Muslim parliament, an accolade, Kalim Saddiqui, one of its sponsors, was happy to accept. This body was established in 1991. Saddiqui claimed that according to purist Islamic theology Allah alone has the right to make laws and therefore the British parliament being non-Islamic has no true jurisdiction. His compromise demand was that any law concerning Muslims must therefore come through the jurisdiction of the 'Muslim parliament'.

At the same time Saddiqui was also proposing that Muslims develop their own board. This would be similar to that which the Board of Deputies for the Jewish community or the Church of England through its General Synod for the Anglican community exercise for their people. In May 1996 representatives from various

Muslim organisations met in Bradford and decided to form a new body. The Muslim Council of Britain held its inaugural meeting in London in November 1997. It represented the coming together of over 250 Islamic organisations. Their intention was to present a common front and to lobby for additional rights for British Muslims. By 2003 it was reported that other Muslims were seeking to form a new Islamic Council of Britain to press for the introduction of Shariah among other aims.[12]

Meanwhile within the official system of national government, by September 1998 there were already four Muslims appointed to the House of Lords. Three were Labor supporters and one is a hereditary peer and a Conservative.[13] Muslim parliamentarians did not support the government's contribution to 'War on Terror' in Afghanistan in 2001.

Contextualised Preaching

Aggressive missionary outreach *(dawa)* has been a feature of Islam in Britain. In 1995 a campaign was launched to reach every home in the UK with 'the pure and pristine message of Islam'. Through house to house visitation, literature distribution and major rallies, the message was communicated that Islam was the only way forward for the future of humanity.[14]

Seminars are held using the mosque as an 'educational centre'. Issues such as Islam being the theological continuity of Christianity, evolution, the meaning of life, the way to happiness and contentment, how to be pure in heart, how to be saved, the importance of family, community and ethical behaviour, the certainty of judgment and the compassion of God, are discussed. Within the Christian context, rather than the death of Jesus Christ being the way of salvation, the 'straight path' of Islam is presented as the means of salvation. Communication methods include sketches, songs, testimonies of reversion to Islam and miracles. Sponsored events of indoor soccer, badminton and martial arts have been used. Post reversion discipling is carried out in mosques for newer believers.[15] (Note: one does not convert to Islam. Muslims believe that we are all born Muslims and what is necessary is for each to revert back to the true faith of Islam.)

For members of the community it is estimated that about 20% of Britain's Muslims now follow the more severe teaching of the Deobandi sect. Approximately 20 religious colleges teach its interpretation of Islam. Its practices include women members not being allowed to attend their own weddings. They instead nominate two male relatives to participate on their behalf. The movement extolled the Taliban of Afghanistan as an exemplary model Islamic welfare state.

Political Process

Islam does not divide life into secular and sacred. Therefore political processes which many Western Christians would rather avoid are to a Muslim simply another means to reach the goal of Islamisation. Not all political systems have the stamp of Islamic approval. But any may be used along the way.

For example within the British context, Islamic leaders have proven to be quite adept at using to advantage the liberties which democracy, asylum laws, Western notions of human rights etc. afford. On the other hand according to Abu Hanza al-Masri, a London based Muslim cleric, the principal of democracy is hostile to God and is therefore to be condemned. He says, 'Democratic means such as elections and dialogue only serve to ensnare us (Islamists).'.[16]

Omar Bakri agrees with him. He described democracy as being 'deceptive, dangerous and unworkable'.[17] Similarly an editorial in the December 1996 edition of Al-Khilafah, a magazine banned in the Middle East but claiming the right of free speech in Britain said, 'All over the world the twin evils of freedom and democracy have wreaked havoc with peoples' lives.'.[18]

This 'evil' of democracy however has been used to good effect to obtain further Islamic rights. The British Education Act of 1988 states that religious education should 'reflect the fact that religious traditions in Great Britain are in the main Christian while taking into account the teaching and practices of other principal religions'.

Under pressure from Muslim groups the Secretary for Education allowed Muslim students to be separated out from others in school during religious education periods. Muslims have additionally been seeking state funding for Muslim schools that teach traditional Muslim values. Funding for the first two applicant Muslim schools has been agreed to and announced.[19] In August 2002 it was revealed that Birmingham City Council was investigating a reported attempt of Muslim governors who had allegedly attempted to try to force out white staff at the Washwood Heath Technology College and to appoint only Asian teachers in their place.[20]

Some see this activity as the implementation of Al-Muhajiroun which means 'the migrants'. Based on the original example of Prophet Muhammad's moving to Medina the concept is expanded 'for those who migrate with the goal of subduing the new locale to Islam and of building up the strength of the Muslim community...in order to serve as a base from which to initiate new projects...'[21]

When an Anglican church declined to hire out their hall for a Muslim social event, the rejected party applied successfully to the Commission for Racial Equality for legal representation. It was later established that under the Race Relations Act, the Church is legally obliged to make its facilities available to Muslims and others. Hiring a mosque for Christian functions would never happen in a Muslim country where not only would Christians not have a hall available for hire but they would seldom be given permission, if at all, to build a church in which to meet.

So Muslim leaders encourage their communities to use the democratic processes when it is to their advantage, but where it is interpreted to be otherwise then the advice is to the contrary. On January 5 1992 Kalim Saddiqui in his capacity as Director of London's Muslim Institute urged that 'Muslims should resist any public policy or legislation that conflicts with the interests of the 2 million Muslims living in Britain.'.[22]

Social Action

The Afro-Caribbean community within Britain has also proved to be a fruitful field for Islamic mission. With a message of hope against the suffering of economic deprivation, racial discrimination and other social ailments, the Nation of Islam (NOI) has been working since the mid 1980s with its message of empowerment, self-determination and self-esteem. This movement emphasises the value of the family, discipline and work and positively acts proactively among society's castoffs of prison inmates, drug addicts and prostitutes.

POWER (People Organising Working for Economic Re-birth) is another Muslim organisation that has done similar work. PACE (Programme for African Cooperative Economy) likewise promoted Islamic principles and teaches self-help as a means of economic improvement.[23]

Finance

None of the significant changes which have come into Britain in the last few years could have occurred without the injection of significant amounts of funds. It is estimated that in the 1980s Saudi Arabians donated US$50 million to fund the upkeep of 800 mosques and monthly payments through the Saudi embassy for nearly

100 religious leaders.[24] More money comes from the Gulf States or the private funds of Middle Eastern rulers. These gifts are always carefully targeted to maximise impact towards goals.

Oxford University, originally established as a centre for Christian learning, now has its own autonomous centre for Islamic studies which rivals its older centres of Hebrew and Christian studies. The buildings and offices of the new centre were purchased with a gift from the ruler of Sharjah. Exeter University has received over 3 million pounds from various Gulf States. Oman gave nearly half a million pounds and Dubai paid 750 000 pounds for a new library. At a time when universities are under considerable financial pressure this money is used 'to establish centres for the study of Islam at the highest level in Britain. By doing so (the donors) are able to promote Islam as a humanitarian and caring religious system and give it academic credibility.'.[25] They are also able to influence outcomes favourable to Islam in the field of academic research and in public debate. It also ensures that Islam will be 'approached with less than academic candour'.[26]

Additional if unintentional help for the introduction of Islamic expansion in Great Britain has come from the highest offices of the realm. In 1976 Queen Elizabeth II, one of whose official titles is Defender of the (Christian) Faith, opened a US$2 million exhibition in London called 'The Festival of Islam and the Festival of Britain'. One of its stated aims was to win England and all English speaking countries and Europe for Islam.

In 1989 Queen Elizabeth's husband Prince Philip established a US$7 million trust to sponsor the first authorised English translation of the Quran. 'Since traditionally Muslims have held the belief that the Quran is untranslatable the approval of this translation by the Muslim World League and Meccan leaders is revolutionary.'.[27]

In 1995, the then Prime Minister John Major officially opened a state of the art US$12 million multimedia studio in the heart of London from which Arabic transmissions go around the world.[28]

In 1997 Queen Elizabeth II during a state visit to Pakistan, announced to a gathering of distinguished guests that 'a distinctive new identity, that of the British Muslim has emerged'.[29] Quite so. Her listeners would have been delighted to hear it and could have thanked her and her government for all their help.

The Church

But perhaps in a spiritual sense the greatest help has sadly come inadvertently from the Church. Islam, the fastest growing religion in Britain,[30] has been able to expand into what might be regarded as a spiritual vacuum. Over the last few decades UK church attendance declined to only 9% of the population. In London where the Islamic concentration is greatest that figure dropped to between 5% and 8%, many of whom are of West Indian origin and therefore culturally distant from Asian Muslims.

Mainline Anglican and Roman Catholic communions provide an example of what has been happening. Over a ten year period, statistics for church attendance, marriages and baptisms have been consistently trending negatively. For example the Anglican Church in Hereford reportedly registers 1000 parishioners, but average weekly attendance is about 60. Not surprisingly belief in a personal (Christian) God has similarly declined in the last half of the century from 43% to 31%.[31]

...there are probably now more Muslim missionaries coming into Britain than there are Christian missionaries going out from Britain.

A church's vitality may well be measured in terms of its missionary outreach. Since 1910 the number of British missionaries has dropped by about 31%. Today only approximately 8500 missionaries go out worldwide from the United Kingdom (26% of whom are short term). The irony is that there are probably now more Muslim missionaries coming into Britain than there are Christian missionaries going out from Britain.

Up to this time the church seems to have developed little by way of apologetic to meet the invasion of Islam. In the public domain of the famous Hyde Park, Muslims dominate while the Church is silent and absent. Still today a mere handful of Christian individuals is designated to work full time amongst Muslims.

Many Muslims claim that the Church is seen as dull, dying and irrelevant. They buy its empty buildings to recycle them into new mosque-based communities. They claim that the Church has lost its way.

From a Muslim perspective Dr Kalim Saddiqui, Director of the Muslim Institute said that 'the great majority of those who speak on behalf of Christianity today have gone back to paganism in their religious life'.[32] Some Christians might well agree with him.

What are the results of all of this?

The Church can take some small comfort that at least their founder will no longer be pilloried quite so easily. When the British theatrical puppet show *Spitting Image* introduced a distorted rubber character of Jesus Christ, Christians were offended. But the program's producer said that 'only nutters' would be offended and that viewers could expect a 'second coming'. 'However when a representative from the Islamic Affairs Committee expressed 'anger and revulsion' at this 'degrading' entertainment the producer quickly back pedalled saying they had no plans to bring it back.'.[33]

According to a report from the Centre for Islamic Studies at the University of Wales, the bottom line result is that during the last decade 10 000 Britons were moved to confess that 'there is no God but Allah and Muhammad is his prophet'. And that is just the start of possibly a permanent change for the formerly Christian and United Kingdom of Great Britain and Northern Ireland which since February 2002, no longer uses the traditional Christian symbols of BC and AD to denote passing of the years but BCE (Before the Common Era) and CE (Common Era). A religious transformation is in progress through ways big and small. In April 2003 the British press was reporting that hot cross buns were banned by about six councils in the north of England because the Christian symbol - the cross - was distressing to Muslims.[34]

Could it be that Britain's greatest twentieth century statesman, Sir Winston Churchill was prophetic when in 1922 he declared, 'The British government is the greatest Muslim state in the world'?[35]

CHAPTER 3

WESTERN EUROPE

As in Britain, Islam has also become the second largest religion in the remainder of continental western Europe.

It has been estimated that in 1989 there were 7 million Muslims living in western continental Europe. By 1995 the number had grown to 15 million. If that is so, this represents the largest movement of Muslim peoples into this part of the world in recorded history. Western Europe has not experienced this sort of movement for five centuries.

The biggest concentration of Muslims in any western European country is in France. There are approximately 6 million around the country with 1 million in Paris itself.[1] Twenty-eight percent of the city of Marseilles is now Muslim. Throughout France in the 1970s there were only 12 mosques. By the end of the 1980s there were more than a thousand.[2] In May 2003 the French Council for Muslim Religion held its inaugural meeting at UNESCO headquarters in Paris.[3] The Council will represent all believers who participate in the network of mosques and French Muslim associations in their interaction with the government.[4]

> Germany has been called the door of Islam to Europe. The city of Cologne is known as the capital of the 'Islamic Republic of Western Turkey'.

The second largest concentration of Muslims in western continental Europe is in Germany. In excess of 3.7 million live there. In the state of North Rhine – Westphalia 'nearly one third of public grade school pupils are Muslim, and the state now offers them Islamic religious instruction.'.[5] Germany has been called the door of Islam to Europe. The city of Cologne is known as the capital of the 'Islamic Republic of Western Turkey'. Throughout the country one new mosque per week is being opened. The Libyan based Society for the Preaching and Spreading of Islam has opened in Bonn. It established an annual budget of US$100 million to promote the establishment of Islamic cultural and training centres for outreach into western Europe.[6]

As it was in Britain so also in Germany. In 1989, the first Islamic political party was formed.

The first mosque opened in The Netherlands in 1949. There are now in excess of 200 places of Islamic worship serving the Muslim community which by the turn of the century had grown to 5.4% of the population.

Spain has a long history of direct contact with Islam. From the eighth to the fifteenth centuries it was under Islamic rule. Some Spanish towns still have an annual celebration to remember the final battles to free themselves of seven centuries of Islamic rule. Similar annual events by Muslims are held in parts of the Middle East to celebrate the expulsion of the 'Christian' crusaders from the eastern Mediterranean.

In Spain the largest concentration of Muslims is most likely in Madrid where over 30 000 live. In Madrid the Spanish government donated 8000 square metres of land for a new mosque to which the Saudis gave US$17 million toward its construction.

In Rome, Italy, about a ten minute drive from St Peter's which is the epicentre for many of the world's Christians, a new mosque has been built on 30 000 square metres of land. It is larger than St Peter's Basilica. It can accommodate 300 000 worshippers and is the largest mosque in Europe.[7] It cost US$50 million, 17 million of which again was provided from Saudi Arabia. The Rome City Council donated the land. In Italy there are over 300 000 Muslims and many small mosques.

Another 300 000 Muslims reside in Sweden. The first mosque has been authorised for Stockholm. Already Islam is the second largest religious group after Protestant Christianity in Sweden.[8] Approximately 200 000 Muslim immigrants live in Denmark. In 2002 one of their organisations reportedly announced a US$30 000 reward for the murder of several prominent Danish Jews. What wasn't as widely reported was an Islamic edict calling on Muslims to drive Danes out of the Norrebro quarter of Copenhagen or an open declaration of the goal to introduce Islamic law once Denmark's Muslim population grows large enough.[9]

The question is how has this rapid expansion of Islam in Europe occurred?

Immigration

The biggest influx has come about through immigration. Europe is undergoing a profound demographic change whereby a Judeo-Christian civilisation is processing toward Islamisation. Bat Ye'or notes that this is happening through 'establishing permanently in Europe a massive Arab-Muslim presence by the immigration and settlement of millions of muslims with equal rights for all'.[10] Most Muslims in continental western Europe are from northern Africa. From the early 1960s they came looking for a better way of life as European colonial powers were granting independence to their former African provinces. In West Germany they have come more recently from Turkey looking for employment and political asylum (Turk 1.61m; Kurds 0.5m; Arab 0.3m; Iranian 0.12m; Afghani 0.07m; Pakistani 0.04m). Italy is under great pressure from the unemployed from Albania and northern Africa. Some Muslims also relocated to western Europe from war zones in the Balkans.

Political Process

Relocated Muslims have prospered because open Western democracies have granted them the same rights as historically they have to other religious communities. For example the Manila Chronicle reported that 'nearly 500 years after expelling all Muslims who refused to convert to Christianity, Spain recognised Islam (in July, 1989) as a major national religion. The Ministry of Justice's Advisory Commission on religious freedom granted Islam the status of a religion "of substantial foothold" in Spain, making Muslim schools and places of worship eligible for tax exemptions.'[11]

In Rome as previously mentioned, it was the local government who granted land for what has become the largest mosque in Europe. Some hoped that Saudi Arabia might reciprocate by allocating land and allowing a church to be built in its country. No such gesture has ever been forthcoming.

In Belgium the government has given official recognition to Islam so that the state now pays salaries for *imams* (ie. religious leaders of mosques). Provincial governments provide maintenance for mosques.

Organisation

Just like Britain, organisation was undertaken on the continent to facilitate growth and to secure a better foothold by promoting the health of the Muslim community in each country. The constitution of the Islamic Council of Europe, article 111, sections 1–3 finalised by 1987, states that the Council exists:

To assist, support and supplement the activities of the member organisations in different fields of dawa (Islamic mission), including the establishment of mosques and Muslim cultural centres, dissemination of Islamic publishing and distributing literature, promotion of Islamic education and the fulfilment of other Islamic duties and obligations.

To make necessary arrangements for the establishment of new centres for organised Islamic activity wherever necessary.

To undertake and promote those activities at European and regional levels which are necessary to strengthen the work of Islamic centres and organisations, such as establishment of central or regional libraries and information and documentation centres, research bureaus, training colleges, schools, etc.[12]

Unity, coordination and cohesion have brought good rewards for the spread of Islam throughout western Europe.

Western society however is beginning to experience the clash of widely divergent cultures in which Islamic practice is a significant issue. There has been considerable debate in France over what is considered to be appropriate dress for women and whether or not girls can wear head coverings in state funded schools. Time off from work to pray on Fridays at the mosque or at other appointed times, appropriate food laws and preparations and other relevant practices are now being reexamined.

In 1987 an eighteen year old Turkish woman after moving in with her West German boyfriend, was beaten to death by her father. The father who was duly sentenced to life imprisonment for murder was quite unremorseful because as he maintained, he had 'executed Allah's will'.[13]

Finance

In continental Europe, Islam is being helped by funding from external sources to secure property and build mosques. Imams are often paid for by the governments of Muslim countries. Turkey sends religious teachers and provides Islamic lessons for children in Germany. Morocco and Algeria have done similarly in France. [14] Even the Church has helped. In Pforzheim, a city in southwest Germany, 16 out of 19 mainline Protestant churches and the Roman Catholic Church participated in raising money to build a local mosque. The supervisor for Protestant churches in the area,

Hanns-Martin Schaefer said that the gift was meant as a sign of their intention to maintain good links and reconcile relationships with the Muslim community.[15]

Evangelical churches however protested against the collection. While some may have accused them of being mean spirited, one can't help but reflect that the motives of those who sponsored the offerings within the Church for the mosque were not so much biblical as political and social, seeking to maintain peace and the status quo at all costs.

Church

The biggest aid to the growth of Islam may have been the same as that in England, the spiritual condition of the Church. Silvana Ferraguti de Cecco, an Italian social worker poignantly commented, 'Our own churches are half empty while (the Muslim) mosques are full. Shouldn't we be asking ourselves some questions?'.[16]

Indeed we should.

At the beginning of the last decade of the twentieth century, the Christian spiritual climate of continental Europe was certainly waning. It has been estimated that at that time in France there were 26 000 Roman Catholic priests and 40 000 professional astrologers registered for income tax purposes. At the same time geographically next door in the area which used to be known as West Germany, there were 30 000 Christian clergy of all types and 90 000 registered witches and fortunetellers. Not only was the Church losing out to paganism it seemed unsurprisingly unwilling, reluctant or ignorant of how to respond when confronted with the influx of Muslims. Characteristically in Germany evangelistic efforts at the time were criticised somewhat by mainline German churches who feared that 'such work would damage inter-faith relations and cause social disintegration of ethnic communities.'.[17]

With ongoing tension and disturbance in the Balkans as well as comparative poverty continuing to the east in Albania, Turkey and northern Africa it could be assumed that the transmigration of Muslims from those countries into western Europe will continue. That in itself is not necessarily a bad thing. It presents the Church of the West with an unprecedented opportunity to awaken from what seems to be spiritual lethargy to bestir itself, by word and deed to bring a powerful witness to these new arrivals. That is more hope than reality. In the meantime the build up continues.

Once more if history is any teacher, what is happening in this time may prove to be irreversible. Time would seem to be on the side of Islam. As one source close to the Muslim leadership in Iran, which was trying to expand (militarily) its base of support in the Balkans said, 'Iran is in no hurry. It does not expect short term results. In time Iran may find that the seeds it has planted are ready to sprout.'.[18] Quite so.

The question is, what will the harvest be?

CHAPTER 4

THE GREAT SATAN

When Ayatollah Khomeini of Iran first labelled the United States of America as 'The Great Satan', he probably did many a greater favour than he realised. For the first time at an international level the double speak of diplomatic niceties was dropped so that we could hear what an Islamic leader really thought of the 'Christian' West in general and the United States in particular. 'There is no God but Allah. America is the enemy of God! Down USA.' has become the chant of the streets, not just in Teheran or Baghdad but in many other Muslim cities.[1] These revelations have shocked many people. But severe shocks can sometimes resuscitate otherwise terminally ill patients.

America is the most powerful political economic entity in the world at this time. In terms of the percentage of population actively affiliated with church and the monies it generates for Christian work, the Church of America, in all probability, is also the most powerful in the Western world. This does not necessarily mean that it is the most powerful spiritually. Numbers and wealth have seldom been significant determinants on God's scales.

Insofar as America is comparatively strong in terms of whatever index is used, we might have expected that the 'foreign' religion of Islam would have been able to make less of an imprint on the fabric of religious life in America compared with other Western nations. This is not the case.

It is somewhat of a paradox that although the US continues to be the world's most technologically advanced nation, it is exceptionally difficult to know precise figures on the religious scene with any degree of certainty. With strict separation between church and state the government is not allowed to collect religious data.[2] This means that one is more dependent on the figures issued by the various religious bodies themselves about themselves. In the competitive environment of America, these figures may not be wholly reliable or statistically neutral to the degree that would be desired. Muslims and Christians both have goals and dreams.

Back in 1984 the Vice President of the Islamic College in Chicago stated, 'My dream is that the USA will become an Islamic nation by the year 2000'.[3] That dream has not been realised but progress toward it is certainly underway.

In 1989 an official publication of the Saudi Arabian government put the number of Muslims in the United States at 5 million.[4] One year later in 1990 the number stated elsewhere was 8 million.[5]

Then in 1993 the official yearbook of American and Canadian churches put the figure at 6 million. A 1997 estimate of 6–10 million Muslims is well within the bounds of possibility. These are concentrated in 22 major cities.[6]

By 1988 Muslims had established 600 centres.[7] By 2000 there were over 1200 mosques and as many again of other Islamic centres such as schools, colleges, etc. Even in Birmingham, Alabama which some call 'the buckle of the Bible Belt', by 2002 there were several mosques and a thriving Muslim community.[8] New York became a type of 'Mecca' in America for Muslims. Entire areas in Brooklyn and the Bronx became Islamic.[9] The nation's capital, Washington DC, had 39 mosques by 1997.[10] There was even a mosque established on the campus of Shaw University, a Baptist institution in Raleigh, North Carolina.[11] Not surprisingly it was built with monies donated by the Saudi Arabian government. In 1999 Muhammad Hisham Kabbani warned the State Department that extremists had taken over 80% of the mosques in the United States.[12]

Some estimate that a new mosque is being built in America every week.[13] Much of the growth of Islam in America has taken place in the last decade.[14] At the current rate, some estimate that Muslims will outnumber American Jews by 2005.[15] It is quite probable however that the number of Muslims in the United States already exceeds that of Jews.

With 165 Islamic schools, 426 Islamic associations and 90 Islamic publications,[16] funding in place from Saudi Arabia, Kuwait, Iran and other oil rich nations, over 300 *imams* (religious leaders of mosques) and other Muslim preachers graduating annually from American Islamic training institutes for the work of *dawa* (mission) in America,[17] there is no doubt that a firm foundation has been laid to achieve the ultimate goal of the Islamisation of the United States.

Twelve national level organisations already exist to facilitate this objective.[18] The most well-known of these is the American Muslim Council (AMC) established in 1990. The AMC and its sister organisations exist to unify the Islamic community, to coordinate and resource its mission thrust and increasingly to effect political change favourable to Islamic interests. The American Muslim Council in particular has been commissioned to search for suitable candidates for public office at all levels of government within the United States.

To influence public opinion it adopted a subsidiary goal of preparing and distributing news releases and public service announcements for 700 television outlets as well as radio and press media. To equip Muslim college graduates for future public service the AMC encourages them to apply for positions as aides to members of Congress.[19]

How has this come about? As in other Western societies the largest increase in the number of Muslims has come through immigration.

> ...there is no doubt that a firm foundation has been laid to achieve the ultimate goal of the Islamisation of the United States.

Immigration

Reportedly one of the first Muslims to arrive in the New World was an Egyptian early in the seventeenth century. He was integrated into an American tribe in the region of today's New York and married one of the chief's daughters. However he fell foul of local cultural norms by treating his wife inappropriately. The locals swiftly applied their version of contemporary anti-discrimination law. They skinned him alive.[20]

Saudi Arabian government publications claim that up to 30% of Africans who came as slaves to America were originally Muslims who after arrival lost their Islamic identity.[21] However Arabs themselves were major suppliers to the trade. They would not have sold their own co-religionists into slavery. The unsubstantiated claim is of no value beyond being an illustration of historical revisionism to serve contemporary propaganda purposes.

What is more certain is that the next major wave of Muslim immigrants came during the 1860s by people wishing to escape military responsibilities in the Ottoman empire. Syrians especially, landed in the north east in Massachusetts and then moved inland to Michigan.[22] In the early twentieth century several hundred thousand more came from eastern Europe including Albania.[23] The end of that century saw more arrivals from this same source, specifically from Bosnia and Albania.[24]

Another major wave of Islamic immigration was in the late 1940s as India and Pakistan, East and West, were being granted independence from Great Britain. In the following decade more came from Turkey. Since the 1960s there has been a steady inflow of the order of about 100 000 per year from the various Islamic countries. In addition to legal immigrants, it is thought that there are probably another 45 000 illegal Muslim immigrants entering the United States annually. An analysis by Khalid Duran and Daniel Pipes concludes that Muslims immigrate to the United States because of ethnic and religious persecution, civil and international wars, for educational advantage, Islamist ambition, and as Muktedar Khan put it to participate in 'the richest Muslim society on earth'.[25]

Biology

The second major cause for the increase in the overall proportion of Muslims in the United States is the higher than average birthrate pertaining to most Muslim families. This comes about because it is desirable in terms of the culture of the countries of origin. But it also has a 'folk Islamic' theological base. Sons are much desired because they are seen as the blessing of Allah. Folk Islam often teaches that the number of children a woman will bear is written on her forehead. Therefore there is nothing that one should do to increase or diminish that predetermined number. Abortion is forbidden and contraception is discouraged because that also would be seen to be attempting to interfere with the will of Allah.

Intermarriage

Linked to the high birthrate there is the third factor of intermarriage. Muslim students who come to the United States, like other third world citizens, desire to remain in the first world for economic and material advantage. One of the ways of assuring residency is to marry an American citizen. Approximately 7000 marriages are completed each year involving American women marrying Muslim men from overseas. Islamic law requires that any children of these marriages must be raised as Muslims.

Social Action

A fourth factor that has facilitated growth among some Americans has been the attractiveness of the security and discipline of the Islamic society as compared to that which exists within socioeconomically deprived pockets of American urban societies. Islam is known to place a strong emphasis on family stability. It aggressively opposes the use of alcohol, promiscuity, gambling, the practice of homosexuality and drug abuse. The disciplines which the religion impresses on its adherents and the way in which the community is self-protective, has proven attractive to those who have not been able to find solutions to these problems elsewhere in society.

In addition to presenting an alternative to American secular society with its attendant good and evil, Islam also presents a strong alternate choice to that other refuge from the difficulties of city life – the Church.

Church

As the fifth factor, the Church itself needs to acknowledge that because of its history and state, it also has contributed even if only negatively, toward the growth of Islam. Significant sections of the Church appear to be historically identified with racism and segregation. Still today some sections could be said to be far too preoccupied with their own existence and indifferent to the plight of many within their cities.

In focussing on legitimate spiritual needs to assure people entry into heaven, some parts of the church seem to have forgotten their responsibility to attempt to meet real needs on earth. These comments would apply especially to needs within the African American community. Not surprisingly it is this community which has provided the largest indigenous contribution to the growth of Islam in America. Estimates vary from 60%–90% of Muslim converts coming from this ethnic group.

It is also calculated that among these African American converts to Islam up to 80% of them had some sort of Church affiliation.[26] Probably they were disenchanted by their contact with practising Christianity, as well as being attracted toward something else that was offered from within Islam, namely its claims to be free from the stigma of slavery and to have been an African religion. Increasingly among African Americans, allegiance to Allah and his Prophet Muhammad has been replacing that to Jesus Christ.[27] At the beginning of the final decade of the twentieth century it was estimated that the number of African American converts was close to 600 000.[28] Other estimates have placed it higher. It can be reasonably assumed that the rate of conversion has been maintained within this community.

Proselytisation

This highlights the sixth factor for growth within the American Islamic community -conversions. One recent Muslim publication claimed that in one year alone there were 8000 conversions in New York City and almost 15 000 in Washington, DC. In

2002 David Barrett, co-author of the World Christian Encyclopedia, estimated that 50 000 Christians per year convert to Islam while 20 000 Muslims adopt Christianity.[29]

In 2003 the Council on American Islamic Relations chairman Nihad Awad reported to the Saudi paper 'Ukaz that 34 000 Americans had converted to Islam following the New York Trade Tower event and in his estimate this was the highest rate reached in the US since Islam arrived there.[30]

This cause is progressed through: airbrushed documentaries such as 'Muhammad: Legacy of a Prophet' which presents Muhammad as 'a model of perfection'[31], the education system, eg in Byron, California parents were surprised to find Islam being taught at their children's school when the teaching of Christianity was forbidden[32], books placed in libraries which present a revisionist view of Islam donated by the Council on American Islamic Relations[33] and even through an Islamic prison program which recruits and trains dozens of chaplains to minister to thousands of inmates.[34] With continued growth the number of conversions will compound.

Finance

Growth and expansion always cost money. Adequate finance has been the seventh growth factor. It is certainly well in place for Muslim work in America, probably even more so than in other Western countries. During the last few decades of the twentieth century Saudi Arabia made available US$87 billion for Islamic mission and ministry in the Western Hemisphere.[35] Iraq, Libya, Iran and Kuwait also contributed handsomely. Prior to the Gulf War, 'Kuwait had budgeted US$25 billion to blanket the US and Canada with Islamic propaganda'.[36]

As in Great Britain so also in America, lump sum grants have been targeted to maximise impact for Islam. For example Saudi Arabia donated US$5 million to establish a centre for Islamic legal studies at Harvard University with a similar program accepted by the University of Arkansas. In both cases a condition of accepting the gifts was that Muslim professors teach the courses. Berkeley received two large gifts from Saudi benefactors. The Alireza family donated US$2 million and US$5 million was given from the Sultan ibn 'Abd al-'Aziz Charity Foundation to broaden understanding of the Arab and Islamic worlds.[37] As in other countries money has been given for the establishment of significant mosques. For example, US$40 million given for a mosque in Manhattan's Upper East side.[38] US$8.1 million was given by King Fahd of Saudi Arabia and his son, Prince Abdul Aziz for a four storey mosque and Islamic centre in Culvar City, Southern California.[39]

Contextualised Preaching

The final factor for the growth of Islam in the United States, which is unique to that country as compared with other Western countries, is what has happened within the African American community. Toward the end of the 1980s the number of converts to Islam from the Anglo community was estimated at between 40 000 and 75 000. Estimates of converts from the African American community were over ten times greater.[40]

'American blacks have traditionally allowed religion to play a major role in their subculture. Because of the white majority's unwillingness to assimilate them into mainstream society, their places of worship became the only institutions where blacks were able to achieve leadership positions. Ministers of religion often became the leaders of the community.'[41]

In terms of religion, this has applied to Islam as it has done for some time within the Christian community.

The genesis of black Islam in America is traced to a sect called the Moorish Science Temple of America founded by Timothy Drew in 1913.[42] As often happens with the death of a founder, so in this case the group divided. Wali D. Fard led the new offshoot. He was also known as Wallace D. Fard, Wali Farad, Fard Muhammad Ali and Farad Muhammad. His credentials are a matter for speculation. One story attributed to him claims that he emigrated from Mecca to Detroit.

Fard could see that real remedies were required to reverse the perennial social ills dogging his section of society. People were looking for answers to their social and economic problems. They were also looking for freedom from injustice, equality with the white society, release from poverty etc. By 1933 he had 8000 followers. The first Temple of what became known as the Nation of Islam (NOI) was established in Detroit. Not much is known about Fard prior to 1930. Even less is known about him after March 19 1934. He somehow disappeared from the scene as mysteriously as he had appeared.

But among his disciples was one Robert Poole who had been an unemployed auto worker. He became the new leader of the movement and took the name Elijah Muhammad. He preached that Fard had been God incarnate who had reappeared as the long awaited *Mahdi* (or second Messiah). The reason claimed for his coming was to reestablish the black nation for whom the universe had been created. Whites were said to be merely an aberration of recent history. It was preached that a mad scientist called Yakub had created them by means of primitive genetic manipulation.

Elijah Muhammad led the movement for 41 years until his death in 1975. He unfortunately left a legacy of deception, corruption and financial chicanery.[43]

During all of his years of leadership the Nation of Islam was never recognised by the major groupings of orthodox Islam around the world.

But during Elijah Muhammad's tenure of leadership, one Malcolm Little learned of NOI while he was in prison. Upon his release in 1952 he joined the movement and proved to be outstandingly successful in recruiting new believers. He was given the name 'Malcolm X' to signify his unknown ethnic origins. His natural charisma was instrumental in seeing him elevated to the position of a national spokesman. Within a few years membership of NOI had grown to 40 000. By 1963 however, Malcolm X had moved close enough to the circles of top leadership to discover enough about the lifestyle of Elijah Muhammad as to become disillusioned. His agitation led to his own suspension. After this he moved to a more orthodox appreciation of Islam by studying its teachings without the influence of NOI.

On March 8 1964 Malcolm X formed another organisation that he called the Muslim Mosque. A month later he undertook his first pilgrimage to Mecca *(hajj)*. This was a life changing experience for him. He assumed a new name El-Hajj Malik El Shabazz and from then on he followed orthodox Sunni teaching and practice. However he was not to follow this new direction for long. Members of Nation of Islam allegedly assassinated him on February 21 1965. Nation of Islam claimed the killing was the result of a government plot.

During Malcolm X's excursion into orthodox Islam he had been accompanied by the son of Elijah Muhammad, Wallace Deen Muhammad. In 1970 the latter was reconciled back to NOI and upon his father's death in 1974 he was elected to lead the movement. At first he sought to honour the memory of Fard and Elijah Muhammad. But gradually he changed the doctrine and the structure of the movement.

Influenced by orthodox Islam Wallace preached that Fard was not God and neither was God black. Temples were renamed mosques and Arabic became the language for prayer as it is in orthodox Islam. He also downgraded the concept of black superiority and deleted the movement's separatism as he repositioned it for re-integration with society at large. He renamed the movement 'World Community Al-Islam in the West' (WCIW). Its members were called Bilalians in honour of Bilal. Bilal was an Ethiopian slave who became a caller to prayer *(muezzin)* in the prophet Muhammad's original group of companions in the seventh century. His significance for his twentieth century equivalents was that he was thought to be the first black Muslim.

Not all within the movement were happy with their leader's new directions. In 1978 Louis Farrakhan led a breakaway group. He resuscitated the name Nation of Islam. Farrakhan preached that contrary to orthodox Islam, the prophet Muhammad was not Allah's 'final messenger'. That was Elijah Muhammad. Under Farrakhan the aims of the restored NOI are not too dissimilar from the original movement. There is still the quest for greater social and economic justice for all black people. They have concentrated on creating employment and education opportunities, especially for those who have been African American prisoners, prostitutes and other similarly marginalised people.

Farrakhan has been accused of extreme racism and promoting segregation as a result of well-known speeches he has given. On October 16 1995 he led the march of a 'million men' in Washington DC. 'Farrakhan's fellow organiser was Benjamin Chavis, former "NAACP" Executive Director, who was stripped of that title in 1994 for alleged misuse of funds and sexual harassment.'.[44] The march was specifically aimed at African American men to inspire spiritual and moral rebirth among them. Estimates of attendees ranged from 400 000 to 850 000.

Farrakhan also attempted to move among the black communities in the United Kingdom and elsewhere. In 1998, he visited Australia specifically to meet with members of its aboriginal community who live in Alice Springs in Central Australia. Because they declined his overture he spoke in the inner Sydney suburb of Redfern to an aboriginal community. His visit was more memorable for rhetoric than substance.

Under Farrakhan's powerful charismatic leadership with his appeal to African American pride, empowerment, segregation, setting community ills right, meeting real needs within the black community and linking this to aspects of power within Islamic theology, the movement became predictably appealing, especially to the disempowered and marginalised of society.

Many blacks have found NOI or orthodox Islam attractive. From their perspective, both Government and Church have failed to deliver. But Islam offers hope of a job, a stable family, a secure environment and solid social structures.

The testimony of Imani Kareema Ellis is instructive. In 1988 she converted from Roman Catholicism to Islam. She said:

As a black woman I find (Islam) to be very liberating to members of oppressed groups. It teaches that there should be no prejudices based on race.

During congregational prayer, on one side of me may be a sister from India, on the other side a sister from Taiwan, in front and behind me an African sister and a Caucasian sister.

It's the most beautiful thing you've ever seen.[45]

Another convert who is now the leader of a mosque put his attraction for Islam thus, 'I used to be a Christian but Christianity's a welfare religion – Jesus paid it all. Black people don't need to hear that. They need to earn it.'.[46]

Political Process

Apart from significant inroads into the black community Islam is starting to make its presence felt across the political and economic spectrum of American life. The American Muslim Council which commenced in 1990 endeavours to give Muslims a voice on ethical and public policy matters. It attempts to adjust the notion that 'American principles of morality and justice are based on the Judeo-Christian tradition alone. They favour the more inclusive idea of such values deriving from the Judeo-Christian-Muslim tradition.'[47] In September 1991 the Council was recognised as the endorsing agency for Muslim clerics for the armed forces. The first Muslim chaplain was accepted on December 3 1993. By 1999 there were approximately 13 000 Muslims in the US armed services with a large number of these being high ranking officers. The armed forces received a severe jolt when black Muslim convert Sgt. Asan Akbar of the 101st Airborne Division rolled grenades into the tents of his commanding officers and then proceeded to shoot those who sought to flee during the second Gulf War of 2003.[48] In 1997 the Islamic crescent was added to the Cross and the Star of David and Law Tablets as a part of the seal of the US Navy Chaplain Corps.[49]

Muslims are starting to mount a significant lobby which in time will probably successfully counter the longstanding pro-Israel Jewish lobby in the United States. They were able to oppose Israel's request for a US$10 billion loan guarantee to assist the resettlement of former Soviet Jews in Israel.

During the time of the Balkan Wars they were able to intervene on behalf of Bosnian Muslims against Serbian 'Christians'. President Clinton seemed to respond favourably to their request by actions he took within days of their representations. The Islamic Society of North America lists amongst its aims 'to assist in the growth of strong, viable, visible, vocal and effective Muslim communities in the local level...to aid Muslim causes in the Muslim world by influencing governmental policy of the US...and providing moral and material support.'[50] In June 1991, Siraj Wahaj became the first Muslim to lead in prayer in the US House of Representatives. In February 1992 Wallace Deen Muhammad did likewise in the Senate.[51]

Miller Brewing, Coca Cola and other major commercial enterprises have been obliged to apologise publicly and to change their advertising when it has seemed to have been insensitive toward an aspect of Islamic religion or culture. Nike was obliged to recall 38 000 pairs of shoes because their squiggly *Air* word could have been misconstrued to be similar to the Arabic script for *Allah*. They were also required to fund Muslim educational centres.[52] In November 1998 Muslims 'took to the streets' to protest the 20th Century Fox film *The Siege,* claiming it caricatured Muslims as terrorists.[53]

In October 1995 Al Gore in his capacity as Vice President was obliged to offer an apology to the Muslim community. Similarly in February 1996 Joseph Kennedy, serving as a representative in Congress was obliged to apologise. Both had used the word *'jihad'* as a figure of speech to describe what they considered to be over zealous activities of their political opposition in the Republican Party. *Jihad* is an Arabic word used by Muslims for religious war mostly against non-Muslims as well as for internal spiritual struggle.

During the Republican Convention of August 1996 Muslim groups sponsored a hospitality suite from which they were able to promote social and political issues of concern to their community. House Speaker Newt Gingrich was sailing the new winds on the political seas when he included reference to mosques in his speech at the Convention.[54] A drive was initiated by Islamic groups to register at least a million voters.

With sufficient critical mass for a support base, the emergence of a new political force has commenced which will have wide ranging ramifications for American policies abroad especially as they relate to its traditional support of Israel and its attitudes towards the Middle East.

What of the future?

Islamic groups will use the open political democratic processes in America more than ever before to further their interests. A circular released from the American Muslim Council in part states: 'Our American democratic system allows us to work together as interest groups and gives us the opportunity to lobby our decision makers. Other ethnic groups have succeeded in influencing American policy. We can do the same.'.[55]

But Islam is much more than just another ethnic lobby group. As its influence grows it is bound to have repercussions on the whole American way of life and not just its political systems, although the strains which will appear in those systems may be useful as an early warning barometer for what is ahead.

So much that is embedded in Islamic theology is inseparable from the Arab culture in which Islam was birthed. Such concepts as 'life, liberty and the pursuit of happiness' as being legitimate ends of government and very important to the American way of life are almost unimaginable within pure Islam. 'The key phrase within the Declaration of Independence that all men are equal before the "laws of nature and of nature's God" cannot be translated into Islamic terms but instead conveys blasphemy and heresy.'.[56]

Dr Mahatir Mohammad as Prime Minister of Malaysia, in common with many other Muslim leaders has vigorously attacked such American icons as capitalism, '…the free market and market forces, globalisation, liberalisation, deregulation, absolute freedom etcetera…'.[57] Even more significant is Islam's well-known stance on secularism which is implemented probably more rigorously in America than in any other Western state. One 'moderate' Egyptian cleric who was appearing on government controlled television to broadcast his interpretation of Islamic law said, 'A secularist represents a danger to society and the nation and must be eliminated. It is the duty of the government to kill him.'.[58] Clearly Osama bin Laden agreed with that sentiment wholeheartedly. In June 1999 two years before the September 11 atrocities, he appeared on Arab satellite TV urging like-minded Muslims to attack Americans wherever they were to be found.[59] He is alleged to have carried out the threat through his al Qaeda organisation operating against American assets overseas and at home.

One American university professor concludes, 'Islam and Democracy simply aren't compatible.'.[60] But one of Iran's leading philosophers, Abdul Karim Soroush is one of a growing number of Islamic thinkers who are at least 'exploring the compatibility of Islam and democracy.'.[61] Such transient intellectual pursuits however give little comfort as they are unlikely to reverse 14 centuries of tradition and some current international Islamic practices.

Whatever the outcome of the rethink, in the interim democracy can serve a useful purpose for Islam. As one Muslim leader said to Giuseppe Bernardini, Roman Catholic Archbishop of Izmir, Turkey: 'Thanks to your democratic laws, we will invade you. Thanks to our religious laws, we will dominate you.'.[62]

Saudi Arabia and the United States represent extreme opposites on a cultural, political and religious world scale. Both would claim to exemplify the best of their hitherto dominant religions, Islam and Christianity. The clash that is likely to occur as Islam increasingly impacts within America is potentially of cataclysmic proportions.

In an article entitled 'The New Ideological Enemy', a think tank of the Pentagon considered that a confrontation with Islam was inevitable. Reflecting on this one Muslim commentator observed:

'...the advocate of the New World Order, the Satanic Bush administration, claiming for the monopoly of World power is eyeing on Islam as the only enemy capable of dismantling its hegemony in the wake of the crumbling communist empire...Unlike other ideologies, (Islam) did not really die out but is now experiencing a revival to challenge the present status quo.'[63]

The threat to 'the American way of life' does not come from some militarily inferior cluster of far off powers. It comes from within. It is already grafted into the body politic, slowly but surely effecting change to achieve its ultimate goals – the Islamisation of America. Ismail Allah-Faruqi agrees. 'Nothing could be greater than this youthful, vigorous and rich continent (North America) turning away from its past evil and marching forward under the banner of Allahu Akbar (God is Greater).'.[64]

> The threat to 'the American way of life' does not come from some militarily inferior cluster of far off powers. It comes from within. It is already grafted into the body politic, slowly but surely effecting change to achieve its ultimate goals – the Islamisation of America.

Whether or not the Church can, as an independent spiritual entity, shake itself free from some of its unfortunately less attractive historical positions, practices and alliances and radically realign itself to face the new challenge remains to be seen. As yet it may even be failing to realise the threat to its own existence. Louis Farrakhan claims to have preached in as many churches as he has in mosques. By 1998 he was claiming to have been visited personally in his home by about 2000 Christian leaders.[65]

Whether cross or crescent dominates the future American skyline is a question only time will answer. But a teacher at the Al Ghazly Islamic School in Jersey City in New Jersey well summarised the Islamic option. 'Our short term goal is to introduce Islam. In the long-term we must save American society…this piece of land is Allah's property.'[66]

The US government perhaps unwittingly gave a significant boost to that prospect, when in late 2002 it issued postage stamps appropriately inscribed in Arabic wishing everyone a happy Eid. This 'Eid' is the festival which concludes the end of Ramadan, the annual month of 'fasting' for all Moslems. If the present trend continues it could well be that one day the stars and stripes may be replaced by the crescent moon.

CHAPTER 5

THE DARKENING CONTINENT

Across the other side of the globe from America lies the massive continent of Africa. With an area of 30 million square kilometres and approximately 750 million people in over 3000 ethno linguistic groups speaking 1800 known languages, it represents a continent where both Christianity and Islam have existed from the first centuries of their respective births. It is on this continent where the irrefutable evidence of history clearly marks the trail of Islam and the changes that it has inevitably wrought.

If there is any doubt as to the permanent and to date, irreversible effects that Islam has had on entering 'Christian' countries, one merely needs to look at Africa. In its first century of existence Islam swept across all African countries north of the Sahara as far as the Atlantic Ocean. These were previously countries where Christianity was well-established. Today apart from Egypt, in each if any, only the faintest flicker of Christian existence may be found. But south of the Sahara the contest is now joined. Each of these major missionary religions has advanced to face each other once more.

The evidence of the process of Islamisation that emerges from Africa, its causes, methods and effects are repetitively reliable. It is littered through the bones of history. It is infused in the wounds of current events. Today Africa continues to be a living laboratory demonstrating the procession of Islam, where it leads and what the anticipated end result may be.

In the far north there are those countries that have been totally subdued. In the immediate sub-Saharan region there are now nine states with the majority of their populations being Muslim. In central Africa on the west, there is Nigeria where an intense struggle is being waged to claim Africa's most populous state for Islam. On the east coast in Sudan, war continues relentlessly involving the continent's most ancient Christian community just as it has been intermittently pursued for the last 1400 years. Away to the south the battle is only just beginning. But begin it has.

In a speech delivered in Kigali the capital of Rwanda, with the whole continent in mind, President Gaddafi of Libya described the Christian Church as 'false, infidel and irreligious'. He went on to say, 'Africa must be Muslim. Christians are intruders in Africa and agents of colonialism; we must wage a holy war so that Islam will spread in Africa.'.

The first adherents to what became Christianity arrived back in Africa having been converted in Palestine. The Church was established several centuries before Arab armies arrived. If these Christians and their descendants are 'intruders', then conversely by what appropriate term shall Muslims be described?

President Gaddafi was speaking at the opening of a mosque and Islamic centre for which Libya and the United Arab Emirates had provided US$5 million. Rwandan President at that time, Juvenal Habyarimana, had recently renounced Christianity to convert to Islam. President Gaddafi went on to say, *'You are hoisting the banner of Islam below the equator in the heart of Africa and declaring that Muhammad is the Messiah of God. You are facing up to the challenge of the Christian Church, which does not recognise the prophecy of Muhammad.'*[1]

So much for below the equator. Other Muslims believe that countries above the equator in the continent's northern most reaches also need Islamic purification.

'Italian sailors, their ship moored in port, are murdered in their sleep; Russian and Romanian oil workers are shot by gunmen disguised as police; Western diplomats venture out only with armed bodyguards. Clearly the armed Islamic group, which last October (1993) warned foreigners in Algeria either to leave or be killed, is being true to its word. Even if they choose to leave, however, as many do, foreigners cannot escape the consequences of Algeria's turmoil.'[2]

Algeria was the heartland of the early church of northern Africa that produced such illustrious leaders as Cyprian, Tertullian and Augustine. With the church in a moribund state in the eighth century Islam entered the region. Algeria is 96.7% Muslim. Henri Teissier, Archbishop of Algiers likens the current church to the tiniest of objects hidden within the centre of a set of oriental resting dolls.[3]

A group of Algerian citizens has called for an even stricter form of Islam and they continue to carry out their bloody threats. During 1992–1999 this struggle between factions within Algeria's Muslim society cost 100 000 lives.[4] This is happening at a distance closer to Europe than is Bosnia from the German border.[5]

In the continent's most southern state, South Africa, former Secretary General of the Islamic Propagation Center, Yousuf Deedat revealed that it was no secret that South

Africa was now also high on the agenda of the Muslim offensive. 'We are going to turn South Africa into a Muslim state. We have the money to do it.'[6] The number of Muslims in South Africa is fewer than 2%. But no one should underestimate Deedat's challenge and legacy.

From Cairo in the north to Capetown in the south, from Dakar in the west to Djibouti in the east, Islam is on the move. It intends to finish the job it started fourteen centuries ago, the Islamisation of the entire continent of Africa. It is now present and growing in many African countries and is already contesting for additional control of some. One of its own commentators, Dr Mozammel Haque concluded that Africa 'is turning into a battleground for the rival faiths of Islam and Christianity'.[7] This 'new presence of Islam is being felt in a wide belt across central Africa from Sierra Leone on the Atlantic to Sudan on the Red Sea'.[8]

A Christian analyst has observed that:

Muslim missionaries are flooding Africa with funding from Saudi Arabia and Iran. They are being encouraged to marry Christian women and raise Muslim children. Mosques and Quranic schools are being built everywhere...Islamic NGOs (Non Government Organisations) train development people and send them into the villages and the urban slums with revolving loans for anyone who will become Muslim. The best students are being recruited actively for the three Muslim universities in Africa...Islamic centres are springing up all over Africa.[9]

Colonel Gaddafi of Libya uses his oil wealth to pay off debts of sub-Saharan nations but at the cost of their being absorbed into the block to achieve his stated desire for a united Islamic Africa.[10]

> **From Cairo in the north to Capetown in the south, from Dakar in the west to Djibouti in the east, Islam is on the move. It intends to finish the job it started fourteen centuries ago, the Islamisation of the entire continent of Africa.**

Africa's connection with Christianity is second only to that of Palestine and Israel itself. Africa provided timely hospitality for Jesus near the beginning of his life. At the end of his earthly life, an African from Cyrene (Libya) carried his cross.

The Christian Church was more substantially and extensively established in Africa prior to its development in Europe. The Apostle Mark is said to have located to Alexandria. In the first few centuries of the Church's existence, some of its most famous bishops and thinkers came from northern Africa. However it did not penetrate beyond the Sahara, except in the east where it went as far as Ethiopia and the Sudan. Then in the seventh century Islam swept out of its home base in the Arabian peninsula and overran Christianity across all of its northern African countries.

Islam also did not proceed beyond the Sahara except down the east coast where, by the twelfth century, Arab and Persian traders had established a series of fortified trading stations. Their intermingling with indigenous peoples resulted in the development of Swahili becoming a major trade language.

At the beginning of the twentieth century, it was estimated that the entire continent's population was 32% Muslim. Christians numbered only 9.2%. These were concentrated more in the sub-Saharan areas primarily as a result of renewed Christian missionary activity that re-entered the continent seriously in the eighteenth century. Their work was among animist tribal groups.

But by the mid 1980s the continental positions were reversed. Christians were numbered at 44.2% while Muslims were 41.2% of the total population.[11] By 2001 Christians were 48.4% while Muslims were 41.3%.[12] But the most significant item was the location of the Muslim population. 160 million were north of the Sahara and 157 million were in sub-Saharan Africa.[13] Islam had grown beyond its northern African base to come down the west coast and the Sahel region. Christianity had grown in the south and to the east. This changing demographic trend had not gone unnoticed.

The 1970s proved to be the opportune time to prepare for the relaunch of the Islamic mission to Africa. The OPEC crisis and the accumulated oil wealth after 1973 would provide the finance. The Iranian revolution of 1979 gave motivation, zeal and a transferable model of operation. An Islamic conference in Abuja, Nigeria, in 1989 codified and formalised the process.

In 1974 as money started to flow in previously undreamt of amounts, the Muslim World League (Rabita-al-alam al-Islam) called a key conference in Mecca. The governor of Mecca, Prince Fawaz bin Abdul Aziz gave the inaugural address at the conference. He called for unity within international Islam for the struggle ahead. The chairman of the conference, Sheikh Muhammad Ali al-Harakan, Minister for Justice in Saudi Arabia, emphasised a need to return to the basics of the Quran and Sunnah (practice of the prophet).

The conference was divided into five sections, the first being 'Islamic *Dawah*: Means and Methods' (*Dawah* in Islamic evangelism is the invitation/call to conversion.)[14] Priority was to be given to increasing the number of educational and cultural centres for the propagation of Islam, its language and its culture. The most modern methods were to be used in repackaging and presenting Islam through educational, health, social welfare and vocational institutions.

At the conclusion of the conference, a new body known as the Supreme Coordinating Council of World Islamic Organisations was established. The main task of this council was to coordinate the activities of all member bodies in their preaching and outreach on behalf of Islam. Representatives to the Council were appointed from each continent. Of the nine available places Africa was given three, thus indicating the high priority that continent was to have in the future spread of Islam.

As Islam looked at Africa it was presented with a conundrum. To the Muslim mind, Islam as revealed is perfect. Therefore it should have influenced the world and specifically Africa much more than it had done in the last fourteen centuries. That it had not done so was a major concern that had to be addressed.

'The issue at stake for Muslims (was) not renaissance, *nadha*, with its sociopolitical and economic overtones, nor (was) it reformation, *islah*, with its theological implications...the key word...(was) *tajdid*, renewal.'[15]

The emphasis on a follow-up conference in Mecca in October 1987 was again stressing the need to return to the Quran and Traditions *(Hadith)*.

One of the specific outcomes of the 1974 and 1987 conferences was the Islam in Africa Conference in November 1989, held in Abuja, the then newly constructed capital city of Nigeria. The conference was sponsored by the Nigerian Supreme Council for Islamic Affairs, the Islamic Council for Europe, whose headquarters are in London and the Organisation of the Islamic Conference.

In a communique issued on November 28 1989 from Abuja, in part the conference resolved to call on all African Muslims:

• to unite,
• to cooperate with international Islam,

- to strive to remove any barriers within Islam,
- to bring the syllabi of educational institutions into conformity with Islamic ideals, goals and principles,
- to encourage teaching Arabic as the lingua franca,
- to cooperate in areas of commerce, industry and finance,
- to intensify efforts to introduce or reinstate Islamic law *(shariah)* and
- to form a permanent body to be known as Islam in Africa Organisation (IAO).

The permanent headquarters for IAO was to be established in Abuja.

The communique thanked the then President of Nigeria, General Ibrahim Babangida, for his stimulating inaugural address. This address had been delivered on his behalf by the then Chief of Army Staff of Nigeria, General Sani Abacha who went on to become the next (unelected) president of Nigeria until his death on June 8 1998.

Among the eighteen specific objectives set out for IAO in the communique were the following:

- To establish Islamic tertiary and vocational centres which are designed to train *dawah* (Muslim missionary) workers.
- To support, enhance and coordinate *dawah* work all over Africa and propagate the knowledge of Islam throughout the continent.
- To support the establishment and application of the *shariah* to all Muslims.
- To ensure the appointment of only Muslims to strategic national and international posts of member nations.
- To ensure that only Muslims are elected to all political posts of Muslim nations.
- To ensure the ultimate replacement of all Western forms of legal and judicial systems with the *shariah* in all member nations...and
- To eradicate in all its forms and ramifications all non-Muslim religions in member nations (such religion shall include Christianity, Ahmadiyya and other tribal modes of worship unacceptable to Muslims).

Above the seal of the president of the Federal Republic of Nigeria on the document, the final paragraph states:

The joint conference finally ratified the admission of Nigeria as a full member of the Organisation of the Islamic Conference (OIC), and thanked the government and people of Nigeria for having generously donated US$21 billion to the Islamic development fund of the OIC and sincerely requested the Federal government of

Nigeria to implement all policies and programmes of OIC to show the whole world that Nigeria is truly an Islamic nation.

One of the immediate implications of the communique was the disenfranchisement of approximately 70 million Christians who already lived within the borders of the 24 participating countries.[16] It applied specifically to Nigerians, the majority of whom were and probably still are Christian but who now were to be subjected to the outworking of resolutions from this conference.

As one observer noted:

This means that a Holy War on the continent of Africa is well on its way! If this agreement is allowed to come to fruition, it will certainly turn Africa into one giant Iran, bringing with it one of the greatest holocausts our generation has ever known.[17]

While 'Holy War' might not complete the conversion of the entire continent during that correspondent's lifetime certainly all the evidence indicates it is well underway. For non-Muslim Africans the indications for the future look anything but calm, peaceful and undisturbed.

CHAPTER 6

DARKNESS GATHERS

The Islamic world (Middle East influence in particular) is putting pressure on the nominal Yao Muslims to become more militant and disciplined in the expression of their faith. Hence the growing presence of Arabic speaking Muslim missionaries, proliferation of mosques in town and village areas and an influx of petro dollars for educational and social development programs. It is obvious that Muslim leaders are using their base in the Yao Muslim community to influence other tribal groups. The Christian Church in Malawi will rapidly lose ground if it fails to act quickly to the growing and aggressive Islamic influence.[1]

Such is the conclusion of a report from inside the southern African nation of Malawi (Christian 80%; Muslim 13%).

The Yao tribe to which the report refers is 90% nominal Muslim. Folk Islam predominates. But with external sources allegedly financially backing nationwide projects of mosque building, strengthening Islamic institutions and training indigenous people in how to preach, Islam is rapidly raising its profile within this nation. Even though the percentage of Muslims is proportionately low, the push is on.

One correspondent concludes that the 'government is about to be Islamised...' Certainly the President of Malawi was in favour of such an outcome. On May 4 1999 E Bakhi Muluzi in his official capacity as President of the Republic of Malawi wrote to Col. Muammar Gaddafi in his capacity as President of 'The Great Arab Republic of Jimuhariya (Libya)'. In his letter President Muluzi is reported as saying:

...The remittance of the equivalent of $9M(MK 405m) would assist and enable my efforts to penetrate the central region [and] donate for more mosques and silence the noise on the arms route to the DRC (Democratic Republic of Congo). The penetration of the northern region would be through the construction of a 136 km road, where as in the central region, there shall forthwith commence the building of Islamic centres...

In general the Islamisation evangelism process is going on well save for financial handicap. For the first time in the history of my country, Arabic has been introduced to the University of Malawi.

Please find enclosed a detailed contingency plan. Inshia Allah.[2]

Kuwait has reportedly accepted responsibility for establishing mosques throughout Malawi at a distance of 20 kilometres in every direction. Saudi Arabia has allegedly undertaken to do likewise in neighbouring Zambia.

An Islamised Malawi would certainly be well-placed geographically to be used as an effective launching pad to thrust north and south into central and southern Africa respectively. But what has happened in Malawi can be said of many other countries in the continent.

In the eastern states of Tanzania (Christian 51.4%; Muslim 31.8%), Kenya (Christian 78.6%; Muslim 8%) and Uganda (Christian 88.6%%; Muslim 6%) attempts are being made to form national level, Islamic based, political parties which would then influence all other parties. Sheikh Ahmad Balala, leader of the Islamic party of Kenya said that if the government should try to impede the establishment of an Islamic voting block then 'millions of soldiers will die in a bloody war that has never been seen in this country'.[3] Conservative Muslims in Kenya are seeking the implementation of Shari'ah Islamic legal code.[4]

The Chairman of the Council of Imams and Preachers of Kenya (CIPK), Sheikh Ali Shee threatened that unless the concepts of Islamic courts were enshrined in the new Kenyan constitution, provinces in which Muslims lived on the coast and in the north-east would break away.[5]

Previously the degree of peace that existed in the east African states, partly because Islam was proportionately much smaller, was such that even if Muslims wanted to convert to Christianity there was little objection. More recently the scene has changed remarkably but not unexpectedly. Christians are branded as being 'unbelievers'. Christian evangelistic activity is opposed. Christians have been ridiculed for their faith. Articles offensive to them have been regularly published in media controlled by Muslims. Libya and Saudi Arabia among others, are said to be the main financial backers for the new advance.

Muslims consider that Islamic law *(shariah)* is more desirable than Christian 'British' law which is still foundational for a number of African states. If the state permits freedom of choice that results in lifestyles considered lax or permissive from an Islamic perspective, then Muslims may claim not to be bound to obey the laws of that state. Observance of religious dictates has prior allegiance over laws of any state in any areas where the two may conflict.

As the duty of the state is to promote (Islamic) good and prevent evil (Surah 9:7), should a Muslim choose to disobey particularly any laws of a secular state for reasons of religious preference then, from a Muslim perspective, that person is exonerated. Similar attitudes are held toward education. In concept and content, Muslims desire it to confirm and conform to Islamic objectives.

Similarly, Muslims with their perspective of the spiritual nature of the state, consider that spiritual exercises should be funded by the state from tax revenue because Muslims pay into state coffers. Therefore, the argument goes, it should be the responsibility of the state to fund pilgrimage to Mecca, Quranic schools, etc. Until these and other religio-social demands are met, agitation for such will probably increase.

> In the period 1991–93, 500 new mosques and Islamic centres were erected with money provided through the Saudi backed Muslim World League and Islamic Bank.

Adjacent to Kenya's northeast are Somalia and Ethiopia. Somalia with 99.9% of its people declared as Sunni Muslim is obviously Islamic. Ethiopia is fast following.

The Christian population of Ethiopia is 65%. The Muslim population is 31%. Following the fall of Ethiopia's former Mengistu communist government, the emphasis of the Islamic movement in the post-war reconstruction period was on securing its religious future in the country. In the period 1991–93, 500 new mosques and Islamic centres were erected with money provided through the Saudi backed Muslim World League and Islamic Bank.[6]

In the centre of the continent to the immediate west of these key east African states, sprawls jungled Democratic Republic of Congo (formerly Zaire). From its trading bases on the east coast of Mombasa in Kenya and Dar-es-salaam in Tanzania Islam has pushed inland. The majority of Muslims in Congo are Sunni concentrated in the eastern towns of the country.

Although they number only 1.1% of the population which is 95.3% Christian, with the usual formula of outside financial, political and educational assistance, they are becoming increasingly influential. New mosques have proliferated. Scholarships have been provided to study within local Islamic institutions as well as those abroad. Converts to Islam have been offered initial capital to start up businesses. As one farsighted person has already concluded, even though it might as yet seem unthinkable, 'If the West does not help, Zaire will become Islamic'.[7] A sampling of the more southern states shows similar trends.

In Mozambique in 1993 the percentage of Muslims was estimated to be 13% with Christians numbering 42% of the population. By 2001 it was estimated that the percentage of Muslims had increased to 18.1% while the percentage of Christians had increased to 57.6%.

In 1996, 59 members of parliament successfully introduced a bill to declare the major Islamic festivals of *Eid Al-Fitr* and *Eid Al-Adhar* as public holidays. Parliament passed that bill even though it was clearly contravening the relevant sections of the national Constitution. In fact in the following year of 1997, the Supreme Court of Mozambique ruled exactly that. The bill was unconstitutional.

At least up to this point in time there had been equality before the law for all religions. Christmas Day also had not been recognised as a day of any religious significance. The country is supposed to be strictly secular according to its constitution. But Muslims are putting on pressure for this to change in their favour.

Although Mozambique was left somewhat financially destitute after its years of experimenting with Marxism, Middle East money has been channelled into one of Africa's poorest states with significant amounts of that money going toward building mosques.

Even though Muslims numbered only 1.6% in 2001 in the neighbouring state of Zimbabwe, the objectives that were communicated through the 1989 Nigerian conference communique are still being vigorously implemented. In this case, cooperation from international Islam in terms of finance is reported to have come from Iran and Malaysia. As is commonly the case, conditions are applied to accepting such help.

In return for the money to reconstruct recording studios for a television company, Malaysian interests were granted free airtime to promote Islam. Where Malaysian companies have built new housing colonies, mosques also were constructed as a part of the project. Islamic schools and cultural centres as well as other forms of training centres in practical skills were built. Free scholarships were awarded to those who convert to Islam. More advanced scholars may be sent to Islamic universities overseas.

Firsthand reports[8] speak of Islam's focus on vulnerable and poor communities. Teenagers are offered educational scholarships the first two years of which must be devoted to Quranic studies in Saudi Arabia. In Mashonaland in the east, vast tracks of land have been given to Libya in exchange for oil. The Commander of the Airforce in 1980–1990 was a Pakistani, Daud Porter. Still today fighter pilots are trained in Libya and Pakistan. Iranians have bought up much of the manufacturing sector while medical practitioners come mostly from Egypt.

To influence the political climate further in recent years, the Presidents of Pakistan and Iran, as well as high ranking members of the Malaysian government have visited Zimbabwe. To change societal norms and culture Muslims have made a major thrust in the food processing area. Religious leaders have been employed to oversee the slaughter of animals and other food processing activities to ensure that matters are carried out in accordance with *shariah* law. Muslims claim that this is part way to seeing the people become Muslims.

The cumulative effect of what is happening is summed up by one internal observer who says, 'Islamic centres throughout Zimbabwe are "now" indoctrinating underprivileged youths so as to turn them against their African beliefs, Christianity and the government if it refuses to bow down to their demands'.[9] As critical mass is built, the future does not bode well for hitherto Christian (61%) Zimbabwe.

Slightly further south and immediately adjacent to Zimbabwe is Botswana. Here the percentage of Muslims is even smaller, 0.2% in 2001. The centre for Muslim activity in Botswana was moved from Lobatse to Gaborone after a mosque was erected there in 1982, this time reportedly paid for by Saudi and Libyan governments. Muslim missionaries focus on prisons, the poor, educated youth and Christians. In 2001 Christians were still 67% of the population. Muslims accuse Christianity of having failed. The evidence cited for this claim is the widespread practices of substance abuse and sexual promiscuity in the society.

This charge is levelled at Christians in just about every country. It conveniently overlooks the same problems in countries such as Pakistan and the widespread common illnesses caused only by sexually transmitted diseases in other south Asian Muslim communities.

At the base of the continent stands South Africa, long known for its granitelike stance as a conservative 'Christian' nation. Islam first arrived in South Africa in the form of imported slaves from what today is Indonesia and Malaysia. The Dutch brought them to the early Cape colony from 1654 onwards.

The British contributed to official immigration of Muslims by bringing Indian indentured labourers into Natal. While the labourers were mostly Hindu, these were later followed by other Indians who were Muslim traders. These later arrivals built their own mosques in Natal and spread their faith, eventually to reach Botswana. As noted earlier South Africa has been moved up the priority scale for Islamic attention. Libya has reportedly been a principal financial supporter in this cause.

In August 1996, 5000 Muslim vigilantes rioted in Capetown. Their chant was *Allahu akbar* (God is Greater). The public reason for the march was the same as that given in the ghettoes of America. The accusation is repeated around the world. Social degradation (in this case attributed to drug abuse) it is claimed, is a result of derelict, decadent Christianity. By associating a symbol of contemporary society's sickness with an alleged cause, 'failed Christianity', Muslims would hope to build the case for the necessity of a new foundation. Christianity – out. Islam – in. The transition would not be peaceful. In August 1998 and January 1999, Muslim processionists were involved in violent clashes. They were opposing Britain's involvement in continued hostilities in Iraq.[10]

In 2001 Muslims in South Africa numbered only 1.5% of the population but in the rush toward the future the past cannot be forgotten. Before the institution of the Truth Commission chaired by Archbishop Desmond Tutu to try to make the South African past right, Muslims were following their own version of that path. An Islamic *dawah* college leader had already threatened to have a Protestant pastor assassinated for remarks he had made in a taped sermon a decade earlier unless he immediately retracted them.[11]

To the northwest of South Africa is Ivory Coast (31.8% Christian, 38.6% Muslim). To relieve financial stress in 2001 it joined the Organization of Islamic Conference to qualify for funding from the Islamic Development Bank. Now Islamic groups are demanding a Muslim government and *shariah* (Islamic) law.[12]

Nigeria in many ways epitomises much of the entire continent of Africa. Within its 924 000 square kilometres is reflected the topography of the continent. In the south are tropical forests and as one moves north these give way to savanna grasslands. Finally from the north, there is the encroachment of the desert moving relentlessly to the south.

Like many other African countries, Nigeria has many tribal groups. There are 426 different ethnic groups within its borders. Because ethnicity is a sensitive political issue, the country has been divided increasingly into ever smaller states within a federal framework. At the moment there are 36 such states which helps to reduce the impact of tribal loyalties on the national political level. The largest indigenous people groups in Nigeria are Hausa, Yoruba, Ibo and Fulani.

When Nigeria gained independence from Britain in 1960 there were great hopes for this, the most populous and richly endowed nation in the continent. It has fertile agricultural land, significant mineral resources and vast reserves of oil. The natural ingredients were there for success. However the opportunities have been largely squandered through incompetent management, corruption and neglect of appropriate expenditure on basic agriculture and infrastructure.[13] The country has also been troubled by political turmoil for much of its independence era. Military coups, civil war and other tensions are endemic.

The Nigerian Church has an outstanding record of growth through evangelism. However within its success lies perhaps its greatest current weakness. According to one analyst, evangelism has not been accompanied by sufficient follow-up. In teaching there have been doctrinal distortions often introduced from abroad. Materialism, as well as seeking after position and power has caused division and fragmentation within the profusion of indigenous denominations. Second generation nominalism and instances of syncretism are the results of inadequate discipleship. Observable divisions and double standards have led to public disrepute of the Gospel.[14] Although there is still much of magnificence in the Body of Christ within Nigeria, there is also much which, unless attended to quickly, could result in its own undoing.

Statistics in Nigeria are always open to question. Probably there are between 110–120 million people in the country. No one can be quite sure what the size of the population is or its major divisions. In the 1991 census it was revealed that Nigeria had 20 million fewer people than it had claimed.[15] The most recent official calculation for the number of Muslims as compared to Christians dates from 1963.

Today, Muslims claim to outnumber Christians and of course Christians counter claim. A 2001 estimate put the number of Christians at 52.6% mostly resident in the south and the number of Muslims at 41% mostly resident in the north.[16]

In recent times the government has not allowed religious data to be collected at official census times. This could be because it is potentially such an explosive political issue. Equally it could have been that hitherto key government Muslim officials fear that their claim of a Muslim majority is wide of the mark and don't want any definitive evidence to the contrary to emerge. Therefore although they have had the authority to direct such questions to be inserted in the census they have not done so. What is more certain is that Nigeria is far closer to becoming an Islamic state than any other sub-Saharan country on the continent that has not already been declared Islamic.

The communique of the Organisation of Islam Conference dated November 28 1989 explicitly claimed Nigeria as already being an Islamic nation. Although Christians and others may have objected to this development, that position has neither been denied nor rescinded. The framework at least is set for its implementation.

In the already predominantly Muslim north, Christian evangelistic activity has been severely curtailed, restricted or banned. In the process of rioting and looting, Christian churches have been destroyed and sadly, Christians have responded in kind. Muslim youth are drawing inspiration from Iran-style fundamentalist militancy.[16] As recently as January 1998 Christians were still wondering whether or not Nigeria was a member state of the OIC and voiced a suspicion that it was although somewhat inactive[18] and the position remains quite clear. Equally clear is that officialdom was implementing the recommendations of the Abuja communique to achieve its stated objectives.

Muslim leaders have repeatedly called for the full establishment of *shariah* (traditional Islamic law) courts in the south where most Christians live. They have insisted that Christians cooperate with their demand as is common in other African states. The Muslim controlled press has accused and abused Christians. The standard international accusation of the failure of Christianity that has resulted in the rise of drug culture, promiscuity etc. has also been levelled. In general, Western values in common with the international trend are denigrated.

The country has been governed by a succession of Muslim military rulers mostly from the north since the failure of the Ibos in the south to secede in a civil war of the 1960s in which a million people died.[19] This resulted in preferential treatment being given to the Muslim community, be it in the form of the financial rewards of government contracts or key positions within government. This often heightened tribal and religious tensions. When the government appointed Muslim Ibharra political leaders over Bassas Christians, when public funds were used to build on government property and Christian religious instruction in schools was disallowed while Islamic teaching was encouraged, Christians reacted.[20]

In the area of finance Nigeria itself is potentially wealthy. Even though the country became almost bankrupt through mismanagement, it hardly qualifies for additional input from Middle East resources. Nevertheless, there has been unique success in persuading other agencies to support financially the aims of Islam within Nigeria. In the period 1997–2002, UNICEF spent up to US$30 million on the rehabilitation of Quranic schools in Nigeria. The chief justice of the Federal Republic at that time, a Muslim, nicely summed up the attainment of this objective as not only significant for Nigeria but for Islam internationally. He said, 'The time has come for Islam to have a place in the heart of the United Nations.'

Obviously he meant an Islamised United Nations because the Supreme Council for Shariah in Nigeria issued a statement published in local newspapers on Monday March 4 2002 which rejected President Obusanjo's attempts to complete the parliamentary process of ratifying UN conventions on human rights' issues. The Council regarded them as a 'plot to destabilise (Nigeria) through the United Nations' covert campaign against Islam'.[21]

The irony of the inconsistency of what has been happening here is clarified when it is known that, over in Islamic Sudan on the other side of the continent, if so much as a single Bible was found on a United Nations relief plane with goods for the Christian south, the whole flight was cancelled and desperately needed supplies of food and shelter were denied those who most needed them. This was allegedly because of United Nations policy.

The situation in Nigeria remains explosively tenuous. Some pressure release may have arrived with the transference of political power to non-Muslim President Olusegun Obasanjo on May 29 1999. But it has been the Northern Muslim majority military and not civilian politicians who have ruled Nigeria for 30 of the last 40 years.[22] In reaction to some of Obasango's appointments of non-Muslims, northern states called for the introduction of *shariah* law in contradiction to the federal constitution which guarantees religious freedom.[23]

The Roman Catholic Archbishop of Lagos, Rev. Dr Olubunmi Okogie responded by stating that the call for the implementation of the *shariah* as an 'option for Nigeria is nothing other than a declaration of a religious war on the country's Christians'.[24] Bishop Okonkwo of the Redeemed Evangelical Mission declared the Islamic legal code as the 'silent killer' of the Christian faith.[25] Even so on October 27 1999, Ahmed Sani, governor of the northern state of Zamfara, unilaterally declared *shariah* law to apply in his state. This was followed by similar declarations in the neighbouring states of Sokoto and Kebbi, which in turn caused rioting and inter-religious killings. In a meeting of the 36 state governors it was agreed not to implement *shariah* law.[26] However the three dissenting states later declared they would ignore the Federal Government order.[27] The states of Kaduna and Oyo subsequently issued similar declarations. By 2002, 12 northern states defied the federal government and the national constitution by declaring *shariah* law.[28] By May of that year the first attempt was made to introduce *shariah* law into a majority Christian southern state.[29] Ibrahim Datti Ahmed from Kano state added 'non-Muslims should understand the fact that *shariah* has permanently come to stay and even the National Council of States headed by President Olusegun Obasanjo has no right to stop its implementation… Christians and other non-Muslims who cannot cope…should leave'.[30] In spite of President Obasanjo's call for prayer and fasting to reconcile Muslims and Christians, tensions continued to explode into violence.[31]

In 2003 Rev. Dr Josiah Fearon, Archibishop of Kaduna[32]reported that in the north:

- No Christian education is allowed in any government school and Christians may not be enrolled unless they convert to Islam.
- Buying land for a church or a pastor's house is disallowed.
- Christians are not given government contracts.
- Public Christian processions, radio and television broadcasts are banned.
- In January 2000 when a Christian delegation put their case to the governor of Kaduna, Al Haji Ahmad Mohammed Makarfi, violence resulted in 1000 Christians being killed.
- In the same state in November 2002 rioting took place as a reaction to a 'Miss World' article published in another state by a newspaper two-thirds of whose editors were Muslim. In Kaduna 130 churches were damaged or destroyed. Five hundred Christians were killed and almost 1000 were injured. The Islamic leaders who orchestrated the attacks were the same ones who had signed a pact three months previously to ensure peace between Muslims and Christians.[33]
- In Kano State government officials requested the demolition of 50% of Christian churches.[34]

If observers of the African scene find it difficult to comprehend what is happening, they need to understand the Muslim mindset. In many countries Islam is still a small percentage but with unity of purpose and external help it is growing rapidly. To understand the conflict between the major missionary faiths of Christianity and Islam, we need to come to terms with that Muslim mindset. As one Muslim put it, 'In the Quran I find nothing to teach us how to be a minority religion, while in the New Testament I find nothing to teach Christians how to be a majority religion.'[35]

Although differently expressed, similar sentiments of triumph have been reported from Islam's heartland. According to two British nurses who were released from Saudi Arabian custody in May 1998, the common taunt they endured from Saudi police was 'British trash. Islam rules.'. This is a succinct summation of some

Muslims' attitudes and aspirations even if somewhat crudely expressed. In the case of Africa it applies not just to those countries formerly associated with the now defunct British Empire. It is applied to the appropriation of the entire continent.

Christian leaders are becoming quite aware of what is happening. The question is 'can the Christian Church unite and take its stand to turn back the tide from the north before it rolls over them?' The outcome will probably be known in the near rather than the distant future.

Islam is unlikely to stop until it is in a majority position, nor will it rest there. If any should doubt the possibility of this future outcome then one need only to examine what is happening in one other African country away in the north – Sudan. This country represents a different and more advanced stage in the centuries long struggle with Islam on the 'Dark Continent'.

CHAPTER 7

DARKNESS DESCENDS

The Republic of Sudan with an area of 2 504 000 square kilometres is the largest country in Africa. It represents 8% of the African continental landmass. Its 30 million people consist of 240 ethnic groups speaking 132 languages. Because many of the northern tribes have been Arabised, 49% of the total population speak Arabic but 45.2% of the people are Arab. Islam entered northern Sudan through Egypt and seeks as well, to encompass the mostly black Christian Central and Southern Sudanese who comprise 54.8% of the national population. In 2001 Muslims numbered 65% of the population while Christians were 23.2%.

Sudan is one of the poorest countries in the world. It has repeatedly ranked among the worst on the United Nations human suffering index. Because of protracted civil war up to 2 million of its citizens have been killed through war, famine and similarly man-made disasters. Five million of its people have been internally displaced.

It is acknowledged that reasons for the ongoing war are very complex. These include the whole gamut of political, economic, ethnic, cultural and religious factors. Some of these are generated domestically. Others are of international origin. However the purpose of this work is to focus on the unique contribution of aspects of religion, specifically Islam to the situation in Sudan.

Egyptians historically referred to ancient Sudan as the land of Cush. For them it represented their main supply of ivory, incense, ebony, yellow gold and black gold – that is slaves. But in 712 BC King Prankhi of Cush conquered the Egyptians. Sudan ruled over Egypt until they lost control in 671 BC to the invading Assyrians. In 23 BC the Romans arrived to the north of Sudan and remained substantially in Egypt until 297 AD. During the Roman conquest to the north Christianised Ethiopians extended their territorial claims into Sudan from the southeast.

During the next three centuries the land which today is known as Sudan, was subdivided into a number of kingdoms. Three of these in the north, adjacent to

Egypt, converted to Christianity already well established in the neighbouring countries of Egypt and Ethiopia.

Prior to the Christian era, their predecessors in the faith, the Israelites were well acquainted with the Sudanese. The second wife of Moses was from the land of Cush (Numbers 12:1). King David knew of them (Psalm 68:31). It was Cushite rulers in Egypt who intervened on behalf of King Hezekiah (2 Kings 19:1–9; Isaiah 37:1–10). Prophecies in Isaiah 18 and Zephaniah 3:10 are thought to refer to Cush. It was a Sudanese official, Ebed-Melech who rescued the prophet Jeremiah (Jeremiah 38:7–13). The first Sudanese to become a follower of Jesus was the treasurer of Queen Candace in 37 AD (Acts 8:26–34). During the third century Christians fled to Sudan to avoid the persecution of Roman emperors, Decius and Diocletian. In the fourth century mass conversions to Christianity were taking place in Sudan. At the same time churches and monasteries were constructed, some of which continue in existence to this day. In the sixth century Christianity became the official religion of Nubia. But in the seventh century there came from the east, the armies of Arabia and Islam.

Having conquered Egypt in 642 AD they swept south and attacked Nubia in 643 AD and 652 AD. It was here that the Arab advance was halted. The Christian kingdoms of northern Sudan although hard hit nevertheless stood firm. As easier conquests were to be found to the west, the invading forces followed a path of lesser resistance. As Sudan and its kingdoms were unlikely to go away, they could be safely left for sharper attention at a later day. That day certainly would come but not yet.

A peace pact *(baqt)* was agreed and ratified between the newcomers from the north and the Sudanese in the south. It held until 1260 when it was broken by a series of attacks launched from Egypt against Sudan. Although territorial conquest was initially denied the northern forces, previous preceding Arab immigration into Sudan as well as a weakened national church had already compromised internal integrity.

Pressured from without and disintegrating from within, the last of the northern Christian kingdoms fell in 1484. Even so, relatively few Nubians converted to Islam. In this case, 'Christianity began to die out because of internal weaknesses in the churches and not because of external attacks of Islam.'[1] What a salutary lesson for the contemporary church to note.

An appeal was made to Ethiopia to send ministers and monks to teach within the faltering Christian community. This was denied. A divided church will always fall before a united attack. It would seem that in seven centuries, the majority of which was spent under the threat of Islamic pressure, the church of northern Sudan still had not learned that lesson. The last we see of her is as a tired defender, battered and worn down as battalions from the north at last breached the defences.

In the seventeenth and eighteenth centuries, several attempts were made by Roman Catholic missions to establish new openings. These all failed through disease or violence committed against the missionaries. A new attempt in 1873 proved somewhat more successful. Also in the nineteenth century Egypt unleashed a new series of attacks against Sudan which were resisted until Britain became the dominant colonial power in the region.

In 1877 General Charles Gordon was appointed by the British to be the Governor of all Sudan. Gordon was a practising Christian. He was offended by the slave trade which was more favoured by long-standing Muslim practice in the area than by current British Christian conscience. Gordon attempted to stamp it out. Instead of seeing it as a reversal to their economic prospects, Moslems declared it as an action against Islam.

> 'Christianity began to die out because of internal weaknesses in the churches and not because of external attacks of Islam.' What a salutary lesson for the contemporary church to note.

When under threat, it is a long-standing practice within Islam to rouse popular sentiment and mount successful counterattacks by declaring the matter to be religious. That being so the only appropriate response is *jihad* – holy war. Muhammad Ahmed declared himself to be the *mahdi,* the long awaited Messiah for Islam. In 1885 Gordon's capital of Khartoum fell and so did Gordon's head – literally by the Mahdiyya movement's sword. The *mahdi's* forces were not defeated until 1898 at Omdurman.

Sudan also knew peace for 60 years under the leadership of Pax Brittanica. In the period 1938 to the 1970s the Church that remained in the south experienced a series of revivals. This was a fortunate preparation for what awaited it in the latter part of the twentieth century.

With the granting of independence in 1956, civil war broke out and the age-old relentless push from the north was resumed. In 1957 the Muslim government of Sudan took control of all mission schools. In 1960 the government decreed that the weekly holiday of Sunday would be replaced by the Muslim Friday. Islamic schools were also built throughout the south. In 1962 the government introduced its Missionary Society's Act which limited Christian evangelism. Two years later in 1964, all missionaries were expelled. Southern resistance continued until 1972 when the Addis Ababa agreement guaranteed autonomy and religious freedom for the south.

As is often the case, the agreement was observed only for as long as it seemed opportune to do so. In 1983 protocols of the agreement were annulled when the nation's military dictator, Nimeiri declared unilaterally that henceforth *shariah* law would be applied throughout the whole country. This was tantamount to declaring once more the whole of Sudan to be Islamic.

John Garang, a Dinka tribal leader in the south, reactivated the Sudanese Peoples Liberation Army (SPLA) to resist the latest religious and ethnic move from the north. Initially the front was able to reclaim much of its southern territory but not for long.

In 1989 Lieutenant General Omar-Al-Bashir of the National Islamic Front (NLF) overthrew the democratically elected government and promised 'national salvation' and Islamisation of the entire Sudan.[2] The common method to unite Muslim peoples to achieve such a goal was employed. *Jihad* (holy war) was declared against those who were non-Muslims in 1992, especially the Nubians. In addition to that a *fatwa* (that is, a religious or judicial sentence pronounced by an appropriate religious authority) was issued which declared 'an insurgent who was previously a Muslim is now an apostate. A non-Muslim is a non-believer standing as a bulwark against the spread of Islam. And Islam has granted the freedom of killing both...'[3]

In the north, Christians who remained were severely discriminated against in terms of occupational or educational opportunities. Aid could be delivered if the recipients agreed to become Muslims. Many were driven out into the desert there to die of hunger or thirst if they chose not to accept the option of becoming Muslims.

1992 was declared not just a year of *jihad* but also a year of the nation's 'righteousness' in upholding Islamic *shariah* law.[4] In pursuit of the religious objective, a ferocious campaign was unleashed to eliminate non-Muslim Nubians as well as to dominate the south once more. While the number of those affected can never be known precisely, some estimates range above 2 million killed[5] with 5 million driven into internal exile.

According to witnesses entire Christian villages have been annihilated. Congregations have been burned to death. Churches were bombed at times when it was thought that most worshippers would be in them. Likewise, clearly marked hospitals and medical vehicles were targeted.[6] Water, food and clothes were all withheld. When Christians were forced to flee to garrison towns, men and women were separated in an additional deliberate genocidal attempt to prevent future births of young Christians.

Young men were drafted into compulsory service with government militias. Children were removed from parents and forced to attend Quranic schools to be re-educated as Muslims. Women were reduced to slave labourers on farms while girls are retained for the sexual pleasures of the government's army.

For reporting some of these activities the UN Special Rapporteur on Human Rights in Sudan, Gaspar Biro was declared persona non grata. He noted that captured boys were used simply as 'cannon fodder'.[7] Of the 1.95 million Nubians, only a quarter remained in their homelands of the Nuba mountains. Where they or other Christians have been driven away their vacant land has been seized and given to Arabs.[8] The cross is regarded as a curse by Sudanese oppressors but it still becomes useful to achieve the purposes for which it was originally intended. Eyewitnesses have reported finding people crucified, some dead, others still alive at the time of finding them.[9]

When the government captured the city of Juba, a major city in the south, they killed anybody between the ages of 14–45 years. All the children between the ages of 9–15 years were taken off as slaves.[10] The United Nations Commission on Human Rights for Sudan also cites an alarming increase in the incidence of slavery since 1994.[11] In the period 1995–1999, the Swiss based Christian Solidarity International (CSI) redeemed more than 11000 slaves by paying US$50 per head to Arab militias organised by the government in Khartoum.[12]

All of this and more has been committed by the Islamic government of Sudan which earlier had officially protested against the alleged practice of ethnic cleansing among states on both sides of the conflict in the Balkan War. Baroness Caroline Cox of Christian Solidarity Worldwide (CSW) who visited the area a number of times said that what was happening was a Sudanese 'government sponsored, government sanctioned ethnic cleansing program.'[13]

'What is happening is a tragedy based on the callous disregard for human life,'[14] declared a World Vision news release. Franklin Graham, founder of Samaritan's Purse, goes further. He said, 'Throughout our relief work around the world over the past 20 years, I can say without a doubt that the worst mass murders, village destruction and religious and ethnic cleansing I've ever seen have been in Sudan'.[15] When Graham, referring to his organisation's Sudanese experience, pointed out that Islam was not the peace-loving movement it wanted to claim to be (after the September 11 2001 bombings in New York and Washington) the response was a *fatwa* against him.

The intellectual and theological framework for the operation in Sudan has been provided by Dr Hassan al-Turabi and the National Islamic Front which he has led. He has said his 'goal is to impose Islam in Sudan along the same uncompromising lines as Iran'.[16] Aldo Deng-Akuey, former deputy speaker of the Sudanese National Assembly, said that 'Turabi's dream is to repopulate the south with Muslims...Slavery is a weapon that serves [a] political objective. Land is the prize'.[17]

One might well wonder why the United States Government and its representatives, the great advocate of other people's human rights, have been so unusually quiet about what is happening in Sudan especially when they are so vocal and proactive regarding other areas of the world of less protracted and extreme behaviour. In America the Congressional Black Caucus (CBC) has not even backed a House resolution requiring the US government to act against nations which engage in the practice or traffic of slavery, which in this instance is so well documented.

In Sudan's case, this inactivity is happening because of the unity and cooperation that now exists at the international level among Muslims. Charles Jacobs, an American research director, has noted that 'black leaders are pressured by the Farrakhanites'. Louis Farrakhan, international leader of Nation of Islam (NOI) in America has gone further. He has applauded the militancy of Sudanese leaders, President Bashir and Dr Turabi. He has visited them in Khartoum. NOI's international representative, Akbar Muhammad attributes much of what is happening in Sudan as simply related to their culture. That exonerates the practice.[18]

In 1994 the Arab League passed a resolution in support of the course of action that the government of Sudan is pursuing. The government which has inflicted suffering on a massive scale such that it ranks amongst the worst in the world and who endures self-imposed famine as a result of its own policies, continues to operate mostly because of massive aid reportedly from Libya and Iran. The object of its ire in part, is one of the oldest Christian communities in Africa and the world, as well as those who are the results of modern missionary activity.

Supply lines from the east through Ethiopia have already been significantly weakened. If Islam can be strengthened simultaneously to the south along the northern borders of Kenya and Uganda, then the enclosure around the millions of Christians in southern Sudan will be complete. After 14 centuries a wall of spiritual and military protection which has withstood penetration from the north for so long will have been demolished. The road to central and southern Africa will be open.

When Pope John Paul officially visited Sudan in February 1993 he was given a message from Sudanese Church leaders begging him to lift the 'curtain of silence surrounding persecution of them'. They said, 'Do not let yourself be blinded by the red carpet in Khartoum...the hands you will shake will be full of Christian blood.'[19]

In April 2001 when Christian evangelist Reinhard Bonnke arrived in Khartoum at the invitation of the Sudan Council of Churches, the government having previously given official permission for his meetings, suddenly reacted with violence forcing Bonnke to depart. As believers met to pray in All Saints Cathedral police fired tear gas into their midst arresting 105 and sentencing 53 people to be immediately flogged and imprisoned. Christians in the north have come to expect such treatment. They have been told to exhume their dead from the sole Christian cemetery in Khartoum because the site is required for a new mosque.[20]

On April 30 2001 the United States Commission on International Religious Freedom issued its annual report. Not surprisingly, it concluded that Sudan was 'the world's most violent abuser of the right to freedom of religion and belief.'.[21]

A few years ago, in his Christmas message Monsignor Macram Max Gassis, Bishop of Al-Obeid, Sudan said:

For millions of people in Sudan this celebration (of Christmas) is totally different. While bells of joy ring elsewhere in the world, in Sudan the drums of war are beating; while music of peace is played, bombs explode and artillery fires thunder; while carols are sung, Sudanese hear shrieks calling for jihad (holy war) being chanted; while churches are decorated with flowers and fancy vestments are worn, Christians in Sudan pray under trees, deprived of their pastors.

While peace to people of goodwill is announced, for Sudanese hatred is inculcated and persecution propagated; while millions wear costly dresses, enjoy plenty of food and exchange gifts, my people go around starving, naked, sick, enslaved, shamefully raped and humiliated.[22]

> As they retrieve charred bodies from bombed out churches, 10 million southern Sudanese know too well the power of the solidarity of Muslim brotherhood as they have become more and more doubtful of the substance of any solidarity existing among the followers of Christ.

At the same Christmas, Bishop Paride Taban of the Diocese of Torit in southern Sudan added:

...(of) the Khartoum regime's policy of forced Islamisation of the south the Christian world either does not care to know or does not care to react...As they retrieve charred bodies from bombed out churches, 10 million southern Sudanese know too well the power of the solidarity of Muslim brotherhood as they have become more and more doubtful of the substance of any solidarity existing among the followers of Christ.[23]

Just as the Christians in Ethiopia of the fourteenth century denied a call for help from the almost obliterated Christians in north Sudan, which denial in part contributed to their annihilation so it would seem that the same could be repeated in the twenty-first century.

The average Christian in Sudan has learned lessons that were well-known to their earliest forebears in the first century. When asked what the cross that adorns their churches, homes and clothing meant, one of them replied, 'The cross testifies that God has placed his spirit in me to follow and obey him in life. It reminds me of the words of Christ – to take up my cross, to follow him and to deny myself. The Cross requires us to pay the price to be a Christian.'.[24]

These are lessons that the Church in the West has yet to learn. If it fails to respond, to unite and to learn, then it may be obliged to do so through direct experience by means and for reasons not too dissimilar from that of the shattered, suffering Church in Sudan. This may happen much sooner than the 1400 years it has taken for Islam gradually to subdue Sudan. For already that power is well established within the West, confidently claiming the twenty-first century as 'theirs'.

CHAPTER 8

THE WORLD WIND

'We shall export our revolution to the whole world. Until the cry "There is no God but Allah" resounds over the whole world, there will be struggle.' Thus declared Ayatollah Khomeini of Iran.[1] Although that Ayatollah is no longer with us, his words and the 'struggle' live on.

Islam first moved into Europe in the eighth century. Crossing the Mediterranean from Africa to Gibraltar it moved swiftly through the Iberian Peninsula to France. It suffered its first major military defeat on the continent at Poitiers in 732. The victor was the Frankish ruler Charles Martel, grandfather of Charlemagne. Islam remained in what is today's Spain until 1492. 'It was not until this (twentieth) century that Islam began another incursion into the West...largely through immigration.'[2] But the expansion is not just into the Western hemisphere. It is as Ayatollah Khomeini suggested, 'over the whole world'.

If one could board ship at Sudan's major port on the Red Sea, sail out into the Indian Ocean and proceed in a southeasterly direction until the next major landfall was sighted, one would probably land on the continent of Australia. It is a matter of conjecture as to how close this continent may have come to being claimed for Islam in the seventeenth century.

Muslim merchants and missionaries from Persia and Gujarat in India had arrived in West Java by the end of the eleventh century. These were joined by Arab Hadrami merchants in the thirteenth century with a further major migration in the late 1700s.[3] By a combination of persuasion and protracted warfare in what is now Indonesia, Hinduism was gradually replaced by a chain of Islamic kingdoms. By 1607 when Portuguese explorers encountered them, they had reached Papua. Had not the colonising Dutch arrived on the scene with their superior technology and sea power, it is reasonable to assume, given the rate of progress westward of Islam, that in the seventeenth century its followers would have claimed, colonised and converted Australia.

The search for the unknown south land *terra australis incognita* had been unsuccessful for centuries. Muslim sailors referred to it as the kingdom of *al Dadjdjal*, the Muslim Anti-Christ. According to some of their traditions and legends, this Anti-Christ was a broad foreheaded, fuzzy haired, unbelieving monster who lived on a more remote island east of Java, attended by demons.[4]

But Pedro Ferdandez de Quiros, a pious Portuguese explorer thought otherwise. He 'prophesied' that this unknown land would be *terra australis del Espiritu Santo*, the south land of the Holy Spirit.[5] But to his prophecy there was attached one caveat. If the new land did not become (Roman) Catholic and was instead taken by Dutch and English heretics, then all the blessings would be converted 'into great evils, and bring everything to ruin'.[6]

Perhaps in observing Australia today, some present day followers of both of these major religious groups might consider there was some truth in their forebears' understandings after all! However one may interpret such historical concepts of previous eras, there is no doubt that at least one new spirit is blowing across Australia, which if successful will certainly recolonise it at last – the spirit of Islam.

In the 1970s, Islamic leaders in the country reportedly set a rather optimistic goal that by the year 2000 Australia would be an Islamic state. Obviously this has not (yet) happened. But a new date for such an outcome has been set for a couple of decades hence. According to Dr Mohammad Wang, a Chinese Muslim in Australia, 'A new phase in the campaign for a greater Islam in Australia is beginning'.[7] The 1991 and 1996 government census statistics showed that the number of declared Muslims grew by 35.81% during those five years.[8] A similar increase was recorded in the 2001 census. In 1996 Muslims were estimated to be 1% of the population.[9] The 2001 census showed they represented 1.5% of the population, an increase of 40% during 1996–2001.

The first recorded Muslim event that occurred on Australian soil was in March 1806. The Muslim crew of the sailing ship Sydney, moored in Sydney Cove at the time, performed the 'festival of Hussan' during the ten days of Muharram, much to the curiosity of the local citizenry.[10]

The first known Muslims to live in Australia were camel drivers who arrived in Melbourne in June 1860. They had been brought with their animals from northwest India to assist a transcontinental expedition of exploration led by Robert Burke.[11] During the period 1867–1910 they provided transport for the development of Central Australia's desert regions. Mostly they returned to the Punjab of today's Pakistan but many remained and settled in Australia.

Similar to Europe and the United States, Australia also has for the most part been a generous host country for immigrants and refugees looking for a better way of life in terms of material prosperity. Thus after the Second World War, the first major Muslim influx came from Turkish Cypriots who were holders of British passports.[12] In the decades of the 1960s, 70s and 80s, Muslim immigrants came mostly from Turkey and Lebanon.[13] Refugees from the strife torn Somalia, Ethiopia and other eastern African regions, as well as the Baltic and Middle East regions represent the latest waves.

The sevenfold increase in Australia's Muslim population that has occurred since 1971 has mainly been due to mass migrations and high birth rates.[14] Although Muslims came to Australia from 63 different countries,[15] 35.01% are Australian born. The next two major categories are from Lebanon (17.4%) and Turkey (14.53%).[16]

The first mosque was built in the city of Adelaide in 1890.[17] By 2003 there were 82 mosques and various Islamic centres around Australia.[18] The largest mosque accommodating 5000 worshippers is in the suburb of Auburn in Sydney.[19] In each state of Australia there is also an Islamic Council, cultural centre and students association. The Australian Federation of Islamic Societies established in Sydney in 1964 and renamed Australian Federation of Islamic Councils (AFIC) in 1975 has a permanent Federation Secretariat in Sydney and is seen as 'a symbol of unity and power of Islam and the Muslim Ummah in Australia'.[20] The King Khaled Islamic College of Victoria in Melbourne was the first to provide complete Islamic education for children from the commencement of their school years through to university matriculation. In the last decade of the twentieth century many similar schools were established across Australia. They offered 'normal state educational curricula within an Islamic ethos'[21] and were partly funded by Australian government grants. In February 2003 the study of the Quran was added as a subject to state government secondary school curricula. Salifu Baba, assistant principal at Minaret College, said, 'We see this as a big step forward'.[22]

Monies for some of these institutions were raised from overseas Islamic funds. For example in the municipality of Broadmeadows in Melbourne an A$20 million centre including a mosque, a school, a supermarket etc. was constructed with a loan from a Saudi Arabian bank with financial assistance being sought from other Muslim countries (except Libya and Iran). All leaseholders at the centre are required to respect relevant Islamic religious laws.[23]

As in most Western countries, so also in Australia, leading tertiary institutions are always in need of more funding. When this is offered from a Muslim country it usually comes with the condition of increasing Islamic influence within that recipient institution. One of Australia's most prestigious universities, the University of Queensland, accepted a grant of A$10 million from the government of the Sultan of Brunei. Shortly thereafter, bilateral discussions were initiated with a view to appointing a (Muslim) professor of Islamic Law at the university.[24] The community has made significant headway in developing its own media outlets in television and radio.[25] It publishes a number of journals, magazines and its own newspaper, *Australian Muslim News*. The last is under the auspices of the Australian Federation Islamic Council (AFIC). Its own financial institution, the Muslim Community Cooperative (Australia) Ltd (MCCA) has enjoyed steady growth since it commenced in 1989 with 10 members and A$20 000. By 2003 it was reported as having 5500 members and A$26 million in cash and secured assets. In the state of Victoria it became the main home lender for the Islamic community. It is also 'a part of a global trend to develop specialist Islamic banking and investment products that observe sharia law.'[26]

Malik Hilweh, the owner of the Islamic mortgage Iskan Finance, has negotiated the first Islamic superannuation investment fund in Australia with a target of A$1 billion.[27] Muslims are encouraged to 'buy Muslim and support the Muslim economy in Australia and worldwide'[28]. Islamic banking and financial services offered in over 50 countries are now estimated to be worth more than US$200 billion a year. According to the Saudi government weekly *Ain Al-Yaqueen* its government revenue had been used to expand Islam in non-Muslim countries. By 2002 it claimed to have funded the building of 210 large mosques and Islamic centres, more than 1500 smaller mosques, 202 colleges and almost 2000 Islamic schools. It had also established scholarships and academic chairs in prominent foreign universities and colleges and printed 100 million copies of the Quran for distribution in non-Muslim countries.[29]

In Australia the Imam Ali mosque at Lakemba in Sydney was built by a donation of US$1.2 million from the Saudi Arabian government. A further $1 million was provided in May 1983 to build the first full time Islamic primary school in Melbourne. [30] In 2002 Saudi citizens arrived with another US$3 million reportedly to establish another school.[31]

As in America so in Australia, Muslims endeavour to work among the socially disadvantaged, especially Australian aboriginals. Although the proposed visit by Louis Farrakhan referred to earlier, was unsuccessful, Bilal Cleland, a spokesman for the Australian Federation Islamic Council, reported that an *imam* (religious leader) was being sent to Alice Springs in Central Australia for ten days every two months to give teaching. In his opinion, 'It is wonderful to see how much confidence the Islamic faith gives aboriginal people'.[32]

In that Islam probably already outnumbers the Jewish community in Australia, media reporters sensitised to the direction of future trends already refer to the 'Judeo – Christian–Islamic tradition which operates in Australia'.[33] Muslims in Australia have learnt well to use the media and the political machinery of state to adjust whatever message is appropriate for the occasion. Although having the support of Australian opposition political parties, when the Australian government decided to enter the 1991 Gulf War on the side of its traditional Western allies in conjunction with some Muslim countries, the Australian Muslim community objected strongly.

In the Gulf War of 2003 the Australian Federation of Islamic Council called even the pre-deployment of Australian troops in the Gulf a 'provocative and illegal act'.[34]

> In that Islam probably already outnumbers the Jewish community in Australia, media reporters sensitised to the direction of future trends already refer to the 'Judeo–Christian–Islamic tradition which operates in Australia'.

Others regarded the war as 'another Muslim capital (falling) to the conquerors from the West'.[35]

Announcing that in future the Islamic community would launch a campaign of political action including backing pro-Muslim candidates in government elections, the secretary of the Islamic Council, Bilal Cleland went on to say that 'Muslims can't stand aside from politics. We have to get our community to understand the power structures in this community and to exercise their democratic right.'. In future the Muslim vote was to be marshalled to serve their unique interests including a long-term concern to get more 'permits to build new mosques'.[36]

Within two years Muslim candidates were selected to stand as representatives of the major political parties. However, in the intervening time, circumstances and public perceptions had changed. In Australia, given its secular nature, religion is mostly separate from politics. Adjusting appropriately in direct contradiction to the previous religio-political stance, the president of the Islamic society of the state of Victoria, Haissan Sidaoui could say, 'It is repugnant to Islam. We do not stoop to politics.' Following a similar line Liberal party candidate, Mr Reza Kosanoglu, a Muslim himself went on to say, 'Politics and religion as far as Islam is concerned should not mix'.[37] However on talk-back radio in Melbourne in the lead-up to the 2001 Federal election, when a Muslim caller was asked which political party he would vote for, he replied he would not support any because Muslims were hoping to put their own Muslim candidate into the Senate to represent their interests.

Truth seems to be sacrificed on the altar of convenient opportunity. To achieve desired ends some Muslim leaders seem not only prepared to say different things to suit different occasions, they will use whatever advantage is available through government democratic systems even though democracy is hardly its end in view. Perhaps this is an example of *al-taqiuua*, 'what some in Islam call the moral right of Muslims to mislead and lie to non-Muslims'.[38]

As in so many other countries, *dawa* is being practised to win a permanent religious footing. To improve the image of Islam liason is maintained with media, the government and other public bodies. 'Carefully worded reading material is circulated to dispel misinterpretations about Islam'.[39] Nida'ul Islam Magazine has amongst its goals to produce a section in the society which understands Islam to its true reality, and which realizes that *jihad* is the only path to establish the Islamic state and that it is the youth generation who form the fuel for the Islamic movement in general and the *jihad* stream in specific.[40] Abu Bakar Bashir has urged the Islamic faithful in Australia to 'endeavour to bring about an Islamic state in Australia even if it is in 100 years from now.'[41]

In the matter of immigration as a means of increasing Islamic presence, Christian immigrants from one Middle Eastern country report that their visa applications were rejected by a Muslim employee of an Australian Embassy in their country of origin. They were advised to reapply through a more sympathetic office in a 'Christian' country in the region thereby to avoid problems. Similarly, a Christian who had to flee for his life from a southern Asian Muslim country and was granted residency in Australia, was unable to have his family join him. His visa applications on their behalf were repeatedly blocked by Muslims well placed in the offices of the Australian embassy in his country of origin and in the capital city of the Australian state through which he was applying. Visa applications from hopeful Muslim immigrants were facilitated.

In one of the suburbs of a state capital city, a local Christian community did what it could to help new Muslims adjust and settle into their newly chosen country. When a sufficient number of Muslim households had been established in a concentrated area, the helping Christian community was confused and dismayed to learn all non-Muslims were being told by the newly established community to sell up and move out because the area was now declared Islamic.

Over an extensive period of time, two Muslims from a Middle Eastern country, of their own volition, made discreet inquiries about Christianity in a local church. Eventually through a vision of Jesus that one of them had they decided to become Christians. Within a very short time Muslims from their former country visited them. They were advised that the local consular representatives knew what was happening. They were then told of all that they had done, who had visited their home, how they had received Bibles, etc. It was quite obvious they had been under close surveillance for an extended period of time. Failure to renounce the course of action they were following could have repercussions on their relatives back in their country of origin.

Another couple who had not yet gained citizenship within Australia, visited their consulate to register the names of their children, desiring to give those children 'Christian' names. They were advised that such registration would not be permitted unless the children had Muslim names. The message was the same. Unless they came into line there could be repercussions on relatives back home.[42]

It would seem that diplomatic outposts, whether they are embassies or just consulates, have been used to monitor the movements of Muslim nationals in their adopted countries as well as being conduits to expand Islamic influence. Not even in their adopted country, in this case Australia, will Muslim immigrants be permitted to leave their faith regardless of the laws of the adoptive country. An Australian lawyer of the more recently formed *Religious Freedom Institute* was called to defend 'two Muslim converts to Christianity who...reported receiving death threats from certain Islamic religious leaders...in Australia.'[43]

Some in the Muslim community have a deep-felt need for preservation of their society and culture. Amir Abdullah sees children's education in government schools as part of a plot to get Muslims to see themselves as Australians first and Muslims second. He sees ceremonies such as daily flag raising or teaching of civil responsibilities or even sex education as part of a plot to dilute Islamic purity. He warns that sending children to preschool kindergartens could result in their being 'suckled by the Shaytan'. He further stresses that Muslims must not change their dress, their appearance or their diet. Nor should there be any friendships with non-Muslims. In summation 'every aspect of Kuffar society is designed to mislead us from the straight path'.[44]

Hizb ut-Tahrir representatives have warned that integration and multiculturalism are Western plots to erode the purity of Islamic belief. 'We are Muslims first and we live in Australia. We must teach our children to live...so that when the state is reestablished their loyalty is to the Islamic state.' They preach their belief that they have been brought to Australia by Allah to help establish a worldwide Islamic state.[45]

Amir Abdullah regards Christian missionaries as 'human shayateen' who attempt to convert Muslims to their false religion. To do this they use the creative approaches of murder, sexual assault, kidnapping and blackmail. In the same article he warns followers to be wary of the Red Cross, World Vision, the Salvation Army and Christian Aid.[46]

Australians need to 'realise Islam is now an Australian religion'.[47] One analyst concludes that 'Australia's religious mosaic has been forever changed...This means not only that Islam is here to stay but also that it will play an increasing influential role in the religious affairs of this nation'.[48] According to a police report, Saudi national Hamand Abaid Alanezi entered Australia in March 1999 on behalf of an organisation believed to be led by Osama bin Laden. He and four Iraqi 'refugees' allegedly were involved in a violent event that was designed to recruit people to assist 'Islamic activities in Kosovo and Chechnya'.[49] It would seem that Islam's influence in Australia would not be confined merely to 'religious affairs'.

During 2001 an Australian husband and wife were on a flight between Lahore and Islamabad in Pakistan. Next to them was a Pakistani gentleman who, upon learning of their country of origin, said 'Australia is ours now. You will all come peaceably or there will be holy *jihad*.'.[50] In 2002 Sheikh Shady Al Suleima commenting on the necessity of following 'the right path' said, 'We want to show that Islam makes you a winner. It will get you to the top in whatever you want.' The question is having arrived at the top what might Islamic (?) Australia look like?

To the immediate north of Australia is a large island now divided into two countries, the western half is Papua now governed by Indonesia. As with East Timor which suffered at least 200 000 civilians killed when Indonesia invaded in 1975, the indigenous population had no say in its island being taken over by Indonesia. With a policy of transmigrating Indonesian citizens from crowded Java into the pristine jungle areas of Papua, the island, formerly mostly Christian, is rapidly Islamising. Not only is there an Islamic university in Papua now but right down to preschool, Islamic education is offered at the village level. To accelerate the process over 2000 members of Laskar Jihad have reportedly moved into Papua establishing 12 military training camps with an office in Sorong. Their stated aims are to destroy all Christian infrastructure. There is additional evidence which suggests leaders of the Indonesian army and others are sympathetic to their activities. In January 2003 the group's leader, Jafar Umar Thalib was found 'not guilty of inciting hatred and religious violence', despite overwhelming evidence, which resulted in the deaths of many thousands. While in jail he had been visited by Indonesia's Vice President, Hamzah Has.[51]

After bloody clashes in Kalimantan,[52] Papua and Ambon, Civil Rights Commissioner Marzuki Darusman concluded that the trouble stemmed from the Soeharto Government's policy of appointing and permitting Muslim political elite to carve up the power, resources and lands of outer island non-Muslim people.[53] A change of government would ensure at best only a pause in the process.

> 'Australia's religious mosaic has been forever changed...This means not only that Islam is here to stay but also that it will play an increasing influential role in the religious affairs of this nation'.

Papua New Guinea on the eastern half of the island made a unique decision in the late 1980s. It declined to allow a mosque to be built within its territory. Like other South Pacific nations, the government considered that as its people were Christian, it would be inappropriate to have such a worship centre within its borders.

However money often allures a change of allegiance. By the mid 1990s Malaysian money had not only bought up vast tracts of untouched tropical forest, it had also facilitated the establishment of a bank which had, at that time, even greater resources than the PNG national bank. Past decisions were reversed. By mid 1990s not only had a mosque been built but a second one was being built in the more remote highlands which were the exclusive province of Enga Christians. As the then Minister of Education was also a Muslim, Islamic teaching was introduced into school curricula. A toehold had been gained.

Across the other side of the Pacific Ocean, Islam has reached various stages of development in most countries of South America. The patterns of operation are similar to those elsewhere.

Venezuela has long been known as a strong Roman Catholic nation. But with a Muslim population of fewer than 0.35%, its first Islamic centre was opened in 1996 at a cost of US$9 million.

In Panama the first mosque was built in 1980. Islamic population in this country is now about 3.5%.

Suriname's population is about 20% Muslim. These Muslims are mostly descendants of the indentured labourers that the Dutch colonial government imported between 1890 and 1940.

Bolivia is possibly the poorest of all Latin American countries. It provides a suitable opportunity. Islamic immigration into Bolivia has begun in recent times from Arab and southern Asian countries. 'In the capital city of La Paz, and in Sucre, Muslims distribute food along with the message of Islam. All that one must do to receive food is to become a Muslim.'[54]

In Argentina, President Carlos Menem was a Syrian Muslim. When he married a Roman Catholic woman and later made his run for the presidency, he conveniently converted to Catholicism. But as president he also made significant grants of land for the building of mosques. Saudi Arabia donated US$10 million for an Islamic Centre to be built in Buenos Aires on government donated land.[55]

It is in Brazil however, that one finds the centre of Islam for South America. The suburb of Sao Bernardo do Campo in the city of Sao Paulo is where its power is concentrated. Sao Paulo is the second largest mega city in the world. On its prestigious Avenida do Estado in the central business district is the largest and most influential mosque in that nation, Mesquita Brasil.

In the central business district of Rio de Janiero, Brazil's second largest city, 'the bulk of businesses and shopping areas are owned by Arab Muslims'.[56] Every month from its area of influence in Sao Paulo, business men raise millions of dollars to fund Islamic work throughout South America.[57]

Initiated by a transfer of Arab funds, which so successfully generated additional funding within South America, the pace of building Islamic centres and schools, training of Muslim missionaries and feeding the poor is bound to increase.

No place is too remote to be brushed by the current worldwide winds of Islam. In the city of Baguio, in the west-centre of the Island of Luzon in the Philippines, a new foreign funded Islamic training centre graduates 40 Muslim missionaries per year to work in that local area alone. In the south of the country, Pakistani missionaries have been busy strengthening the Muslim movements in Mindanao and beyond.

In the west central Pacific Ocean there are eight inhabited atolls. In the local Polynesian language the word meaning eight is 'tuvalu'. That is the name of this tiny speck of a country in the middle of the ocean. In 1861 a Cook Islands' chieftain by the name of Elekana landed in Tuvalu with the message of the Gospel. On each atoll there is a church in this totally Christian environment.

However, although this comparatively microscopic country might be unknown or forgotten by the rest of the world, it is not unnoticed by Islam. Today within sight of the small airstrip, minarets of a Muslim mosque rise above the coral into the azure blue of the clear Pacific sky. By the middle of the 1990s, 50 Tuvaluans had been converted to Islam.[58]

Much closer to home base, the best opportunity for expanding Islam during the twentieth century has been virtually on its back door step. With the collapse of the Soviet Union possibilities reopened for the re-Islamisation of what could be up to 60 million former Muslims[59] in the newly independent states of Kazakhstan, Uzbekistan, Kirgistan, Turkmenistan, Tajikistan and Azerbaijan.

As these republics are far 'closer to Mecca than Moscow'[60] inevitably cashed up Islam responded swiftly. Within a year of the Soviet demise, Saudi Arabia and Jordan had shipped more than 1 million copies of the Quran into Uzbekistan alone. These presumably rolled off what is reportedly the largest printing press in the world. It is located in Saudi Arabia and used (exclusively) for printing the Quran.

Other monies were made available for the refurbishment and rebuilding of mosques and new Islamic centres. Turkey, hardly known as a major economic power or as a significant international aid donor, offered US$1.2 billion aid to the new central Asian republics when its premier, Suleiman Demirel toured the region in April 1992.[61] Iran commenced broadcasting the Quran and other Islamic teaching into the republics through 38 of its own radio stations.[62]

As Islam regained its hold after 70 years of suppression under communist rule, the hope of religious freedom[63] disappeared as quickly as immediate post-independence euphoria. Within a year Islamic leaders *(mullahs)* in Tajikistan were preaching that in this republic where perhaps 90% of the population would be claimed to be Muslim, democratic rule would mean Islamic rule. Tens of thousands of Christians and Jews realising what lay in front of them started to flee the republic.[64] Within two years the situation had changed even more. The practice of Islamic government was being implemented.

On December 31 1993 nine members of a Russian Baptist family were murdered in Tajikistan by a group of armed men. They also burnt the family's house to the ground. This family had received threatening letters because the husband who was working with young people in a local Baptist church had begun evangelism among Muslims.[65]

By 1996 Uzbekistan had passed a new law that even blocked the distribution of Christian literature.[66] In the same republic, the Baptist Union of Churches faced media charges that they were involved with violence, bribery, the breakup of families and anti-government 'insubordination'. In Kirgistan churches have been closed and enabling legislation has been introduced to legitimise such official activities. In Turkmenistan young Christian believers have been threatened with expulsion from universities.[67]

At least in these countries the common international charge of a failed Christianity causing descent into drug addiction, sexual promiscuity etc., cannot be levelled at Christians. But Christianity has been branded and opposed by being tagged as a 'Russian religion'. Needless to say, where these republics have been subjected to suppression primarily from Russian communism, this is an association that the struggling new churches could well do without.

Within the Russian confederation, oppressive communism has been rapidly replaced by an equally zealous Islam. In 1994–96 Shamil Basaye led a violent campaign to convert Chechnya into an Islamic nation. 80 000 people were killed in that conflict. The country was renamed Ichkeria and adopted the *shariah* code as the supreme law of the state.[68] In August 1999 he led his Islamic Wahabite forces into neighbouring multi-ethnic Dagestan with the aim that it would become the next Islamic republic.[69] Russia reacted with greater military force and determination than before. Within three months of intensive fighting the Russians re-entered the Chechen capital of Grozny.[70] In spite of the brutality of the conflict, not all Muslims were disappointed with the outcome. One couple summed it up this way: 'We're not just fleeing the war in Chechnya. Our fundamentalist government wanted to make Chechnya another Afghanistan. We'd rather be ruled by Russians.'[71]

In neighbouring Turkey, the seat of centuries of rule for the Ottoman Empire, things have hardly improved. Although Turkey is constitutionally a secular nation, in practice it is fully Islamic. Turkey would hope that the world would forget the massive genocide it perpetrated on Armenian Christians early in the twentieth century. On April 24 1915 on this one day alone, as many as 600 000 Armenians were killed. The only means of escape offered was conversion to Islam.

So keen are Turkish authorities to obliterate the memory of these matters from the mind and attention of the international community, that for many decades they have embarked on a process of destroying even the oldest historically significant Christian buildings within their country. In 1914 the Armenian patriarch of Constantinople completed an accurate inventory of ecclesiastical buildings used by Armenian Christians. The total was 2549. A 1974 survey of the remaining '913 buildings whose location could be accurately indicated showed that of these, 464 had completely disappeared, 252 were in ruins and only 197 were still standing in any sort of sound state'.[72]

More recently in 1993–94 the oldest known place of Christian worship in the world, existing from the time of the Apostle Paul at Urfa, the Church of St John and St James, was converted into a mosque.[73]

On September 12 and October 3 1999 security police surrounded worship centres in Izmir and Zeytinburnu districts of Istanbul. They arrested Turkish nationals, foreign residents and tourists and charged them with attending illegal meetings in spite of the fact that both congregations had met publicly and openly for more than five years with full government awareness. The buildings were closed and sealed. The Turkish

> More recently in 1993–94 the oldest known place of Christian worship in the world, existing from the time of the Apostle Paul at Urfa, the Church of St John and St James, was converted

constitution grants freedom to meet for worship to people of all religions but administrative laws have been used to harass at least Protestant Christians who have steadily grown in number.[74] Likewise police harassment has continued. On May 24 2000 eight men were arrested from a meeting in a place registered for Christian worship.[75] Previously such meetings were held only in secret in people's homes. In 1998 a Government minister actually participated in the opening of one new church building.[76]

A snapshot of what has happened in central Asia in the final decade of the twentieth century provides a reasonable picture of what, in the event of their becoming fully Islamic, other nations might expect along the way. For that picture of the final scene we need merely glance at Islam's traditional heartland.

Closer to the epicentre of Islamic power in the Middle East, it is no longer a matter of expansion. These lands are well held.

In southern Asia, Bangladesh came into being in December 1971 when it won its war of independence (with India's cooperation) from what was then West Pakistan. Its constitution declared that it would be a secular state. But in 1988 with 87% of its population being Muslim it re-declared itself as an Islamic state.[77] In Bangladesh there are an estimated 64 000 madrassas reportedly funded by proselytizing Arab charities. Reflecting that which is taught in these schools Maulana Ubadaidul Haq, in December 2002 preaching to a congregation of hundreds of thousands including government ministers, called for a *jihad* against Americans. He said, 'President Bush and America is the most heinous terrorist in the world. Both America and Bush must be destroyed. The Americans will be washed away if Bangladesh's 120 million Muslims spit on them.'[78]

On October 23 1991 Muslims attacked a Christian village in southern Bangladesh burning down its church, several homes and destroying furniture and belongings in more than 20 other homes. They were incensed because they had a report that some of their number had become Christians and were allegedly to be soon baptised.[79]

Although the constitution of the Republic of Bangladesh guaranteed religious freedom, in 1996 the government announced that, in future, bibles could only be given out to Christians and that in translations of the Holy Bible into the Bengali language certain 'Quranic' words were not to be used. By that the government meant that translators were not to use Bengali words which were based on Arabic. They were to use words based on Sanskrit, the language of Hinduism in India.[80]

In 1997 a Muslim convert was tortured to coerce him to revert to Islam. He remained steadfast to his new allegiance to Jesus Christ. Sections of his hands were amputated and he was tied to a tree and left overnight. By the next morning he was dead. Before newspaper reporters arrived from the capital city Dhaka, his body was hung by the neck from a tree. The reporters were told that he had reverted to Islam but because he was so ashamed of his temporary lapse into Christianity he had committed suicide.[81] Without hands, this would have to be considered a 'miracle' of devilish proportions.

In Dhaka on April 28 1998 an unruly crowd ransacked St Frances Xavier Girls High School (Roman Catholic), Holy Cross (Anglican) Church and the nearby Baptist Church compound. The crowd then moved on to attack the 175 year old St Thomas' Church (location of the former Anglican bishop of Dhaka). A religious leader in a nearby mosque had falsely announced over his public address system that Christians were dismantling the mosque.[82] An appeal to religious sentiment is a dangerous but frequently used ploy to effect revenge of any sort on those who are not Muslims.

In Pakistan in February 1997 approximately 15 000 Christians were left homeless after Muslims rampaged through their village of Shantinagar. Buildings, businesses, vehicles, churches and homes were all destroyed. Holy Bibles were confiscated and burned. Again this attack was instigated by Muslim leadership giving out false information.[83]

In the same year on December 6, Maulana Habib Ullah Dogar, after Friday prayers, urged his congregation to demolish a partly built Christian church. In 1995 a small group of village Christians had bought a piece of land for their church for 12 000 rupees. The United Presbyterian Church of Pakistan gave the money to erect a modest building. A mob led by its cleric smashed the partly finished building, tore down its cross and threw it into a cesspool. Pastor Noor Alam reported the event to the local authorities. On the night of January 28 1998 he was stabbed to death in his home in Sheikhupura. The 'act was carried out as a religious duty in the name of Allah'.[84]

In the same country Christians have been greatly victimised by having questionable charges of blasphemy levelled against them. The law required the death penalty for such an offence. In October 1997 Judge Arif Iqbal Bhatti overturned a lower court blasphemy conviction against two Christians, Salamat and Rehmat Masih. He himself was shot and killed as a result of his decision.[85]

Although Pakistan's founding father, Muhammad Ali Jinnah preferred a secular democracy, its first Prime Minister, Liaqat Ali Khan commenced the process of Islamisation. In 1956 Pakistan was declared an Islamic Republic. In 1973 Zulfikar Ali Bhutto took steps to Islamise the nation further, presumably to silence (unsuccessfully) his opponents. General Zia ul Huq established a Federal Shariah Court and later, Prime Minister Nawaz Sharif completed the process with Constitutional Amendment No.15.[86] In December 1998, 35 Muslim organisations banded together to push an Islamising relevant Bill through Parliament in the following year, declaring that any member of Parliament who opposed it would be disqualified from Parliament and accused of treason.[87] In October 2002 the Muttahida Majlas-i-Amal (MMA) came to power in Baluchistan and the North West Frontier Province. They are insisting that all existing legislation must be brought into line with *shariah*. All economic development work is to take place only in areas where the local population correctly prays five times a day. Promotion within government institutions is to be based solely upon candidates' Islamic credentials.[88]

In the Margalla hills of Islamabad, the International Islamic University has been located, financed by King Faisal of Saudi Arabia. 1500 students mostly from central and southern Asia are in training to become 'the future leaders of the Islamic world.' They are being prepared to take 'the message that the 21st century will belong to Islam.'[89]

Certainly there will be little room for non-Muslims in Pakistan.

On May 6 1998 (Roman Catholic) Bishop John Joseph shot himself to death at the same spot where one of his parishioners, Ayub Masih had been shot in November 1997. Ayub Masih had had the 'blasphemy' death penalty pronounced against him for allegedly insulting Islam and the Prophet Muhammad. Locals claim it was a trumped-up charge related to a land dispute. While Dr Joseph's funeral was being conducted Muslims attacked and burned Christian homes and shops. They also destroyed Holy Bibles and smashed (mourners') pictures of Jesus. Bishop Joseph's last words may prove prophetic, 'It is no longer possible for my people to live in Pakistan.' [90]

Closer still to the Middle East in Afghanistan, the Taliban who first emerged as a military organisation in late October 1994, in the last few years substantially militarily reconquered the country with external assistance. A reclusive mullah named Muhammad Omar, a Pashtun from Kandahar, led them. He took the title Amir-ul Momineen – the supreme leader of the faithful. Their goal was to establish the world's purist Islamic state. Girls' schools were shut down. All females over the age of ten were required to wear the veil. All women were stopped from working in most occupations.[91] Stereos, tape recorders, cassettes, music and watching television were all banned.

Although 'the Taliban came to power with a pledge to end the heroin traffic from Afghanistan', wars are expensive and poppies pay.[92] During the last decade of the twentieth century, under various revolutionary governments, poppy cultivation tripled. Afghanistan was producing three times more opium than the rest of the world with 96% of production under Taliban control. The Taliban regime became the world's largest producers of heroin even to the point of establishing model farms in Herat to teach the best methods of cultivation for the raw product.[93] Then in July 2000 for reasons still unclear, with stockpiles in place, Mullah Omar suddenly reversed previous practice by ruling that growing poppies was a sin against the teachings of Islam.[94] Opium dealer Mirakbar asserted that 'the Taliban may have tried to prevent farmers from growing it but then stockpiled it in warehouses and were involved in trading it.' The raw opium is transported into Pakistan where it is processed into heroin. With the fall of the Taliban, poppy fields bloomed once more.[95] Among the end users, Christians were frequently blamed by Muslim preachers for allowing such a practice within Western nations.

As a government minister surveyed the destruction of Afghanistan's capital city, Kabul, he stretched his arms wide and remarked, 'See, this is what Islam has done for us!'[96] To another foreign visitor an Afghan man held out an empty cartridge case and said, 'Here! Accept a gift from Islam.'[97] According to one highly placed Afghani official, just to be found in possession of Christian literature would be cause for imprisonment.[98] On January 8 2001 Mullah Omar announced that anyone converting from Islam would be subject to the death penalty, those responsible would be similarly dealt with and that anyone found 'selling material critical of Islam or books about other religions' would be jailed for five years.[99] Later that year, eight foreign NGO workers and 16 Afghanis were arrested on a charge of preaching Christianity. After months of imprisonment without trial, they were released by Northern Alliance and foreign troops during the 'War on Terror'.

In the Middle East itself, Islam seeks to diminish any remaining vestiges of Christianity within any countries where it still exists. In present day Iran the Christian church was an established institution until Arabs conquered the territory in 642 bringing with them the new religion of Islam. With their arrival persecution and oppression began. In the period 1291–1304 Ghazan, a Muslim, ordered the destruction of all churches. With the arrival of Tamerlane in 1369 the church was completely swept aside. Despite extreme persecution and many threats the church has nevertheless continued to exist and is seeing more converts from Islam than ever before - but at a cost.[100]

In Iran within the first four years of its post Shah Islamic revolution, 27 pastors were executed. In 1994, its fifth year, in the first six months, three more national level Christian leaders were killed: Mehdi Dibaj, an Assemblies of God pastor, Reverend Tateos Michaelian and Bishop Hovsepian Mehr. A senior official of the Ministry of Islamic Guidance succinctly summed up the government's position when he told Christians, 'From now on either we kill all of you quietly or we make your lives so difficult that you will have no choice but to leave the country.'[101] In Iran Muslims are forbidden to enter Christian churches for worship. Such church services as there are, are not even allowed to be conducted in Farsi, the official language of Iran.[102] In neighbouring Iraq in 2003 with the fall of the Saddam Hussein regime, Christians started to report harassment, intimidation and violence from Shia Muslims who quickly wanted to impose *shariah* law on Muslims and non-Muslims.[103]

With constant pressure of this magnitude exerted upon Christians it is hardly surprising that their communities grow smaller and smaller. Even in the newly created semiautonomous area on the West Bank under Palestinian control, matters are hardly easier. An Israeli government report says that Christian cemeteries are vandalised, churches are robbed and Islamists particularly harass younger Christians.[104] In the town of Bethlehem, a major focus in Christianity's history, 30 years ago there were five mosques. By 1998 in greater Bethlehem there were 72. Christians reported that it was wiser to stay indoors, particularly on their annual religious festival days of Christmas Eve and Christmas Day than go outside and risk abuse.

It has been estimated that the number of Arab Palestinian Christians has been reduced to fewer than 30 000 among the 3.4 million inhabitants of territory controlled by the Palestinian Authority.[105] Fifty years ago the Palestinian population was approximately 25% Christian.

It has been further estimated that partly because of the pressure on Christians to either convert to Islam or to get out, some 2 million Christians left their homes in the Middle Eastern countries during 1993–97.[106]

In neighbouring Jordan in 1998, what was probably the only uniquely Christian shop and showroom for the whole of the country was deliberately torched in the capital city of Amman a few days before the end of the Muslim month of Ramadan.[107]

Around the world Muslims have regarded Christians as 'the enemy'. They are considered historic enemies supposedly because of the behaviour and actions of the Crusaders in the Middle Ages. They were considered colonial enemies because of the political expansion of Britain and France into Islamic heartlands in the nineteenth century. They were regarded as neo-colonialist enemies because the West exploited the oil resources of Muslim states. They were ethnic enemies when viewed from a position of Arab superiority. They were secular enemies because their governments did not acknowledge *Allah*. They were considered political enemies because Western 'Christian' nations mostly align with Israel. They were religious enemies because in the eyes of Islam they are infidels, unbelievers according to the Quran and the Prophet Muhammad and are therefore suitable only for conversion or conquest.[108]

Around the world Islam has taken every opportunity to expand. The symbol of its presence is the mosque. Christians may lament the fact that often mosques and Islamic centres are built with the seeming 'cooperation' of governments who have sold their inheritance for petro dollars or votes. But have Christian denominational or local congregational leaders been any different when countless formerly Christian church buildings in the West have also been sold, undoubtedly for a good price, to have them recycled into centres of Islamic activity? Did they not understand that whenever this has taken place it certainly changed the landscape irrevocably at that time if not for all time?

In the city of Perth in Western Australia, a case went to court regarding a hall which had been erected at a declared Islamic centre. Construction for the hall did not have appropriate government approval. Its location also contravened local building and other regulations. Because of this, in accordance with state law, the order was given for it to be demolished. The senior managing trustee of the local mosque defended the Muslim position by saying, 'In our religion that place (the attached hall) remains to the Day of Judgment as a place of worship. You cannot do anything. That's our religion. You can't sell it. You can't demolish it. The mosque remains a mosque as long as the world exists.' [109]

In 1913 Ottoman Celal Nuri said that as a Muslim he considered the whole world of non-Muslims as infidels and enemies. 'Friendship (with) the West is the vilest of crimes I can imagine. A nation incapable of hating the West is doomed to extinction.'[110]

No Muslim nation has ever become 'extinct'. However many non-Muslim nations with increasing numbers of Muslims and mosques, are perceptibly approaching that cultural and religious point. The same may be the fate of the formerly 'Christian' West unless it comes to grips with what is happening and commences to resource and implement appropriate responses.

PART 2

WHY IT'S HAPPENING

If it is important to understand what is happening, it is equally necessary to understand how and why Islam must operate the way it does. In Part 2 we examine the origins and history of Islam as revealed through its prophet Muhammad, its holy book the Quran, its basic theology, practice and development. The evidence of the centuries indicates that Islam has not, cannot and will not change.

CHAPTER 9

SHIFTING SANDS

During what has been probably the longest continuous international war in the twentieth century, the Iran–Iraq conflict, President Saddam Hussein of Iraq ordered the restoration and rebuilding of the ancient city of Babylon. Fourteen million bricks were produced for the project. Modern house bricks certainly gave Babylon a somewhat updated and contemporary appearance. To further identify with other great leaders of the area's rich history, a Babylon festival was conducted in 1989. As a part of this Saddam Hussein's head was superimposed on a silhouette of King Nebuchadnezzar who reigned for 43 years of Babylon's Golden Age until just before the city was captured by the Persians (today's Iranians) in 538 BC. Iraqi historians also busied themselves tracing Saddam Hussein's personal history from his birth as the son of a landless peasant family outside of Tikrit, 125 kilometres north of Baghdad, right back to the Prophet Muhammad of Arabia.[1]

History is very important to most Muslims. Knowledge of the past can help to explain attitudes in the present. Linkage to the past often provides the rationale for actions in the present. To understand Islam today, as well as to anticipate its future directions, we need to understand something of its origins and from where it has come. Inevitably this leads to what is today known as Saudi Arabia.

Whatever else might be desirable objectives or performance indicators for the Saudi Arabian government, competition for the international tourist trade is certainly not one of them. Unless one is a Muslim on pilgrimage or is involved in commercial, professional or political enterprises considered vital to the kingdom's interests, then the legendary Arab hospitality may not apply. This means that for most, the Arabian peninsula will remain somewhat of a mystery shrouded behind a veil of ultimate Islam.

It also means that the popular perception of the geography of the Saudi Arabian peninsula remains one of unrelieved desert. This in turn romantically suggests endless hills of shifting sand. This is hardly Arabia as it is in reality. Down the western side flanking the Red Sea from Palestine in the north to Yemen in the south there is the Hijaz. *Hijaz* means barrier. This is a rugged mountain range obstructing easy penetration to the hinterland from the west. East of the Hijaz stretches the Najd, which are the highlands of Arabia.

The country can be divided into four well-defined regions. In the north there is Arabia Petraea home of the Edomites and Midianites of old. Then there is the Hijaz proper in which the city of Yathrib, later named Medina, is found. Toward the south is the province of Tihama where Mecca is situated as well as its principal port Jeddah, which is an arrival point for many who undertake the annual pilgrimage to the sacred city. Entry into Mecca is prohibited to non-Muslims. The southernmost region is Asir and it borders the Yemens and Oman.

The first mention in recorded history of an Arabian is on an inscription of the Assyrian ruler, Shalmaneser III. The battle of Karkar was fought in 854 BC. Shalmaneser defeated a coalition of small western states in which the Israelite King Ahab was included. Also on the losing side was an Arabian Gin Dibu who had joined Bir-'Idri of Damscus (the Biblical Benhadad II) against Shalmeneser III. He not only lost his honour but 1000 camels as well.[2]

From that inauspicious entry into the written annals of human history, Arabians were more frequently mentioned in the records of Assyria and Babylon. They were referred to as Aribi or Aribu, a nomadic people who lived in the northern Arabian Desert.[3] The first mention of Arabs in the Bible is found in 1 Kings 10:15 recording trade between Israel and Arabia.

There is no convincing explanation of the meaning and use of the word *Arab*. They are described as one of the Semitic peoples. This designation is given to those who were reputedly descendants of Shem the son of Noah who is claimed as the most ancient ancestor of Arabia's inhabitants.[4] The peoples who have populated the peninsula throughout history are variously divided into three major categories.

The first is the *Arab ul-Baidah*. They are sometimes referred to as 'the lost Arabs'. They are thought to be the extinct Hamitic Kushites who preceded the Semites. According to the Quran, their extinction was caused by a hot wind which blew continuously for eight days, accompanied by an earthquake. They had invoked the displeasure of the Supreme deity because of their idolatry and were accordingly punished for such (Surah 7:63; 11:53).

The second phase of development was through the *Arab ul-Ariba* referred to variously as the original, true or pure Arab Semites. They are said to be descendants of Joktan, the great grandson of Shem mentioned in the Jewish Torah and the

Christian Bible (Genesis 10:1,21,25). These people are thought to have known and to have been worshippers of the true God of Shem (Genesis 9:26). They divided into two branches. Ya'rub founded the kingdom of al-Yemen. Juhum founded the kingdom of al-Hijaz.

The third wave of Arab population takes us from the eras of ancient legend into more examinable history. The *Arab ul-Mustaribah,* mixed or naturalised Arabs, claim to be descendants of Ishmael and the daughter of ul-Muzaz, the king of al-Hijaz. Ishmael is identified as the son of Abraham. He and his descendants are said to have settled among the Joktanites and intermarried with them. The Prophet Muhammad is said to have been able to trace his lineage back to these ancestors.

According to the Islamic interpretation of history, al-Hijaz is the district where Abraham and his people settled. Mecca is claimed as the place where Ishmael's life was saved and where Hagar and Ishmael were later buried. The place where water was provided for them is said to be the Well of Zamzam and it still operates in Mecca today. It is further claimed that to commemorate God's miraculous preservation of Ishmael, God commanded Abraham to build the Kaabah, the holy shrine in Mecca. Muslim historians believe that from this high point of history, for 50 years prior to Ishmael's death at age 137 years, he preached about the one true God.

Following his death it is said that Jurhamites seized the shrine and retained control of it for 300 years. When the Ishmaelites eventually drove them out, the Jurhamites used the sacred items of the temple to fill up the Well of Zamzam. Muslims calculate the time between the erection of the Kaabah and the coming of Muhammad to be 2740 years.[5]

Jewish and Christian records tell a different story. They were originally and separately (revealed and) written many centuries before the appearance of the Quran. The human instruments of the Judeo – Christian written accounts were much closer to the actual events and they produced the only known written record in existence for most of the common material prior to the Quran. Not surprisingly, Jewish and Christian records are in complete agreement on the material in question. But both significantly disagree with later Quranic 'revelations'.

Furthermore, twentieth century archaeological discoveries and the recovery of very ancient manuscripts thousands of years old continue to confirm the veracity of Jewish and Christian Scriptures. In spite of millennia of transmission, reproduction and translation they are virtually unaltered and very precise in whatever they record.

According to the Biblical record, Abraham was directed by God to emigrate from Ur (in modern Iraq). He was promised that he would become the father of a great nation

(Genesis 12:1–3). Having no natural heir, his wife Sarah in keeping with the custom of the day, offered her Egyptian maid Hagar to Abraham. According to the Midrash, a collection of very early Jewish commentaries on the Old Testament, Hagar was a daughter of Pharaoh who was given to Abraham to appease divine wrath (Genesis 12:17).

After Hagar fell pregnant to Abraham, animosity developed between her and Sarah. Hagar consequently fled into the desert where an angel of the Lord found her beside the road to Shur. The word *shur* means a wall of fortification and is identified with a series of forts that were built on the Egyptian borders in Sinai.[6]

In the theophany at Shur roadside, an angel instructed Hagar to return and submit to her mistress. He encouraged her by saying that she would have a son whom she was to name Ishmael but 'his hand would be against everyone...and he would live in hostility toward all his brothers' (Genesis 16: 11–12).

Ishmael's mother Hagar was a very special person in Biblical history. She was the first post-Fall woman to whom there was a divine appearance. She was the first to record that not only does God see but he also hears. Her son Ishmael was the first person to be given a name by God himself.

Thirteen years later Sarah gave birth to Isaac (Genesis 21:5). Because of the continuing feud between Sarah and Hagar and the jealousy and animosity that their two offspring were likely to promote in the competition for Abraham's notice, favour and blessing, Abraham reluctantly sent Hagar and Ishmael off into the desert. He was comforted by the knowledge that Ishmael also would lead a nation which would become great (Genesis 21:13–18). Ishmael grew up, became famous for his archery and subsequently married an Egyptian woman obtained for him by his mother Hagar (Genesis 21: 20–21).

When Abraham died, his two sons Ishmael and Isaac were obviously on sufficiently good terms and living within geographical proximity to one another to the degree that they jointly buried their father near Mamre (Genesis 25:9). Abraham had earlier bought the field of Ephron the Hittite, with its cave of Machpelah, for a family burial place (Genesis 23). Sarah, Abraham, Isaac, Rebekah, Jacob and Leah were all buried there. The site was appropriated in the seventh century by invading Muslims. The Mosque of Abraham in the southeastern part of the town of Hebron is built over the burial cave.

Even today, these ancient sites are of great significance to Muslims and Jews and the possession of these sites is hotly contested. In October 2000 after days of fierce fighting, Palestinian forces gained control of Joseph's tomb in Nablus, Biblical

Sechem, about 65 kilometres north of Jerusalem. It was then converted into a mosque with a painted green dome. This was followed by an attempt on December 5 2000 to take over Rachael's tomb in Bethlehem. The three-pronged attack fell short by 10 metres.[7]

After Ishmael died aged 137 years, his descendants settled in the area which stretched from Havilah to Shur over near the border of Egypt and according to the earlier promise (Genesis 16:11–12), 'they lived in hostility toward all their brothers' (Genesis 25:17–18). None of this or any other events recorded in the Bible regarding Abraham's life and activities place him anywhere on the Arabian peninsula with or without Ishmael.

In every respect God's word regarding Ishmael was fulfilled. As promised (Genesis 21:18,20), Ishmael did have 12 sons who went on to become princes of tribes of East Palestine, Jordan and later around Aqaba in Arabia.[8] Ishmael's eldest son Naboath (Genesis 25:13) became the founder of the tribe of Nabat. The Nabateans were neighbours to an Arabian clan descended from Ishmael's second son Kedar (Isaiah 60:7). The Nabateans founded Babylon and Ninevah. They built reservoirs, dams and aquaducts in current Iraq. Petra in today's southern Jordan

> Ishmael's mother Hagar was a very special person in Biblical history. She was the first post-Fall woman to whom there was a divine appearance. She was the first to record that not only does God see but he also hears. Her son Ishmael was the first person to be given a name by God himself.

became one of their great fortresses to control the caravan routes. The Judean king, Herod the Great, was also of Nabatean lineage through marriage.

As the legal heir, Abraham's and Sarah's son Isaac, obtained his father's inheritance. Prior to his death, as Abraham had earlier done with Ishmael, he sent all his other sons of concubines away to the east of later Israel (Genesis 25:5–6). With the assurance of Abraham and God's blessing (Genesis 25:11) Isaac went on to marry Rebekah. Like Isaac's mother, she was initially barren until God intervened (Genesis 25:21–22). This marriage produced twins, Esau and Jacob. Esau, through his own weakness and prompted by Jacob's seductive opportunism, lost his inheritance to his younger brother Jacob (Genesis 25:33). 'To spite his parents',[9] Esau went and married Canaanite women, one of whom was Basemath (Genesis 36:3) who was a daughter of the also disinherited and disaffected Ishmael.

According to the Bible, God's blessing continued on through his chosen line of Abraham, Isaac and Jacob. But that sort of favour was not accorded to Ishmael (Malachi 1:3; Romans 9:7; Galatians 4:21–31) and his descendants. They would fulfil other divine purposes on their way to promised 'greatness'.

It is hard to discern the degree to which the conjunction and co-mingling of the descendants of Ishmael and Esau established a bed where seeds of rejection, resentment and bitterness would germinate. This bed that would later result in such an awesome, endless harvest of habitual raiding, rivalry, ransom and death as their descendants lived 'in hostility toward all their brothers'.

In the Rabbinic commentary known as Midrash it says, 'When Esau was getting old he called in his grandson Amelech and said: "I tried to kill Jacob but was unable. Now I am entrusting you and your descendants with the important mission of annihilating Jacob's descendants - the Jewish people. Carry out this deed for me. Be relentless and do not show mercy."' In Jewish understanding Amelech has come to represent the spirit of hatred against the Jewish people with which it is impossible to reason and which seeks only their destruction. This was exemplified by Haman, a descendant of Agag, the Amalekite (Numbers 24:7) who is infamously mentioned in the book of Esther (Esther 3:1ff). Fighting within and hatred without especially toward the Jewish people is one of the hallmarks of many contemporary movements within Islam.

Observing tribal life in the area as recently as the twentieth century Michael Asher concluded:

...the tribes were violently independent and quite often in a state of hostility with one another...Yet while the more mobile tended to sneer at the more settled, they were kinsmen... The tribes which were most powerful at any given moment were considered the most 'noble' and altered their genealogies accordingly...(For the individual) his hand was turned against every man unless it suited him.[10]

It is impossible to estimate the huge amount of money which has flowed into the Arab world in our time in the forms of aid, grants, loans and investments, let alone the countless billions of dollars earned by them through the export of oil and natural gas. Yet 'something is still amiss. Money and opportunity and goodwill (are) to little or no avail.'[11] Fouad Ajami, a Lebanese Shiite Muslim, in attempting to come to terms with Middle East history describes it as 'a chronicle of illusions and despair, of politics repeatedly degenerating into bloodletting.'[12]

David Pryce-Jones analysing the twentieth century regional state of affairs at an international level said that:

...every Arab state is explicitly Islamic in confession. Religious and ethnic minorities have been persecuted everywhere. Nowhere is there participation in the political process corresponding to any conception of representative democracy. No parliament or assembly except by appointment of the power holder, no freedom of expression throughout the rigidly state controlled media, no opinion polls, nothing except a riot to determine what public opinion might be. Nowhere in the Arab world is there security guaranteed under the law for persons and property. The same is true for non-Arab and Shia Iran where the difference between the rule of the late Shah and his successor Ayatollah Khomeini may be posed as a question of who is persecuting whom and according to what principle?[13]...Time after time another bout of inter Arab fighting produces a flurry of further metaphors about socialism and revolution, which fade out as yet another absolute ruler takes power exactly as his predecessor had done. National interests are not at stake. Territorial adjustments do not follow...Tribes and religions do not have institutional mechanisms for compromise and mediation. Instead they resort to war in a perpetual process of adjudicating issues outstanding between them.[14]

In February 2002 President Musharraf of Pakistan in an international radio broadcast stated that 'while Muslim nations were involved in fratricidal conflicts, they were the poorest, most illiterate, most backward, most unhealthy, most unenlightened, most deprived and the weakest of all the human race'.[15] In reaching his conclusion President Musharraf was uncharacteristically candid for a Muslim commentator in that he chose not to blame the 'crusading West' or 'evil Jews' as scapegoats for all Islamic ills. In 1996 Harvard Professor Samuel P. Huntington released the findings of his ground breaking analysis. By tabulating late twentieth century conflicts he demonstrated that Muslims were involved in more intergroup violence and more intercivilizational wars than any others. He also demonstrated that Muslim countries are approximately twice as militarized as are Christian countries. Back in 1989 James Payne had concluded that there is a connection between Islam and militarism.[16]

Huntington noted that 'quantitative evidence from every disinterested source conclusively demonstrates' Muslim bellicosity and violence. He concludes 'Wherever one looks along the perimeter of Islam, Muslims have problems living peaceably with their neighbours...Muslims...have been far more involved in inter-group violence than the people of any other civilisation. The evidence is overwhelming.'[17]

He attributes the causes for this. From the start Islam has glorified military virtues. It was spread by different peoples being conquered and converted. It merges religion and politics by distinguishing only between Muslims and 'the rest'. Finally there has been a demographic explosion in the twentieth century society which has produced in Muslim societies large numbers of often unemployed males.[18]

There is no doubt that the ancient prophecy regarding Ishmael becoming a great nation, however one understands greatness, has been fulfilled. Could it be that the other part of the prophecy relating to his descendants 'living in hostility toward all their brothers' also continues to be fulfilled?

Regardless of interpretations of prophecy and history, what is more certain is that those who claim to be descendants of Isaac and Ishmael are in fact all sons, and therefore brothers, descended from a common ancestor. A study published in the Proceedings of the (US) National Academy of Sciences by genetic researchers demonstrates that Jews are the genetic brothers of Arabs and others in the immediate area. They share a lineage dating back several thousand years to one ancestral group. Harry Oster of the New York University School of Medicine and a co-author of the study concluded 'Jews and Arabs are all really children of Abraham.'[19]

Some might want to accuse God of being somewhat unjust choosing a special relationship between himself, Abraham, Isaac, Jacob and their descendants (Genesis 21:12–13, 28:13). But it needs to be kept in mind that for the children of Ishmael and Esau good provision was also made. For example, they were allotted far more vast territories to the east and south of the much smaller amount of land which was allotted to Abraham's other line of descendants. The Bible holds that these allocated territories were inviolate and coveting territory which belonged to the other was forbidden (Deuteronomy 2:3–5, 19).

In October 2000 as yet another round of the Israeli–Palestinian conflict raged on, the then Prime Minister of Israel, Ehud Barak was asked about the possibilities for peace. He replied, 'We will never lose hope of making peace with our Palestinian neighbours. There is no other alternative. They are here forever as we are.'[20]

During the same week Jaffar, a Palestinian Hamas field leader attacked and wounded members of an Israeli military patrol. But when interviewed after the event he said, 'This land…belongs to Muslims. I don't think in terms of happiness when I kill an Israeli or wound him. I think in terms of carrying out my religious obligations. I am asked by my God to fight the enemies until the last spot of blood.'[21]

It is also intriguing to note that many great peoples of the immediate region, Babylonians, Assyrians, Chaldeans, Arameans, Phoenicians and many others…were, but are no more. The Arabs (and their religious relatives in Israel) were and remain.[22] But the description of their relationships may be best summed up in the Arab proverb 'I and my brothers against my cousin. I and my cousins against the stranger (ie. the world).' If history past and present is any guide, could it be that these 'brothers' seem destined to continue to 'live in hostility'?

CHAPTER 10

STORM WARNINGS

The socio-political structures that existed on the Arabian peninsula at the beginning of the seventh century of the Christian era could best be described as constantly changing alliances among war-like tribal confederations. Because of tribal addiction to *razzias* (raids) on neighbouring oases or passing caravans (to the point where brigandage had become almost a national pastime) a system of ransom and protection monies provided a type of economic interchange between the tribes as well as a ranking of intertribal hierarchies. From time immemorial:

To an Arab honour and respect by the community are interchangeable concepts. Honourable behaviour can be reflected in manifestations of manliness...There is a strong correlation between honour and group cohesion and group survival. Honourable behaviour is that 'which strengthens the group...while shameful behaviour is that which tends to disrupt, endanger, impair or weaken...'.[1]

Weaker tribes were obliged to pay protection money to the stronger, who in turn grew even stronger. Both in the south and the north of Arabia, semi-sedentary tribes engaged in cultivation. Craftsmen, artists, debaters, scholars, philosophers and merchants had their place in society. Greek and Phalavi were official languages to the west and the east of the peninsula. Aramaic was also widely spoken. A small minority could read and write. The all-important oral tradition of the tribes was preserved through their respective highly esteemed bards.

To the north, two empires had been locked in conflict for some time. From the northeast came pressure from the Persian Empire. From the northwest there emanated the power of the Byzantines. They faced off across the peninsula. To diminish incursions by nomads who had nothing to lose by conducting raids along northern Arabian tribal borders, both Byzantine and Persian officials recruited mercenaries to achieve their own ends. The Byzantines drew support from a Christian Arabian tribe, the Ghassanids. The Persians did likewise from another

Christian tribe, the Lakhmids. Each client tribe was paid in weapons, horses and other appropriate items of trade by their respective imperialist puppet masters.

The economy of the peninsula in both northern and southern regions depended on the careful use of water. Close to the Euphrates and Tigris Rivers in the north intensive irrigation permitted the development of gardens and orchards. In the far south watercourses were dammed for similar purposes. Castles, temples and other signals of society developed alongside agriculture. However for the vast central area of the peninsula traversed ceaselessly by Bedouin, trading and raiding formed the basis of economic and social life.[2]

Bedouin prosperity was related to those timeless twin measures of peninsular wealth – camels and date palms. From the camel they obtained milk for drinking, flesh for eating, skin to provide covers and warmth, hair for tents, dung for fuel and urine for hair tonic and medicine. Town dwellers depended on this 'ship of the desert' more as the means of transport for goods and personnel between trade centres.

Major caravan routes traversed the peninsula from the north taking the goods of Palestine, Syria and Persia through to the south, on to Africa in the west and India in the east. Twice yearly, large caravans passed north and south. At its northern reaches the caravans passed through what were the great cities of Palmyra (in Syria) and Petra (in today's Jordan). But the centre where the trade routes crossed was Mecca.

By the fifth century of the Christian era Mecca had superseded other towns as an important trading centre. It was governed by a committee of prominent merchants *(mola)*. At the time of Muhammad the dominant confederation around Mecca was the Quraysh.

Typical of trading centres of any age there had rubbed off on Mecca some of the wealth and culture of the neighbouring countries whose trade it handled. Not all of that was good. Slave girls, gambling, singing, dancing, female infanticide, immorality, drunkenness and general carousing as well as idolatry had become part of its life.[3] Material prosperity is often the forerunner to moral depravity, the correction of which is the province of religion.

Although the original Semites might have known of and even worshipped the true God of their ancient ancestor Shem, with the passing of time that knowledge and practice had been well and truly lost. Muslims refer to the era prior to the coming of Prophet Muhammad as *Jahiliyah* (the time of ignorance or barbarism).

Bedouin polytheistic paganism of antiquity centred chiefly on the moon god, the symbol for which still appears in much of Islam. By the fourth century of the

Christian era, some began to accept a form of monotheism, that is a belief in one supreme God. In southern Arabia this God was known as *al-Rahman* (the merciful).[4] Belief in jinns and ghouls, minor spirit beings, was also prevalent. Oracles were consulted. They interpreted the desires of deities as exemplified in various idols by the use of pointed arrows. Custodianship of the Kaba was also highly prized.

Gods or spirits were thought to inhabit blocks of stone, rocks, trees, wells and other outstanding features. Tribesmen danced around altars made of stones upon which victims were slaughtered and their blood poured out. Well-known religious sanctuaries existed at Nejrun on the Yemeni border and at Sana in (today's) Yemen Arab Republic. But the best known sanctuary was that of the Kaba at Mecca.

It was considered the most holy and contained 360 idols, one for approximately each day of the calendar year of that time. Tribes made annual pilgrimages to this sanctuary. Included in the shrine ceremonies were activities such as kissing the black stone and making seven circuits of the temple naked. Apart from the nakedness, both these practices were incorporated into Islam. Regarding the black stone Caliph Umar was later to say, 'Had I not seen the Prophet kiss you, I would not kiss you myself.'

The oldest known name attributed to God in the Semitic language of ancient Babylonia consists of just two letters, the consonant 'l' preceded by a smooth breathing pronounced 'Il'. In ancient Israel it was pronounced 'El'. These became generic terms. The Arabic term 'Allah' results from the conflation of the definite article with the generic term for gods expressed in singular form. The process of transition from ancient generic to contemporary specific is not clear.[5] What is better known is that the title for the dominant moon god in southern Arabia was Ilah. Meccan pagans knew of Allah as the Supreme deity. This name was also known to other practitioners of the main religions of the Arabian peninsula, Christians and Jews.

What became the international Jewish dispersion into various other countries beyond its homeland, began with the fall of Samaria in 721 BC. Fugitives fled from the old northern capital and its surrounds and shortly thereafter colonies appeared elsewhere. One such colony was as far away as Aswan in Egypt. The fall of Jerusalem in the sixth century (586 BC) was cause for an even greater scattering from Israel. With the destruction of the temple in Jerusalem in the first century of the Christian era (70 AD) and severe Roman repression that continued into the second century, far fewer Jews dared to remain in their homeland. Well-known Jewish colonies sprang into existence in Arabia as far south as Yemen.

By the time of Muhammad, according to their historic practice Jews had come to dominate the economic life of the Hijaz. They also held much of the best land in the various oases. They controlled finance, trade and industry and almost had a monopoly on the all-important production of iron items. Although fewer in numbers, with their superior knowledge of agriculture, irrigation and facets of industrial production, they also managed to dominate much of the economic life of the peninsula. Jews had been uncharacteristically zealous in evangelism and many proselytes had been made among various tribes. Half of the population of Medina was Jewish.[6]

There is also evidence suggesting a Christian presence to some degree. Just as Judaism had very early associations with the Arabian population through Abraham, Moses and his marriage to an Arabian woman (Exodus 3:1; 18:10–12) and so forth, so Christianity had some Arabian contacts from its earliest days. The apostle Paul preached first in Syrian Damascus (Acts 9:20) before repairing to Arabia (Galatians 1:7). St Thomas is said to have founded the first church in what is today known as Iraq.

By the time of Muhammad in the seventh century some tribes had become Christian. They were located in Syria in the north, Egypt to the west and Yemen in the south. At least two Christian tribes lived in the Hijaz. The Christian Abyssinian general Abraha was known to have built a church in Sana when he was viceroy of Yemen.[7] He invaded Arabia from Yemen in 570 AD. Among the Quraysh of Mecca there were known to be individual Christians. When Muhammad returned to Mecca in 630 AD paintings of Jesus and Mary were still visible inside the walls of what became Islam's holiest shrine, the Kaabah. On the Arabian peninsula there were settlements of Christians and fully developed communities with their own bishops, monasteries and church buildings. Some of these were within short distances of Mecca.

But seventh century Arabian Christianity in belief and practice was significantly dissimilar from much of that of our era. It was still struggling to define and defend what represented orthodoxy. Decisions being made in other places were certainly affecting local expressions of belief, practice and relationships. Arab Christianity was divided between Greek (becoming Orthodox), Monophysite (Jacobite) and Nestorian. Arguments revolved mainly around attempts to understand and explain the person of Christ and principally how could human and divine natures co-exist in a single person while that person remained a human being.

Traditional Nestorianism implied a split within the person of Christ into two natures, divine and human.[8] Nestorians were active in evangelism. Although their position was outlawed at a Council held in Ephesus in 431 AD, they continued to expand, moving down the east coast of Arabia to Bahrain and Oman. Eventually they reached Afghanistan and further east into China.

Monophysites believed that there was only one nature in Christ who was the divine Word. The Quran would later describe the office of Jesus as 'a word from Him' which is reminiscent of Monophysite theology. Their position was proscribed by the Council of Chalcedon in 451 AD. However, like the Nestorians, they also had been zealous in preaching on the peninsula and had established many churches.

Arab Christians were far less enthralled by the theological niceties, subtleties and endless attempts to define the indefinable than were their co-religionists in the West. Theirs was a more robust expression of the practicalities of faith in a harsh environment. While Greek theologians might attempt to dissect their opponents with the pen, Arabs would resort to the sword to defend their stand. They held to their Monophysite position refusing to accept the doctrine of the two natures in Christ.

A well-known Arab chieftain, Harith, even went to Constantinople for an audience with the Emperor to request a Monophysite bishop for his people. On his death his successor Mundhir took up the cause and in the best tradition of tribal leader became the protector of their theological stance.

All of this was being played out against the volatile political background of the ongoing contest between Byzantium and Persia. Because the Byzantines had prohibited Nestorianism in Persia, it was encouraged. Political wars became infused with theological overtones, which in turn contributed their own impetus for further fighting.

Mundhir and his people had been loyal allies of the Byzantines. He had intervened where necessary to defeat Persian incursions. However, when he also travelled to Constantinople expecting a reward as a loyal ally, he was treated insultingly. Later he was betrayed and taken in chains back to Constantinople. From there he was sent into exile. His son, Numan was also later captured and exiled along with his father.

In the sphere of human enterprise, personal relationships frequently influence outcomes far more than commitment to (theological) truth. Such treachery, tyranny and injustice would not be forgotten by those who had lost their beloved tribal leaders in such a shameful way.

The professional clergy hardly provided a more exemplary model than their political and social counterparts. The endless heresy hunts and anathemas, imprecations and excommunications which they engendered, were outdone only in shame by arguments among high officers of the Church over such matters as primacy, controls over dioceses, the extent of bishops' territories, finances and so on. Endless disputation among clergy seeking power, prestige and other worldly attainments was parallelled by the frequency with which they broke their own commitments. Dissension among those who certainly should have known better was ruining the prospect of a longer lasting vibrant church remaining as an attractive witness among the tribes of Arabia.

In the pressure of Church and state upon its people Jews also were not neglected. At the encouragement of the bishop of Jerusalem, the Emperor Heraclius (610– 41 AD) decreed the conversion of all Jews in 632 AD which increased killing and persecution. Another group therefore was prepared to react with hostility against the Byzantines.

The Lord of the Church had instructed his first followers to love one another (John 13:34 –35) even their enemies (Matthew 5:43– 44). These seventh century counterparts however, chose to unleash on one another waves of persecution, confiscations of churches, monasteries, dioceses and other treacheries in an attempt to establish by force belief in truth, which was only ever meant to be accepted by the persuasion of exemplary perfect love. When both empires, West and East made the same mistake of withdrawing subsidies to their mercenaries and then murdered and imprisoned Arab kings, friends and allies were finally turned into permanent enemies.

From the Church, Islam may have imbibed something of Monophysite theology. Islam's practices might also have been influenced by that same group's practice of hospitality, almsgiving, fasting and obliging their Christian women to be veiled when out of doors. It may have even been influenced by the Nestorian clergy prostrating themselves to the ground and facing eastward whenever they prayed. But little else of value had been demonstrated or would be considered desirable for adoption. History shows that whenever princes of the Church ally with kings of state the result is often disastrous for both. Seventh century Arabia would provide no exception.

Muslim historians are seldom noted for their high praise and generous interpretation of Christian history. But of this particular time and place one could hardly disagree with one Muslim historian who describing the times of the seventh century in Arabia concluded that, 'A demoralised and degraded state of society (existed) all over Christendom.'[9] Murder, rape and treachery at the highest levels provided 'an index to the morality of the Byzantine Christians.'[10] 'The followers of Jesus, instead of alleviating, intensified the evil...and converted western Asia into a wilderness of despair and desolation.'[11]

When the time for change came peoples of Arabia, Syria and northern Africa would welcome anyone as deliverer from the depredations and oppressions initiated by the Byzantine Empire and Western Church axis.

The Bible records how in bygone times whenever God's people, the Israelites perverted their worship, practised injustice or in various ways broke their covenant and forsook him, he reacted. He raised up Babylonians, Assyrians, Persians, Egyptians and whoever wished to stride the stage of momentary magnificence. He allowed them to attack, invade and crush his people as he had forewarned. This was divine chastisement. That being so, why should God's more recent people the Church be excluded from the practice of such a timeless principle? Could there be sufficient reason to invoke God's mercy on behalf of a Church which had seemingly, selfishly, wilfully forsaken the way of its Lord, Jesus Christ?

A hammer was about to fall on Church and state alike.

Both Christian tribes, the Lakmids at Hira and the Ghassanids nearer Damascus had

> From the Church, Islam may have imbibed something of Monophysite theology. Islam's practices might also have been influenced by that same group's practice of hospitality, almsgiving, fasting and obliging their Christian women to be veiled when out of doors.

been forsaken and had therefore withdrawn their loyalties to their former paymasters, thus throwing open the northern gateways. Up until this time the invasion traffic had mostly been from north to south on the Arabian peninsula. Now it would be reversed. The next time the Bedouin came forth it would not be merely another *razzia* for purposes of raiding, recruitment or ransom. The Persians and the

Greeks might think so. But in this they would be gravely mistaken. For this would be something that the world had neither expected nor had yet experienced. This would be *jihad* (holy war). And the war cry would be:

There is no god but Allah and Muhammad is his prophet!

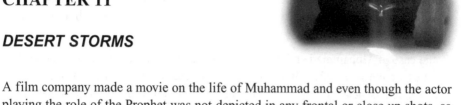

CHAPTER 11

DESERT STORMS

A film company made a movie on the life of Muhammad and even though the actor playing the role of the Prophet was not depicted in any frontal or close up shots, so great were the objections to the movie that it had to be withdrawn from distribution. This film had the official stamp of approval of the Egyptian government.

In Pakistan, the implementation of that nation's blasphemy law, which prohibits any hint of negativity to be said about Islam, its prophet or its 'inspired' writings, has resulted in numbers of Christians being sentenced to death. In some cases, where the state has not succeeded, the implementation of its laws has been swiftly administered by passionate religionists regardless of whether or not those accused were justifiably guilty as charged. This sort of environment is hardly designed to promote freedom of speech, open and honest enquiry or assist in objective research.

Therefore the modern biographer who wishes to go beyond simply recording any historical events as are recoverable and tries to interpret these matters, faces considerable difficulties. Most Muslim writers, as an article of faith, would want to profile Muhammad as the epitomy of compassion and mercy similar in character to the titles attributed to the God who is worshipped. This is understandable. The faithful of every religious tradition tend to sanctify their heroes of history almost to the point where they are beyond human recognition. Popular purveyors of both oral and written forms related to religion, produce more hagiography than biography, as it is understood in modern Western methodologies. In such ways mere mortals are converted into sanitised saints. Christian authors are not immune from this tempting tendency.

In addition to the social and theological difficulties associated with writing about Muhammad, there is the normal problem that he lived so long ago. Unfortunately, in that era there was not the always present, ever intrusive video cameras to record everything he said or did with irrefutable accuracy. Even if that were so it would be insufficient to dissuade the converted toward another conclusion they were reluctant to accept.

In December 2001 the United States government released a video purportedly found in Afghanistan which, by his own testimony, implicated Osama bin Laden directly in the September 11 2001 events in New York and Washington. Many Muslims still refused to regard it as reliable evidence. They preferred to believe the bombings were part of a Zionist plot.

In the case of Muhammad and the times in which he lived we are mostly dependent upon oral records. His friends and followers collected many thousands of anecdotes that became associated with his belief and practice. Over the years these have been collated into six major collections generically known as *Hadith*. The problem for Islamic historians and lawyers has been the vast amount of material available, some of which because of its contradictory nature, cannot be authentic. Various criteria to substantiate authenticity include whether or not the material is attributed directly to Muhammad, the quality of the Arabic used and additional evidence of external support.

The most important source for the recovery of information regarding Muhammad's life and ministry is the Quran. But the problem with this is that its contents permit no chronological arrangement. Nor does it convey personal information regarding the Prophet's personality and other factors that could help us understand him better. Finally of course, there is the personal and often unintended bias any writer brings to his subject.

In spite of these challenges an attempt needs to be made to know and understand this man Muhammad who without question, is one of the great figures of human history. That which his life has bequeathed to the world is his overwhelming conviction that there is only one God and that there should be only one community of authentic believers.[1] This conviction is matched only by his belief in his unique status as a prophet of God, the last of that line.[2]

The foci of Muhammad's activity were two cities known today as Mecca and Medina. Mecca huddles in a low-lying, north-south oriented valley in western Arabia. To the west it is bordered by a range of hills. To the east are high granite rocks. In the centre is Islam's principal shrine, the Kaba. Prior to the time of Muhammad, guardianship of this sanctuary was the responsibility of the Jurhamites. Their chief carried the title *Malik* (King). The Jurhamites lost control to the Khuzaites who in turn were replaced by the Quraysh, a powerful tribe allegedly descended from Ishmael.

By the time of Muhammad within the confederation of the Quraysh, the clan of the extended family of Hashim was specifically involved in the custodianship. The Hashimites however were losing power to a rival branch, the Ommeyya who were gradually taking over provendering pilgrims to the shrine. Members of the royal family of today's kingdom of Jordan are direct descendants of the Hashimites.

Abdul Muttalib, known to belong to one of the higher class families of Mecca, was custodian of the Kaba. He was to become grandfather of the Prophet. One tradition has Abdul Muttalib being instructed in a vision by a spirit as to the location of the ancient well of Zamzam. On the departure of the Jurhamites they had reportedly dumped some of the treasure of the Kaba into the well and covered it with sand.

> ...an attempt needs to be made to know and understand this man Muhammad who without question, is one of the great figures of human history.

Again according to a tradition, Abdul Muttalib is said to have prayed for ten sons, one of whom he would dedicate to be offered as a sacrifice in thankfulness for the granting of his prayer. Infanticide was practised in ancient Arabia. Abdul Muttalib's prayers were answered and his youngest son was named Abdullah. Divination designated this son for sacrifice. But a spirit medium is said to have advised Abdul Muttalib that the sacrifice of 100 camels would be acceptable in the place of his son. Divination through the use of arrows and spirit mediums was also a common practice of the times. Abdullah became the father of the Prophet Muhammad. Whether or not such traditions are true, they are indicative of practices of the time and give important insights into the spiritual heritage and environment of Muhammad.

Muhammad was born in Mecca on the 12th of Rabi I, in the Year of the Elephant. Attempts made to calculate from the calendar of that time and place it into modern Western dating systems, often yield different conclusions. Islamic historian Ameer Ali calculated that the equivalent date was August 29 in the year 570 AD.[3] The Year of the Elephant was so named because Abraha al As Ashram, the Abyssinian viceroy of Yemen, attacked Mecca in retaliation for the desecration of a church he had built in Sana. This had been done by a Meccan. Abraha used an elephant in his attack force. This was the first time such an animal had been seen locally and made such an impact as to have the year identified by its appearance. This event occurred approximately 55 days before the birth of Muhammad.

From the beginning life was difficult for the new child. His particular clan was in economic, political and social decline. Also two months prior to his birth his father Abdullah had died on a journey to Yathrib (later renamed Medina). After the baby was born Muhammad's mother Aminah notified the boy's grandfather, Abdul Muttalib. He in turn took the newborn to the Kaba for, presumably, some form of dedication. Against the advice of his colleagues he chose a name for the baby outside of the family, but one nevertheless relatively common in society. Muhammad means 'the praised one'.

In keeping with the custom of the time where relatively better off families did not perform nursery duties, a slave girl from the home of Muhammad's uncle Abu Lahab, was secured to suckle the child for the first few days. He was then handed on to Halimah of the Banu Sad tribe, to be his foster mother in the desert for the next two years.

Abul Fida recorded an event which, if true, is of singular spiritual significance for Muhammad's later spiritual journey. The event is widely acknowledged by Islamic historians but later writers prefer to place it during Muhammad's adulthood prior to his claimed ascension to heaven.[4] The story as related by Abul Fida occurred during Muhammad's stay with Halimah. It is as follows:

When some time passed Muhammad and his foster brother went out to a distance from the house. When Halimah's son came to his mother and said, 'Two men clothed in white raiments have taken hold of the Quraysh boy and have thrown him down and have ripped open his belly.' So Halimah and her husband went to the place where the child was but found him standing on his feet. And they said, 'What has happened to thee, child?' And he answered and said, 'Two men came to me and threw me down and ripped up my belly.' Then Halimah's husband said to her, 'I greatly fear that this boy has got the epilepsy.' So they took him to his mother Aminah. And Halimah said to Aminah, 'I am afraid he is possessed of a devil.' But Aminah said, 'What in the world can Satan have to do with my son that he should be his enemy.'[5]

Possibly Aminah's musing was foresight that only a mother might intuitively draw. Later commentators reassigned this intervention to the angel Gabriel (Surah 94: 1).

When Muhammad was just six years of age his mother took him on a journey to al-Medina. She died during the return journey and was buried at al-Abwa. His grandfather Abdul Muttalib once more became his guardian. He died two years later when Muhammad was eight.

The responsibility for the child now passed to his paternal uncle, Abu Talib, who became like a father to him. One can only guess at the degree of emotional deprivation, psychological stress and uncertainty which was produced in this boy so frequently bereft of those appointed most dear to him. Mention is made in the Quran of the impoverished state of his frequent orphanhood. (Surah 93:6–11). It is understandable then that in young adulthood he preferred his own company to the company of others. He often withdrew to solitary places in the desert to contemplate the meaning of life.

Abu Talib was an excellent model of ancient Arabian cultural practice. He committed irreversibly to all of his family members providing them with immunity and protection from others, come what may. This was vital to Muhammad's later ministry. Even though Abu Talib did not accept Muhammad's prophethood or the new message that he preached, he was, until his death, the principal protector of his nephew from others who conspired to effect vengeance against him. Families or tribes were prepared to pay fines or forms of agreed compensation but would seldom, if ever, hand over their own kith and kin. In the event of death 'blood money' was an acceptable compensation.

This is still a tenet of Saudi Arabian law as was evidenced by the payment of monies to the family of an Australian nurse allegedly murdered by two English nurses in the kingdom. When the payment process was completed in 1998 the two convicted women were released from their sentences, even though one had been sentenced to death.

When Muhammad was 12 years old (582 AD) he journeyed to Busra in Syria. It is thought that on this journey he may have met with the Christian monk Buhaira, others of that Palestinian religion as well as Jews. Like many of his time who were in similar economic circumstances, Muhammad spent much of his boyhood as a shepherd and goatherd.

Apart from accompanying his uncles on local skirmishes known as the 'sacrilegious wars', so called because they were carried out during the sacred months when fighting was normally forbidden, all authorities agree that Muhammad's youth was otherwise uneventful. By his behaviour and character he built a reputation for being one known for his good manners, honourable attitudes and correct behaviour. His behaviour was so exemplary he was given a title in youth, 'al-Amin' (The Faithful or Trusted One).

When he was 25 years of age, an event took place that was to have a profound influence on him over the next quarter of a century. His uncle Abu Talib, recommended that he accept employment with a comparatively rich widow named Khadijah. She had been married twice before and already had two sons and a daughter. She herself was the daughter of Khuwailid ibn Asad of the Quraysh tribe.

Muhammad was accepted into service and on behalf of his employer journeyed to Busra, a town 96 kilometres (60 miles) east of the Jordan River. It is said that during this journey he once more came in contact with those peoples who honoured and revered Abraham who professed to abhor idolatry and who worshipped the one true God – Jews and Christians. If that is so, he would have also closely observed their unfortunate mutual animosity of that era.

Having successfully completed this commercial mission for Khadijah he accepted her next offer, that of marriage. She was 40 and he was 25. The marriage by all accounts was excellent. By her, Muhammad fathered two sons (some say three) and four daughters and all, with one exception, died before Muhammad's own death. The sole survivor of Muhammad was his daughter, Fatimah.

The marriage certainly brought stability and security into Muhammad's life, enough to free him from the anxieties and uncertainties of relative poverty. It also afforded him adequate time to reflect on deeper issues and the meaning of life. He was concerned about the state of society in and beyond Mecca. Gambling, drunkenness, lawlessness, endless quarrelling, widespread immorality and a general decline in religious ethics troubled him greatly.

In 595 AD, to arrest some of this, he and others took the praiseworthy step of establishing *Hilf ul Fuzul* (Federation of the Fuzul). The Fuzul had been an earlier ancient society with similar objectives. This commitment taken by a number of leading families was an attempt to restrain lawlessness in Mecca and to defend the weaker or oppressed members of that society wherever possible.

At age 35 Muhammad's reputation was further enhanced. The Quraysh had agreed to reconstruct the Kaba. Disagreement arose over who should have the honour of repositioning the sacred black stone in the Kaba and precisely in what position it should be placed. The sensitivity of the issue combined with the volatility of the persons involved could easily have led to bloodshed. This in turn would have degenerated quickly into the threat of war. Muhammad's wise advice solved the matters to the satisfaction of all.

About this time Muhammad officially adopted the son of his former guardian and uncle, the deceased Abu Talib. Ali was six years of age at the time. He also befriended and adopted one of Khadijah's slaves, Zaid. Both these boys would grow to play a very significant role in later events.

As Muhammad approached 40 years of age he still could not shake free from his concern about the debased state of his people with their endless fratricidal rivalries and wars, intertribal dissensions, disputations over creeds and sects etc. He was also aware of those other less than perfect shadows of truth, Judaism and Christianity. By this time he had developed a habit of frequently withdrawing to a cave called Gharat on Mount Hira.[6] Here he spent time in contemplation and prayer. He was occasionally joined in this exercise by other *hanifs* (those inclined toward seeking truth). These were probably times of deep agony of soul, mental turbulence and emotional turmoil. It was on one such occasion in his fortieth year that Muhammad believed he received his first revelation and calling from God.

> During the month of Ramadan there is a night that has been called laylat al Qudr (night of power). On this night Muhammad is reported to have had a visitation by a spirit being of light later considered to be the angel Gabriel.

During the month of Ramadan there is a night that has been called *laylat al Qudr* (night of power). On this night Muhammad is reported to have had a visitation by a spirit being of light later considered to be the angel Gabriel. During the visitation Muhammad was ordered to read (or recite or cry out). Muhammad's response was to enquire as to what he should read, recite or cry out. After this he was squeezed until his chest was constricted. He was commanded as before. The sequence was twice repeated then Muhammad commenced to recite redolent in style of 'the form of speech of rhymed prose of old Arabian soothsayers'.[7]

This event was a defining moment in human history. No matter how others might interpret it, for Muhammad there was absolute certainty. He was completely transformed in his understanding of who he was and his mission in life. He came to the conviction that he was called to proclaim a new (he would say the original) Word of God. In time this conviction would be an unshakeable certainty for him which would drive him relentlessly forward for the rest of his life (Surah 2:185; 44:3; 97:1).

Understandably, at first Muhammad was somewhat confused and hesitant. He thought that he could be a *kahin* (soothsayer) or *madjinun* (one possessed) (Surah 52:29). His wife Khadijah took him to Waraqah, the son of her uncle, to seek his interpretation of what had happened. Waraqah was one of several hanif who from time to time, were in Khadijah's house and were friends of Muhammad. Waraqah was of the opinion that Muhammad had been visited by the *Namus al Akbar* that is, the messenger and message who was thought to have visited both Moses and Jesus. Muhammad received no further 'revelations' for some time and this served to increase his bouts of depression and confusion. Spiritual encounters such as these were not unknown within his own and neighbouring cultures.

In well established Jewish tradition there was already a long history for the role of *nobi* (prophet). Historically this person, somewhat similarly to Muhammad, had an intense preoccupation with God, out of which arose a compulsion to declare the will of God regarding moral issues of the day. The spoken medium was frequently in poetic form.

Among pagan Arabs there was no correlating tradition. Their nearest equivalent was the *shair* (knower or magician). These were men who communicated mysterious knowledge which was generally attributed to that revealed to them by a familiar spirit called a *jinn* or *shaytan*. As these men communicated their message often in rhymed prose, the rhythm of which was preserved, *shair* later came to mean a poet.[8]

As indicated Muhammad initially thought of himself in these terms. Those who disagreed in Mecca were less generous and gentle in their evaluation. They categorised him as one possessed, a soothsayer or a magician. But Muhammad and others close to him came to believe otherwise.

His wife Khadijah as was usual in her role, had implicit faith in her husband. Initially she was his major source of encouragement in believing that he was indeed a special messenger, an apostle, a prophet from God sent with a message to reclaim his fallen people. It is generally agreed that she was the first convert to what became known as *al Islam* (the surrender).

Although his preaching aroused opposition, it nevertheless brought some positive results. After Khadijah, among the next converts were those of his own household. The first of these probably was his cousin and afterwards son-in-law, Ali. Then there was the manumitted slave who became his adopted son, Zaid. Also in this earliest group was his trusted friend and later father-in-law, the respected merchant Abu

Bakr of the family of Taym ibni-murra. He was two years younger than Muhammad. There was also Usman, the grandson of Abdul Muttalib. Abu Bakr later became the first Kaliph and Usman became the third. Talha, a warrior and another merchant Abdur Rahman, who later became conqueror of Persia were next. In time this group would become known as *ashab* (the Companions). At the time of their 'conversion' they were young and relatively uninfluential.

Conversions to the newly emerging religion were held secret until the community's habit of daily prayer became known. The initial 50 followers were people of mostly humble origin who were primarily family members and close friends. The background of the community's first *muezzin* (the person who summons Muslims to prayer), Bilal, was typical. He was another slave, manumitted by Abu Bakr.

By this time Muhammad was preaching that the Meccan sanctuary, the Kaba, belonged exclusively to Allah. While Meccans acknowledged the supremacy of Allah (Surah 31:25; 39:38) they were unprepared to admit his exclusivity. Muhammad encouraged them by saying that if they would submit, Allah would protect, bless and make them prosperous (Surah 28:57; 29:67).

Recognising the threat to their position and power, not to mention income, Meccans tried to discredit Muhammad by accusing him of sorcery, fraud or merely parroting ideas obtained from foreigners, especially Jews or Christians. The *Hadith* (Traditions) record at great length, persecutions and ill treatments of the budding community. Although the object of many of these traditions was clearly to glorify the early body of believers while conversely demonising unbelievers, nevertheless there is sufficient evidence to indicate that the persecutions were often real and physical.

Said was a converted youth who was attacked while leading prayer. He defended himself by striking one of his attackers with a camel goad. This was the first of much blood spilt in the cause of Islam.

By the fourth year of Muhammad's mission, he was holding meetings in the house of Arqam, a recent convert. This was situated in close proximity to the front of the Kaba. It became known as the birthplace of believers and was given the title of 'House of Islam'. Then three unusual events took place. The whole explanation for these events is difficult to obtain.

As enmity against Muhammad and his group increased, he recommended to those who were his followers and were without adequate tribal protection or were not personally strong enough to maintain faith under persecution, to seek asylum elsewhere. Eleven families, involving 83 men and 18 women, moved to Abyssinia where they were given hospitality and granted protection by the Christian authorities of that place. This became known as the first *hijrah* (flight).

However Muhammad's advice seemed to be at variance with the message he had been preaching up to that time, namely that the sovereignty of God was adequate and must be accepted and relied upon by all who would trust in him. Muhammad personally held to that line. From about this time on, not only did he preach the exclusive unity of God but to that was added the demand for obedience to his apostle. Failure in this evoked the punishing pain of hellfire (Surah 72:23).

The second unusual event of this time was an attempt by the opposing Quraysh to annihilate not just Muhammad, but the entire clans of Hashim and Muttalib to which he was related by birth. A confederacy was formed, the object of which was to completely isolate Muhammad, his followers and his relatives. This was to be done through a total boycott where all other Quraysh would refrain from all social, commercial, political and religious intercourse with the offending party. It was thought that in this way the community would disappear. Muhammad and his followers endured great hardship for three years before the boycott was lifted, which only came about because the results were proving to be counterproductive. Sympathy for, rather than animosity against, Muhammad was increasing.

The third unusual event was actually reported by Muhammad himself. He claimed that either in the course of a dream or a vision he was carried on a winged steed by the angel Gabriel, from Mecca, past Medina to Jerusalem where he was welcomed by all the former prophets. From there he ascended to the highest heaven into the very presence of Allah and received the instruction that his followers were to pray five times a day. Recollection of this nocturnal journey (Surah 17:1) still receives high prominence in the annual calendar of Islamic events.

Of more immediate benefit to the strained community in year six of Muhammad's mission, two powerful Meccan citizens joined his band. One was an uncle and foster brother, Humzar. The other was Umar. Umar became known as the 'Lion of God'. From a Christian perspective he could have been titled the St. Paul of Islam. He was a man of great courage who, having once given his word would never retract it. In time he would also succeed Abu Bakr in the Khalifate and would leave 'the stamp of his warlike spirit on Islam'.[9]

As if the troubles Muhammad already faced were insufficient, he was about to receive two more quick personal blows. When he was 50 years of age and in the tenth year of his mission, his beloved wife of 25 years, Khadijah, died aged 65. For all these years she had been his only wife, his great counsellor and his strongest supporter. A blow of this magnitude was bound to weaken the strongest, and Muhammad was no exception. Not only that, a few weeks later his uncle and faithful guardian Abu Talib also died. The significance of that was that he was now bereft of communal protection while living in the midst of his enemies.

Muhammad quickly regrouped and recovered. Within two months of Khadijah's death he had married Saudah, a widow from the group who had gone to Abyssinia. He also became betrothed to Ayishah, the daughter of Abu Bakr. At the time she was only six years of age. He married her three years later when she was just nine.

Being exposed without adequate protection at Mecca and discouraged at the lack of positive response, Muhammad attempted outreach at another centre. The selected town was Taif, 96 kilometres (60 miles) east of Mecca. The reception that his preaching received there was even more hostile than that in Mecca. He was derided, ridiculed and stoned. He had to flee from the town to save his life. There was now no automatic rite of passage for him to return to Mecca where he was still unwelcome. He had to seek protection of one al Mutin before he could re-enter the city. Fortunately such was accorded to him.

In the midst of his despair and the apparent hopelessness of his mission, encouragement came from an unexpected quarter which some might question. Approval of his preaching was expressed by some *jinn* (spirits) (Surah 46:29; 72:1). Shortly thereafter, six men of the Khazarj tribe visiting from the city of Medina were attracted to his teaching. The following year when they returned, they and six others took the oath of allegiance which became known as 'the first pledge of Aqabah'. Aqabah was the name of a nearby hill where the oath was taken. The pledge given to Muhammad which many others would also take, was:

We will not associate anything with God; we will not steal, nor commit adultery, nor fornication; we will not kill our children; we will abstain from calumny and slander; we will obey the Prophet in everything that is right; and we will be faithful to him in weal and in sorrow.[10]

The new group returned to Medina with a *musab* (teacher) to instruct them in the new way. The following year, when Medinans returned for the annual pilgrimage to Mecca, their number had grown to 70–75 who secretly allied with Muhammad and pledged their very lives to him. This was known as 'the second pledge of Aqabah'.

However their activities had been observed by a Meccan spy who revealed all to the opposition party. They in turn decided to remove the threat of Muhammad permanently. To avoid a vendetta of intertribal bloodletting they planned that several from different groups should stab Muhammad simultaneously. But before this plan could be effected Muhammad, fearing for the lives of his Meccan community, encouraged them to depart for Medina. Their departure strategy was successfully implemented.

After about 150 had left Muhammad, Abu Bakr, Ali and their families were all who remained in Mecca. They in turn escaped by heading south rather than north along the Medinan road where searchers after discovering their absence would be likely to hunt for them. For three days this party remained hidden on Mount Thaur, while being provisioned by Abu Bakr's son who also brought news of enemy Meccan movements.

After this, by circuitous and less used routes, Muhammad and his little party headed northeast toward Medina, the city to which they had been invited to repair. This journey became known as the *hijrah* (flight, migration or breaking of old ties). This 450 kilometre (280 miles) journey of migration on June 20 622 AD has been adopted by Muslims as the starting point of Islamic chronology. It was but the first stage which, in hindsight, would be seen to be a movement of such significance as to alter permanently the course of world history.

CHAPTER 12

THE NEW FRONT

At that time, the city that Muhammad went to was known as Yathrib and had been established by the Amalekites. It would be fully renamed *as al Medina un Nobi*, the City of the Prophet.

Medina, not unlike Mecca, was a cesspool of intrigue. It was constantly unsettled by tribal rivalries led by the Aus who were supported by local Jews and the Kazraj. Benu Qurayza Kazraj were supported by al Nadir. Medinans did not want or need so much an ecstatic preacher as a political leader who would mediate their disputes and bind them into some sort of internal cohesion. Muhammad would be welcomed into their midst and granted protection as one of their acknowledged citizens.

Up to this time, functioning mostly in the role of religious leader, Muhammad had patiently absorbed insult, verbal and physical attack and in summary, anything that was handed out to him by the oppositionists. He had only advocated quite modest resistance (Surah 16:126). He had preferred to rely upon the sovereignty of God, the justness of his cause and to allow all retribution to be a matter for Allah. Now comes a transformation.

While he had been but a persecuted citizen within hostile Mecca and the leader of an insecure, emerging religious community, the face he presented was both modest and mild. He had sought to persuade by all means and to admonish verbally where appropriate. Now, as an honoured citizen, he would become principal legislator, not just for his own community but for the welfare of all at Medina. The movement which he had up to this time sought to lead, 'was a religion within a state. Now it would be more than a state religion. It would become the state (itself)'.[1] Religion and politics would be seamlessly fused.

Muhammad's poetic pronouncements as prophet would give way to the prose of civil administration. The form might change but his authority would increase as he issued edicts on matters not just relating to spiritual and ethical behaviour but on all manner of everyday life matters. From this power base under construction, he would in future allow no compromise with idolaters. For them it would be either Islam or the sword.

Monotheists, mostly Jews and Christians, could at least have a choice. If they chose not to accept Islam they would be discriminately taxed for the civil protection which Islam allegedly would provide for them. But all of this would not come about without resistance.

In Medina the idolaters and oppositionists of Mecca were quickly replaced by a party that became known as *Munafiqun* (the hypocrites (Surah 63:1– 6)). These were the ones who welcomed Muhammad to Medina and, on the surface at least, warmly embraced Islam. With time however, as they realised the implications of their commitment, it became clearer that they had little intention of fully surrendering to Allah or his Prophet.

Muhammad appreciated that he had a very divided city, which could be injurious to his cause and terminally dangerous to his health. He quickly demonstrated the brilliance of his political genius by requesting the various parties to join him in a treaty. Broadly speaking the parties involved were:

- the *Munafiqun* (the Hypocrites). Headed by Abdullah ibn Ubay. He harboured pretensions of city leadership. They were frustrated and temporarily put on hold because of the arrival of Muhammad.
- the *Muhajirun* (emigrants or refugees), erstwhile of Mecca.
- the *Ansar* (allies, assistants or helpers). This group consisted of local converts at Medina prior to the Prophet's arrival.
- the Jews whom Muhammad hoped to graft into his new movement.

In a masterly stroke he had the four groups enter into a treaty binding them all to:

- Not participate in sedition
- Proclaim the Quraysh of Mecca to be outlaws
- Grant religious toleration to Jews and require their support whenever the Muslim party had need of it.

With respect to the Jews, Muhammad went even further. He related Islam to their progenitor, Abraham and other of their prophets. He followed practices of fasting and animal sacrifice as well as praying toward Jerusalem. The Jews however would not respond to his claim of prophethood.

In time, as they remained aloof, Muhammad would charge them with having concealed and misrepresented the content of their scriptures (Surah 2:140). Still unable to elicit positive response he would go even further and attempt to intimidate them with terrible threats (Surah 4:55–56). When the breach with the Jews finally came he was inspired to change religious ceremonies of Islam eg. altering *quibla* (direction of prayer) from Jerusalem to Mecca (Surah 2:142–145).

Of necessity, in the first year at Medina, Muhammad was busy overseeing the building of houses for his self-contained community as well as commencing construction of the Great Mosque, which still bears his name today. He also married Ayishah. For the first time he had more than one wife simultaneously and this threatened the unity of his family. This was gradually replaced by a plurality of wives. To attempt to be fair, he had to build separate houses for each wife. He was then obliged to visit and give equal time and attention to each wife. But, for some time, the demands of the expanding community would take precedence over personal domestic matters.

Medina was ideally located as a theatre of operation to sever the commercial artery binding Mecca to Syria. If that could be achieved his old enemies would be weakened. The obvious means was to watch for and raid Meccan camel caravans as they passed nearby.

> Monotheists, mostly Jews and Christians, could at least have a choice. If they chose not to accept Islam they would be discriminately taxed for the civil protection which Islam allegedly would provide for them.

Toward this end six Muslims ventured forth and attacked a caravan guarded by the Quraysh. One of the guards was killed and two were taken prisoner. This happened in the sacred month. Previously it had been agreed that during this month war and hostility were banned. To Muhammad and his followers, engagement in such an unprecedented activity was a bold masterstroke. To the Meccans it was a breach of sacred trust.

To achieve his end Muhammad had to overcome two major obstacles. The first obstacle was the desirability of breaking the truce of the sacred month. Secondly even more beyond any norms of tribal morality, was the act of attacking one's own tribe and blood relatives. Both of these concepts were quite revolutionary. Hitherto they were probably even unthinkable. At a more mundane level, Muhammad and his followers had been virtually expelled from Mecca and as such had suffered shame. This humiliation had to be redressed especially as he had promised the Meccans divine punishment for what they had done.

To protect Muhammad from unnecessary criticism, Islamic historians have stated that he sent his small force into the field foraging for 'opportunity' with permission to use their own judgment. Be that as it may, there was no doubt of the destination of any plunder thereby profited. It was taken directly to the needy Muslim community in Medina.

This double breach of custom incensed the Quraysh at Mecca. Approximately 1000 warriors came forth engaged by only 305 who could be mustered from Medina. But to gather even this number Muhammad had to remind them of the treaty into which they had entered by mutual consent.

To justify breaking the truce in the sacred month, a precedent was introduced which became a practice in the future as the need arose. Muhammad invoked a 'special revelation' (Surah 2:217). He preached the concept of *jihad* (holy war) against idolaters as a sacred duty of the faithful. It was better to 'slaughter' any who impeded access to Mecca and its Mosque than to tolerate anything else. (Surah 2:216–217).

He decided to intercept another caravan at Badr. Muhammad himself would lead. But the Meccans had already reacted and were waiting. Again, Muslim scholars sought to exonerate Muhammad from initiating any military activity by claiming that he was responding to traitors in his ranks. This is how the Quraysh were already in the field. But this overlooks what provoked the Quraysh to react in the first place. It also leaves unanswered the question of why would a Quraysh caravan heavily laden with merchandise, so far away from its destination and support base in Mecca risk provoking a Muslim attack on its exposed flank as it passed nearby Medina.

Early historian, Ibn Hasham, says that before the battle of Badr in 624 AD, Muhammad had sent out a force to capture the caravan but the Meccans foiled his plan by despatching an army to rescue and protect their property. Muhammad interpreted the circumstances they faced as Allah forcing them into battle. As a charismatic preacher he was able to inspire his troops. He was well aware that the fate of Islam would hang on the outcome of this battle.

Fortunately Muhammad had chosen the most favourable terrain and demonstrated that he was emerging not just as a great politician but as an astute military tactician as well. In the fight which followed, many of the Quraysh from Mecca and some of

Muhammad's bitterest opponents were killed. Meccan leader, Abu Sufyan, saved his caravan and its precious cargo. But he failed to general the disorderly group from Mecca into anything like a disciplined army able to overcome the smaller Medinan band inspired by its leader.

The Meccans were routed. Booty of 115 camels, 14 horses, carpets, items of fine leather, vestments, armour and other appropriate articles of the time were all taken to Medina. The head of one of Muhammad's severest foes, Abu Jahl, was also delivered to him and cast at his feet. Tradition has it that Muhammad's reply regarding this head was, 'It is more acceptable to me than the choicest camel in all Arabia.'

> Muhammad invoked a 'special revelation' (Surah 2:217). He preached the concept of *jihad* (holy war) against idolaters as a sacred duty of the faithful.

As a field commander, Muhammad had demonstrated exceptional daring and courage to commit his troops against such a numerically superior force. Loss for the Muslims would have ended everything including the life of their Prophet. For the Meccans, it seemed but a temporary if unexpected setback at the time. Muhammad attributed this victory to the intervention of Allah. By association he was confirmed as Allah's appointed Prophet. A marked change was effected in the minds of his followers (Surah 3:123–127).

Just as sudden crises often trigger extraordinary acts of human endeavour, so with their resolution the more normal characteristics of human behaviour re-emerge. A dispute arose over the distribution of booty. Muhammad frequently used life situations to great advantage to establish principles for the community and to teach life lessons to guide them well into the future. This would be one such occasion.

He therefore decreed, like King David before him in a similar situation (1 Samuel 30), that all should share equally in the booty regardless of their role in battle. There were two exceptions to this. Mounted cavalry would receive an extra portion because of the obvious added expense of their commitment. And for Allah and his messenger, according to the dignity of the prophetic office, Muhammad would, in the first instance, be apportioned 20% and would have the first choice from all booty (Surah 8:41). It was understood that the leader or ruler would re-allocate his portion in ways similar to that of a public treasury. He would accept responsibility for the support of the poor and other needy. Muhammad chose as his portion the famous camel of Abu Jahl and a well-known sword *Zul Fiqar* (the Lord of the backbone).

Apart from the revolutionary break with custom and the theological interpretation of the victory obtained by the Muslims at the battle of Badr, in terms of history, another significant stage had been reached. This was the first time that the Prophet had drawn the sword in support of his assertion that he was commissioned as the special messenger on earth of the Most High God, Allah (Surah 3:11). It would not be the last. Indeed by his choice of *Zul Fiqar,* he clearly signalled his expectations and role for the future.

As Muhammad's position strengthened, so his pronouncements also changed in tone. Having started as a simple searcher after truth, he now undergoes a transition to one who demands unhesitating obedience, not just from his tribe or even his city, but from the whole country of Arabia. No longer would it be adequate to commit to obey Allah. One must obey Allah's prophet, Muhammad (Surah 3:132, 172). And whoever obeys the messenger obeys Allah (Surah 4:80).

As the Jews continued to resist, Muhammad changed the *quibla* (direction of prayer) from Jerusalem to Mecca. He introduced the prospect of a return to pilgrimage to Mecca. He changed the time and duration of the fasts. The Jews were more highly educated. They were in possession of much of the most fertile oasis land. Not unexpectedly, they were economically dominant in terms of trade and capital accumulation. They were also still unimpressed by this Prophet whom they regarded as pretentious. Muhammad ominously once more warned that disobedience would bring hell fire (Surah 9:63). It was to no avail.

When a Muslim girl was insulted by Jewish youth, by way of response the whole Jewish tribe, the Quraiza, was attacked. At the intercession of another tribal leader, death sentence over them was commuted to life banishment. Their houses and lands were confiscated and redistributed among the growing number of Muslims. Again this was no accident. It was a portent of what lay ahead in future for all who disobeyed the decrees of the Prophet.

Because of continued interference with their caravans, the Meccans once more ventured forth under Abu Sufyan. This time the Quraysh approached Medina with a strength of 3000. Muhammad responded with 1000. But Abdullah as chief of the *Munafiqun* (hypocrites) withdrew from the field with 300 of his followers.

Muhammad again demonstrated his outstanding natural abilities. He encouraged his troops on in the face of adverse odds and then took up a well chosen position at the foot of the hill Uhud. Additionally, he carefully positioned his archers to protect the Muslim flank and ordered them not to vacate that position under any circumstance.

At first in spite of the smaller numbers, the battle favoured the Muslims. However the Muslim archers eager for spoil among any of the vanquished, left their position prematurely. This allowed Khalid, the Meccan, to attack from the rear with cavalry. The Muslim force was further destabilised by the battlefield rumour that Muhammad had been slain. Abu Bakr, Umar and Usman effected an excellent retreat. Ali, Abu Bakr and Umar were also seriously wounded.

It was fortunate that the Quraysh chose not to press home their victory. Probably they were operating on the older Arab conception of the purpose of war, namely the defence of honour. Shame earlier inflicted upon them had now been redressed. Muhammad also had been wounded. He had been hit by stones and further injured by nails in his own helmet. Nevertheless the next day, in spite of his wounds he pursued the enemy from a safe distance. In this way honour, tarnished in battlefield defeat, was somewhat restored.

Unwisely the Jews did not try to hide their delight at Muhammad's defeat at Mount Uhud. Several Muslim expeditions were subsequently carried out against the Jewish tribe of Bani Nadir at their base five kilometres (three miles) from Medina. They were suspected of treachery. They also declined to accept Muhammad and Islam. Therefore they were forced into exile. They had to leave all their weapons, gold, silver and other possessions behind. On this occasion the accumulated booty Muhammad reserved for himself with the right of distribution (Surah 59:6).

When the dust settled Muhammad was still faced with a theological challenge. If, according to his earlier pronouncement, the victory at Badr was accepted as proof of Allah's being with them (Surah 3:126) and that Muhammad was his prophet, then how was the defeat at Uhud to be interpreted? The 'revelation' provided through Muhammad served to silence the doubts of at least the faithful. It was said that on this occasion Allah permitted defeat so that he could sort out precisely who were the true believers (Surah 3:140).

In the fourth year of his Medinan era (4AH) Muhammad married two more women, both widows of his companions in arms. Meanwhile Meccans continued to be agitated because of the ongoing harassment of their caravans. Encouraged by Jews at Khaibar in the district of Medina they decided once more to attempt to put an end to Muhammad and his followers. After negotiating additional support from various other tribes, they approached Medina with a force of 10–12 000 men at arms including men from two Jewish tribes. Again the battle was an opportunity for Muhammad to display his inventiveness and skill at deploying his outnumbered troops to maximise his own advantage.

Acting on advice received from a Persian named Salmon, Muhammad ordered a trench to be dug as defence for an unprotected part of the wall of Medina. With 3000 troops he faced his foe who, instead of aggressively assaulting their target, opted indecisively for a siege. During the siege Muhammad conducted what today would be called psychological warfare. He tried to undermine the enemy's morale through secret negotiations.

Because of the harshness of the terrain and the time of the year, after 25 to 30 days, the numerically superior Meccan led force was obliged to withdraw because of a lack of water and exposure to the elements. This became known as the 'Battle of the Ditch' or the 'War of the Trench' (Surah 33:9). In spite of the large numbers and the length of hostilities only eight warriors were killed.

With the withdrawal of the besieging forces, Muhammad initiated a move against the last Jewish tribe of any size in or near Medina. They had continued to resist him and his claims. From his perspective they represented a fifth column in his midst. This tribe was the Banu Quraizh. He concluded that Jews (and Pagans) were his worst enemies (Surah 5:82). They had been previously warned of the consequences of breaching their treaty with him (Surah 59:2–5). Their recalcitrance would now be punished.

Claiming divine direction Muhammad rode with a force of 3000. After a siege lasting between 15–25 days the Jews surrendered. At the time they hoped for the same clemency that had been offered the tribes of Nadir and Aus before them. The fate of the former had been banishment. The Quraizh hoped that this would be the worst that might befall them.

On this occasion however, Muhammad did not grant clemency. Instead he delegated sentencing to one of his companions, Sad. He was not tenderly inclined toward these Jews. He ordered that all men be executed by beheading and that all women and children be sold into slavery. Sentence was carried out on all the men except one Jew who abjured his religion to save his life. 600–800 men were beheaded on that one day alone.

Ameer Ali, a twentieth century Muslim historian, speculates that only 200–250 were killed. He also argues that what happened to them was just in that they were traitors who 'were sentenced according to the laws of war in operation at the time'.[2]

By way of mitigation some Muslim scholars point out that Jewish and Christian armies have carried out similar atrocities. They also refer to examples of this type of operation in the Bible attributed to King David and others. Various traditions place responsibility onto Sad for what happened. Others indicate Muhammad was directly involved. Regardless of the chain of command, Muhammad was field commander. Ultimate responsibility always rested with him. In the light of this, some struggle to understand and to reconcile the apparent paradox of such an outcome being associated with one who claimed to come in the name of Allah, the Compassionate and Merciful.

In the distribution of captives Muhammad kept for himself a Jewess, Rihanah. Also in this period he married his cousin, Zainab. Muhammad had previously given Zainab to his adopted son Zaid. Muhammad had encountered her accidentally when visiting Zaid who happened to be absent at the time. Upon learning of the Prophet's attraction toward her, Zaid agreed to release her to his benefactor by effecting a divorce. However, relationships among Arabs and their children, natural born or adopted, were strictly regulated and custom certainly prohibited such a marriage as was proposed taking place.

The problem was resolved in Muhammad's favour by another 'revelation' declared through him that 'There can be no difficulty to the Prophet in what Allah has indicated to him as a duty' (Surah 33:37–39). (Muslim commentators attribute cause of the dissolution of Zaid and Zainab's marriage to mutual incompatability.)

Subsequently and according to one tradition, Zainab was given to boasting that she had been given in marriage by God, himself. Shortly thereafter Muhammad was led to issue a new set of injunctions which involved the seclusion of women, and more stringent rules applied to his own wives along with the threat of double punishment for failure to obey (Surah 33:28–34).

In the sixth year after the *hijrah* (6AH) there were more military expeditions. Muhammad, in person, led against Banu l-Mustaliq. They were taken by surprise. Booty of 1000 camels, 500 sheep and many women and children were seized by Muhammad's troops. From among the women taken, Muhammad personally ransomed one, Juwairyah, from Sabit ibn Quais. He married her. She ultimately outlived him by 45 years.

While the exact date is uncertain, it is thought that around this time Muhammad broadened his horizons beyond Arabia. He invited foreign sovereigns and princes to embrace Islam. Kasna-Parwiz, the king of Persia treated Muhammad's missive with contempt. He tore it to pieces. This invoked a prophetic curse of like kind from

Muhammad who declared that the same would happen to the Persian's kingdom. Islamic invasion after the Prophet's death brought it to pass.

Mukawkis, governor in Alexandria in Egypt, was more circumspect and exhibited a classic Middle Eastern diplomatic response. He didn't give a direct answer. Instead he begged the Prophet to accept as a gift from him two especially chosen Coptic slave girls. One of these, Mariyam, Muhammad reserved for himself. She later bore him a son, Ibrahim.

By this time, although the divine word decreed that only up to four wives at any one time were allowed the faithful, discounting personal concubines, the Prophet himself was significantly in excess of the permitted number of legal wives. This created difficulties not least of which was the challenge of his giving equal attention to each of his women folk. Domestic bliss was shattered by their objections to his favouring one against another. The problem was resolved by Muhammad receiving another 'revelation' which absolved him from conjugal restrictions previously placed upon him by his wives (Surah 66:1–6).

The attitude and comment on such practices by Muslim commentators is most instructive. Summing up for many of them, commenting on Surah 66, Pickthall states:

'For Muslims, monogamy is the ideal, polygamy the concession to human nature. Polygamy is of the nature of some men in all countries and of all men in some countries...Whether monogamy or polygamy should prevail in a particular country or period is a matter of social and economic convenience. The Prophet himself was permitted to have more wives than were allowed to others, as head of state. He was responsible for the support of women who had no other protector.'[3]

By the end of the sixth year, having virtually systematically encircled Mecca by overcoming various tribes and thereby claiming their allegiance, Muhammad was able once more to turn his attention towards Mecca. Somewhere near the beginning of 7AH he had declared that the pilgrimages to Mecca and their attendant ceremonies were a sacred ordinance commanded by God (Surah 22:26–29). Muhammad decided to perform *umrah* (the lesser pilgrimage to Mecca). It gains less merit and omits the sacrifices of the hajj.

He invited several Bedouin tribes to join him in this enterprise but they refused. Bravely undaunted he nevertheless set out with 1400 men. Not surprisingly, he was checked by the Quraysh who exercised their responsibility as custodians of the Kaba. Ameer Ali is of the opinion that according to law because they were only custodians, they had no right to interdict the approach even of an enemy.[4]

Negotiations were undertaken to break the deadlock. Usman who was entitled to protection in Mecca because of his blood ties with relatives, was despatched as representative negotiator for the approaching Muslims. A compromise was achieved. The truce agreed to was known as the Treaty of *Al Hudaibiyah* (Surah 48).

According to this treaty, although the Muslims would not be permitted to enter Mecca for this year, in future they would be allowed annual visits, unrestricted and unmolested for a period of three days. During this time they were permitted to worship at the Kaba and the idolaters would withdraw to prevent the possibility of conflict. In addition to this it was agreed that hostilities would cease between the parties for a period of ten years.

In their frustration Muhammad's followers were at first, angry at what seemed a defeat for their position. Their hopes were dashed. In this they failed to appreciate the political skills of their leader. At first what seemed a frustrating compromise, in fact turned out to be *Al Fath* (victory) for all *Al Islam*.[5] For the first time the Meccans had been obliged to give full recognition as an equal to one they had pursued as a despised fugitive. Not only that, the Muslims had regained a foothold and annual legal entry into Mecca. Even though initially it was for only three days per year, it was still a start.

> By this time, although the divine word decreed that only up to four wives at any one time were allowed the faithful, discounting personal concubines, the Prophet himself was significantly in excess of the permitted number of legal wives.

Muhammad also effected another brilliant victory in 7AH (628 AD). He marched against one of the last remaining Jewish strongholds, six days northwest from Medina. Khaibar was a very fertile oasis area and was well fortressed. It represented a great challenge for Muhammad's now finely honed skills.

The oasis of Quamus was defended by Kinanah, a powerful Jewish chief who styled himself as 'King of the Jews'. According to custom, Ali using the Prophet's sword, engaged in single combat with a representative from the besieged tribe. Ali won. Within days all of Khaibar had fallen to Islam. Only the chief who had hidden his precious metals and other valuables was subsequently executed.

Among the captives, Muhammad noticed the beautiful Safiya who was the widow of a fallen chief. He claimed her for his own household. Another Jewess of the vanquished tribe Zainab, who had lost all of her menfolk in the battle, invited Muhammad and Abu Bakr to feast on lamb she had prepared. It was poisoned. When this was discovered she was killed immediately. All other inhabitants were exiled to Transjordan.

During the Khaibar campaign, in response to the demands of his troops, Muhammad instituted *mutah* (temporary marriage). According to this arrangement a Muslim was able to engage in sexual activity with a woman for a limited period of time after which she was to be paid a sum of money. Others beyond the Muslim community might justifiably interpret such activities as prostitution renamed. In later divisions over the issue, Sunni Muslims claimed that Muhammad subsequently prohibited the practice. But Shia Muslims, quoting Surah 4:24, claimed it was permissible.

The Khaibar campaign was also significant for the introduction of another practice which continues to this day. It is used wherever Jews and Christians may capitulate. After the battle Muhammad did not kill the Jews. They were only banished to another country. There was, of course, the option of converting to Islam. Those monotheists who chose and still choose not to accept Islam became subject to *jizya* (a special annual capitation tax). This granted them 'protection' within Muslim countries. Surah 9:29 says:

Fight against such as those who have been given the Scripture as believe not in Allah nor the Last Day, and forbid not that which Allah hath forbidden by his messenger and follow not the religion of truth, until they pay the tribute readily, being brought low.[6]

Under the original terms of agreement at Khaibar, Muhammad allowed Jews and Christians to keep their land but half of their produce had to be sent to Medina. This increased the wealth of the Muslim community. Umar later expelled all Jews and Christians from the Arabian peninsula, seizing their entire wealth for the Muslim community.

In 8AH Muhammad with 2000 of the faithful, proceeded to Mecca where they fulfilled all the obligations of the lesser pilgrimage. During his stay he negotiated for an eleventh and final wife, Maimunah. Also during this visit, two very important converts came into Islam. One was Khalid ibn Walid who later because of his reputation as a mighty warrior and his military genius, became known as 'the Sword of Allah'. The other was Amr who would facilitate Islam's entry into foreign nations. During this visit Muhammad's old nemesis, Abu Sufyan, endeavoured to prepare for the inevitable, through secret negotiations, to forge a way most favourable for the future.

Later in this year an envoy of Muhammad who had been sent to the Christian prince of Bosta in Syria, was slain by the chief of Mutah in Transjordan, southeast of the Dead Sea. Three thousand troops were sent to exact retribution. For the first time the Muslims encountered the Byzantine military machine and were badly mauled. Amazingly, a month later, Amr marched into the same area unopposed and received the offender's submission.

On all sides Islam continued to gain as tribes submitted. Territory increased and the number of adherents grew. Once more the attitude of Muhammad changed. He was no longer satisfied with political treaties that kept a degree of order among the tribes. He demanded that they adhere to Islam. This in time would provide the ultimate social contract, defection from which, by tribe or individual would always be allowed only on pain of death.

Until things settled however, there would be incidents and skirmishes threatening peace. Muhammad was ready to exploit any advantage, such as the one which allowed him to break the treaty with the Meccans and to march on the city once more. In an incident between the Bakr and Khuza tribes some belligerent Meccans supported the Bakr. But the Khuza were allied to the Muslims. Muhammad moved swiftly.

Although he secretly prepared for war, the word got out and the Quraysh of Mecca sent a delegation under Abu Sufyan seeking to maintain peace according to the treaty agreed to earlier. Muhammad knew he held the upper hand and on January 1 630AD marched with Muhajirun, Ansar and Bedouin and an army that had grown to 10 000. Abu Sufyan, the chief negotiator for Mecca, realised the superiority of the force against him. Having failed a second time to secure peace, he reluctantly submitted to that which he had fought against all his life. He repeated the *Kalima* (the confession) saying the words binding him and his city for all time to the Prophet, 'There is no deity but Allah. Muhammad is the Apostle of Allah.' It was over at last.

Muhammad's years of daring, tenacity and unflinching commitment to his cause had paid off. He entered Mecca triumphantly with almost zero resistance as most of the citizens capitulated. He demanded the keys to the Kaba from its custodian. As one of his initial acts he had the shrine cleared of its idols.

Then in a brilliant stroke of masterly diplomacy he acted with great generosity, granting large gifts to significant Meccans. When his own people objected to this excessive zeal with their community's resources, Muhammad responded justifying his actions by declaring that this new use of alms was ordained by Allah (Surah 9:60). He also returned the key to the Kaba to its hereditary custodian and confirmed others in their offices. For any who disagreed with the new order of things, there was always that great persuader, the sword of Khalid, ready to annihilate any who saw things differently. It was estimated that Khalid was responsible for the death of only 350 or so people on this occasion.

To other Medinans who complained regarding the Prophet's largesse, he remarkably persuaded them to accept his actions because they had already received the blessings of the Almighty in terms of peace within their community and Allah's promise of his presence along the way. Of material rewards they had already received much. The Meccans were assembled at Mount as-Safa and took the oath of allegiance to abstain from theft, adultery, infanticide, lying, backbiting, etc. Also there was the codicil to obey Muhammad.

After two weeks Muhammad and his troops departed from Mecca. Along the way to Taif they encountered Beni Saqif and Beni Howazin tribes which almost proved fatal. His large army of new converts possessed more enthusiasm than military discipline. Taif remained unsubdued. But shortly thereafter it also moved with the trend of the times and surrendered to Islam.

Muhammad's ninth year in Medina became known as 'the year of deputations'. Nothing succeeds like success. As remaining uncommitted tribes saw advantages for both this life and the next, they despatched their envoys to signify their allegiance to the now dominant movement (Surah 110:1–3). Kingdoms further afield would not yet appreciate the need to submit to the new force. But those on the Arabian peninsula fully realised the advisability of submitting sooner voluntarily rather than being compelled later.

An original example of this religious diplomacy is still on display at Sohar Fort in the Sultanate of Oman. Muhammad sent the message to the Omani Julanda brothers through his personal intermediaries, 'Amr bin al-'As al-Sahmi and Abu Zaid al-Ansari. Translation of the Arabic original reads as follows:

Peace be upon the one who follows the right path! I call you to Islam. Accept my call, and you shall be unharmed. I am God's Messenger to mankind, and the word shall be carried out upon the miscreants. If, therefore, you recognise Islam, I shall bestow power upon you. But if you refuse to accept Islam, your power shall vanish, my horses shall camp on the expanse of your territory and my prophecy shall prevail in your kingdom.[7]

Given the clear import of the message, additional persuasion was hardly necessary.

As in every other year there were always more conquests to be made. When a rumour spread that the Byzantine emperor Heraclius was assembling an army to invade the Arabian peninsula, Muhammad assembled a counter force of 20 000 plus a cavalry of 10 000. He dispatched them to Tabuk on the Syrian border. The supposed invasion by Heraclius turned out to be just that. It was no more than a rumour. But the opportunity was not lost to bring Christian and Jewish tribes in the north into submission.

By now the movement had started to reach out from the peninsula, in the north as far as the borders of Syria and in the west toward Egypt at Aqaba. The submission of all who remained on the peninsula was a foregone conclusion. Religious teachers and tax collectors were being despatched to the far corners of the new kingdom on earth. Even within Bahrain and Oman in the farthest reaches of southern Arabia, the new teaching penetrated, claiming their allegiance and their taxes. Those who declined to forsake their pagan ways were quickly persuaded otherwise by the threat of *jihad*.

The end for other options and freedom of choice for any of the peoples of the Arabian peninsula was at hand. At the annual pilgrimage in the following year (631 AD) Muhammad deputised the faithful Ali to announce that after the period of the sacred four months, all who had not already done so must choose. Muhammad would no longer hold himself obliged to fulfil any prior treaty commitments that he may have enacted with tribes who chose to remain idolaters. It was Islam or merciless warfare.

At the expiration of this time no unbeliever, that is none who did not already belong to the new religion would be allowed to perform pilgrimage or even visit any of the holy places. Those who did not capitulate would be killed wherever found. If they repented and paid the obligatory alms they could be dismissed and allowed to go free within the constraints of the new order.

It was further announced that 'Jews and Christians were to be fought against until they paid tribute and were brought low (Surah 9:29). This is the mission of Islam'.[8] These monotheists would be tolerated but held in subjection under what would often become unbearable taxation. For the rest, it was conversion or dispatch into the

It was further announced that 'Jews and Christians were to be fought against until they paid tribute and were brought low (Surah 9:29). This is the mission of Islam'. These monotheists would be tolerated but held in subjection under what would often become unbearable taxation.

nether world immediately. 'The sword was not to be sheathed until all submitted to Islam which was to become superior to every other religion.'[9]

In the middle of this year Muhammad's sole surviving son Ibrahim, died. To an emerging culture and religion which banned infanticide (today that includes abortion which is considered as murder within Islamic countries) the loss of a daughter is painful enough. The loss of the last remaining son and male heir would be even more so, particularly to the Prophet who had endured such unjust insult over his lack of such. Ibrahim's death must have been a severe blow of the highest order to Muhammad.

About this time Muhammad's attitude towards the other two contemporary monotheistic religions changed once more. There was no doubt where he stood in the matter of idolaters. In the case of Christians however, an unfortunate application was made which was to have horrendous effects for the next 1400 years. They were to be declared guilty of the sin of *shirk* (associating another with God).

To the Muslim mind and still today the misconception of the Trinity has prevailed. It is preached that Christians regard the Trinity as Father, Mother (that is, Mary) who through sexual union birthed the Son (that is, Jesus). This concept from the mind of the Prophet is naturally grossly distasteful to all Muslims. It is even more so to all Christians who know that assertions of this nature represent a hideous distortion of the theological concept of the Trinity. For people who are guilty of the sin of *shirk*, it is decreed at the last judgment that they will be punished and doomed to hell (Surah 28:62–67). Indeed they are no more than fuel for the fires of the nether regions (Surah 21:98).

In March 632 AD (10AH) with his family of wives, Muhammad set out for *Hijjatu l, Wada* (the valedictory or farewell pilgrimage). What he did on that occasion became the standard of practice for all future ceremonies related to pilgrimages greater and lesser, including such as were carried over from former pagan practices (eg. casting stones at Mina).

Perhaps Muhammad knew that for him the end was near. To the people in Mecca he gave a farewell address urging them not to depart from the exact observance of 'the straight road'. This was the culmination of his long career (Surah 5:3). The religion of *al Islam*, the surrender, was complete.

And yet, although the stresses upon him had been great for so long, peace was not quite at hand. As rumour spread regarding the possibility of his end, with no means of succession decreed, three rival claimants quickly emerged. Just as Muhammad himself had done 23 years previously, each of these claimed to be authentic prophets of Allah. But Mussailima, Aswad and Tulaihah would not be accorded the same protection and patience Muhammad's contemporaries had granted him. Their claims were denied and the pretenders were swiftly despatched.

As Muhammad's health continued to deteriorate his other wives granted his request to remain in the home of his youngest wife, Ayishah. On Monday June 8 632 AD as pain and fever increased, the end approached rapidly. According to one tradition, concerned lest any memorial be constructed which might encourage people to worship him, the Prophet intoned, 'The Lord destroy the Jews and Christians. Let his anger be kindled against those that turn the tombs of their prophets into places of worship...'.[10]

Even though many hold that a part of the miracle of the Quran is that Muhammad was completely illiterate, one of the traditions relating to his final hour records him asking for ink and paper so that he could record for posterity 'a writing which shall prevent (them) going astray forever'.[11]

He ensured that he left no debt outstanding by demanding that gold be given to one immediately to whom he still owed something. When the time came to render an account of his life to the one whose messenger he professed to be, he prayed asking for pardon. He died in Ayishah's arms.

As with the death of any great person, when the expected news finally broke people could hardly accept it. Those in Medina were no exception. Mindful that Muhammad had previously instructed that he should be buried on the spot where he died, his ever obedient followers carried out his wishes to the letter. A grave was dug underneath the bed on which he lay.

Shiite Muslims have transmitted a slightly different account of Muhammad's final days with the purported object of promoting Ali. Sunni Islam notes that Mariya's son, Ibrahim predeceased Muhammad on January 27 632 AD thus leaving no male heir. Therefore he left no legal successor. That meant that the struggle for succession would now begin.

CHAPTER 13

THE GREATEST?

A few years ago the then World Heavyweight Boxing Champion, Muhammad Ali, repeatedly proclaimed that he was 'the greatest'. Of course he was referring to his pugilistic skills. They have since faded as disease and age have taken their toll upon his once magnificent body. The title of being the greatest man who has ever lived is frequently given to another man by many millions who follow his teaching today. This was Muhammad Ali's much earlier namesake, the Prophet Muhammad. Claimants to this title come and go. It is a frequently attributed but short-lived accolade. Disagreement with the sometime fanatical followers of such 'greats' is never welcomed and sometimes dangerous.

A few years ago a newspaper in Indonesia ran a survey among its readers asking them to list whom they considered to be the greatest people in the history of the world. When the newspaper collated its readers' responses and published the results, Muhammad did not come out as number one. Reaction to the publication of this finding was swift and sure. The newspaper was immediately closed down as if it was in some way to blame.

It is certainly not easy to comment on or to try to evaluate the life and work of the one to whom over a billion Muslims ascribe the title Prophet. There is usually significant divergence of opinion between precise scholarship and popular sentiment. Within that gulf of difference there frequently lurks dangers to any commentators.

The Grand Imam of Al-Azhar University in Cairo, Sheikh Muhammad Sayyed Tantawi, at a dialogue organised by Pusat Islam in Malaysia in August 1998 said that 'contrary to popular belief, not a single mention of punishment, especially the death penalty is ever mentioned in the holy book of Islam' relating to the matter of apostasy from Islam. For scholars Islam is a faith that is based on persuasion rather than compulsion. But religious leaders and experts seldom adopt such a view on religious freedom.[1] Between text and tradition there are many shoals upon which commentators may founder. Nevertheless in spite of the dangers the journey needs to be undertaken, even though there are no indisputably reliable charts.

There is no documentary evidence or even an early known copy of the Quran in existence from the period of the first one and a half centuries of the existence of the Muslim communities. Earliest Islamic literature and documentary evidence are from late in the eighth century.[2] In the face of a lack of original documentary evidence for the life of Muhammad, we are obliged to rely upon traditions concerning his person and work. Unfortunately some of these are often contradictory and therefore unreliable, but not all are so.

In general terms it must be agreed that what Muhammad achieved during his lifetime was quite remarkable. However, what has been accomplished subsequent to his life in his name has been nothing short of spectacularly beyond imagination. None could have foreseen how his life, his example and his teaching could have so affected the entire world in the intervening centuries.

From a very inauspicious beginning overshadowed by poverty, he became successful in business and in marriage, firstly to Khadijah and then to others. After his spiritual encounter, his conviction from that point on was absolutely consistent. Amazingly he was able to withstand severe persecution and a three year boycott. Although he never wavered in his sense of call he was able to speak frankly of his faults (Surah 9:43; 40:55; 47:19; 48:1; 80:1).

Through his call he saw what he believed to be truth about God which his fellow men did not see. This created within him an irresistible impulse to proclaim the truth that was revealed to him. For this he risked his life. He unselfishly endured years of hostility and humiliation in Mecca in the unshakeable conviction that he had been given a unique task.[3]

In pursuit of his calling, according to some traditions he suffered persecution, loss of property, the goodwill of fellow citizens, the confidence of friends, and was even forced to flee for his life on more than one occasion. Neither bribe nor threat nor inducement of any kind could persuade him from his mission of proclamation. He believed that he was called to preach the unity of God and was absolutely determined that all others should hear and respond to this message.

In keeping with the ancient prophets of Israel, idols, for Muhammad, were of death and darkness, useless lumps of wood and stone. Allah was light and life.

From time to time he forsook the comfort of home and hearth for the spartan cave on Mount Thira to commune with Allah's angelic messenger. Initially, like Jeremiah and Isaiah before him, there was a reluctance to believe that he could have been especially chosen and called. There was no doubt regarding his sincerity. Whether the calling was truly of God is left for others to judge.

One of the tests of a person's sincerity and consistency of life must surely be found in the reactions of those who live and work closest to him. The record of Muhammad's life is that even unruly Arabs who knew him came to respect and to revere him. They came to call him Prophet. They were best placed to see what sort of person he was. In an era of compromise and connivance he was known as someone who led a simple life, paid all of his debts, was faithful and loyal to his associates and as one who emancipated slaves. With such personal positive habits it is easily understood how, although he himself claimed to be only a man and no miracle worker, other well-intentioned followers may have deified him and attributed to him feats of suprahuman dimension.

Non-Muslims have characteristically criticised Muhammad negatively for the number of wives he had. But this overlooks the fact that most were widows. It also

> In general terms it must be agreed that what Muhammad achieved during his lifetime was quite remarkable. However, what has been accomplished subsequent to his life in his name has been nothing short of spectacularly beyond imagination.

overlooks the times in which he lived. Those who had lost husbands in battle had little alternative but to live lives of wretched poverty or prostitution. By being incorporated into a household by marriage rather than being just booty from warfare, even if they were only one of many wives, there was an undoubted improvement in their social standing and security.

Also non-Muslim commentators need to remember some of the history of their own heroes of the faith. King David had six wives and concubines (2 Samuel 5:13; 1 Chronicles 3:1–9). Rehoboam had 18 wives and 60 concubines (2 Chronicles 11:21).

King Solomon had 700 wives and 300 concubines (1 Kings 11:3). These were kings of Israel. Such office had been specifically forbidden (Deuteronomy 17:17). Yet they came to rule and be regarded with honour by people then and since.

There is no conclusive record of the strength of Muhammad's personality or persuasiveness. It is necessary for us to read between the lines of history to reach conclusions on that. While transforming from someone unknown to one of the most influential people of his day and in human history, Muhammad never forgot his own humble beginnings. Stories abound of his mending his own clothes, cobbling his own shoes, riding on an ass and often taking others behind him. He had a deep hatred for lying. His ability to endure hardship was legendary. He maintained priorities which are admirable and unfortunately followed by few others, certainly not those in his position of responsibility. For him Allah was first. Some of his own needs often took a lesser place than the needs of others.

He dressed simply, avoiding silks and other fineries of the time. He is known to have accumulated some property eg. armour, swords, coats of mail, shields, lances, barns and nine houses in which mostly he accommodated his wives separately. Such accumulation would hardly be considered excessive for a person in his position and the times in which he lived.

It is said that he was illiterate. This enhances the claim that the Quran is a 'miracle'. Counterargument to this, is that if Muhammad was illiterate, without scribal assistance he would not have been able to conduct the extensive business affairs of his first wife. Nor would he have called for writing materials when he was close to death.

What Muhammad achieved through the social reorganisation of the Arabian peninsula was unprecedented. He formed the community of believers *(ummah)* on a religious, cultural and political basis. Many of the differences between tribes with their endless feuds and reactionary blood vengeance were finished. There would be no distinction between believers except for degrees of piety (Surah 49:13). Whether new converts came for economic and political advantage or fear, admission into the new community would be by the recitation of a common creed and maintenance of the basic five times a day. prayers. There had never been unity on the Arabian peninsula prior to Muhammad.[4] Now all would coalesce around the call, course and commitment to this new religion. Religion and the state would be fused into one. Islam would transcend all tribal allegiances.

For those who accepted the new order, probably one of the most notable social changes would be that of the status of women. Henceforth they would be veiled in seclusion (Surah 33:53, 55), although this practice was not unprecedented or unique to Islam at the time.

In matters of marriage, polygamy (Surah 4:3) would be permissible but not polyandry. Men would have more rights than women (Surah 2:228) to the point of being permitted to beat them for suspected disobedience (Surah 4:34). One authoritative tradition records that by revelation, Muhammad was shown that the majority of the inhabitants of hell were thus imprisoned because they were ungrateful to their husbands.[5]

For Jews and Christians within the new Islamic society their position would be reduced to second-class citizens with a curtailment of what, today, is called Human Rights. They would be required to pay taxes in excess of those which were required of Muslim citizens for the privilege of being 'protected' by the Islamic society. Their

> For Jews and Christians within the new Islamic society, their position would be reduced to second class citizens with a curtailment of what, today, is called Human Rights.

places and practice of worship would also be carefully circumscribed. Those 'peoples of the Book' ie. Jews and Christians, who would not accept the new order would be banished from their homelands. The outcome for any, once having accepted the faith but choosing to defect, would be death.

As part of the religious transformations of the times, economics was not left untouched. Taxes were to be levied and redistributed according to the needs of the faithful, initially through the wishes of the community leader, Muhammad. Usury was outlawed once more. Booty from war including any form of riches, land, women or children was redistributed from among non-Muslims, to the faithful.

As an Arabian peninsula military leader Muhammad was without parallel. He showed great daring, courage and flexibility, sometimes winning against all odds, such as the Battle of Badr (Surah 3:13). He also fought his way out of difficult positions as in the Battle of the Ditch (Surah 33:9). He showed great ingenuity and flexibility even in what today would be called psychological warfare.

With outstanding diplomatic skill he was able to advance his religious causes by weaving together political and military objectives. When he first attempted *umrah* (the pilgrimage to Mecca) with 4400 men, this resulted in their being checked for two days outside of Mecca at Al-Hudaibiyah. Muhammad was able to conclude a treaty with the hostile Quraysh which, although disappointing to his troops, nevertheless gave him great satisfaction for the long-term benefits it gave him. For the first time he had recognition as an equal with the Meccans and was guaranteed future entry into their town to have access to the Kaba unmolested, for three days per year. All hostilities were to cease for ten years.

Using the excuse of smouldering hostilities between tribes which inhabited the Meccan neighbourhood, Muhammad seized the opportunity to declare the treaty broken within a couple of years and thereby justified his marching upon Mecca on January 1 630 AD. Given that Muhammad's army had swelled to 10 000, the Meccans saw the writing on the wall and sued for peace. Muhammad wanted their submission.

In victory he was magnanimous, granting gifts to the Meccans (Surah 9:60) and confirming office holders in their previous roles. Later, when a threatened approach from the north of an army under Heraclius did not materialise, not wanting to waste the expedition of his 20 000 troops, Muhammad used the opportunity to bring the local tribes into submission. He used treaties gained through diplomacy as means to an end. For example at the Battle of Ocba in 631 AD, he showed neither compassion nor mercy claiming that the reason for his harshness was his opponents' unwillingness to fulfil previous treaty obligations.

When a Muslim girl was allegedly insulted by youth of the Jewish tribe he took the opportunity to attack, proscribe and banish the entire tribe. He seized all of their property and land for redistribution as booty which won great prestige for him amongst the faithful.

As his military prowess increased so did the frequency of revelations that later were collated to form the Quran. From what we know of Muhammad's life, the tone of those 'revelations' became more dictatorial. 'He who at one time spoke only as a searcher after truth now demanded unhesitating obedience from the whole country of Arabia.'[6] His ascendency would become so complete that ultimately he would 'stand above the law' to which he would proclaim all others must submit.[7]

Having commenced with the ideal of the suppression of idolatry he was rapidly moving on to visions of world conquest. Muhammad achieved victories in the fields of military operations, diplomacy, politics, economics and social change. That which he attained in the field of religion, in the context of place and time would cumulatively become quite revolutionary.

As the new religion of Islam evolved there were similarities with other religions. For example in common with paganism Islam shared a belief in jinns, Satan and evil omens. Before the lesser pilgrimage of umrah he declared that the pilgrimage of pagan Arabs to visit the Kaba was a sacred ordinance of God (Surah 2:142–150; 22:26–30). Activities associated with the pilgrimage such as touching the black stone, circumambulations of the former idol house, journeying seven times between As'safa and Al'marawah, sacrificing animals and fulfilling all other ceremonies of the lesser pilgrimage were also previous pagan practices.

In keeping with Jewish practice he declared the tenth day of the month of Muharram-ashura as a fast day corresponding to the tenth of Tishri, the Jewish Day of Atonement. Also there were ceremonies of purification prior to prayer. Friday was declared a day of prayer somewhat similar to the Jewish day of preparation for the Sabbath. At first he chose Jerusalem as the direction for prayer, although popular tradition holds that when he fell out with the Jews the direction was changed to Mecca. Fasting in Ashura came to be replaced by fasting throughout the month of Ramadan (Surah 2: 185) which bore similarities with contemporary Manachian practices.

> As the new religion of Islam evolved, there were similarities with other religions. For example in common with paganism, Islam shared a belief in jinns, Satan and evil omens.

Eventually however, the greatest conflict between the new religion and other religions existed between Islam on the one hand and Christianity and Judaism on the other. Ultimately, this would come down to a battle of the holy books, the Quran and the Bible. Muhammad had a distinctive understanding of divine revelation. In Judeo–Christian history, divine revelation was conveyed through human intermediaries. But for the Muslim 'the Quran in its totality originates and ends in God, not man. Human involvement in divine inspiration is inconceivable'.[8] However in Judeo–Christian terms, once the word of the Lord had been spoken it was irrevocable and unchangeable. But what is slowly revealed through the Quran seems to change according to the exigencies of the situation, later passages sometimes 'abrogating' earlier ones. The changes usually authenticate action which Muhammad himself was desirous of undertaking or which he had just completed.

Regarding aspects of Judaism, where variants occurred between the older Jewish texts and the Quran, Muhammad asserted that the Jews had received only part of the revelation (Surah 4:44). He further asserted that that revelation was meant only for a particular time (Surah 6:146; 16:118). He went on to say that Jews had also concealed some of the revealed truth in their scriptures (Surah 2:42) and that they had deliberately falsified Scripture (Surah 2:59; 4:46; 5:13). Similar claims were made for differences in the revelation of the Quran as compared with uniquely Christian Scripture. For example although there are similarities in the birth miracles relating to Jesus and the doctrine of the logos (Surah 3:39; 4:171) yet Muhammad rejected the Biblical concept of sonship and the event of the death of Christ (Surah 4:157).

In the Quran followers of Islam are exhorted to ask Christians and Jews if in doubt about what has been revealed (Surah 10:94). But the only acceptable answer for Muslims is that which is given in terms of Muhammad's interpretation of Judaism and Christianity and not how it stands in the Biblical record.

Muhammad claimed that the only true revelation was his (Surah 2:109–121) and that he was the seal of the prophets (Surah 33:40). As a test Muhammad required Jews and Christians to bring proof of their positions. Their own claims were considered to be invalid unless substantiated by some external documentation or support. Unless Jews and Christians had such external support then it was considered that they were only proclaiming their own desires (Surah 2:111). The same test of validity however was not applied to his claims.

To reach the conclusions for what he claimed for himself, his office and his revelation, Muhammad virtually had to do what he accused Jews and Christians of his day of doing, that is changing Scripture. He claimed to be the last prophet to whom Jesus had pointed and that the original Greek used in the New Testament referred to the 'praised one' as a derivative of the Arabic *Ahmed*. But this necessitated changing the Greek word 'Counsellor' of John 14:16, 14:26, 15:26, 16:7 (Surah 61:6). Even if the word used for 'Counsellor' in Greek could be changed to 'praised one', there is no way Muhammad could fit the description of that person and work of the one described by Jesus. The Bible not only declares that those prophecies were fulfilled in the New Testament period, but it describes who the

'Counsellor' would be in very specific terms as one who would be 'with' and 'in' Jesus' disciples (John 14:17) and this could not apply to Muhammad. To claim otherwise would necessitate deleting large slabs of the New Testament not to mention changing key words in the 5336 Greek manuscripts of the New Testament[9] which predate Muhammad's revelation.

The apparent convenience of Muhammad's revelation is worrisome. Although all other followers of Islam were permitted a maximum of up to four wives at any one time (Surah 14:13), the same was not applied to Muhammad. He was exempt. When he spent a disproportionate amount of time with Maryam this caused the others to object. The problem was solved through another 'revelation' (Surah 66:1–6). For the sexually deprived troops at Khaibar a new revelation was declared. Muslims could effect a temporary 'marriage' through payment of a 'dowry' (Surah 4:24). As noted previously, in every other society throughout history payment for sexual favours outside of marriage has always been called for what it is – prostitution.

> After Muhammad's accidental encounter with Zainab that led to her divorce from Zaid and subsequent marriage to Muhammad, a new set of directions were 'revealed' regarding the seclusion of women.

When Muhammad desired to marry Zainab who had previously been given by Muhammad to his adopted son Zaid, the latter agreed to part with his wife to favour his friend and benefactor. But relationships between adult Arabs and their (adopted) children were so strict that the resultant union would have been regarded as incest, against which there was severe prohibition.

Nothing short of unprecedented divine revelation could have surmounted such sanction or diminished the difficulties attached to such a union. Appropriately it is claimed that Allah revealed through Muhammad that 'there can be no difficulty to the Prophet in what Allah has indicated to him as a duty' (Surah 33:37–39).

After Muhammad's accidental encounter with Zainab that led to her divorce from Zaid and subsequent marriage to Muhammad, a new set of directions were 'revealed' regarding the seclusion of women. Even more stringent restrictions were applied to Muhammad's own wives, breach of which resulted in double punishment (Surah 33:28–34).

To justify attacking the Meccan caravan in the sacred month, it was retrospectively revealed that Allah permitted it (Surah 2:217). Under pressure from Meccan demands a revelation came that it was necessary to adhere not only to the doctrine of the unity of God but to obey his prophet. Failure to do so resulted in hellfire (Surah 72:23).

To explain why there may have been a mistake in the utterance of an original revelation regarding pagan deities (Surah 53:19ff), it was claimed that all preceding prophets and their utterances in the name of God also suffered from Satanic interference which Allah subsequently corrected. In Christian theology, to attribute to Satan that which is exclusively of God is blasphemy. This is the one unforgivable sin to which Jesus referred, blasphemy against the Holy Spirit (Matthew 12:31). The *umrah*, previously regarded as a pagan practice was revealed to be a sacred ordinance of God (Surah 22:26–33).

For these sorts of decisions, in today's commercial arena at least, one might be forgiven for presuming there was significant conflict of interest involving the outcomes even though authority was claimed to be derived from extrajudicial sources. Within the context of Arabian religion however, perhaps an apt explanation is coyly given through a tradition attributed to Ayishah. Regarding the frequency of revelation which seemed usually to resolve matters in terms favourable to Muhammad, Ayishah commented, 'Thy Lord seems to have been quick in fulfilling thy prayers'. A nice observation indeed! The demand to obey Allah and his prophet (Surah 3:132) or suffer hellfire (Surah 9:63) inevitably raises the question of the validity of Muhammad's prophethood.

A True Prophet?

In Islamic, Jewish and Christian theology a prophet is a human being vulnerable to human foibles. But Islamic thought advances the concept further. It postulates that a prophet is sinless or at least free from all major sins.[10]

Each religion will obviously apply its own critera in assessing claims to prophethood. For Christians (and Jews) those claims will be codified within their respective scriptures.

The word 'prophet' appears 149 times in the New Testament. Twelve times it speaks of New Testament prophets and more than 100 times it refers to John the Baptist, false prophets and Old Testament prophets and their writings.[11] It is little wonder that there are so many references to prophets and prophecy because prophecy itself is probably the most important of the supernatural gifts mentioned in the New Testament.[12] There are four places in which a list of gifts of various kinds appears in the New Testament (Romans 12:6ff; 1 Corinthians 12:7ff; 1 Corinthians 12:28ff; Ephesians 4:11). The gift of prophecy is mentioned in all four lists.

The prophet is someone who proclaims and declares God's revelation to a community. This person speaks on the basis of what God has made known through audible or visible means (Jeremiah 1:9ff, 5:14; Isaiah 8:11, 22:14; Ezra 9:15). Prophets are those who stood in the council of the Lord, who shared the Lord's secrets about what he was going to do (Amos 3:7), who spoke the Lord's message in the Lord's words (Deuteronomy 18:18; Jeremiah 1:9). Sometimes they showed the Lord's message by means of visual aids (Isaiah 20:2–3; Jeremiah 13:1–11, 19:1–15). Messages they delivered were received either through visions that they saw or words spoken directly to them by the Lord. This is obvious when one looks at the opening verses of the 16 books of the Prophets in the Old Testament.[13]

Of course problems would arise if prophets were false in themselves or in their proclamations. In New Testament times, false prophecy could bring great confusion to the saints of God (Revelation 19:20)... 'The effect on people resulting from the emergence of a false prophet was so disastrous that the penalty for false prophecy was death (Deuteronomy 13:5; 18:20).'[14] The test of whether or not a prophet or prophecy was genuine was always a live issue in both Israel and the Church. The distinction between truth and falsehood was absolutely critical. This was not only so for the hearers but also for the speaker. To speak falsely evoked God's wrath (Jeremiah 23, Ezekiel 13, Micah 3:5).[15] In the Old Testament, Abraham was the first prophet (Genesis 20:7). Moses was the paradigm of a true prophet (Deuteronomy 18:18). In the New Testament, it was John the Baptist (Matthew 11:11f).[16]

In view of the importance of the issue, it is not surprising therefore, that several tests to distinguish between true and false prophets and their prophecies were developed in the Bible.

First, Christians are to test the spirit behind which words are spoken (1 John 4:1–3). The question to be answered is: Is this an operation of the Holy Spirit, a human spirit or an evil spirit that is giving utterance on this occasion? Christians are warned that there will arise false prophets (Matthew 24:24) and that deception will occur (1 Timothy 4:1–3).

Second, believers are urged to test the prophet himself (or herself). Their lives were an integral part of their message eg. Hosea was instructed to marry a prostitute (Hosea 1:2). Ezekiel was forbidden to mourn when his wife died (Ezekiel 24:15–18). Jeremiah was forbidden to marry at all (Jeremiah 16:1,2).

False prophets would appear as wolves (Matthew 7:15–16). Their lives would also be characterised by covetousness (Micah 3:11; 2 Peter 2:1–3). If their manner of life did not measure up to the words they spoke in the name of God, then their message and their person were invalidated.

In the case of Muhammad, questions arise therefore over the command that none should be married to any more than four women. But in his case he married eleven or some say thirteen. There is residual anxiety over his marrying the wife of his adopted son as well as his marriage to a child and women taken captive as prisoners of war.

A third test was the degree to which the prophet's words inspired worship of the true God. Even if a prophet performed miraculous deeds but drew people away from the worship of God he was to be declared false (Deuteronomy 13:1ff). All true prophets shared God's love for Israel but always within the setting of justice and power (Ezekiel 3:12–16; Amos 5:14). This in turn inspired true worship of God. There is no doubt that Muhammad had a great interest in justice and power. But the question is, did he share God's love for Israel and its people and did this in turn inspire worship of their God?

Fourth, believers are required to test the actual words of a prophet to see to what degree any words purportedly spoken in the name of God are in general conformity with preceding Biblical revelation (Acts 17:11; 1 Cor 14:37–38; Gal 1:8; 1 John 4:2–3, 6).[17]

More specifically, such utterances had to be in agreement with doctrine as previously taught (1 Corinthians 12:3).

Jewish and Christian scriptures are in agreement about the unchangeability of God's word (Deuteronomy 4:1–2; Isaiah 8:20; Matthew 5:17–18, 24:35; Revelation 22:18–20). The Quran agrees with this principle (Surah 6:34; 10:64; 50:28–29). The Quran goes even further saying that God's word does not change. It claims that it was sent to confirm and to guard former revelations (Surah 5:44–48).

However the Quran itself is widely divergent from previously attested Biblical accounts. For example regarding Abraham:

- Abraham's father is wrongly called Azar instead of Terah (Surah 6:74 cf. Genesis 11:26).

- He did not raise his descendants in the Valley of Mecca but in Hebron (Genesis 13:14–18).

- His hometown was not Mecca but Ur in Chaldea. Even the recently discovered secular Ebla tablets found in Syria agree with the Biblical account (Genesis 11:31).

- Abraham wandered through Haran not Arabia and went to Canaan not Mecca (Genesis 11:31; 12:5). The Ebla tablets refer to this as well.

- Abraham was willing to sacrifice his son Isaac with whom the Lord was to make a covenant. The Quran claims it was Ishmael who was the son of his Egyptian slave woman, Hagar (Genesis 17:18–21; 22:2) who was the favoured one.

In the case of Muhammad questions arise therefore over the command that none should be married to any more than four women. But in his case he married eleven or some say thirteen.

- It is unlikely that Abraham and Ishmael ever went near Arabia or built the Kaba in Mecca (Genesis 12:10).

In the Quran, Mary is recorded as the daughter of Imran, the sister of Aaron as well as the mother of Jesus (Surah 3:35–37;19:28, 34). But in the Bible, the time difference between the sister of Aaron and the mother of Jesus is approximately one and a half millennia.

The Quran refers to Haman as a minister of a Pharaoh (Surah 28:6; 29:38; 40:24, 36). The Bible identifies him not as an Egyptian but as a Babylonian official of King Xerxes (Esther 3:1) living about a millennium later.

The Quran describes the Holy Spirit as God's own breath (Surah 15:29), the divine inspiration (Surah 16:2) and the angel Gabriel (Surah 19:17) (see particularly

> When it comes to the person of Jesus, the Bible says that every spirit that acknowledges that Jesus Christ has come in the flesh is from God (1 John 4:1–6).

Pickthall's translation of the Quran). This is a confused and contradictory view compared with that in the Bible.[18]

Regarding the death of Jesus the Quran, in one place, claims Jesus was not killed (Surah 4:157–158). The Bible emphatically disagrees (Matthew 27:35, Mark 15:25, Luke 23:33, John 19:18).

When it comes to the person of Jesus, the Bible says that every spirit that acknowledges that Jesus Christ has come in the flesh is from God (1 John 4:1– 6). The person who denies that Jesus is the Messiah is a liar and antiChrist (1 John 1:22). It also decrees as false any person that does not accept that he is the Son of God (1 John 5:10–12). The Quran not only denies the sonship of Jesus, it virtually places a curse upon all who hold such a belief (Surah 9:30).

In the Quran, wives for reproductive purposes are likened to farmland (Surah 2:223) and if disobedient to husbands they are to be beaten until they are submissive (Surah 4:34). In the Bible, wives are to be treated with love, honour and respect to the point of self-sacrifice of a husband for the good of his wife (Ephesians 5:25– 28). To not do so, may mean God will not even hear their prayers (1 Peter 3:7).

Differences between the Quran, 'revealed' several centuries after the New Testament and millennia after sections of the Old Testament are innumerable. This new revelation came when tens of thousands of Biblical documents in various languages were in consistent agreement and were preexistent to revelation through Muhammad.

A fifth test of prophethood is seen in whether or not that which is proclaimed comes to pass (Deuteronomy 18:21–22). Muhammad made no futuristic predictions beyond the possible outcomes of some military engagements which of course rank as a fifty/fifty win–loss chance.

A sixth test was the effect of the proclaimed word upon God's people. Did this word cause people to turn from wickedness back to God or not (Jeremiah 23:18–23)?

There is no doubt that in some of what Muhammad preached was the elimination of idolatry at least. Whom the people turned to is another question.

The seventh test of prophethood is accountability. What is the judgment of other prophets (1 Corinthians 14:29)? If prophets also are known by their fruit (Matthew 7:15–20; 24:11, 24), then true prophets are seen to be in submission to other prophets and local leadership (1 Thessalonians 5:20–21). There is no record of Muhammad submitting his prophecies for testing and discernment of others.

An eighth test of prophethood is that it was the prophet's duty only to deliver the message. The believer must decide what to do with it. For example when Agabus proclaimed a famine was on the way, it was up to the local believers to determine how they would respond (Acts 21:10ff).

> The Quran not only denies the sonship of Jesus it virtually places a curse upon all who hold such a belief (Surah 9:30).

Prophets never coerced, manipulated or sought control. Certainly they never demanded obedience to themselves. To disobey words spoken by the prophet brought punishment from God (Deuteronomy 18:19) and not from the prophet himself. It was not the prophet's place to arrange punishment through some self-fulfilling mechanism.

A ninth test was that... 'true prophecy will always manifest itself in bearing witness to Jesus' (Revelation 19:10).[19] It would be assumed, of course, that the witness to Jesus would be in accordance with that which he himself inspired in the New Testament. But Muhammad denied critical aspects of Jesus' life, death and resurrection. He denied aspects of his sonship and his divinity (Surah 4:157–158; 9:30). In some ways, undoubtedly Muhammad brought peace to Arabia which had suffered bitterly from Christological disputes. 'But the price was the unconditional surrender of the essence of Christianity.'[20]

Was Muhammad a true prophet?

The answer to that is found in the criteria applied. Those which apply to prophethood within the Judeo – Christian tradition would obviously be different from those which apply within the Islamic tradition even though Islam claims commonality with many

> Muhammad founded a nation which became an empire and through its religion has encircled the world. Having demanded obedience he claimed to be no more than an Apostle sent to convert the world with a teaching that claims to supersede all else.

prophets of the Jewish and Christian religions.

There is no doubt that the Romans were great colonisers. Followers of Muhammad became greater. There is no doubt that Alexander the Great was an outstanding military commander. Muhammad's followers would declare he became greater. There is no doubt that Socrates and Aristotle were supreme in their day and in their influence upon subsequent world thought. The thinking of Muhammad has become of greater influence. There have been many great popes, kings and emperors but the influence of Muhammad has become greater.

Muhammad founded a nation which became an empire and, through its religion, has encircled the world. Having demanded obedience, he claimed to be no more than an Apostle sent to convert the world with a teaching that claims to supersede all else. This warrior, legislator and poet has timelessly remained a hero for many. In human terms, he remains a leader without equal. He provided a specific orderly lifestyle of prayer, fasting and guidance under religio-political authorities. He was more than a politician, an economist, a religious leader or a cultural and societal iconoclast. Every prophet of old was first sent to his nation but Muhammad considered that he had been sent to all mankind.[21]

Muhammad died without a legal heir. The struggle to appoint a successor is what caused bloody division within Islam that continues up to the present. Of Islam's first four Caliphs only one lived to die of natural causes.

As a tale of two towns, the Prophet's biography is finally the story of a crucial choice...It is the decision arising from the question: how should prophethood succeed?...It was a decision for community, for resistance, for external victory, for pacification and rule. The decision for the cross–no less conscious, no less formative, no less inclusive–was the contrary decision.[22]

The effects of those choices were exemplified in the lives of the earliest followers of Muhammad and Jesus and continue to be so to this day.

CHAPTER 14

REVELATION OF REVELATIONS

When Syed Ashrim Ali wrote a very well-researched letter to the editor of a capital city newspaper in Dhaka, Bangladesh, inquiring as to the whereabouts of authentic copies of Caliph Uthman's first edition of the Quran, within a few days he was rebuked in the columns of that same newspaper.[1] A.N.M.Jahad, a (retired) Deputy Secretary of the government of Bangladesh, took him to task. Jahad asserted that even asking such a question appeared to be nothing more than 'a subtle device to create doubt about the authenticity of the Holy Quran'.

The inquirer's question went unanswered. His honest search for additional information was arrogantly swept aside. Denigration and abuse crushed his quest for knowledge through the hoped-for dialogue. Fundamental questioning of the Quran is not permitted. Even comparison of it with other books is hardly encouraged.

When an Arab commander first captured the Egyptian city of Alexandria in 641 AD he asked Caliph Umar in Medina for instructions regarding the city's world famous, priceless library of manuscripts. The reply Umar is said to have given was, 'If the books are in accordance with the Quran, they are unnecessary and may be destroyed; if they contradict the Quran they are dangerous and should certainly be destroyed.'[2]

In January 1985 76 year old Sudanese theologian Mahmud Muhammad Taha was publicly hanged because 17 years previously he had allegedly minimized the role of the Quran as a source of law while trying to develop more appropriate law for people in the twentieth century. As a declared apostate his writings were also burned.[3]

When Palestinian scholar Suleiman Bashear argued that Islam developed gradually rather than emerging fully formed from the mouth of the Prophet as recorded in the Quran he was thrown from a second storey window by his students at the University of Nablus.[4]

When Indian writer Salman Rushdie wrote a fictional novel and attempted to provide only a context for a few controversial verses within the Quran, his speculations resulted in his having a *fatwa* (a religious judicial sentence pronounced by the appropriate authority) issued against him by Ayatollah Khomeini in February 1989. They demanded his death and posted a significant reward to encourage success in that enterprise. In his adopted country of Britain there were denunciations of him in many mosques 'by Mullahs and crowds who had only handled a copy of the book to burn it.'[5]

This was because Muslims do not regard the Holy Quran as just another sacred book in the traditional or sentimental sense. It is held to be an exact perfect reproduction of the original, errorless, uncreated prototype kept in heaven on tablets (Surah 5:15; 16:89; 25:1; 46:2; 56:80; 85:21–22).[6] The original heavenly template was known literally as the 'Mother of the Book' (Surah 3:7; 13:39; 43:4).[7] The Quran 'has no parallel outside of Islam…It is unlike anything known to Christianity.'[8] For all Muslims, not just 'fundamentalists' the Quran remains the uncreated Word of God himself which is to be believed and obeyed but never questioned or critiqued.[9] In Christianity the Word became flesh. In Islam it became a Book.[10] That Book has come to be regarded as 'the world's most ideologically influential text'.[11]

The superlatives with which Muslim scholars historically describe their sacred volume are without parallel in descriptions relating to other religions' texts. Badru D. Kateregga, a Muslim scholar, states that:

the Quran as the final revelation, is the perfection and culmination of all the truth contained in the earlier scriptures (revelations)…It is the book for all times and for all mankind…The Quran is the very word of Allah. It was revealed to the Prophet Muhammad (PBUH), through the archangel Jibril (Gabriel) from an archetype preserved in the seventh heaven…Every letter, word, content, form and meaning is divinely revealed.[12]

It is therefore considered to be beyond both culture and translation.

The word *quran* is derived from the Arabic *qara* which in turn is related to the Hebrew *kara*, which means 'to read' or 'to recite'. It is said to be the first word of the first chapter (surah) revealed to Muhammad (Surah 96:1). It is also commonly referred to as *Quran al Majid*, the Glorious Quran; *al Quran ash Sharif*, the Noble Quran; Furqan (distinguisher); *Kalamu'llah*, the Word of God or simply *al Kitab*, the Book.[13]

The Quran is considered to be the eternal, uncreated word of God, inseparable from him, written in a volume, read in a language and remembered in the heart. Since its compilation, it has spoken powerfully and convincingly to the heart of Muhammad's first hearers until this day's contemporary Muslims. Its message welded antagonistic elements into one united organised body which became animated by ideas far beyond those that had until then, ruled the Arabian mind. Its hold is no less today. In the hearts and minds of its Muslim hearers it is considered to be the Word of God himself.

In the Islamic community the Quran is always held in the highest regard and handled with the greatest of care. Usually it is not even opened unless the reader has completed appropriate preparatory religious ablutions. In any room it is stored in the highest place. No other book should be above it. When it is read it will usually stand on a *rehel*, an ornately decorated or carved small bookstand.

It is never to be lowered below the waist because the nether regions of the body are considered to be unclean. Certainly it must never touch the floor. It is usually wrapped in cloth. As it is opened it will be kissed as a mark of respect. While customs vary from country to country, in southern Asian countries, if it is accidentally dropped then the penalty for the poor may be a donation in rice in weight equivalent to that of the Holy book. For the rich the equivalent weight may be paid in gold.

Armlets consisting of verses of the Quran wrapped in leather or metal containers may be worn around various parts of the body as protection against evil spirits. Historically portions have been fixed to lances to ensure victory in battle. Plaques with words from the Quran are a common feature in many houses or on modes of transport. Religious

The Quran is considered to be the eternal, uncreated word of God, inseparable from him, written in a volume, read in a language and remembered in the heart. Since its compilation, it has spoken powerfully and convincingly to the heart of Muhammad's first hearers until this day's contemporary Muslims.

merit is obtained through reading, recitation or memorisation of the Quran. The degree of merit is independent of whether one understands it or not. It is a book sworn by and consulted on all or any occasion.

Unlike Biblical prophets who usually established their claim to prophethood by the performance of miracles or declarations of a predictive nature, Muhammad never made any explicit predictions nor did he perform miracles. To overcome this problem his followers have ascribed to the Quran the status of a perpetual miracle bearing witness therefore to the truth of Muhammad's mission and prophethood. However this claim is an assumption based upon Muhammad's own statements in the Quran (Surah 10:38; 11:17; 52:29–34).

The Quran is organised into 114 chapters or *surahs*. *Surah* means *a step*. Within each surah is a number of verses or *ayats*. *Ayat* means a sign. The order of the *surah* is independent of chronology. The Quran in general starts with the longest surah and concludes with the shortest. Each *surah* is named after some word near its beginning or a subject majored on within it. There is a continuing difference of opinion regarding the numbering and divisions of *surahs* and their *ayats*.

Within this amalgam of theology, treatise, law codes and collected sermons there is no obvious progression of thought. In fact, there is the frequent repetition of the same ideas reminiscent of the Old Testament's book of Proverbs.

Muslims believe that Allah always wanted to communicate with humanity. They say he did this throughout history using his Prophets (*rasul*, sent ones). Muhammad is claimed to be the last of the line of the prophets. The claim is that God's final revelation to mankind existed, uncreated for all time, on tablets in heaven (Surah 17:105; 85:21–22). Some additionally claim that the extent and exactitude of this timeless revelation extended to and included even punctuation, division of chapters and the subtitles given to them. Those revelations were sent down *(Tanzil)* (Surah 17:105; 32:2; 39:2,41) in the month of *Ramadan* on the night of power or destiny *('lailat al Qadr)* (Surah 44:3; 97:1–2). From this highest heaven they were subsequently revealed to Muhammad in instalments by Gabriel (Surah 2:97; 17:106; 25:32).

While the revelation is claimed to be free from any human influence it is said that '…Muhammad did have to fight the whisperings of Satan (Surah 7:20; 23:97; 41:36) and that these sometimes endeavoured to mingle with the revelations seems to be indicated by Surah 16:98.'[14] At least once, Muhammad allowed himself to be tempted by Satan to some extent when he acknowledged the Meccan goddesses al-Lat, al-Uzza and al-Manat. Afterwards he realised his error and received an appropriately amended revelation (Surah 53:19f).

The claim of divine origin for the revelations is attributed to a sole source, Muhammad himself. There is no external evidence to corroborate or authenticate this which became the 'mother of books' (Surah 43:3–4), which no other book can equal (Surah 2:23; 10:37–38). This mutual self-authentication conveniently places both the Quran and the Prophet beyond conjecture, criticism or even examination.

The Quran is said to have been revealed to Muhammad during three separate periods spanning just over two decades. The first of these was at Mecca during the years 611–615 AD. The second period was also at Mecca during the years 616–622 AD. The final era of revelation was at Medina 623–632 AD. The content of these 22 years focuses on Muhammad's establishing nascent Islam and therefore it offers little that is unrelated to the personal and political affairs of the Prophet and his companions. The highly contextualised nature of the revelations and the claim that they are unrelated is meant to convey divine intention to all of Muhammad's actions.

One of the main challenges for commentators seeking to understand the meaning of various portions, is to try to determine in which period *surahs* were revealed. The Medinan surahs are easier to identify because they give divine approval to Muhammad's leadership, have identifiable instructions regarding matters of local events and contain frequent imprecations against Jews. The non-initiated are often surprised by the number of items appearing to personally advantage Muhammad. Also one is frequently startled by the discovery that this religious movement which is said to prefer peace, actually enshrines the practice of war. Muhammad himself conducted 27 battles and planned 39 others. Subsequent Islamic expansion into northern Africa, the Middle East, Europe and southern Asia was carried out, it would seem, hardly for defensive purposes nor by means of peaceful diplomacy. Associated with the religious practice of war, there are enormous rewards promised for the warriors (Surah 4:74; 48:16–17). These are still invoked today in war zones such as Algeria, Iraq, Iran, Sudan and Afghanistan. Leaders commonly inspire and inflame the zeal of their troops by reference to such passages even if the enemies are fellow Muslims.

Also the modern non-Muslim reader is somewhat taken aback to find that the Quran delivers divine sanction for practices such as slavery, polygamy and concubinage similar to that which used to exist in the world of the Old Testament. This in part, explains why some Muslim nations are reluctant to adopt United Nations protocols that outlaw some of these practices.

Furthermore, the Western reader at least, is rather surprised to discover that this religion which preaches the brotherhood of all mankind and particularly the equality of the sexes, in fact, in its holiest book enshrines superiority of the male over the female eg. women qualify for only half the inheritance compared with their male counterparts (Surah 4:11, 176).

Furthermore, the Western reader at least, is rather surprised to discover that this religion which preaches the brotherhood of all mankind and particularly the equality of the sexes, in fact, in its holiest book, enshrines superiority of the male over the female eg. women qualify for only half the inheritance compared with their male counterparts (Surah 4:11, 176). Not only are these inequalities a part of this life but they exist in the next as well. The Quran contains vivid pictures of sensual pleasures of perpetually virgin maidens *(huris)* awaiting the arrival of righteous males in paradise along with rich libations of wine, all of which are prohibited on earth. However wives, according to one tradition, find their salvation only under their husband's feet.

Early in his mission when the position of the new Islamic community and its continued existence were extremely precarious, Muhammad delivered a revelation which encouraged religious toleration (Surah 2:256). But as his political and military power increased so the revelations changed, instructing followers to suppress by violence those who would not comply with the call to embrace Islam (Surah 8:39; 9:5, 29; 47:4).

Arabic is considered to be the language of heaven and this, not coincidentally, elevates the Quran in Arabic to be an exact representation of the very words of Allah. This also means that it is impossible to translate the Quran into another language, no matter how skillful or literal that translation may be. In any other language the Quran is regarded as a non-authoritative 'interpretation'. In spite of the claim of linguistic purity, loan words from at least nine other major languages are found within the Quran's text.

Transmission of the Quran from tablets in the seventh heaven to the lowest and thence via Gabriel and two other spirit beings (Surah 16:2, 102; 26:192–200 and 40:15) to Muhammad, is a process of communication which is wrapped in secrecy. Muslim tradition teaches that Muhammad received the revelations while he was in some form of trance. Some of these were later written down on whatever was available eg. palm leaves, parchments, paper, skins, mats, stones and bark. Muhammad believed he spoke under the official stamp of divine revelation (Surah 4:163–166).

Some of the earliest disciples tried to memorise some of the *surahs*. Notable among these were Muhammad's principal companions, Abdullah ibn Mas'ud, Abu Musa and Ubayy ibn Ka'b. Reliable traditions agree that at the time of Muhammad's death there was no collection of 'revelations' in any final form. Many were not even written down. With his death of course, the source of new revelations ceased.[15]

The Quran itself contains only a few and very obscure hints regarding the process of the communication of the 'revelations'. The main thing was not so much what it is thought that Muhammad may have seen, but what he heard from the spirit intermediaries. Once 'revelation' had been announced no one was permitted to alter the words thereafter. It was impossible so to do (Surah 6:34; 10:64), although one tradition reports that one of Muhammad's Medinan scribes, Abdollah b. Abi Sarh, renounced Islam because Muhammad frequently accepted textual changes on Sarh's suggestions.[16]

After Muhammad's death, at the battle of Yamama where followers of the Prophet were fighting against Musailima whom they judged to be a false prophet, a number of those who had memorised various surahs were killed. Seeing the danger a companion of Muhammad, Hazrat Umar, proposed to Caliph Abu Bakr that a collation of such revelations as were recoverable be undertaken.

Abu Bakr was originally reluctant to accept this suggestion because Muhammad had not specifically suggested that such a task should be carried out. Eventually he commissioned one of Muhammad's former secretaries, Zaid ibn Tabit. Other traditions include Quairaishis Abdullah ibn Az Zabur, Sa'id ibn Alas and Abdur Rahmin ibn al Haris ibn Hisham in the original editorial board.

At first Zaid was overwhelmed at the enormity of the task. However, he persevered to at least his own satisfaction. His composition was later entrusted to the keeping of Hafsah, one of Muhammad's wives. She was also the daughter of the second Caliph Umar.

By the reign of the third Caliph, Uthman, different editions had come into existence in different provinces of the expanding empire because companions of the Prophet had compiled their own editions from their own recollections and sources.

Abdullah ibn Mas'ud's manuscript was most authoritative in Kufa, Iraq. Ubayy ibn Ka'b's version was the standard text in Damascus, Syria. Al Ashari's version was supreme in Basra. There were significant differences among these three major codices with no codex being in agreement with the other two.

Later on Hudhaifa considered that quarrels existing among his Syrian and Iraqi troops who were campaigning in Armenia and Azerbaijan, were dangerous. They quarrelled over which edition was superior. He therefore appealed to Caliph Uthman to rectify the situation so that a standard authorised text could be produced and be acceptable to all. The Caliph did this by fiat. His preference was for Zaid's edition, which was still held by Hafsah because of its alleged use of Meccan Quairaishi dialect.

After copies were made of Zaid's compilation, copies were sent to Kufa, Basra and Damascus while one was kept in Medina. Orders were then issued to destroy all other texts that were at variance with Zaid's authorised edition.

Even after all of this, significant difficulties remained. Following the dispatch of Zaid's text he suddenly recalled a verse which he had inadvertently omitted (Surah 33:23). Furthermore, all major traditions speak of Zaid's edition as having omitted an authoritative reference to stoning as a punishment for adultery.

Such additions and omissions only highlight the fallibility of relying on one scribe's memory and choices, particularly in the light of other authoritative versions.

Ibn Mas'ud of Kufa in Iraq had been one of the first Quranic teachers authorised by Muhammad himself. He had personally memorised 70 surahs. According to tradition none knew or understood the Quran better than he. Not surprisingly Ibn Mas'ud declined to destroy his version.

On the other hand, Ubayy ibn Ka'b of Damascus, another outstanding early authority, agreed to destroy his codex including its two extra surahs not included in Zaid's edition. The codex of Abu Musa of Basra also contained additional surahs. Other companions of the Prophet had their own primary versions. But the authorised version gradually gained acceptance and ascendancy especially since it was backed by no less an authority than the Caliph himself. But even Uthman's authorised version was not the final edition. After his death, al Hajjaj, the Governor of Kufa made eleven additional corrections and alterations to the text. Thus, through a long process of repeated redaction, was a standard text canonised. Even that rested on the preference of a single somewhat fallible scribe employed by one Caliph.

There have been frequent assertions by Muslims themselves that the standardised version is corrupted. Kharidjis have rejected a love story of Surah 12 as being unworthy of the Quran.[17] Shiites have consistently maintained that passages relating to Ali and his claim to leadership were suppressed by the 'godless Uthman'.[18] Quarrels and questions remain over the discarded surahs of Abu Musa and ibn Abbas.

The Sunni Muslim claim that today's version of the Quran is the very word of God, infallible, unchanged even in its pronouncement and chapter divisions, does not seem to rest on very solid foundations when one understands how this version was developed. Even today in modern Islam there are at least two versions of the Quran. One is the Egyptian edition adopted in 1924 and the other is that which was traced to Warsh (D. 812) from Nafi of Medina, which is used in other parts of Africa.[19] Certainty is often the progeny of unexamined zeal. Just one of the difficulties for those who would assert that the Quran is an exact replication of God's uncreated word of tablets existent in heaven, is the number of contradictions which exist within the text. The revelations were received within a 22 year period and during that brief time it would seem to the casual observer, that the Almighty was frequently changing his perfect will and word.

To extract themselves from this obvious difficulty Muslim scholars have developed the theory of Abrogation. The means to explain contradictions within the text is that later revelations *(nasikh)* may annul earlier revelations *(mansukh)*. However this device raises further difficulties. If the uncreated status of the Quran is inherent within the being of Allah then the Quran is part of the essence of Allah. If abrogations are allowed within the Quran, an implication must be that there are abrogations and contradictions within the essence of Allah which is impossible. If also God's words are eternal and uncreated, how could they be superceded into obsolescence?

One theological explanation of the device of Abrogation asserts that it was developed to protect the Prophet from remaining in error. Hence, a second revelation was sent to annul the first. But the question is where does that stop and how many more may have been needed but for Muhammad's death?

A further problem with this theory is that there is little agreement on which surahs were earlier and which were supposed later revelations. Moreover the Quran itself states that none can alter the words of Allah (Surah 6:34). Its text is said to be without contradiction (Surah 4:82). In spite of this there is convenient support also within the text itself for abrogation or the substitution and replacement of one revelation for another (Surah 2:106, 108; 16:101; 17:86).

The number of abrogations is variously estimated at between five and 500.

Some of the better known examples include:

The change of the direction of prayer *(quibla)* from Mecca to Jerusalem and back to Mecca (Surah 2:142–144).

Inheritance laws granting equal shares for men and women (Surah 2:180; 4:7) later changed so that men receive a double portion (Surah 4:11).

Changes to nightly prayer formulas (Surah 73:20, 24).

Punishment for adulteresses from life imprisonment (Surah 4:15) to 100 lashes (Surah 24:2). Homosexuals were not punished at all if they repented (Surah 4:16).

Changes to retaliation laws for murder (Surah 2:178; 17:33).

Days for the creation of the world are increased from six (Surah 7:54; 25:59; 32:4) to eight (Surah 41:9–12).

There was to be no compulsion in matters of religion (Surah 2:256) but those who do not submit to Islam are to be slain wherever they are found (Surah 9:5), beheaded (Surah 47:4) or warred against (Surah 8:39; 9:29).

Widows are to remain separate from society after the deaths of their husbands for four months and ten days (Surah 2:334). This period may also be one year (Surah 2:240).

Dietary and Sabbath laws (Surah 16:114–119, 124) are also contradicted (Surah 16:101).

Abraham and his progeny (Surah 2:132), all earlier prophets (Surah 28:52–53) and the disciples of Jesus (Surah 3:52) were all regarded as earlier Muslims. But Muhammad was the first to bow to Allah (Surah 6:14, 163; 39:12).

Allah cursed all liars but Muhammad is permitted to break his own oath (Surah 66:1–2).

Pharaoh was drowned with his army (Surah 17:102–103) but was also rescued (Surah 10:90–92).

Muslims, Christians and Sabians are all saved (Surah 2:62). Elsewhere only Muslims are saved (Surah 3:85) while Jews and Christians have the curse of Allah on them (Surah 9:30).

Jesus did not die (Surah 4:157) but elsewhere he died and rose again (Surah 19:33).

The Bible does not agree with the Quran because, it is claimed, Jews and Christians have corrupted it. But the words and revelations of Allah can never be altered (Surah 6:34; 10:64).[20]

If the Quran has been sent down from the highest heaven and is unaltered in any way – a perfect copy of uncreated tablets preserved in heaven – obviously the question arises as to how all the changes and contradictions of Allah appear within the text. It becomes more difficult when one is reminded that all these changes were effected within the span of a couple of decades. These facts cannot but help challenge the claim that the Quran represents a revelation for all time.

> If the Quran has been sent down from the highest heaven and is unaltered in any way – a perfect copy of uncreated tablets preserved in heaven – obviously the question arises as to how all the changes and contradictions of Allah appear within the text.

Because the Prophet Muhammad is the sole source for authorising the Quran to its unique status and the Quran in turn is the sole source for authenticating Muhammad's prophethood, it becomes somewhat difficult to break into this circuitous process. Obviously for truth to be established, it is hoped that there might be some other signs external to the two primary mutual self-authentications which could objectively increase credence of such claims.

This becomes possible where, for instance, the Quran might refer to historical events or geographical places. Archaeological tests have repeatedly enhanced the reputation of the Holy Bible that has been under close scrutiny for a long time as to the validity of its own claims. However, where the Quran does mention events or locations that can be cross-checked from other verifiable sources, the reader is surprisingly left with an even greater heightened sense of uncertainty as to how the claim that the Quran is an exact revelation from Allah who is incapable of error, can be sustained. Some of the commoner items which are demonstrably at variance with known more easily verifiable facts of the natural world are:

The Quran claims to follow, protect and confirm the Scriptures of Jews and Christians which preceded it (Surah 3:81; 6:92; 35:31; 46:12). The word of Allah is also unchangeable (Surah 6:34; 10:64). These things being so, one would naturally expect a degree of consistency where the Quran refers to events recorded in the Scriptures of its two religious predecessors. However such is not the case. For example the Quran claims it was Pharaoh's wife who rescued Moses (Surah 28:9). Christian and Jewish Scriptures say it was not his wife, but his daughter (Exodus 2:10).

The Quran asserts that Christians worship three gods, the Father, the Mother (ie. Mary) and the Son (ie. Jesus). It further claims that this is what Christians mean by the Trinity (Surah 5:73–75, 116). Yet Christianity has never known any such teaching. Like its Jewish forefathers it has always held that God is one (Deuteronomy 4:35; 6:4, Mark 12:29; James 2:19). It is interesting to note that the Quran not only speaks frequently of Allah but also of his uncreated word (Surah 16:40; 36:82). It also speaks of his spirit (Surah 58:22), 'our spirit' (Surah 66:12) and the Holy Spirit (Surah 2:87, 253). These three elements are precisely that which Christian theologians have grappled to understand over the millennia and to which they have attributed the theological concept known as the Trinity.

In the Quran Mary is the sister of Aaron as well as the mother of Jesus (Surah 19:27–28; 20:25–30; 66:12). But, in fact these are two different women whose lives were lived at different times separated by approximately one and a half millennia.

The Quran portrays Haman as being in an Egyptian Pharaoh's employ and building a high tower to reach God (Surah 28:38; 29:39; 40:24, 36). But the attempt to build such a tower belongs to a different era (Genesis 11). This was approximately 750 years earlier in the Biblical chronology than the time of the conflict between Moses and Pharaoh. Haman of course, was never in the service of Pharaoh. His is uniquely a Babylonian name. He was a civil servant of King Xerxes (Esther 3) who lived approximately 1100 years after the Pharaonic events.

The Quran states that the calf worshipped by the ancient Israelites (Exodus 32) was cast by a Samaritan (Surah 20:85–87, 95–97). But this ethnic subgroup was not identified nor did they have any known separate existence till many centuries after the incident of the golden calf. They were descendants of the Israelites in the northern kingdom of Israel.

In accordance with folk tales of the time, the Quran agrees that the sun sets in a spring of murky water (Surah 18:86). Today we know differently.

The Quran says mountains are used by Allah as weights and tent pegs to stabilise and prevent the earth from shaking (Surah 16:15; 21:31; 31:10; 78:6–7; 88:19). Again, today we know the opposite to be true. Mountain ranges result from the earth's shaking as tectonic plates collide. Rather than holding the earth down the opposite is true. They result from the earth being pushed up.

Stars and meteorites are said to be used as missiles shot at evil spirits who try to eavesdrop on Quranic readings in heaven (Surah 67:5; 72:6–9). Astronomy indicates otherwise.

As noted earlier, not only was the Quran meant to protect the earlier writings of Jews and Christians, it was also meant to confirm that which had been revealed (Surah 3:81; 6:92; 35:31; 46:12) ie. the law of Moses, the Psalter of David and the Gospel of Jesus. However it is said that the Jews received only part of the heavenly revelation (Surah 3:23; 4:44). But of that which they received they are said to have 'forgotten' some (Surah 5:13), 'concealed' (Surah 2:174) or even perverted the Scriptures (Surah 4:46; 5:16, 43).

Christians are similarly regarded as participating in some international conspiracy to belittle the new, full, final, exact revelation. If that was so, what does one say regarding the Scripture that remains? There are many thousands of pre-Islamic manuscripts of the Christian Scriptures of various lengths and translations still in existence.

Unlike Islam, Christianity never had an equivalent of a Caliph to centrally order the destruction of all copies, translations or commentaries of its sacred Book. The Scriptures were widely distributed long before anyone had ever thought, dreamed or even heard of the concept of a new international religion. And they are all in essential agreement. Consequently the claim that the Quran both confirms and protects Scriptures that have preceded it is seriously undermined through these disagreements.

Not only is there disagreement among Judeo/Christian and Muslim Scriptures, there are further items which call into question the validity of the revelations received by Muhammad. For example large flights of birds are alleged to have dropped bricks on Abyssinian General Abraha's army so turning it back from Mecca (Surah 105). Secular history records that his withdrawal was due to an outbreak of smallpox within his army. In a reversal of Darwin's theory of evolution, fisherfolk are said to have been turned into apes because they broke the Jewish Sabbath (Surah 2:65–66; 7:163–167).

In addition to the above list of anomalies which are but a few from a much wider selection, linguistic experts have identified 'more than one hundred aberrations from the normal rules and structure of Arabic'.[21] But to Muslims the absolute perfection of the language of the Quran remains as an impregnable dogma.[22]

All of this could naturally lead one to conclude that the claims of the Quran being an exact replica of God's inerrant word in heaven remain open to question. Furthermore, so many of the unusual stories in the Quran are easily traceable to non-Biblical sources. There were many Jewish and Christian Apocryphal writings largely of the second century which were rejected from the respective canons of both of those religions, because they were not only non-authoritative but had no basis of fact or in history. In many cases these stories can only be described as fanciful. Yet these are seemingly the primary sources for a number of Quranic stories.

Included among these are:

Satan's refusal to worship Adam (Surah 2:30–38; 7:11–18; 17:61–63) and his expulsion from God's presence. Its parallel is found in the second century Talmudic Jewish writings.

An aberrant account of the murder of Abel by Cain (Surah 5:27–32). The parallel is found in the Targum of Jonathan-ben-Uzziah and the Mishnah Sanhedrin 4:45.

A story about Abraham destroying idols (Surah 21:51–71) is also found in a second century collection of Jewish folk tales known as The Midrash Rabbah.

The account of God threatening to squash the Jews by dropping Mount Sinai on them (Surah 2:63; 7:171) is also found in a second century Jewish collection known as Abodah Sarah.

The story of King Solomon, the hoopoe bird and the Queen of Sheba (Surah 27:17–44) is sourced in the II Targum of Esther, another second century Jewish creation.

The story of Mary, Imram and Zechariah (Surah 3:31–41) is found in a second century Christian folktale included in The Protoevangelion's James the Lesser.

Fables regarding Jesus' birth (Surah 19:16–28) are traceable to a second century work known as The Lost Books of the Bible.

A story recounting the infant Jesus being able to talk (Surah 19:29–33) is originally found in second century Egyptian Apocryphal writings known as The First Gospel of the Infancy of Jesus Christ.

Jesus creating birds from clay (Surah 3:49) is from yet another second century work, Thomas' Gospel of the Infancy of Jesus Christ.

The use of a balance to weigh believers' good and bad deeds on the Day of Judgment (Surah 42:17; 101:6–9) is found in the earlier Testament of Abraham.

Concepts of paradise in which the righteous will be rewarded by access to perpetually virgin beautiful maidens *(huris)* (Surah 2:25; 3:15; 4:57; 44:54; 55:56–58; 56:22–24, 35–37) are also found in Persian Zoroastrianism.[23]

What may one conclude from all of this?

There is a unity of thought, a directness and simplicity of purpose, a peculiar and laboured style, a uniformity of diction coupled with a certain deficiency of imaginative power, which indicate that the ayats (signs or verses) of the Quran are the product of a single mind.[24]

But that is precisely the nub of the problem. A single mind has produced a single book that authenticates that single mind as being the seal of the prophets which in turn gives a final revelation. One exclusively authenticates the other.

Furthermore the collection and collation of the material today known as the Quran, is largely the product of a single redactor who admitted to omission and mistake. Not only that, as we have seen, this volume went through many additional changes. Still it is claimed that although all other variants were destroyed, that which remains is the very perfect word of God. 'While it may be true that no other work has remained for twelve centuries with so pure a text, it is probably equally true that no other has suffered so drastic a purging.'[25] The question of course, remains open as to whether Abu Bakr's recension was complete and represented an authentic edition.

That many believe it was and accept it as such is a faith statement undergirded by little more than sincerity. Members of the Flat Earth Society were equally convinced of their belief in the shape of the earth until overwhelmed by contrary facts. Even so some still hold dogmatically to their earlier position regardless of masses of

> In excess of a billion people regard the Quran incomparably highly. But this is not a contributing fact as proof toward its veracity. Claims are not proof. They are a measure of people's sincerity and faith.

empirical data to the contrary. As in other areas of human endeavour, to those who believe no proof is necessary, to those who don't or won't no amount of proof is ever sufficient. [26]

In excess of a billion people regard the Quran incomparably highly. But this is not a contributing fact as proof toward its veracity. Claims are not proof. They are a measure of people's sincerity and faith. As for others, as it has been since Muhammad first claimed to be speaking revelations from God, serious questions await answers. Since those questions have not been answered in the last 1300 years, it is unlikely that they will be answered to the satisfaction of others in the near future.

CHAPTER 15

THE BASICS

One of the functions of mankind's various expressions of religion is to gain heaven and to avoid hell. Islam is no exception. When compared with Christianity it is unique among other world religions. It is the only major religion to appear later in time than Christianity. It is the only religion which, when confronted with Christianity's beliefs, not only specifically rejected them but virtually eliminated the Church in several countries in which it was established prior to Islam's arrival. In the process centuries-old Christian communities subsequently submitted or were mostly extinguished. Where adherents of that ancient national church survived, they were reduced to the status of second-class citizens and were obliged to pay 'protection' money for the privilege of being allowed to exist. Greek and Latin, languages of the Church, were relegated for use in ancient liturgies. Arabic, the language of the victors, became and remained the official language.[1]

Muhammad set out to recall his people from polytheistic paganism to worship only one invisible God, Allah. He preached that

> Muhammad set out to recall his people from polytheistic paganism to worship only one invisible God, Allah. He preached that all the prophets followed this particular monotheism right back to and including original man, Adam.

all the prophets followed this particular monotheism right back to and including original man, Adam. He asserted that what he preached was the original religion of all Arabs whose progenitor was Abraham through his first-born son, Ishmael.

By the time of Muhammad's death virtually all the Arabian peninsula had accepted Islam's creed, 'There is no god but Allah and Muhammad is the apostle of Allah.' Within another 50 years Muslim armies had conquered the whole of the eastern Mediterranean and northern Africa. Apart from Islam's military conquests, one of its attractions to the uninitiated is its apparent simplicity of doctrine and the direct demands of its duties.

There are five basic doctrines all Muslims must believe. There are also five duties to be performed.

DOCTRINE

1. Belief in God

Islam teaches that there is only one true God (Surah 2:163; 6:19). His name in Arabic is Allah. 'He is numerically and absolutely one. He is beyond human understanding. Only his will may be revealed and known.'[2] Allah is all-seeing, all-knowing, all-powerful, self-existent, without equal or partner. He created and maintains the world.

This belief in God is Islam's most fundamental tenet.

Muslims refer to God in terms of 99 'beautiful names'. These outline characteristics attributed to him. A common frequently observed practice is the use of a 99 bead rosary (subha) which is used as a memory aid in reciting the 99 names of God.

A popular folk belief is that the one hundredth name for Allah has not been revealed to mankind. It was told only to the camel explaining that animal's haughty bearing. Muhammad is said to have stated that 'whoever called upon God by that exalted one hundredth name would receive all his desires'.[3]

2. Angels

Islam believes in angels. They are the servants of Allah through whom he reveals his will (Surah 35:1). The chief among them is Gabriel (Jibril) who is said to have appeared to Muhammad (Surah 2:97). There are also fallen angels, the chief of whom is named Shaytan (Surah 15:28–35). Followers of Shaytan are known as jinn although not all jinn are demons. Two angels are said to remain in attendance on each human being. One records good deeds, the other sins. Their record will form the basis of judgment upon that fateful future day (Surah 50:17–23).

3. Scripture — the Books of God

Muslims believe that there were 104 sacred books of direct divine revelation, only four of which are still in existence in compiled form. These are:

- The law books of Moses *(Torah)*. These correspond to the first five books of the Bible.
- The *Zabur* of David. This corresponds to some Psalms.
- The *Injil* of Jesus, a single book which corresponds to some of the material in the Christian Gospels.
- The Quran.

In addition to the Quran, there are the Traditions *(Hadith)*. These are collections of teachings and actions attributed to Muhammad. They are a very important source for Islamic history and law.

A popular folk belief is that the one hundredth name for Allah has not been revealed to mankind. It was told only to the camel explaining that animal's haughty bearing.

The Quran is held to be Allah's final word to mankind. Therefore, it is said to supersede and overrule all previous writings. If one accepts the principle that the last or latest must be a further and fuller revelation from Allah then according to the logic of that principle the holy books of Sikhs, Baha'i and Mormons are all progressively superior because each of these chronologically appeared even later than the Quran.

In the Bible there are no contradictions between material attributed to Moses, David and Jesus. In contradistinction to this, the Quran is in frequent and significant disagreement with these three blocks of data that have preceded it. For example there are wide differences in the common stories relating to Creation, Abraham, Ishmael, Isaac and Jesus. This disruption of progressive, harmonised, divine revelation is rationalised by Muslims by declaring that the first three are corrupted and this is why they are no longer in agreement with the Quran.

No attempt is made to explain who did this and how or when it was done around the world. Nor is there explanation of why there are still so many thousands of copies of these three texts in existence, which when originally produced, predate Islam. Texts from the Dead Sea Scrolls that predate Christianity are in remarkable agreement with what is used today. The same is true for Hebrew, Greek and Latin manuscripts rediscovered during the Renaissance after being overlooked for a millennium.[4] These transmissions and translations of the copies are the same as what was in existence before and since the advent of Islam. Muslims sometimes assert that original copies agreeing with the Quran are in existence but are held for safekeeping at various holy shrine sites. But to date none have ever been produced.

4. Muhammad

Islamic popular tradition claims that Allah has sent 124 000 prophets *(nobi)* and 315 messengers or apostles *(rasul)*. Six have been given special titles: Adam, the Chosen of God; Noah, the Preacher of God; Abraham, the Friend of God; Moses, the Converser with God; Jesus, the Spirit of God; Muhammad, the Messenger of God.[5]

The Quran names only 28 prophets of Allah of whom Muhammad was the last and greatest. On Muhammad himself has been bestowed approximately 200 honorific titles, the best known of which is Seal of the Prophets (Surah 33:40). One of his other titles is Peace of the World, an intriguing title considering how much warfare is associated with Muhammad himself and the expansion of Islam.

5. The End Times or the Day of Judgment

Muslims believe that on the 'last day' the dead will be resurrected. Allah will judge all and each person will be dispatched to either heaven or hell. Paradise is a place of sensual pleasure (Surah 44:51–55; 55:46–78). Hell is a place of physical torment for those who have opposed Allah and his Prophet Muhammad (Surah 44:43–50).

The Day of Judgment is anticipated to be a terrible day. Each person's destiny will be determined on the basis of the balance of their good and bad deeds (Surah 21:47; 23:101–104). To each will be given a 'book of destiny'. If this is placed in the right hand then a person may be saved. If it is placed in the left hand that one knows he is lost. To reach Paradise there is an additional test. All must cross a bridge as narrow as a single hair and as sharp as a razor. The righteous may cross successfully but unbelievers will fall into hell.

All hope that good deeds recorded by angels during their lives, when weighed in the scales of justice, will outweigh similarly recorded bad deeds. However, Allah will judge according to his own will rather than according to any human concept or precedent for justice. Allah reserves the absolute right to send individuals to wherever he pleases. Therefore even for the most sincere believers and for those who have also most diligently followed all of the prescribed practices there is still never any assurance of salvation. There is only one way that each might approach certainty of bliss and that is to die as a martyr during a war declared as an Islamic Holy War *(jihad)*. Such declarations serve as an incentive for military recruitment and promote zeal in battle.

Predestination

Closely linked to the outcomes of the Day of Judgment, sometimes listed as an additional foundational faith, is belief in the concept of predestination. 'The dominant mood of the Quran is determinist. God decides, man accepts.'[6]

'Islam' means submission to the will of Allah. A 'Muslim' is one who submits. Everything is to be in submission to Allah. This includes good and evil. Even faith and unbelief are considered to be preordained. Concepts such as free will or an individual's right of choice and response are mostly alien to deterministic Islam. A good example of this is what usually happens when Muslims study the Genesis account of the fall of Adam and Eve. When Muslims are asked why did Adam and Eve fall, the most frequent answer is that Allah deceived them.

> There is only one way that each might approach certainty of bliss and that is to die as a martyr during a war declared as an Islamic Holy War *(jihad)*. Such declarations serve as an incentive for military recruitment and promote zeal in battle.

Sin also is foreordained. This removes personal moral accountability and responsibility from the individual. In part this explains why, from a Western values perspective, an Islamic state may appear to be more rigorously religious but at the same time seem to be more corrupt in some of its practices. If sin is not the result of moral choice but is foreordained by Allah, then the individual is helplessly non-accountable.

A common belief is that on the fifteenth night of the eighth lunar Islamic month, Allah determines the fate of all mortals for the coming year. This overriding concept of predestination and the individual's sensitivity toward it explains why the common response to every incident is 'Allah willed it'. Similarly to every suggestion or invitation the opening or parting remark usually is 'if Allah wills it'.

Along with the Muslims' faith and belief in Allah, his angels, the authority of the Quran, the Prophethood of Muhammad, the inevitability of the end times and the Day of Judgment, there are additional obligations or duties which each believer must perform to increase hope for salvation. Neglect of any invokes dire consequences.

The five duties commonly known as Pillars *(arkanu'd-din)* are:

1. The Statement of Belief or Confession of Creed *(Shahadah)*

Islam demands its believers have faith *(iman)*. Faith is defined as confession with the tongue and belief with the heart. The full form of the fundamental confession of faith is:

I believe in Allah, his angels, his books, his prophets, in the last day, in the predestination by the Most High God of good and evil and in the resurrection after death.

The shorter form of the Confession is:

There is no God but Allah; Muhammad is the Apostle of Allah.

This confession of faith is known as the *Shahadah* or *Kalima*. As part of the process of becoming a Muslim a person must repeat publicly the *Shahadah*. This creed also is repeated five times a day in the call to prayer from towers attached to mosques *(minarets)*. It is also repeated in all prayers and in every home.

2. Prayers *(Salat)*

Salat refers to the obligatory prayers that must be said every day. The Quran makes reference to prayers being said only three times a day, morning, noon and night. But because Muhammad said prayers five times daily, after his death this became the custom. Similarly some of the bodily postures which are assumed during prayer are not Quranic injunctions. They arise from Traditions associated with the Prophet.

The times for obligatory prayers are:

- At dawn but before sunrise *(Fajr)*
- Between sunrise and noon *(Zuhr)*
- Midafternoon *(Asr)*
- Soon after sunset *(Magrib)*

- Well after nightfall *(Isha)*.

For congregational prayer, five times a day from the towers *(minarets)* of mosques around the world, prayer callers *(muezzins)* call the faithful to prayer. Their formula is:

God is most great.

God is most great.

I bear witness that there is no God but Allah.

I bear witness that Muhammad is the Apostle of Allah.

Come ye unto prayer.

Come ye unto good.

Prayer is better than sleep.

Come ye to the best deed.

To pray, clean space sufficient to kneel and touch one's forehead to the ground is required. Shoes are removed and often the head is covered. The space must be sufficient to allow one to face in the direction of the sacred mosque in Mecca in which is housed the Kaba said to have been built by Abraham and Ishmael.

Obligatory prayer may be said anywhere. Therefore, Muslims will often unroll their special prayer mats or other suitable materials on trains, ships, at the roadside or even on planes. Computerised compasses have been developed specifically for the purpose of showing the direction of Mecca *(quibla)* from whatever point the traveller finds himself.

Before any Muslim recites prayers ceremonial ablutions are required. There may be some variation according to circumstance. The lesser ablution *(wadu)* involves washing with water the face especially the orifices of mouth, nose and ears, hands and arms up to the elbows and feet up to the ankles. Unless all is performed strictly according to preset formulae then prayer is rendered inoperative and ineffectual. A more complete washing *(ghusl)* of the entire body is required after certain sexual functions or menstruation. Unless scrupulously carried out one remains ritually impure. Muhammad's son-in-law reputedly related that Muhammad once said regarding this ceremony, 'He who leaves but one hair unwashed on his body will be punished in hell accordingly' (Mishkat bII.c.vii).

In the event of water being unavailable or unwise to use because of ill health, sand or earth may be rubbed over face and arms as a substitute ablution.

Prayer begins with a silent intention *(niya)* of sincerity. The abbreviated confession 'God is most great' is repeated. A passage from the Quran is recited. This is followed by a series of prostrations, recitation of other Quranic passages and private personal prayer.

Spontaneous prayer *(du'a)* may be said at any time. Friday is the day of congregational prayer. Midday is its appointed hour. Prayers are led in the mosque by an *Imam*. Congregational prayers are usually for men only. But some mosques do have specially screened compartments for women who may wish to pray. Women are normally expected to pray at home.

Orthodox Muslims disapprove of closing one's eyes during prayer.

Mosques *(masjid* means place of prostration) are always oriented toward Mecca. The direction is indicated by a niche *(mihrab)* in the end wall. Recent archaeological evidence from Iraq and literary evidence from Egypt however, seem to show that the earliest mosques up to about the middle of the eighth century were directed not to Mecca but to Jerusalem.[7]

Although Islam teaches strict monotheism, at the popular or folk level veneration is given to relics, tombs and places associated with saints, mystics and founders of religious movements. To these places people come to offer gifts and to pray. Prayer is also offered in cemeteries for the dead. Muhammad is believed to be the great intercessor but appeal is made also to many other saints and holy men.

The twenty-seventh night of the month of Ramadan is celebrated as the Night of Power or Destiny *(lailat al qadr)*. It is thought that this is the night on which Muhammad received his first revelation of what was to go on to become the Quran. This night is kept as a prayer vigil. Many believe that on this night God hears their prayers either directly or by the angel Gabriel. On this occasion the intercession of Muhammad or others is unnecessary.

On the matter of prayer one tradition teaches that to miss just one of the five obligatory daily prayers invokes punishment in hell for 5000 years!

3. Almsgiving (Zakat)

Almsgiving (zakat) is the third pillar of right religion *(din)*. Zakat means 'purification' or 'growth'. It is a term used to express that portion of property which is given as alms, an act which purifies the remainder of one's possessions (Surah 2:43, 110, 117, 277; 4:162; 5:55). Believers are required to give approximately 2.5%

of capital wealth. It is levied on capital and some goods that have been in one's possession for twelve months or longer.

Zakat is distributed to widows, orphans, the sick, other unfortunates and for the propagation of Islam. It may also be given to help the needy make pilgrimage to Mecca. It must not be used for expenses involved in building mosques, funerals, the liquidation of debts of a deceased person or for the needs of immediate relatives. A person whose debts are equal to or exceeding the amount of his whole property is not required to give. Nor is it due from a person's immovable properties and necessities of life such as house, clothing, books, tools or weapons.

Examples of levies are:

- One goat for five to nine camels.
- Two goats for 10 to 14 camels.
- None is levied on fewer than 30 cattle.
- For 60 cattle, two calves must be given.
- For sheep and goats, none is levied on fewer than 40.
- Horses, silver and gold attract varying amounts of levy.
- On merchandise, the calculation is 2.5% if in excess of 200 dirhams.
- On all fruits of the earth, 10% is levied except on wood, bamboo and grass. Hand or artificially watered produce attracts a 5% levy.

Zakat is not collected in mosques. It is received by appointed collectors or the donor may distribute it directly himself. Sometimes Islamic governments have tried to establish other procedures to assist national economic reform, eg. the Pakistan government some years ago seized 2.5% of all bank accounts over a fixed amount. The government of Bangladesh struck a levy equivalent to a day's grain needs per person ie. 1.75 kilograms.

Freewill offerings or charitable gifts *(sadaqa)* (Surah 2:263) may be given at any time. They are particularly given at the annual festival at the end of Ramadan known

> Although Islam teaches strict monotheism, at the popular or folk level veneration is given to relics, tombs and places associated with saints, mystics and founders of religious movements.

as *Eid al-Fitr.* That which is given is granted as merit and counted among good deeds to facilitate entry into Paradise.

4. Fasting (Saum)

The fourth pillar or practice of right religion is fasting *(saum).* This is especially focussed on the ninth month of the Muslim lunar year called Ramadan (Surah 2:184 –187). The name for this month is said to be derived from *ramz* which means *to burn.* The inference is that during this month if right practices are followed one's sins may be *burnt away.*

Ramadan is that month in which the Quran is said to have been sent down from the highest to the lowest heaven in preparation for communication to Muhammad. For each day of this month a fast is rigorously kept during the daylight hours. It begins at first light as soon as a white thread may be distinguished from a black one. It is meant to continue until dusk which is calculated by one thread being indistinguishable from another. In Muslim cities often a cannon will also signal the official beginning and end of each day.

The month of fasting ends with the appearance of the new moon. This is celebrated by a festival known as *Eid al-Fitr.* This is a day of great feasting and of giving alms to the poor. People, especially children will normally wear new clothes. This feast is second only in importance to *Eid al-Adhar* (Surah 22:34–38), also known as Eid al-Kabir, the Feast of Sacrifice which occurs 70 days later.

Keeping this month long, daylight hours fast is obligatory for all Muslims who have reached puberty and are of sound mind. However there are some exemptions. Temporarily exempted are those who are engaged in heavy labour, travellers, prepubescent children, the sick, pregnant or nursing women, the very elderly or soldiers engaged in Holy War *(jihad).* The expectation is that each day's fasting missed during Ramadan will be made up later or alternatively extra alms will be given to the poor.

During daylight hours the expectation is that nothing may pass through the throat. The most rigorous will not even swallow their own saliva. No food, drink, smoking, medical injections, socialising, smelling fragrances or sexual activity is permitted during daylight hours. Additionally it is expected that playing games of chance, coarse language, anger, wearing makeup and other such activities will also be eschewed.

In many Muslim households the women rise during the night to prepare a meal *(sahur)* which is eaten before dawn. Immediately after sunset special parties to break the fast *(iftar)* are held with friends, neighbours and virtually anyone who cares to drop in. This is a time of relief especially if the lunar month occurs during the summer months when the days may be long and hot.

Ramadan preachers usually tour the towns to deliver special messages of religious or social significance to encourage the faithful. In this month of heightened spiritual activity, special prayers *(tarawith)* are offered. These are usually performed by groups of people. One of the objectives of the month is to read through the entire Quran. If done in this month extra blessing is accrued. It is a month when those normally irreligious can suddenly become very religious because it is good to be seen as such.

The purpose of the fast is to deny one's physical appetites, to bring passions under control so that time might be set aside to read and meditate upon the teachings of the Quran and thereby learn about Allah. Some consider that the fast is a debt owed to Allah. In this way one may partially atone for one's own sins.

Identification with the poor is enhanced and of course merit gained contributes toward earning a place in Paradise. Some believe that during this unique month the gates of Paradise are opened and the gates of hell are shut. Also it is thought that devils are chained by one leg.

A wider purpose is achieved. 'By fasting together, the worldwide community of Islam *(ummah)* affirms its brotherhood and equality before Allah'.[8] Other fasts are voluntary eg. on the tenth day of the month of Muharram. But the fast of Ramadan is obligatory. For those who breach this requirement, not only are there social sanctions that may quickly apply, but there are also spiritual ramifications.

If during the fast a believer commits any unworthy act then his fasting is considered meaningless. One tradition teaches that if a keeper of the fast does not abandon lying then God does not care about his fasting. The severity of strictures which apply during the month are more than rewarded by the joy of being released at the end of the month.

5. Pilgrimage to Mecca *(Hajj)*

The fifth pillar of right religion is the pilgrimage to Mecca which all believers are expected to make at least once in their lifetime (Surah 2:196–203; 22:26–33). If pilgrimage is too difficult or too dangerous, a believer may send someone else in his place. No non-Muslim may participate in this event or for that matter ever enter the holy city of Mecca. Lesser pilgrimages may be undertaken at any time but this

Greater Pilgrimage is fundamental and is undertaken at the time of the new moon in the twelfth month of the Islamic lunar year.

Pilgrims are required to wear no other clothing than two seamless white cloths. One is for the lower part of the body. The other is for the upper part of the body. Women are completely veiled. Pilgrims upon arrival circumambulate the Kaba seven times in an anticlockwise direction. The former pagan practice was in the opposite direction. During these circumambulations pilgrims try to kiss the black stone embedded into the corner of the Kaba.

There is procession to the two hills, Safa and Marwa, and to a locally named Mount Arafat on which a night is spent. Pebbles are cast at a stone pillar that represents Satan. Extra trips are made around the Kaba.

Day ten is a time of communal confession of sins and the slaughter of animals in the Valley of Mina. The meat from these sacrificed animals is shared with the poor. This practice is replicated throughout the Islamic world at the time of the Great Festival known as Eid al-Adhar or Eid al-Kabir.

Finally the head is shaved. At departure time from Mecca many pilgrims take holy water from the well of Zamzam which in Islamic lore, is associated with Hagar and Ishmael. Some, prior to departure, visit the Prophet's tomb in Medina. The Hajj is considered essential to salvation even though the vast majority of the world's Muslims, Saudi government subsidies notwithstanding, can never hope to make such an expensive journey.

The basic doctrines and pillars of Islam are its formal face of orthodoxy. But ultimately religion is more about people than doctrine. Part of Islam's attractiveness as well as its ability to hold people, is that obviously for some it meets real needs in their lives, even if only the desire to belong to a community.

Adaptations of Islam vary from country to country according to local history, culture and custom. At the local level there is often incorporated pre-Islamic religious beliefs and practices. Adherents however are expected to accept the basics without question. To suggest otherwise could result in threat, hostility or even retributive violence.

Muslims believe that by the performance of their obligatory duties, salvation just might be attained. But by salvation a Muslim is not anticipating a restoration of a broken relationship with the Almighty. Allah is so infinitely different from mankind as to make him inaccessible and unknowable. Therefore no relationship with him is ever possible no matter how righteous the believer.

Christians seek salvation from the state of sin itself. For Muslims salvation is escape from judgment and punishment for sin (Surah 78:31–40). Against this background the words of the Apostle James speak devastating truth, a death knell of all hope. 'For whoever keeps the whole law and yet stumbles at just one point is guilty of breaking all of it' (James 2:10).

Professor Riaz Hassan of Flinders University, Adelaide, Australia in a pioneering study found that 'for a large majority of Muslims the experience of Allah was one of fear'.[9]

Within a context of uncertainty or fear many Muslims as they age, regardless of how they may have spent or misspent their youth, become more scrupulously religious in striving to attempt to fulfil all the letters under the considerable weight of all the law. As the Quran says '…those whose balance (of good deeds) is heavy, they will be successful. But those whose balance is light, will be those who have lost their souls; In Hell will they abide' (Surah 23:102–103).

> Part of Islam's attractiveness as well as its ability to hold people is that obviously for some it meets real needs in their lives, even if only the desire to belong to a community.

Those who struggle under the multiple weights of uncertainty, fear and unbearable law are yet to learn of the glorious release and discovery made by an earlier searcher after truth, the Apostle Paul. He summed up this situation when he wrote to the Church in Ephesus, 'For it is by grace you have been saved, through faith…not by works, so that no one can boast' (Ephesians 2:8–9).

What a relief! What a release from the war within and without.

It is this matter of warfare which some regard as a sixth pillar of Islam. Holy warfare is *jihad*.

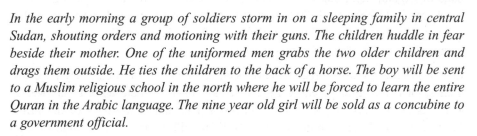

CHAPTER 16

WAR WITHOUT END

In the early morning a group of soldiers storm in on a sleeping family in central Sudan, shouting orders and motioning with their guns. The children huddle in fear beside their mother. One of the uniformed men grabs the two older children and drags them outside. He ties the children to the back of a horse. The boy will be sent to a Muslim religious school in the north where he will be forced to learn the entire Quran in the Arabic language. The nine year old girl will be sold as a concubine to a government official.

The mother is molested repeatedly and disfigured before the soldiers leave.[1]

In the country of Sudan, apart from an 11 year cessation between 1972 and 1983, civil war has raged since 1955. One of the reasons for this war is that the Arab led Islamic government in the north wants to impose Islam on the south which is inhabited mostly by Christian and animist groups.

In Sudan when Lieutenant General Omar Ahmad al Bashir seized power in June 1989, he promised a revolution of Islamic salvation through an Islamic army guided by the principles of *jihad* or religious warfare. This has resulted in mass crucifixions, hangings, burning Christian villages and churches, systematic persecutions and mass drownings. At one point the Nile River washed up 500 bodies in a single day. Sudan became an incubator for radical Islamic movements with at least 35 known training terrorist bases.[2]

One aspect of this warfare has been that tens of thousands of children have been abducted from the south, many of whom have been subsequently sold at slave markets in the north for as little as US$15 per child. It has been estimated that approximately 2 million people who would not convert to Islam have been killed, while 3.5 million have been forced to flee their homes.[3]

In 1993 Christians in nine villages in Tehsil Kot Adu, District Muzaffargarh, in the province of Punjab, Pakistan, applied to the relevant government authority to be registered as owners of the land they had occupied and developed for the preceding 16 years. During this time they had built roads, clinics, schools and housing accommodation. The government, according to its own laws agreed with the legality and rightness of their case, but when it reached the local level Muslims drove off the Christian occupants and seized the land and property. Government authorities took no action.[4]

In the same country of Pakistan in February 1997, a somewhat frenzied mob of 20 000 people led by local members of a Sunni group of Muslims, accompanied by a band of Afghanistan trained *Mujahuddin*, took just six hours to ravage and destroy 13 churches, 150 homes, 1500 Bibles and hymn books and any domestic items left after systematic looting of the properties. Fifteen thousand Christians were left homeless.[5]

In Iran in recent years Christians have been arrested and tortured. They have lost homes, jobs, and employment. Christian schools have been closed or taken over by Muslims as was also the case for colleges in Pakistan in the days of the Prime Ministership of Benazir Bhutto's father, Zulfikar Ali Bhutto. In Iran in June 1993 all churches were ordered to sign a statement that they would not evangelise Muslims. They were banned from holding church services in the national language of Iran, Farsi. Christian communities were obliged to use the more ancient and almost defunct languages of Armenian or Assyrian. A senior official of the Ministry of Islamic Guidance in Iran reportedly said, 'From now on either we kill all of you (Christians) quietly or make your lives so difficult that you will have no choice but to leave the country'.[6]

In Egypt in September 1997, 40 Christians were killed outside St George's Church in the village of Arroda in the province of El-Minyah. Within days five more were killed in the same vicinity. Then in the town of Mallawi two men and a 15 year old boy were killed. Nine of these were killed during attendance at Sunday School. Like dozens of other killings in Egypt 'all seem to have the same motive – reprisals for Christians' failure or inability to pay *jizya*, the traditional Islamic tax levied on all non-Muslims.'[7]

Appeals to the police and other government authorities have been of little or no effect. When Bishop Wissa and two other clergymen spoke out about the torture and detention of more than 1000 Christians in the Egyptian province of Sohag that occurred in August–September 1988, they were arrested and charged with damaging national unity.[8]

In countries adjacent to Israel and within its borders, the Islamic organisation *Hamas* operates. *Hamas* is an acronym for *Harakat al Muqawama al Islamiya.* It also means zeal. It is an Islamic resistance movement founded after the outbreak of the Intafada in December 1987 in Palestinian sections of Israel. Their literature describes Jews as:

- Brothers of the apes
- The killers of the prophets
- Bloodsuckers and whoremongers (Leaflet no.1,30)
- Cancer expanding…threatening the whole Islamic world (Leaflet no.16)
- The enemy of God and mankind (Leaflet no.78).

At a 1994 Muslim Youth Association Conference in Los Angeles a Muslim spokesman was reported as saying 'I'm going to speak the truth to you. It's simple. Finish off the Israelis. Kill them all! Exterminate them! No peace ever!' An FBI report says US$207,000 was raised after this speech for 'the cause'.[9] In March 2002 the Saudi Arabian newspaper *al-Riyadh* ran a column by 'an academic claiming Israeli Jews were 'mixing the blood of Muslim children in their pastries.'[10]

In November 2 2002 Australian Muslim, Jack Roche said that Israeli Prime Minister, Ariel Sharon had 'a nickname in Arab circles...the pig'. Not 'a pig', 'the pig'.[11] In May 2002 prominent Saudi cleric Sheikh Saad Al-Buriak in a government mosque in Riyadh was reported as saying 'Muslim Brothers in Palestine, do not have any mercy neither compassion on the Jews, their blood, their money, their flesh. Their women are ours to take, legitimately. God made them yours. Why don't you enslave their women! Why don't you wage jihad! Why don't you pillage them! People should know that Jews are backed by the Christians, and the battle that we are going through is not with Jews only, but also with those who believe that Allah is a third in a Trinity, and those who said that Jesus is the son of Allah, and Allah is Jesus, the son of Mary.'[12]

The speaker is a close friend of Prince Abdul Aziz Ben Fahd and hosts a government television programme in Saudi Arabia. In a two-day telethon in Saudi Arabia he raised over US$100 million for the Palestinian cause. It's obvious Jews are not the only object of Islamic ire. Christians are likewise threatened. In October 2002 in a sermon in a Tabriz mosque Iranian cleric, Ayatollah Mohsen Mujtahed Shabestari called for the death of prominent Christian Americans, Jerry Falwell, Franklin Graham and Pat Robertson. The Iranian Farsi daily 'Abrar' made clear that this was because these three had dared to be critical of Islam.[13]

In Afghanistan when a Christian believer invited his friends to a Christmas pageant, shortly thereafter his home was rocketed and he lost his employment. Another Christian believer who was open about his faith was killed by gradual torture.

In Turkey, a national pastor was taken into prison on eight separate occasions. Each time 'he was whipped and harshly interrogated for outright sharing of his faith'.[14]

What motivates these activities?

Islam identifies five enemies against whom it must wage war:

* The nafs or lust, the invisible enemy
* Satan (another invisible enemy)
* Hypocrites (munafiq)
* Sinful Muslims ('asi)
* Infidels (Jews, Christians and all other non-believers in Islam).[15]

Sheikh Taj Alddin Hamed Al Hilali - the Grand Mufti or spiritual leader of Australia's Muslim community is widely reported as identifying Muslims as having three enemies: 'the white pigs in America, the red dogs in Russia and the black snake of the Jewish nation'.

Sheikh Hilali who likes to be known as a man of peace additionally expanded on his attitude towards Jews by reportedly saying that they 'try to control the world through sex, then sexual perversion, then the promotion of espionage, treason and economic hoarding'. Although he reportedly said that in 1998 despite numerous requests 'he has never apologized for nor rescinded those comments'.[16]

The warfare that is waged is sometimes called the sixth pillar of Islam. It is known as *jihad*. Doctors Emir and Irgun Caner both formerly Muslims state that 'Islam does in fact have an essential and indispensable tenet of militaristic conquest at its heart. In both the teachings of the Quran and the Hadith the infidel (Kafir) must either be converted or conquered (in the struggle of) jihad'. They point out that even a cursory reading of the Quran or the Hadith gives evidence of a missiological endeavour to expel or destroy infidels (Surah 3:85). They are to be seized and slain and no friends are to be made of them (Surah 4:89). They are to be regarded as enemies (Surah 4:101). Allah has prepared a humiliating punishment for them (Surah 4:102) and will instill terror into their hearts (Surah 8:12). Therefore they are to be fought against (Surah 9:29). Christianity is seen as a specific enemy of Islam and thus held out for specific scorn in the Quran (Surah 4:171; 5:14, 17, 72-73, 75).[17]

In recent times in the West for reasons of political expediency or correctness, there has been a certain reluctance to examine or even acknowledge the existence and the effects of such activities as if this 'would be a sort of dark stain on the greatness and purity of Islam'.[18] Amnesty International claims that Saudi Arabia (and others) escape international condemnation for human rights abuses because of other countries' dependence on them for oil supplies.[19] Whether it is a matter of political reluctance or innocent ignorance, either way such a lack of knowledge of the fundamentals of Islamic theology and how this undergirds all activities toward the non-Muslim world is something we ignore to our own peril. The meaning and practice of *jihad* changes in explanation and application according to the environment in which it operates.

In its original pre-Islamic sense the word refers to effort, striving or struggling. In some contexts it therefore becomes a figure of speech to illustrate how a believer needs to wage war against his own sinful inclinations as defined within Islam (Surah 9:20). This interpretation of *jihad* is promoted particularly by mystics. This usage and practice is both understandable and innocent in itself within the confines of Islam. Another interpretation of *jihad* emphasises the clash of world views 'in which Islam will ultimately prevail'[20] (Surah 2:190–193).

But these meanings and usages hardly account for the whole. Within the Quran and the Traditions, *jihad* has been established as a religious duty. It is invoked specifically not just for the excision of evil from within individuals or from within the Islamic society. It is also the divinely appointed means for the advancement of the cause of Islam through war against all unbelievers (Surah 8:37–39).

The Holy War as it is known in Islamic Jurisprudence is basically an offensive war. This is the duty of Muslims in every age when the needed military power becomes

> Amnesty International claims that Saudi Arabia (and others) escape international condemnation for human rights abuses because of other countries' dependence on them for oil supplies.

available to them. This is the phase in which the meaning of Holy War has taken its final form. Thus the apostle of God said: 'I was commanded to fight the people until they believe in God and his message....'[21]

From its earliest days the non-Muslim world has been more aware of the military application of *jihad* than of any other meaning associated with the concept, thus Jerusalem was captured by 638 AD. Through military expansion Islam rapidly spread across northern Africa, on to Spain. The advance of the Muslim army was finally arrested between Tours and Poitiers in France, by Charles Martel in 732 AD. Similarly around the other side of the Mediterranean basin Islam expanded to the fall of Constantinople in 1453. All of this in terms of religious allegiances was achieved militarily at the expense of Christianity.

The notion of *jihad* is fired by another fundamental principle, the worldview that believes in the inevitable universality of Islam.[22] Towards this end, the world is divided into two groups, Muslims and non-Muslims, or those who have submitted to the will of Allah and those who continue to resist. Territories where Islamic law governs are known as *dar al-Islam* ie. the house of Islam. Where non-believers, non-Muslims or infidels as they are most commonly known, remain in control, these areas are known as *dar al-harb* ie. the house of war.

Those who inhabit such places are described as *harbis* because they live in territories where either war is being waged or is yet to be waged by whatever means to bring them into submission. Muslims have a sacred duty, an obligation to participate in subduing *dar al-harb* to become *dar al-Islam*. Therefore consistent with Islamic theology Habib Rizieq, chairman of Indonesia's Front Pembela Islam, prior to the 2003 Gulf War could declare 'Every citizen who directly supports the US (specifically Australians and Britons) is considered kafir harbi', an Arabic term for non-Muslims who can be legally killed.[23] Pakistani Maulana Fazl ur-Rahman, Secretary General of the Islamic Muttahida Majlis-i-Amal; Saudi Arabian Ahmed bin Abdullah al-Madi, a professor of Islamic law, Sheikh Faysal Mawlawi, Deputy Chairman for the European Council for Fatwa and Research and many others expressed similar opinions.[24] In a similar vein accused Bali bomber, Imam Samudra, could testify that he felt grateful after seeing the carnage caused by that incident. His gratefulness was that not Muslims but Americans and their allies had been killed because of their involvement in Afghanistan and Australia's 'efforts to separate East Timor from Indonesia which was an international conspiracy by followers of the Cross'.[25]

Muslims believe that all peoples of the world must ultimately submit to the law of Allah as conveyed, interpreted and applied by the prophet Muhammad and his followers. A means for achieving this is *jihad*. The world and all that is in it legitimately belongs only to Allah (Surah 3:180), the Prophet and his followers.

According to Jurisconsult Ibn Taimiya (14ᵗʰ century) the property of non-Muslims must revert legitimately to the sole followers of the true religion (Islam). Consequently the jihad is a means whereby possessions considered illegally usurped by non-Muslims are restored to Muslims. That is why every act of war in the dar al-harb is legal and immune from censure.[26]

Until the entire earth and all of its inhabitants are both returned to the rulership of Allah and acknowledged as such by all, then war must be pursued against those who have yet to submit. Peace is impossible. From time to time for tactical reasons, it may be considered appropriate to pause in advancing the Islamic cause. But this can only ever be a temporary diversion until impediments to advancement have been removed or overcome. To think or act otherwise would be tantamount to denying Quranic teaching, Islamic traditions and history.

If, for political, economic or military reasons, a state of permanent war cannot be overtly or aggressively prosecuted then and only then may a truce be agreed upon (Surah 9:1–5). However according to the model of the Prophet's own example such a truce cannot be maintained beyond ten years. Furthermore at any time during that truce decade it may be unilaterally abrogated whenever the Islamic position becomes favourable to resume an advance. An *imam* is expected to notify the adversary accordingly.

Within these theological constructs the notion of peace is excluded. Objectives of warfare may be postponed but never surrendered. An illustration of the process and how it applies even in contemporary times, is the well documented struggle that has continued for many decades between Jewish settlers and local inhabitants over territory now subdivided into Israeli, Palestinian and Jordanian territories. The ultimate outcome of this struggle is never in doubt to Muslims. It was succinctly expressed by a Muslim merchant in the Old City section of Jerusalem. Overcoming speechless anger he shouted at an Israeli lady 'We will get your country one day!'[27]

In a speech made to South African Muslims, six days after signing the Gaza/Jericho Peace Accord between Palestinian and Israeli authorities, Yasser Arafat, the leader of the PLO faction, challenged his South African co-religionists to declare themselves *mujahuddin* (warriors of the faith) to rejoin *jihad* to regain total Islamic control over Jerusalem. In so doing he was, in his mind, not in any sense being irresponsible or traitorous toward the agreement signed in good faith a few days earlier. Much later in July 2000, when Israeli Prime Minister Ehud Barak made an unprecedented concession to give up virtually all of the West Bank, divide Jerusalem and even to renounce Israeli sovereignty of Judaism's holiest site, the Temple Mount, Arafat declined the offer. With seeming political illogicality but with theological consistency he judged circumstances favoured more the resumption of war than continued peace, hence the Palestinian state controlled media sounded the call to arms. To USA President Clinton and many other world leaders who were calling for negotiations and peace, Arafat replied, 'Our people do not hesitate to march to Jerusalem'.[28] To Barak, Arafat was reportedly even more direct. He told him 'to go to hell'.[29] Barak later commented that for years Arafat talked 'in English about his readiness to make peace and in Arabic about eliminating Israel in stages.'[30]

Former President of Indonesia, Abdurrahman Wahid later revealed that Arafat had told him that 'even if it takes 150 years we'll throw the Jews into the sea'.[31] Later Arafat himself would be even more explicit. On January 27 2002 he publicly declared 'To Jerusalem we will march – millions of martyrs…Al-jihad, al-jihad, al-jihad, al-jihad, al-jihad, al-jihad.' The next day the first Palestinian woman blew herself up in an Israeli restaurant.[32]

Arafat had renounced terrorism in Oslo in 1993. He promised to dismantle Hamas and Islamic *jihad* and to punish those who attacked Israel.[33] But despite this and other commitments Arafat made to renounce violence and terror, he continued to tolerate both, releasing conspirators from jail and glorifying suicide bombers by calling them martyrs.[34]

This was not just because of internal political pressures as Western observers concluded. In adopting this strategy, Arafat was following the practice of the Prophet Muhammad in effecting the Truce of Hudaibiya in 628 AD. At that time, unable to advance and overcome his enemies, Muhammad pledged peace with the Meccans and vowed that it should last at least ten years. But after only two years he unilaterally resumed the offensive by attacking Mecca until he had completely overrun it. During the lead up to the final battle he even refused to meet with delegations from Mecca who were pleading for a resumption of peace and resumption of the truce conditions. Muhammad's strategy has become a model within Islamic law for all agreements with non-Muslim infidels.

With complete Islamic theological consistency, in January 1995 Sheikh Abdel Aziz Bin-Baz as mufti of Saudi Arabia, ruled that according to Islamic law, peace with Israel was allowable but only 'on condition that it is a temporary peace, until

Muslims build up the (military) strength needed to expel the Jews'.[35] Muhammad Sayyid Al-Tantawi, the Sheikh of Egypt's most famous al-Azhar University in a weekly sermon in April 2002 as one of the most significant Sunni Muslim leaders in the world, described Jews as 'the enemies of Allah, descendants of pigs and apes in keeping with Quranic verses (Surah 2:65; 5:63; 7:166).

Tantawi went on to confirm that any suicide attack against any Israeli including child, youth or women was a legitimate act and Islamic duty. Just three months earlier Tantawi had signed an historic agreement with Anglican Archbishop of Canterbury. Dr George Carey at Lambeth Palace to form a joint committee of dialogue pledging to 'encourage religious leaders to use their influence for the purpose of reconciliation and peace making...'.[36]

> For a Muslim peace...implies the extension of...Islam to the entire world...The quest of converting the entire world to Islam is an immutable fixture of the Muslim worldview.

The problem seems to be that many non-Muslim authorities seem to be ignorant, forgetful or to suffer from delusory optimism in negotiating with muslim leaders. The Assyrian born Muslim scholar who claims to be a direct descendent of Muhammad, Professor Bassam Tibi, says the West is gullible.

For a Muslim peace...implies the extension of...Islam to the entire world...The quest of converting the entire world to Islam is an immutable fixture of the Muslim worldview. Only if this task is accomplished – if the world has become Dar al-Islam – will it also be Dar a-Salam, a house of peace.[37]

Toward that objective leaders within Bangladesh's many thousands of madrassas are calling for an expansion of their territory to include northeast India and northern Burma.[38] Indonesian leaders are calling for an enlarged Islamic state embracing not only their country but Malaysia, southern Thailand, southern Philippines and perhaps northern Australia.[39] In Indonesia a manual for Jihad has even been published.[40] Author, Dr Hilmy Bakar Almascaty reminds readers never to work together with the heathen, hypocrites or other enemies of Islam except if they can be used as tools or subordinates. He advises that if the enemy asks for peace that may be made providing conditions favour Islam, based on the historic example of Abu Bashir and Abu Jandal who were companions of Muhammad who waged war on non-Muslim Arabs while Muhammad and the rest of the community was at peace with them. He approves of jihad fighters waging war on non-Muslims even when the majority of the Muslim community is at peace with them. Abu Huraira, a graduate of one of Pakistan's 20 000 madrassas said, 'We believe in the clash of civilizations and our jihad will continue until Islam becomes the dominant religion'. Massoud Ansari reports that these all support the 'concept of *ummah* - an Islamic world without frontiers'.[41]

Western analysts seem to want to ignore the well documented facts of history which demonstrate that Islam's expansion by means of military conquest is not an occasional event but an institutionalised process of normative religious obligation. Egyptian Sayyid Qutb who is regarded as 'one of the major architects and strategists of contemporary Islamic revival', saw *jihad* as 'a mandatory, proactive activity that seeks to establish Allah's sovereignty over the whole earth.'[42] It is an integral part of Islamic missions' *(dawa)* drive for world conquest.

When Islam controls, infidels historically have had one of three choices. They may:

- accept Islam after which their lives and property are spared,
- surrender by a treaty, accepting inferior status and a discriminatory tax,
- be killed by the sword if they are males or be enslaved if they are women or children. For children and often for women too, this has meant forcible conversion to Islam.

The command of the Quran in various passages is quite clear.

When the forbidden months are past, then fight and slay the Pagans wherever ye find them, and seize them, beleaguer them, and lie in wait for them in every stratagem (of war); But if they repent, and establish regular prayers, and pay Zakat then open the way for them; For Allah is Oft-forgiving, Most Merciful (Surah 9:5).

The pursuit of *jihad* is not exclusive to historically normal military means of destruction of property, taking hostages, annihilating or driving out inhabitants as an army advances. It can also be waged by peaceful means through proselytism, propaganda, gratuities paid to 'win over hearts' etc..

With such theological underpinnings non-Muslims need to understand that values and assumptions they bring to negotiating tables or by which they analyse Muslim activities are quite invalid from an Islamic perspective. For Muslims the massacre of enemies is not a heinous crime against humanity. It simply represents victory for Islam. It is not a moral issue at all.

Recent history is replete with Arab expressions of admiration for the holocaust that occurred against Jews in Europe during World War II. When Adolf Eichmann was captured in South America and abducted to Israel in 1961 the banner headline of a Saudi newspaper read, 'Capture of Eichmann who had the Honour of Killing Five Million Jews'.[43]

Similarly, Abu Hassan of the *Islamic Army* having received orders on December 28 1998 to abduct 'Nazarites' (Christians), subsequently killed four foreign hostages in Yemen. At his trial on February 22 1999 he declared he did not feel sorrow for killing any Christians and that he and his group would continue to fight against the (Christian) United States of America and the West because Allah was on his side. (He also said that he would rather die than be defended by a woman.)[44] He 'did not fear the death sentence as it would be martyrdom for Allah's sake'.[45]

A few weeks later, an Islamic group issued a warning through Dubai that the ambassadors of the United States and Britain needed to leave Yemen immediately because they were enemies of Islam. This group was the Aden-Abyan Islamic Army who published their statements through the Saudi owned, London based al-Hayat newspaper.[46] Saudi Islamist leader, Osama bin Laden had two months earlier issued a statement saying it was the duty of Muslims to kill Britons and Americans because they generally supported their leaders' military operations against Iraq.[47] Such expressions and activities while seeming shocking to Western observers are not improper within the Islamic context because they reflect consistency with Islamic theology.

For a Muslim, killing or even dying for the cause of Islam is not only an honour, it is a unique way of pleasing Allah. It is also the only way by which a Muslim, according to Islamic teaching, may have assurance of salvation and a wonderful life in the hereafter of Paradise. Hence, Laskar Jihad, an Indonesian group based in Java, which claimed to have raised 15 000 warriors for war, firstly against non-believers in Indonesia, had a website with a logo of two crossed scimitars and the motto READY TO DIE, and the exhortation 'Never Surrender'. Another website, Hardcore Muslim Hacker Elite (cyber-djihad.net) gave instruction on 'training for jihad in your local country'.[48]

During the Iran/Iraq war of the 1980s when Iranian leader, Ayatollah Khomeini appealed for 10 000 volunteers to fight in that war, within 24 hours even numerous young boys had responded to his appeal. These youths knew in advance that they would not be returning home. Lacking appropriate technology, the practice of Iranian army officers was to use the very bodies of these youths to clear minefields or to short-out high voltage border fences. A note found on the body of one of these young would-be soldier martyrs by the name of Mohseu Naeomi said it all:

My wedding is at the front and my bride is martyrdom. The sermon will be uttered by the roar of the guns. I shall attire myself in my blood for this ceremony. My bride, martyrdom shall give birth to my son, freedom. I leave this son in your safe keeping. Keep him well.[49]

Inspired by the concept of *jihad*, enthused by the prospect of martyrdom, assured through Islamic theology of the certainty of salvation and its sensual rewards beyond this life, this youth went to battle. He died along with at least a million[50] of his contemporaries on both sides of the battle lines. Each believed the declarations of their respective national leaders who somehow persuaded the volunteers to overlook the fact that they were going to fight against fellow Muslims. Two decades later the allure was undiminished. In Azhadkhel Bala, Pakistan, lives trained pharmacist Ijaz Khan Hussein. In October 2001 he went into Afghanistan as a medical orderly to fight alongside the Taliban. Of the 43 men who went with him, 41 were killed. Commenting on this he said:

We went to the jihad filled with joy and I would go again tomorrow. If Allah had chosen me to die I would have been in paradise, eating honey and watermelons and grapes and resting with beautiful virgins, just as it is promised in the Koran. Instead, my fate was to remain amid the unhappiness here on earth.[51]

The call to *jihad* has a powerful capacity to exclude all other rationality. Even the suicide bomber believes that he ascends directly to heaven as a martyr in the holy war against infidels.

Islam forbids suicides…It prefers to speak of martyrdom operations. After a bombing…the gathering is not a funeral but a celebration, a kind of wedding with God. Visitors approach the bereaved parents with the murmur of Mubruk or Congratulations and are offered sweets.[52]

When Ibn Omar Muhammad, a volunteer commander in the Popular Defence Force of (northern) Sudan was killed, his family did not hold a funeral. They celebrated a wedding. The corpse was the bridegroom and the virgins of paradise were the brides.[53]

On October 6 1981 at a military parade in Cairo, four army personnel assassinated President Sadat of Egypt. The lieutenant in charge of the hit squad shouted out, 'I am Khalid al-Islambuli. I have killed Pharaoh and I do not fear death'.[54] All the assassins were members of an underground movement appropriately named Jihad. They were led by Abdul Salam Faraj. They validated their action by declaring Sadat's regime as un-Islamic thus making it a lawful duty to kill its leader. Islambuli's diary entry of 3 September 1984 summed it up: 'The greatest good for the believer is in killing or being killed in the name of God.'[55]

Explaining the zeal of Iranian Muslims, one commentator noted, 'the desire for martyrdom is translated into boldness and competition for it'.[56] It was also certainly no idle boast when Muhammad Taki Moudarrissi, an Islamic Amal leader claimed, 'I can, in one week, assemble 500 faithful ready to throw themselves into suicide operations. No one will stop them'.[57]

The immediate effects of militarily successful *jihad* are usually traumatic in the extreme for any conquered people.

From 652 AD, until its final conquest centuries later, Nubia was forced to send slaves to Cairo.

In 781 AD, when Ephesus was taken, 7000 Greeks were deported.

In 903 AD, when Thessaloniki was overrun, 22 000 Christians were sold into slavery.

In 1064, Seljuk Sultan Alp Arslan devastated Georgia and Armenia destroying property and either killing or removing entire populations.

In 1144/45, Zangi overran Edessa. 6000 adults were killed and 10 000 youth were enslaved.

In the thirteenth century, the Mamaluk rulers of Egypt similarly devastated Armenia/Cilicia. The town of Sis was obliterated. 22 000 of its inhabitants were killed. [58]

The military advance of Islam into Europe in more recent times was only halted by means of superior force at Vienna in 1683.

Probably the best documented process of relentless *jihad* concerns what happened to the Armenians. Seljuk Turks ravished Armenia in approximately 1050. Christians moved to the Taurus of southwestern Anatolia. But the Byzantine overlords who controlled that area were defeated by advancing Muslim armies in 1071. Turkish Muslims then obliged the Armenians of Anatolia to become subject to several emirates. Other Armenians were able to escape to live under Russian authority.

Regardless of the authority under which Christian Armenians lived they were often regarded as a threat to Muslim authority.

Eventually Sultan Abdul Hamid II (1876–1909) was obliged to sign the Treaty of San Stefano which ostensibly provided some relief for Armenians living in Muslim dominated areas. The Sultan however was not about to forsake historic Muslim theology or practice. He engineered the movement of large numbers of refugees into the Armenian areas to seize their land and increase pressure upon local inhabitants to move out. It is estimated that during 1894–96 as many as 200 000 Armenians were exterminated in Mesopotamia. In 1909, 30 000 were killed in Adana.

When western Europe was preoccupied with World War I, the Turkish government determined to liquidate the Armenian problem[59] just as Hitler would attempt to do to Jews a couple of decades later. In 1915, 1.5 million Armenian Christians in territories under Turkish control were eliminated.[60] Two hundred and fifty thousand Assyrian Christians were also killed.[61] The entire male population over twelve years of age in central Armenia were all exterminated. Women and children were driven out into the desert of Dayr al-Zur between Syria and Iraq. They were robbed, raped and finally slaughtered by Kurdish tribes. Some escaped death by enslavement and forced conversion to Islam. Although the deportation, enslavement, forced conversion and massacres are chronicled by Muslim and other sources,[62] in November 2000 the Turkish government was still insisting that the events of 1915 were internal matters which should not be investigated by others and that all that had happened were 'civil strife' events.[63] However these and other well-documented facts of history may be categorised, the end result will probably be the same. In 1997 Father Dimitrios was of the opinion that 'after fifteen hundred years the Ecumenical Patriarch will have to leave Constantinople because there would be none left in his community to minister to.'[64]

The ferocity of Serbian atrocities against Muslims in Kosovo in 1999 although inexcusable, must be understood against the background of history. Western memory is increasingly abbreviated to whatever was on the last television news bulletin. But Serbs remembered that on Kosovo Field a few miles north of modern day Pristina, on 28 June 1389 their leader Prince Lazar was captured and beheaded by invading Turkish Muslim armies. Their 'state was effectively annihilated' on that date.[65] For three centuries, Christian families were compelled to surrender their children to be Islamised and trained for the Ottoman Empire's administration and military service.[66] On June 28 1989 1–2 million Serbs gathered to commemorate their six hundredth anniversary of the battle in 1389 and what Islam had done to them. When Kosovo was placed under an externally imposed 'peace', pressure was again applied to rid the province of Christian presence.[67] The United Nations took control of Kosovo in June 1999. By November 2002 at least 110 Serb Christian sites were either damaged or destroyed.[68]

The same techniques have been used in Sudan. And the longer term outcome will probably be similar. Young non-Muslim children have been captured in slave raids by militias armed by the Khartoum Government. Often through starvation and beatings they were indoctrinated at *khalwas* – strict religious schools until they became Muslim. With time, they were so completely changed that they could be then used in Muslim militias against their own people.[69]

Such activities have not been isolated phenomena. Even with access to significant numbers of official documents that are still

> The arrival of Islam inevitably has resulted in the destruction of pre-existing cultures and where non-compliant, of pre-existing indigenous peoples.

available, it is impossible to calculate the number of non-Muslims who have been enslaved or exterminated over the centuries. The arrival of Islam inevitably has resulted in the destruction of pre-existing cultures and where non-compliant, of pre-existing indigenous peoples. In February 2001 the US Commission on International Religious Freedom received testimony on Indonesian Muslim officials destroying historical records of Christianity in that region.[70] 'The process of total Islamisation of captured territories from behind the new borders has continued uninterrupted over the centuries whereby Dar al Harb became Dar al Islam.'[71]

Dr Amir Ali in a paper 'Jihad Explained' published by the Institute of Islamic Information & Education claims 'that Islam does not teach, nor do Muslims desire, conversion of any people for fear, greed, marriage or any other form of coercion.' He claims that Islam in its military operations may be carried out by leaders who see potential dangers ahead of time and that 'the mission of the Prophet Muhammad was to free people from tyranny and exploitation by oppressive systems. Once free, individuals in the society were then free to choose Islam or not.'[72] Doubtless those who have been on the other side of the sword might be more in agreement with Patriarch Siphronius of Jerusalem (634–638AD) who upon encountering the

Islamic invaders described them as 'godless barbarians who burnt churches, destroyed monasteries, profaned crosses and horribly blasphemed against Christ and the Church.'[73]

Where direct military confrontation is inadvisable, contemporary Islam resorts to other methodologies to pursue its objectives. Some of these include:

a. Propaganda

Free booklets and copies of the Quran have been widely distributed as aids to influence 'reversion' to Islam in targeted Western and other currently non-Islamic countries.

While Islam is positively promoted, that which is non-Islamic is caricatured through demeaning stereotypes. In this way values, practices and lifestyles of the non-Muslim world are recast to be the enemies of humanity. Any modernising or secularising state even if it is friendly to the Islamic world is a target for such propaganda treatment. This was so for the Pahlavi dynasty of Iran (1925–1979) for the government of President Sadat of Egypt and for Kemalist Turks.

The closing declaration of the representatives of the 55 member countries of the Organisation of Islamic Countries (OIC) of December 11 1997 expressed concern about non-Muslim tendencies to portray Islam as a threat. They declared they would portray Islam as historically grounded in peaceful co-existence, cooperation and mutual understanding amongst civilisations! That was certainly their position and the publicly stated position of various Western leaders immediately after the September 11 2001 bombings, but it is hardly the record of history.

b. Political Processes

Where Muslims are present in significant numbers they have been encouraged to join the political process with the objective of the adoption of or return to Islamic law, the *shariah*.

Political and military commands have been unified, eg. in Pakistan and Indonesia. This has facilitated state instrumentalities such as military and police forces which are supposed to protect citizens during disturbances but in practice they have combined against Christian populations as was the case in various Indonesian disturbances in 1999–2000.[74]

The non-Muslim world was to be portrayed as being oppressive, manipulative and exploitative. The world conquest by Islam and the supremacy of Islamic law have been declared as the only way to overcome non-Muslim civilisations. What remains is to be integrated into full Islamic statehood.

c. Social engineering

In many Muslim countries there exist small wealthy Westernised elites. Resentment has been stirred against these by associating them with colonialism and the history of the (Christian) West's treatment of Muslim indigenes. They have been also accused of holding non-Islamic values and of pursuing non-Islamic processes. Whether Islam is in the majority or the minority, anything non-Islamic is to be opposed. Hamza al-Masri, a Muslim cleric, has stated that the very principle of democracy is hostile to God. 'Elections and dialogues only serve to ensnare us (Islamists). Democracy is deceptive, dangerous and unworkable...All over the world the twin evils of freedom and democracy have wreaked havoc with people's lives.'[75]

d. Demographic Change

In the last 40 years Islamic centres have been established in great numbers in non-Muslim countries to take advantage of those countries' liberal freedom of religion laws. These centres become bases from which to operate. Conversions are sought by encouraging Muslim men to marry local non-Muslim women. Immigration has been actively encouraged from Muslim to non-Muslim countries.

In some Muslim countries where appropriate, transmigration has been practised. Muslims are moved into non-Muslim areas. In the latter part of the twentieth century in Bangladesh, Muslims were moved into northern and eastern Bangladesh, forcing non-Muslims across the border into India. In a similar way Islam was introduced to Papua by the Indonesian government. In the same country on the majority Christian island of Ambon, after a decade of supported 'infiltration' to the point where Muslims from Sulawesi controlled the channels of government authority and trade, Christians reacted.[76]

When 200 homes of Christians were destroyed on Christmas Day 1998, at first Christians did not respond. But by the next month violent action and reaction by both Christian and Muslim communities had commenced. By May 2000 thousands of trained Laskar Jihad warriors arrived in the area armed with equipment available only to the Indonesian military. On May 23 the *jihad* plan to eliminate all Christians over the age of twelve in Ambon, Sulawesi, the Mulaccas and Papua was revealed.[77]

Similar transmigrations have been followed in East Malaysia with similar reactions. Further east, Madurese Muslims moved into west Kalimantan to wrest control of the local economy and politics from Christian Dyaks.[78]

Islamic leaders are aware that historically whenever it has entered into a new theatre of operations, it has always commenced from a minority position. But with time and determination Islam has triumphed. What is today known as Pakistan is a good example.

Islam first arrived in the region in 710 AD when Sind and southern Punjab were conquered by Umayyad Arab general, Muhammad bin Qasim. He introduced Islamic law. During 1000–1026 Mahmud of Gazni extended Islamic control further eastward through military expeditions. The Delhi Sultanate (1206–1526) and the Mughal rulers (1526–1858) consolidated Islamisation. Britain (1848–1948) protected Islam's status while at the same time discouraging Christian missionary activity.

In 1948 Britain agreed to create a separate Muslim state to be known as Pakistan, by partitioning from India its northwest provinces and by dividing Bengal. In the east, East Bengal became East Pakistan. After a civil war in 1971 this province became Bangladesh. In 1990 Nawaz Sharif, Prime Minister of Pakistan, 'introduced controversial legislation to make Islamic law, the *shariah*, paramount'.[79] After 1280 years the process was well nigh complete. All that remained was to mop up a rapidly diminishing non-Islamic presence.

e. Terrorism

This has been a means employed particularly against states that might be immediately adjacent to or hostile toward current Islamic states. As a means it has been supported by Iran, Iraq, Syria, Libya, Afghanistan and other places. Some regarded Afghanistan as the 'womb of global *jihad*'.[80] Amal, Hamas, Hezballah (Palestine), Abu Sayeff (Philippines), Laskar Jihad (Indonesia), the Muslim Brotherhood (Egypt), GIA and FIS (Algeria), Mujahuddin and Taliban (Afghanistan), Harakat ul Ansar, HUA (India and Pakistan), Al-Muhajiroun (UK), al Qaeda (internationally) and others have become household names around the world.

What non-Muslims may regard as repugnant can be legally and morally acceptable under Islamic laws of *jihad*. Thus hostages may become military assets. If properly managed they can benefit the ongoing struggle against those who have yet to submit. Breaking treaties with infidel states, if beneficial for Islam, is legal. The summary execution of captured enemy soldiers is entirely legal. Indonesian Abu Bakar Bashir accused of heading Jemaah Islamiah said 'All Ulamas (Muslim leaders) agree with martyrs' bombs...In Islam there is no word for hands up. There is no word for surrender; there are only two things, win or die.'[81]

Where the values of combatants hold so little in common, international covenants which may apply through the Geneva Conventions or rulings by the United Nations and its subsidiary bodies from the Islamic perspective are inapplicable, inadmissible, inappropriate and irrelevant. In such an all-encompassing ongoing war, civilians are regarded as active enemy assets simply because they are not yet Muslim.

The resurgence of contemporary Islam even in its more violent expressions is hardly a passing phenomenon. Its methodologies are well documented and demonstrated through

> Although the vast majority of Islam's followers desire nothing more than peace and prosperity yet because of theological imperatives a state of war must remain until all submit.

14 centuries of its own recorded theology, history and cultural transitions. The vast majority of Islam's followers desire nothing more than peace and prosperity yet because of theological imperatives a state of war must remain until all submit. Nurulla, a student at Markaz-e-Islami seminary near Peshawar Pakistan, commenting on the latest list of 'martyrs', summed it up for many when he said, *'Jihad'* will continue until doomsday...'.[82]

In June 2003 when multiparty negotiations were once more underway between Palestinians and Israelis, Hamas leader, Ismail Abu Shanab surprisingly agreed to a ceasefire and its implication of lasting peace. When asked to comment whether Hamas' unexpected gesture really implied recognition of a peace plan and an ultimate two state solution he reportedly replied, "If you like, yes...This is satisfactory for the time being."[83] In so saying he was being precisely consistent with historical Islamic practice and theology. There may be temporary pauses, setbacks or even withdrawals for strategic reasons, but apparently the hoped for end is seldom doubted.

Islam remains a religion whose followers believe that Allah requires them to send their sons to die for him. Christianity is a faith that believes God sent his Son to die for us.

CHAPTER 17

OPTIMISED OPPRESSION

1998 was the fiftieth anniversary of the United Nations Declaration of Human Rights. Article 18 lists a number of freedoms considered definitive for human existence. But many of these self-evident rights are still non-existent for non-Muslims living in Muslim countries. The situation in Pakistan is a case in point.

Most Christians in Pakistan are poor, despised and suffer from institutionalised discrimination and abuse. They are consigned the lowest, dirtiest and most dangerous jobs. They are exploited by powerful land owners. They are frequently evicted from their homes. They are victimised by the police and the law courts. They are discriminated against in the education system. The Christian faith is ridiculed and misrepresented in the media. Women are often abducted, raped and may be forced to marry their abductor. They live in fear of the infamous blasphemy law with its mandatory death sentence which is often employed against them for little other than personal gain by their accusers.[1]

One international survey has concluded that 'of the 41 countries whose population is at least 70% Muslim 26 are considered not free and 13 are considered only partly free.'[2]

By April 1999 a Swiss human rights group, Christian Solidarity International (CSI) had freed 1783 slaves in Sudan. To buy their freedom CSI paid US$50 per head to the Islamic Government in Khartoum. Those enslaved had resisted forced conversion to Islam.[3]

Human rights as defined by the United Nations Charter are denied to citizens in Islamic Jurisdictions. Only rights sanctioned by Allah as ratified by the Quran are acceptable except where it is to Islamic advantage to argue otherwise. When Muslims in Melbourne, Australia, determined to establish a mosque in an area which local government authorities had already ruled as being unsuitable, they appealed to the Human Rights and Equal Opportunity Commissioner. Australian Islamic Association president Ali Altunsoy 'denied his community was breaking the law. He accused the local government of interfering with rights to practise religion freely.' He declared, '...we didn't decide to practise in the mosque at these times. It is a decision from God...not anyone can change that.'[4]

Back in 1948, when the original United Nation's Charter of Human Rights was being debated, Charles Malek the Lebanese delegate and a prominent Christian, insisted on inserting a clause that guaranteed freedom of religion and worship. Muslim delegates objected. But Mr Malek having lived in close proximity to Muslims all his life knew better than Western delegates. Half a century later things are hardly changed. Edicts of the Quran are not likely to be overturned by those of the United Nations.

'If anyone desires a religion other than Islam (submission to Allah) never will it be accepted of him; and in the Hereafter he will be in the ranks of those who have lost' (Surah 3:85). As if to enforce the point Iran, Qatar, Saudi Arabia and Sudan legislated the death penalty for any who wish to change from belief in Islam to any other religion. In 1981 UNESCO was used to proclaim the universal Islamic Declaration of Human Rights. In August 1990 at the 19th Islamic Conference of Foreign Ministers of the then 45 OIC countries the Cairo Declaration on Human Rights in Islam (CDHRI) was adopted. In the document Article 25 confirms that *shariah* 'is the only source of reference for the explanation or clarification of this Declaration'. Thus its supremacy over all other UN covenants or universal instruments was declared. In December 1991 Adama Dieng, a Muslim Senegalese jurist of the International Commission of Jurists judged that the CDHRI Declaration introduced intolerable discrimination against both non-Muslims and women.[5]

Whenever Islam gains control of any people those people are confronted with a choice. They may choose:

- to submit and become Muslims
- to die by the sword or suffer enslavement
- to continue to live as second class citizens discriminated against for life.

With Islamic conquest, 'populations change status (they become *dhimmis*) and the Islamic law (the *shariah*) tends to be put into effect integrally, overthrowing the former law of the country'.[6]

Jihad is the first phase of Islamisation of conquered peoples. The second phase is *dhimma*, the government of conquered peoples whereby a complex political, economic, religious and cultural process is initiated to replace totally any vestiges of pre-Islamic culture or religion. It is a relentless process that may take centuries.[7]

The precedence for the practice was established by Muhammad's example at the oasis of Khaybar. He attacked the oasis in 628AD, had leaders tortured to find hidden treasure and when the Jews surrendered he agreed to allow them to continue cultivation provided half their produce was given to him. Muhammad also retained the right to cancel this treaty and expel anyone whenever he liked. This treaty was called a 'dhimma' and those who accepted it were known as 'dhimmis'. This established the principle in which protection money would be paid by all non-Muslims to conquering Muslims. The practice was codified in a summarisation known as the 'Pact of Umar' concluded in the eighth century under Umar b. Abdal-Aziz who ruled during 717-720AD.[8]

In February 638AD after a 12 month siege by Muslim armies, Jerusalem was obliged to surrender. As Patriarch Sophronius handed over the keys of the city to Caliph Omar, through his tears he murmured, 'Behold the abomination of desolation spoken of by Daniel the Prophet'.[9]

To many non-Muslims who have lived in Islamic countries that gloomy assessment may still seem true.

In May 1998 65 year old Dr John Joseph, Bishop of Faisalabad in Pakistan committed suicide in an attempt to bring to the attention of the world the relentless pressure on and discrimination against his fellow Christians in that country. More than 200 of them had been sentenced to death in recent times after being accused of blasphemy ie. criticism of Islam in some form.[10] The Bishop regarded his death as a 'sacrificial protest' against the victimisation of Christians under Pakistan's controversial blasphemy laws.[11] How could a bishop of the church be driven to this ultimate action?

Naimat Ahmer, a Punjabi scholar was employed by the Pakistani government as a school headmaster. Some of the Muslim teachers resented the fact that a Christian was supervising them. One day as he walked out of his office with a group of friends, a Muslim attacked him. He chopped the headmaster to pieces. His throat was cut so severely that his head was practically removed…Naimat was dead before he hit the ground. The man who killed him yelled, 'I have rid the world of this evil…' When the assassin was jailed people came from all around to lay garlands and flowers at his cell because they thought of him as a great hero.[12]

The Quran says:

Fight against such as those who have given the Scripture as believe not in Allah nor in the Last Day, and forbid not that which Allah hath forbidden by His messenger and follow not the religion of truth, until they pay their tribute (jizyah) readily being brought low (Surah 9:29)(Pickthall's Translation).[13] *Fight those who do not believe in Allah until they pay Jizya with willing submission and feel themselves subdued. (Abdullah Ysuf Ali's translation).*[14]

The result of successful *jihad* is *dhimmitude* for the survivors. Religious apartheid that discriminates severely is put into effect.

Lieutenant General Omar al-Bashir, President of Sudan, summed up the general attitude and teaching of the Quran toward non-Muslims when he said, 'How do you expect us to introduce equality when inequality is the will of God?' In his country buying and selling non-Muslim slaves has been officially tolerated. Selling them into freedom became punishable by death.[15] Official 'inequality' represents an accurate and honest reflection of classical Islamic teaching. Muslim women are not equal with Muslim men. No non-Muslim is considered equal to any Muslim.

In the Gulf War of 1991 King Fahd of Saudi Arabia reportedly called together 350 Muslim theologians to consider whether or not it was allowable for Muslims to be defended by non-Muslims. One Egyptian theologian answered, 'If a Moslem is attacked by a murderer he can be defended by an unclean dog – so why not by a foreigner?'[16]

While there are variations in practice among Muslim states and even within single states, the effects of *dhimmitude* on non-Muslims has often been devastating. Muslim authorities place severe restrictions upon all non-Muslim religions. Worship by Christians and Jews (Peoples of the Book) may be permitted but with wide-ranging limitations. The propagation of any non-Muslim religion is disallowed. The construction of new churches, convents and synagogues is normally forbidden. Restoration of pre-Islamic places of worship may be permitted but these are not to be enlarged. Obtaining permission is extremely difficult. In Egypt until 1998, this permission could only be given by the President himself. It is virtually impossible to obtain.[17] It is more usual for non-Muslim places of worship to be demolished than restored. In Sudan, in one Episcopal diocese there were previously 586 places of worship. By 1998 only one remained.[18] In 2002 the Indonesian province of Aceh declared *shariah* law. By September of that year 17 churches had been closed and destroyed depriving more than 10 000 Christians of their places of worship.[19]

Another common practice has been converting churches into mosques. There may be prohibitions against the use of bells, burials, ceremonies and further construction. Churches may be pillaged or confiscated. The import of Bibles is often prevented. The wearing of crosses, the placement of Christmas trees and the postage of cards may be restricted. In Saudi Arabia not only do such practices attract arrest of the offender but a Christian is not even permitted to be buried within its borders. The chronicles of history are filled with the details of religious harassment by Islam of those who decline to submit.

For six centuries, from 1266 onwards, Jews and Christians were denied access to the cave of Machpelah in Hebron, burial place of the Hebrew patriarchs. Then in 1862 the Prince of Wales was permitted one such visit. However Jews continued to be forbidden to visit the shrine until after the Six Day War of 1967 when the Jewish army recaptured control of the territory. For seven centuries they were denied access to one of their more holy places.[20]

In Indonesia 131 churches were attacked in the period 1995–1997. This continued an accelerating national trend that had been developing since independence in 1945,[21] as the following table demonstrates.

1945–1954	no churches attacked
1955–1964	2 churches attacked
1965–1974	46 churches attacked
1975–1984	89 churches attacked
1985–1994	132 churches attacked.[22]

The trend of church destruction greatly accelerated during the interreligious disturbances of 1998–2000 (in which Christians were not blameless either). 1 January 2001 saw four more churches targeted for bombing in central Sulawesi, and the province of Aceh declared Sharia Law.[23]

Muhammad Bashrie, the head of Indonesia's Ulema's national board called for *jihad* from March 1998 onwards. This created instability and a most uncertain future into the next century.[24] Ja'far Umar Talib trained at an international jihad university in Lahore, Pakistan. From his modest house in Yogyakarta he formed the 10 000 strong Laskar Jihad whose insertion into the Malaku islands directly resulted in fighting which caused thousands to be killed. He is on record as declaring, 'Islam is the highest religion and the best...There is no way to get respect from non-Muslims for Muslims except through *jihad'*.[25]

Professor Bassam Tibi, a Syrian political scientist, thought the best country in which to pursue a Muslim–Christian dialogue on the subject of human rights was

Indonesia. There was 'genuine tolerance for different religions in this overwhelming Muslim society!'[26] United Nations and other investigations after East Timor gained independence in 1999 clearly showed otherwise.

In West Sumatra, Salmon and Lisa Ongirwalu agreed to accommodate a young woman who had become a Christian. Rev. Robert Marthinus allowed her to enrol in the high school of which he was Principal. Rev. Yanuardi Koto thought such help would be appropriate. In 1999, Koto was sentenced to seven years in jail. Marthinus received a six year sentence. Ongirwalu's sentence was increased to ten years after he appealed against his eight year sentence. The wives of Salmon and Marthinus along with the secretary of the local church Yenni Mendrofa were all sentenced to six years. This is the contemporary reality in a Muslim country of 'genuine tolerance'.[27] In Jordan *shariah* law applies. Therefore when Siham Qandah's Muslim brother-in-law applied to the court for guardianship over his deceased brother's children to bring them up as Muslims rather than Christians as they had been to date, the courts ordered Siham to surrender them or face imprisonment.[28]

In the period 1990–1993, 329 Christians were arrested in Saudi Arabia. Some were flogged. All were deported for the 'crimes' such as praying together, possessing Bibles, pictures of Jesus, rosaries or tapes of hymns.[29] Saudi Law and response remain unchanged.

Despite the Quranic injunction that there should be no compulsion in religion (Surah 2:256) conversions to Islam have been frequently forced. In Yemen until the Jewish exodus to Israel in 1950, Jewish orphans were removed by law from the families of relatives and brought up as Muslims. The same has continued for many years in East Africa with the abduction of Christian children. In the Armenian massacres of the nineteenth and twentieth centuries, Christians converted to Islam to avoid execution.

Not only are there religious implications for non-Muslims, there are other matters which are equally restrictive. Almost without exception non-Muslims are forbidden significant public office. Were they to achieve such it would mean that a non-Muslim could exercise authority over a Muslim. This is not allowed. The same principle applies to employment. Non-Muslims are not to hold management positions. Again this would give infidels authority over Muslims. 'There is no authority of the infidels over the Muslims…In addition a non-Muslim should be humiliated as an infidel.'[30]

In Saudi Arabia Muslim workers asked authorities to give a ruling on the question of whether or not it was permissible for a Muslim company owner to appoint a Christian who would have authority over them. On February 5 1993 Sheikh Mannaa

K. al-Qubtan, professor of higher studies in the School of Sharia, Dr Saleh Al-Sadlan, a professor at the same school and Dr Fahd Al-Oseimi, professor of Islamic studies in Riyadh all ruled that not only was it not permissible to appoint a Christian as a manager over Muslims based on Surah 4:140 but that the Christian should be removed from his job immediately a suitable replacement was found. The other guiding principle in the ruling was that a 'Muslim is honest whereas a non-Muslim is dishonest and does not fear Allah'.[31] In 2003 it was reported that a Muslim Lebanese army conscript shot his fellow army conscript who was a Christian for religious reasons. He later put a question to his Sheikh, 'Isn't it our duty to kill infidels, Christians?' The Sheikh replied, 'Yes. But now is not the time because we have to finish with the Jews first.'[32] Even shared communal hardships do not diminish these theologically based attitudes. In the detention centre for illegal immigrants in Woomera, Australia, Amnesty International gathered reports of Muslim Afghan and Iraqi males stoning, assaulting, sexually harassing, abusing and defecating upon non-Muslim inmates.[33]

> Almost without exception non-Muslims are forbidden significant public office. Were they to achieve such it would mean that a non-Muslim could exercise authority over a Muslim. This is not allowed.

In a sample of Egyptian office holders taken in 1998 it was found that among the nation's 28 governors, its hundreds of city mayors, its 15 university presidents, 300 deans of higher institutes, highest ranking positions in the police and security forces, in the most powerful positions in the media there was not a single office holder who was a Christian.[34] The Christian population of Egypt is officially estimated at 6% and unofficially up to 20%.[35]

In the practice of law, evidence against a Muslim by a non-Muslim is unacceptable. The validity of the non-Muslims' oath is not accepted because they are regarded as of perverse character in that they have denied the superiority of Islam.[36] A Muslim cannot be put to death for murdering a non-Muslim. He may pay blood feud money to the family of the murdered man. However if a Muslim kills another Muslim then he may be killed himself.[37]

In 1964 a law enacted in Pakistan decreed that the witness of a Christian man would be equal to that of half of a Muslim. The witness of a Christian woman would be equal to a quarter of that of a Muslim man.

Nageena, as a seven year old Pakistani Christian girl was raped at 11.30 one morning as she walked home from a friend's house. A crowd of witnesses who gathered around the cowshed saw the four men who did it. Shekhupura hospital confirmed immediately afterwards that the girl's internal injuries were so severe she would never bear children. Nageena's parents filed a case with the police. Dozens of witnesses confirmed who the culprits were. The four men were eventually arrested but later released because 'the police could find no evidence against them'. As far as Nageena's attackers were concerned 'her religion made her worthless, vulnerable and unlikely to be believed…in a judicial system in which the word of a Muslim is worth more than that of a Christian.'[38]

Nineteen months later Nageena's father, Ghulam, was arrested and charged with the murder of an elderly woman. Villagers declared Ghulam had been working in the fields with them at the time of the alleged murder. The men who brought the accusations were his daughter's rapists. The process of Ghulam's imprisonment and maltreatment was supervised by Inspector Mustaq Ahmed, the same officer who released the rapists. Inspector Ahmed told reporters that those accused of rape were good Muslims whom he therefore had no reason to disbelieve. But Ghulam was a Christian. 'My first duty is to Islam. The courts will take a similar view and Ghulam will be hanged. You'll see.'[39]

As the Quran exhorts to *bring low* or subdue those who are non-Muslim, personal denigration has often been employed. Historically, many Muslim cities have been divided into various quarters. Non-Muslims may be confined to live in smaller, lower, shabbier houses than Muslims. In some cases they have not been permitted to own possessions. Honorific titles have been disallowed.

Often non-Muslims have been obliged not to use camels or horses but only donkeys for transport. Up until the seventeenth century at the approach of a Muslim, non-Muslims were obliged to dismount even from their donkeys or suffer being thrown to the ground. In some countries non-Muslims have been obliged to walk with lowered eyes, to pass to the left of a Muslim, the impure side, or to remain standing in the presence of a Muslim. Even in the twentieth century in Iran and Yemen the doors of non-Muslim homes had to be low so that they would have to bow or knock their heads. Jews in Yemen were locked in their quarters at nightfall until 1950.

Personal invective has been habitually targeted at non-Muslim peoples. They are shamed by negative images. Christians have been commonly called pigs while Jews are associated with apes or dogs. As a Jewish beard was regarded as defiling to an executioner's sword, so in Cairo therefore Jews were hanged. A well-known formal curse is, 'May God curse me like a Jew...' In Morocco a traditional belief is that if a Jew enters the house of a Muslim the angels will depart from it for 40 days.[40]

In sexual relationships a Muslim man could marry a *dhimmi* woman. A Muslim man can marry an already married Christian woman. Automatically the Christian marriage is dissolved. No non-Muslim man can ever marry a Muslim woman. In Malaysia in 1997, when Nor'aishah Bokhari, a 25 year old former Muslim woman wanted to marry Joseph Lee, a Christian, she was imprisoned by her family for 41 days. The police were also involved. On December 30 Bokhari escaped and went into hiding with Lee.[41]

Muslim authorities have exploited non-Muslim minorities financially by enforced payment of a capitation tax *(jizyah)*. This is in keeping with the Quranic injunction to humble or subdue them (Surah 9:29). This concession, an alternative to death or enslavement, applied originally only to Jews and Christians but it was later expanded to include Zoroastrians and other minority faiths of central and southern Asia.

Throughout the Middle Ages it was compulsory for *dhimmies* to wear the *jizyah* receipt around the neck or on the chest or wrist. To be caught without this receipt automatically invoked the death penalty. In the Ottoman Empire, it was either produced on demand or immediate imprisonment of the offender was effected.

The essential feature of the constantly changing process of *dhimmitude* has always been to ensure the inferiority of the non-Muslim. Through humiliation and pressure brought to bear by whatever means, it is intended that *dhimmies* will ultimately understand the ignorance of their ways and accept the enlightenment of Islam. Likewise this acts as a disincentive against Muslims adopting other faiths.

Hamas is one of the politico-military religious organisations active for many years mostly within the Middle East theatre of conflict. One of their objectives has been the annihilation of all Jews and of Israel. One of their all time heroes is the famous Muslim general, Saladin. He inflicted defeat upon those medieval marauders known as the Crusaders. Hamas spokesmen say, '*jihad*...is the only way to liberate Palestine. There is no solution to the Palestinian question except through *jihad*. There is no doubt about the testimony of history.'[42] In their last assertion they are certainly quite accurate. *Jihad* and the relentless process of *dhimmitude* which inevitably follows victory continues apace in their part of the world.

The Palestinian Authority (PA) in their Basic Law in Article 4b states that the principles of Islamic *shariah* are to be 'the main source of legislation'.[43] An Israeli government report reprinted in the international edition of the Jerusalem Post claimed that Christians who, since 1995, came under the jurisdiction of the Palestinian Authority also quickly came under increasing pressure. Their cemeteries were vandalised and their churches robbed.[44]

Much was made of Bethlehem millennial celebrations. This was good for international propaganda as well as for attracting tourist dollars. But inevitably after the tourists depart the locals know what awaits them. In 1968 there were five mosques in Bethlehem. By 1998 there were 72. Building continues apace. In Bethlehem on Christmas Eve and Christmas Day, Christians often stay indoors for fear of abuse, although for international media consumption, on such Christian festival days President Arafat frequently appears at Christian functions. The locals know day to day reality is different for Christians living under Muslim 'protection'. Muslims preach anti-Christian messages over their mosques' loud speakers with impunity. Under constant Muslim pressure, the Christian population of this once most Christian of centres has fallen from 80% to 30% in the last half of the twentieth century.[45] Palestinian Christian, Abe Ata, concluded that Christians are treated with suspicion in the Arab world in general, and in Bethlehem, they 'are subject to the indignities heaped upon (them) as a subject population'.[46]

During the twentieth century across the region of the Middle East, the number of Christians in the entire population dropped from 11.6% to 3.5%. This has come about not just through Christians emigrating for economic advantage but also to escape the pressure of being second class citizens, pressure to convert to Islam and more prolific growth patterns in Muslim families. If the present trend continues there will be virtually no church left in the Middle East by 2040.[47]

On the subject of diminishing Christian populations, the Conference of Catholic Patriarchs and Bishops in the Middle East issued a statement from their General Assembly of May 9–20 1999. In it they requested that Muslims reassure 'Christians that they are (still) an integral part of national society, with all that implies by way of both enjoying rights and bearing responsibilities.' The President of the Higher Shi'ite Council in Lebanon, the Imam Shaykh Muhammad Mahdi Shams-ud-Din, took exception to the phraseology. In reply he declared that 'Muslims are not involved in a political act; they are fulfilling a religious commitment springing out of their faith and based upon Quranic revelation.'[48] Quite so. And in as much as history can be a reliable guide the trend of diminished Christian presence in Muslim countries is bound to continue.

What is happening in the previously Christian centre of Bethlehem is typical of what has happened and continues to happen wherever Islam controls or seeks to control. For example in the Israeli town of Nazareth, the childhood town of Jesus, the population in 1999 was approximately 65% Muslim. In April 1999 Muslims used their numerical superiority to press new demands for religio-cultural advantage. They rioted and demanded that a mosque be built adjacent to the Christian Basilica of the Annunciation. The city authorities had planned a small park for the site which would have also incorporated a tomb of a revered Muslim, Shihab-al-Din. But having illegally occupied some of the site and erecting a 'temporary' mosque, made from a tent, the local Islamic religious ruling body then wanted the tent replaced by a permanent mosque. The more zealous wanted a five storey, four minaret mosque. Moderates would settle for one that would have a minaret taller than the church's steeple.[49]

> During the twentieth century across the region of the Middle East the number of Christians in the entire population dropped from 11.6% to 3.5%.

Unless their demand was met they threatened to prevent any millennium celebrations (by Christians) in the town.[50] 'Christians are more our enemies than the Jews,' declared one protestor.[51] On March 3 2002 the Israeli cabinet ratified an earlier Court decision and ordered a permanent halt to the construction of the mosque. Nazareth's deputy mayor, Salmon Abu Ahmed immediately responded declaring, 'We refuse the decision totally. We will continue staying in the Square of Shihab-al-Din until we finish the building. We defeated the Crusaders 800 years ago and we will defeat the enemies of Islam today.'[52]

The Muslim Brotherhood of Egypt and Syria was founded in Egypt by Hasail al-Banna in 1928. It has as its slogan, 'The Quran is our constitution, the Prophet is our guide; death for the glory of Allah is our greatest ambition'.[53] Inspired by such principles and fired with appropriate zeal Abu Hamza al-Masri said, 'Our fighters

> It is obvious that Islam is
>
> not about to collapse ...
>
> Islam continues to grow
>
> in strength and
>
> confidence ... the
>
> question is will Christians
>
> respond, and if so, how?

will fight until the heretics have disappeared...even if this means the death of all human beings.'[54] Muslims believe that Islam is the one true religion. Its goal is the establishment of a united universal theocracy, in which Islamic law *(shariah)* will prevail over every other system. All will revert to Islam or face the possibility of subjugation or elimination.[55]

Faced with such a relentlessly aggressive challenge many non-Muslims slide into unspoken quiet fear. This is precisely a hoped for response engendered by verbal jousting, militant posturing and hostile sabre rattling. But 'fear is the darkroom in which Satan develops his negatives. The purpose of fear is manipulation and control'.[56]

Muslims are no strangers to fear. They fear Allah, Satan, demons, breaking the Quranic code, slipping into doctrinal impurity, non-compliance with the *duties* of Islam, non-Muslims in their midst and societal non-conformity. Some Traditions allege that Muhammad feared the messenger Gabriel and that he hated that ultimate symbol of Christian presence – the Cross. All Muslims especially fear death.

However Christians have nothing to fear except fear itself. As our own holy book says, 'Perfect love drives out fear'. (1 John 4:18). The writer of the book of Hebrews reminds us '...(Jesus) shared in (our) humanity so that by his death he might destroy him who holds the power of death – that is, the devil, and free those who all their lives were held in slavery by their fear of death.' (Hebrews 2:14 –15). What a message! What a hope! It is that which all Muslims need to hear.

It is obvious that Islam is not about to collapse as have the significant Western politico/philosophical movements of the twentieth century: Fascism, Nazism and Communism. Islam continues to grow in strength and confidence. Muslims confidently claim the twenty-first century as 'theirs'. Faced with the enormity of such history and the immediate challenge of the future, the question is will Christians respond, and if so, how?

PART 3

RESPONSE
GOD AND US

God has been launching many exciting supernatural initiatives among Muslims to reveal himself, his love and his purposes. If we can catch his winds of the Spirit, and grasp the opportunities he is presenting, we could well see the greatest ingathering of these people like never before. If the church will release and resource its best, it will advance, not to defeat but to victory.

CHAPTER 18

CONTINUING CONFLICT

On July 9 1935 Winston Churchill warned his countrymen, 'There lies before us a period of strain and peril which I do not think has been equalled – no, not even in the Great War (World War I)…'[1] But neither people nor parliament wanted to face the obvious. The signs were increasingly clear for anyone to see. Hitler was rearming for aggression. But in England people and their leaders wanted to believe that there would be only peace and prosperity ahead.

In a national election campaign later that year, Prime Minister Stanley Baldwin dismissed Churchill as being alarmist and promised in his election manifesto that Britain would not rearm. But within his own electorate, throughout the election campaign, Churchill continued to warn of the aggressive nature of the enemy emerging across the channel. Two days before the election on November 12 1935 Churchill wrote in the Daily Mail:

Terrible preparations are being made on all sides for war…I do not feel that people realise at all how near and how grave are the dangers of a world explosion. Some regard the scene with perfect equanimity; many gape stolidly upon it, some are angry to be disturbed in such thoughts in their daily routine and pleasures.[2]

Churchill warned that all the signals demonstrated danger and that red lights were flashing through the gloom. 'Let peaceful folk beware. It is time to pay attention and to be well prepared.'[3]

No less a call should be sounded in our time as Islam organises, finances, equips and implements its strategies around the world. The question is, 'Will we be like the leaders of Europe in the lead up to what became the Holocaust of World War II or will we respond more appropriately while there is yet time?'

Initially what is required is that we at least acknowledge we are facing an unprecedented challenge of immense proportions. Next, by way of preparation, we need to confront our own attitudes. The danger is that we may react out of fear rather than love. Anything less than this would not only be counterproductive, it could be disastrous. Muslims may have their own theological justification for some of their attitudes and actions but Christians can have little or no justification for some of our un-Christlike initiatives or responses towards Muslims in the past. We need to remind ourselves that Jesus told us that even to those we may see as 'enemies' we are to respond neither in anger nor malice but in love (Matthew 5:44).[4]

Obviously to be well informed is commendable. The more one knows the better. But as Professor Anderson, when head of the department of Islamic Law at the University of London, said, 'You don't need to know a lot about Islam to be able to talk to a Muslim...You don't need to know a lot to tell a Muslim that Jesus loves him'.[5]

We need to get to the place where we can look beyond the activities of the comparative few who carry their automatic weapons, kidnap or terrorise in the name of Holy War and who appear so regularly on television screens. We need to ask God to help us see that irrespective of religious persuasion, all people are the same. They are like us. They are searching for God and looking for answers to their questions and release from fears and supply of needs.[6] When Jesus said, 'God so loved the world...' (John 3:16), God's love was not meant to exclude a fifth of the world's population who are Muslim.

In Indonesia when a 20 year old Sundanese Muslim girl accepted Christ, she automatically shared her new faith with her family. As was to be expected however, her family greeted the good news with dismay and even hostility. Her father was angry because of the loss of honour this would bring to his family. But as is often the case new believers have faith equivalent to that of little children which Jesus so commends and to which he always responds (Mark 10:14–15). The new believer prayed that her whole family would accept Christ within the next month. During the first three and a half weeks nothing changed, nothing happened. Then a couple of days before the end of the month:

...the father turned to his daughter and said, 'Why aren't you dead? I have poisoned you three times. Each time I increase the dosage. I don't understand why you are not dead.' To this the young woman replied that she was unaffected by the poison because Jesus was now her protector and had taken care of her. Upon hearing this, the whole family placed their faith in Jesus as their Saviour.[7]

Clearly God loved these people to intervene in abnormal ways, to paint signs as clearly as any could understand, that he is who he says he is and that Jesus' claims of divinity, of being risen from the dead, of remaining with his disciples etc, are all true. God will go to extraordinary lengths using all manner of circumstances to involve his people to demonstrate love to Muslims. Love is a longed for, missing component of their religious structures. It is seen as a weakness and yet their hearts yearn for it.

Among the most common titles attributed to Allah is that 'He is the All Merciful', 'The Compassionate One'. The paradox is that there is no instance of his evidencing that in any of the events recorded within the Quran. When God's divine love impacts upon a Muslim the results are often startling to him and surprising to the Lord's representatives. One gentle east Asian Muslim scholar summed up the difference thus, 'Christianity is a religion of love. Islam is a religion of rules'.[8]

> When Jesus said, 'God so loved the world...' (John 3:16), God's love was not meant to exclude a fifth of the world's population who are Muslim.

In the former Soviet Union a Baptist pastor was approached by a Muslim family who asked for help. The father of the family had died and although it was a Muslim village there was no resident Islamic religious leader to conduct a funeral service. The Baptist pastor agreed to perform an appropriate ceremony and this 'so touched the heart of the Muslims' that after the funeral they returned to the pastor and said, 'We have no mullah, so may we visit your church!' As a result of that single act of compassionate kindness, 14 Muslims later became Christians.[9]

Information from elsewhere in that part of the world shows that since 1992 the number of indigenous Azeri believers has increased from 10 to up to 5000 – the majority previously were Muslims.[10] In another former Soviet Republic, a woman on a prayer walk asked God for evidence that he was affecting change in her area. She was shortly afterwards invited to a service in another village where she found 200 new Christians, all ex-Muslims, who wanted to be baptised.[11]

A little further south in neighbouring Turkey, it is generally estimated that there are now about 1000 Muslim converts in 20 Turkish congregations all of which have happened in the last few decades.[12] The sales of New Testaments are increasing and a Christian radio station is reaching about 20 million listeners.[13]

Nearby in another part of Central Asia, Baigul brought her alcoholic sister Zhana to the Christian group for help. She watched as her sister gave her life to Christ and was subsequently transformed in the following two months. Baigul obtained her own copy of a Kazak Bible and in time she also had a life changing encounter with Jesus Christ. Previously 'she was a very independent, self-assured Muslim business woman, but now she literally shines with the light of Jesus'.[14]

God is also replicating the initiatives that he is undertaking in central Asia and in Africa. In an eastern Ethiopian, predominantly Muslim town, 25 former Muslim religious leaders have become Christians and meet regularly for Bible study and prayer.[15]

In that same area a young preacher had been working on the Sudan Ethiopian border. One day he visited a home to share the Gospel of Jesus Christ with about ten Muslim men. When, with their permission he was praying, the Spirit of God so came upon him that he began to pray in a language unknown to him. After he had finished his prayer a man in the room who had been crippled for many years advised the evangelist that he had been praying in the cripple's mother tongue and that the evangelist had in fact said, 'Jesus of Nazareth will heal you if you will stand to your feet'. The cripple stood up and was healed. As a result of this many accepted Jesus Christ including the Muslim religious leader of that area.[16]

In a recent three year period, immediately to the south in the city of Mombasa in Kenya, 22 000 people became new believers in Jesus. Twenty-five percent (ie. 6500 people) of the new believers were former Muslims![17]

For many centuries the toughest place in the world to have seen the Spirit of God at work was the various countries of the Middle East. The countries of this region seem locked into permanent conflict within and among themselves. But in an area controlled by the Palestinian authorities, 30 people in one village who were formerly Muslim now follow Jesus. Two former Muslims brought the message to them. There are 50 new believers in a neighbouring village.

A Sheikh came to one of the evangelists in an attempt to cause him to revert to Islam and after two hours the Sheikh departed with a portion of the Bible to read. A month later he also came to faith in Christ. He was so determined to take a public stand that he even shaved off his beard resulting in his being driven away from his home village. In another West Bank town where previously there were three believers, within a few months 30 were gathering.[18]

In Kuwait, as a young Asian paced back and forth on a motorway overpass contemplating suicide, a passing car suddenly screeched to a halt beside him.

A sophisticated Kuwaiti man jumped out, his *dishdasha* robes flowing behind him and called, 'Are you all right? What's the matter?' With care the man persuaded his desperate young friend to let him drive him home. Just before he got out the driver asked, 'By the way, are you a Muslim or a Christian?' The Asian youth who had a Christian background said, 'I am a Christian.' To the young man's astonishment the man reached out and shook his hand saying, 'So am I. No one knows. Not even my family. I will pray for you.'

Although Christianity was planted as a visible presence in Kuwait in the early part of the twentieth century there was almost no visible fruit. Now people are amazed at the run of reported conversions among Kuwaitis.[19] In 1999 the National Evangelical Church in Kuwait even appointed its first indigenous pastor to head the Church.[20]

In the war torn country of Iraq, at the conclusion of the Iran/Iraq war reports indicated that one church grew from 30 to 600 members in one month.[21] In Iran, on March 25 2001, 24 Iranians from a non-Christian background were baptised. Those who officiated considered it the largest number of such people to be baptised in one meeting for centuries.[22] After the 1991 Gulf War against the Allied Forces, a church in Baghdad grew from 250 to more than 1200 believers.[23]

Even from Saudi Arabia reports filter through of discreet believers in Jesus amongst its citizens. Punishment for any sort of Christian activity in Saudi Arabia is similar to that for murder, rape and drug trafficking; 70 lashes and six months to 20 years in gaol. In extreme cases it may result in death by beheading. Yet when 'Pastor Daniel' prayed for a paralysed man in a Saudi hospital and the man was healed, many of the hospital staff subsequently committed their lives to Christ.[24]

Clearly God is on the move. While he waits for his church to respond he is already responding. But such should hardly surprise us. Regardless from which spiritual kingdom a person is transferred into the kingdom of light (Colossians 1:13), this has always been a spiritual, supernatural process. The initiative is always with God. It is the Father who draws (John 6:44). It is the Holy Spirit who convicts (John 16:8–11), causes confession to be made (1 Corinthians 12:3), and completes conversion (Titus 3:5). It is he who guides into Truth (John 16:13) and who effects miraculous signs for unbelievers (1 Corinthians 14:22) which cause repentance within them (1 Corinthians 14:24). He is constantly at work to reveal the very essence of himself – love (1 John 4:8). This in turn attracts other unbelievers (John 13:34,35) to move from death to life (John 5:24).[25]

God is making his response. 'If God shows me that Christianity is the right way, then I will follow it!' said an east African attending a Bible study group. 'I said the same

> The Gospel is 'the power of God for the salvation of everyone who believes' (Romans 1:16). And that must include all Muslims.

thing last month,' grinned the newest convert.[26] God is on the move even in the toughest places of the world. His Word is unchanged. He does not expect that Word to return to him void (Isaiah 55:11). The Gospel is 'the power of God for the salvation of everyone who believes' (Romans 1:16). And that must include all Muslims. The Spirit that is in us 'is greater than the one who is in the world' (1John 4:4). As God makes his response he expects us to respond with him. It is his will that we pray continually to him (1 Thessalonians 5:17,18) and that we present all of our requests to him (Philippians 4:6). These requests must include Dar al-Islam.

It was S.D. Gordon who said, 'The greatest thing anyone can do for God and man is to pray.'[27] As Christians commence with expectancy, hope and faith to face this new challenge, as we are prepared to be motivated by love and surrender our own lives, we will see God go before us continuously responding to the needs of the Muslim world in ever more amazing ways.

Sudan is surely a difficult place in which to live and to witness for Jesus Christ. In 1989 the Government implemented a ten year plan to eradicate the Church. 'But God is doing miracles, not only among Christians but even among Muslims and many Muslims are becoming Christians...because Christians are ready to lay down their lives for Jesus Christ.'[28] In southern Sudan Christians erect crosses above their meagre homes and other buildings. They say they do this so that when the (Northern) Sudanese airforce conducts its bombing and straffing raids they would more easily identify Christians as targets. Christians who have no fear of death prefer to attract danger to themselves so that non-Christians might be spared and thereby have extra opportunity to discover Jesus for themselves.

When Muslim commentators declare that the twenty-first century is 'theirs', that it 'belongs to them' they are right but not in the sense they anticipate. Rightfully it belongs to Jesus Christ and he undoubtedly desires to see the greatest inflow from Islam into the Kingdom of God that the world has ever known (2 Peter 3:9). Whether or not that happens depends on the response of the Church, its leaders and its people.

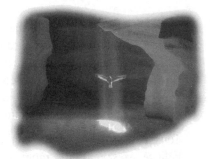

CHAPTER 19

IN THE HEAVENLIES

Said was crying. Muslim women had stabbed his beloved wife Suad as she was conducting a Bible study group in southern Israel. Her unborn child was killed and her left lung had been punctured and had totally collapsed. Surgeons assumed that she, at least, would need a plastic tube to assist her breathing for the rest of her life. As the surgeons worked Christians prayed. Doctors were amazed when Suad awoke from her operation and her breathing was quite normal and no tube was needed. The miraculous healing power of God astounded them.

The next day God spoke to Said and Tabari. He told them to drive back to the village where the attack had taken place. After encouraging the discouraged believers, Tabari stepped outside to address the crowd that had gathered. As Tabari began to preach the rain stopped. The heavy dark clouds parted and left Tabari standing in the midst of a circle of light.

At this point a crowd of angry shouting Muslim men arrived armed with knives, sticks and weapons. They started to throw rocks and stones but these were stopped in midair and reversed back on those who had thrown them. Appearing in the form of bright light Jesus instructed Tabari to speak the words of the Lord boldly and to be unafraid. He promised his protection.

One of the angry attackers struck a believer from behind hitting him on the head with a hammer. The victim collapsed with a deep gash at the back of his head as blood oozed out. Tabari placed his hands on the wound and prayed. The man was instantly healed so that not even a scar remained.

Another attacker threw a knife cutting off the ear of a believer. Tabari picked up the ear, pressed it back onto the victim's head and immediately it fused and was healed. On seeing this the Muslim men fell to the ground and begged for mercy. At least 75 of them believed and gave their lives to Jesus.[1]

Although the above report was carefully recorded in writing and duly signed by those who submitted it as a means of attesting its authenticity, the question remains at least to many Western readers, is it true? It begs credulity because such supernatural phenomena are comparatively rare in contemporary experience. In many pockets of Christianity in the West we may be so bereft of faith as to be considered atheists if not in name then in practice.

To some degree we are the victims of our own belief or lack thereof. Even if we do believe, we seem to live more according to what we value than what we believe. The New Testament records the story of how Jesus was very limited and dishonoured in his time because those present would not or could not believe in him (Matthew 13:53–58).

The Western version of Christianity and our inability to believe has been affected by our materialism purchased through continuing affluence. Church members after their worship is over often gather in the precincts of their buildings. If one listens to their conversations they are hardly ever about what might have just happened in the service. Rather they are studded with our preoccupations of repairing our cars, paying off our homes, ranking our favourite sporting teams or rating our preferred television programmes. Frequent reference will be made to financial and health stresses within our families.

Western missionaries when they gather together will frequently be preoccupied with items such as their children's education, personal health, relationships with friends back home, difficulties of having repairs done to equipment, homes or vehicles. They will talk about decisions made by field leaders or headquarters staff and share opinions about national colleagues, support levels etc.

Comparatively, how often do we hear in our conversations the name of Jesus, new understandings from the Word of God or instances of the Holy Spirit using us in recent days? Materialism undergirded by affluence has come to dominate our thinking and desensitise our spirituality.

A second influence affecting our belief is scientism.

To effect change in our physical environments for good or ill, our first recourse is usually to science. Our continued dependency on our science and its admitted benefits has led us not just to accept uncritically its worldview but also led us to downgrade supernaturalism to the point where we at best ignore it or at worst deny it.

So when, say, a Muslim enquirer approaches with an illness which he may attribute to spiritual interference, almost automatically we deny and downgrade his perception and replace it with our own. Instead of bridging into his world by offering at least to pray for him, we neutralise his theology by substituting our technology in suggesting he report first to a (missionary?) medical centre for perhaps a course of antibiotics or similar medication. Should that line of action prove ineffective, as a last resort we may offer to pray. We do this without thinking whenever confronted by illness in our well endowed medical environments in the West.

> In many pockets of Christianity in the West, we may be so bereft of faith as to be considered atheists if not in name then in practice.

We continue the practice whenever we move to other cultures and countries as well. Only that which can be examined and explained may be believed. For us, often only seeing is believing. But a biblical worldview suggests the opposite – believing is seeing (John 20:29; Hebrews 11:1).

A third influence contributing towards our diminishing ability to believe is secularism.

Since the Renaissance we have increasingly allowed our view of reality to be divided into the spiritual and the natural. This has resulted in religion being increasingly diminished into irrelevance or sidelined to the point of extinction as secularism has increasingly dominated our worldview. Having been born into a society that uncritically accepts this Neo-Platonic dualism, we have lost Biblical perspective. The dominance of this paradigm and its powerful linkage with materialism and scientism has led us into increasing layers of denial of the supernatural in everyday life. But the domain of (Folk) Islam includes such things as jinn, (prayers to) saints, sacred animals and shrines, the evil eye, omens, divination, amulets and magic.[2] Muslim Bedouin life is described as living in a different space-time continuum from the European. It is a world not measured in kilometres or miles. In their world while every tree, stone or pool has an individual spirit, everything is related to God. Whatever happens is the will of Allah. The answer to every question is not in reason but in faith.[3]

Therefore, in an encounter with Islam, it is at this point that the Western witness is often compromised or disadvantaged. A review of the history of Western philosophy and thought shows that since the Enlightenment, prior to the rise of Postmodernism, our 'tradition places importance on articulation of the logical reasons for faith based on scripture'.[4] Everything 'beyond the scope of cognitively reasoned faith'[5] is suspect to the point that many believers in the West do not even believe evil as personified or personalised in a devil, or demons which may be still active in the world today.

However, regardless of the origins and conditioning of our often non-biblical presuppositions, after a lifetime spent living and working within Muslim communities, Vivienne Stacey concluded that Christians have underestimated the spiritual dimensions and hold which Islam has over its followers. 'In reality we are contending with the powers of darkness and not just with people or concepts', she said.[6]

What we must both understand and believe is that in confronting expanding Islam we are faced with spiritual forces of almost 'unbelievable' strength. What other explanation can be given to this movement? As evidence consider its foundations, its history and its contemporary footprint.

As any biography of the Prophet Muhammad clearly demonstrates, this religion was founded and maintained physically by the exercise of power through warfare. Behind its greeting of peace is the paradox of sustained warfare and violence. Upon the death of its Prophet Muhammad, the Companions of the Prophet agreed to elect Abu Bakr as their leader. Revolt and disunity were the immediate result. Reunification however, was achieved during his leadership (632–634 AD).

Abu Bakr had at least nominated his successor as Umar. He led from 634 AD to 641 AD when he was stabbed by a Persian slave. In the midst of dissension, Uthman accepted responsibility as the third Khalifate. Unfortunately during his time (634–656 AD) he succumbed to the fatal weakness of appointing members of his own Umayyad family to most significant positions within the movement. Unsurprisingly rebel forces formed, attacked and slew him in Medina.

The Medinans then elected Muhammad's son-in-law, Ali as the fourth Kalif. But one of the former wives of the Prophet, Ayishah charged him with complicity in the murder of Uthman. Ali was assassinated in 661 AD after just five years in leadership.[7] With his death a great schism within Islam was established which has never been reconciled.

A cursory survey of activity within the heartland of twentieth century Islam reveals that the violence has hardly diminished from its first century beginnings. During the latter part of the twentieth century, Morocco and Algeria fought each other. Algeria continued to finance the Polisario Front to destabilise Morocco from within.

Libya raided its neighbours, Egypt and Tunisia. It has also been heavily involved in military operations in Sudan. Syria twice invaded its neighbour Lebanon, from where it refused to withdraw and also once invaded its other neighbour, Jordan. Iraq invaded its neighbours, Syria and Kuwait and twice sent its troops into neighbouring Jordan. On another front it also fought Iran to a standstill. Jordan, North and South Yemen, Oman, Algeria, Iraq and Afghanistan all experienced brutal civil wars.

If Muslim rulers seem to be merciless to those beyond their borders, the same could be said of their actions toward those under their direct rule. There is little evidence of compassion shown for fellow citizens notwithstanding the great claim that they are brothers of the same Islamic faith.

In 1982 Syrian president Hafez Assad slaughtered tens of thousands of his fellow countrymen in his hometown of Hama. President Saddam Hussein of Iraq and successive leaders of Turkey have inflicted violence of similar magnitude on peoples within their borders. Saudi Arabian authorities summarily executed people without trial as a deterrent to others who might be so unwise as to question government authority. The crime of the executed (in 1982) was only a demand for better living conditions. In 1986 Kuwait deported 26 898 people after its Head of State was assassinated. Even more extensive was its sudden and similar deportation of tens of thousands of Palestinians after the Gulf War of the early 1990s.

> ...Christians have underestimated the spiritual dimensions and hold which Islam has over its followers. 'In reality we are contending with the powers of darkness and not just with people or concepts'.

Libya seized assets of 32 000 Tunisians and deported them in a fit of pique at the failure of a bilateral agreement between the two countries. Sundry terrorist groups in their own and other countries stab, shoot, bomb, hi-jack, kill and maim a wide range of innocent people who happen to be unpitied pawns on the constantly shifting chess board in a vast and relentless thrust for personal power. Public floggings and amputations, executions with attendant crowds in Libya, Sudan, Saudi Arabia, Iran and Afghanistan are often used as the climax to Friday midday prayer times. Instead of construction, (there is) destruction; instead of creativity, wastefulness; instead of a body politic, atrocities.[8] This is often committed by indistinguishable despots. Fouad Ajami reminds us that it is '…a chronicle of illusions and despair, of politics repeatedly denigrating into blood letting…'.[9]

In October 2001 Sudanese Hashem Hassan wrote a letter published in the London Arabic daily newspapers, Al-Quds Al Arabi. He said that Arabs blame others for everything. '…we (have) gained independence…See what we have done with our free will. We became lost in a labyrinth of corruption, economic backwardness and civil wars…'[10] Commenting on the letter Tony Pearce adds: 'The main reason for the lack of freedom in the Arab world is Islam itself.'.[11]

Since the Genesis record of Adam and Eve, one of the surest signs of a rebellious spirit is the ascription of blame to any other than the perpetrators who have caused such unfortunate events to unfold. If the hypothesis is correct that spiritual forces are at work, then it is hardly surprising that when one looks at the previous or contemporary history of Muslim countries, any downturn in fortune is blamed on external factors. Any action is justified under whatever guise. But in reality such activities in the human level are thinly veneered covers for the legitimisation and aggrandisement of personal power. What history often reveals is that the current power holders commit even more atrocities and injustices against their own people than what they denounced for dethroning their predecessors. (It needs to be said that this is not the exclusive province of Muslim rulers.)

The remarkable thing is the extent to which Muslim societies resemble each other.[12] Regardless of what political descriptors are applied to respective Islamic states, republic, democracy, monarchy, emirate, sheikhdom, Khalifate, sultanate, revolutionary or socialist, the end product is often the same.

Dynastic power holders relentlessly fend off and suppress all challengers. Minorities are persecuted. Political assemblies exist only for purposes of rubber-stamping the wishes of leaders. There is limited or no freedom of speech. There is no freedom of religion other than to accept and submit to Islam. The only difference between successive regimes even within single countries is the question of who is suppressing whom.[13]

Rather than accountability, liberty or equality, fundamentals that earthed the political processes of other modern states, Muslim states and societies are characterised by control often accompanied by violence. The history of such is not unique in our times.

For example, between 1671 and 1818, 14 of the 30 rulers of the Ottoman empire rose to power as a result of the murder of the incumbent.[14] In its 184 years as an Ottoman city, Damascus had 133 governors of whom no more than 33 held office as long as two years.[15] In many Muslim states the trend continues unabated. How else can such prolonged irrational violence and instability be explained unless it is in spiritual terms? It defies natural explanation.

Beyond the twentieth century, after decades of political independence from colonialism, countless billions of dollars in foreign aid, development and private investment funds and, in the case of many Middle Eastern Muslim countries, internal wealth of Croesus proportions generated through the sale of oil, little has changed for the masses of inhabitants of these countries. There is still grinding poverty, wars, coups d'etat, suppression, posturing, instability, internal and external aggression.

So widespread and constant are these trends that former Egyptian foreign minister and later United Nations Secretary General, Boutros Boutros-Ghali said:

One of the saddest episodes in modern history is that one of the richest and most promising regions of the world, with one of the oldest and most authentic civilisations known to man, is becoming the permanent field for local wars and internal strife...[16]

At a personal level, Syrian Usama Aboujundi sums up the situation on behalf of tens of thousands who annually join the ranks of refugees, 'The troubles start when you are born, and [continue] until death.'[17]

On July 2 2002 a United Nations Development report was released in Cairo, Egypt. The report was specific to the 280 million people of the 22 Arab countries that constitute the heart and homeland of Islam. It was co-sponsored by the Arab Fund for Economic and Social Development, a finance institution established by the Arab League. The report was prepared by Arab intellectuals from a range of disciplines. It referred to a lack of political freedom, repression of women and isolation from the world of ideas common across the region. It noted that in spite of the oil income of some countries, income growth per capita had actually shrunk in the preceding 20 years, productivity had declined, research and development were weak or non-existent, intellectuals were fleeing repressive political and social environments, women – half of whom were still illiterate – were mostly denied advancement and maternal mortality rates were double that of Latin America and four times that of eastern Asia.[18]

The question is why are these things so? Boutros Boutros-Ghali attributes it to 'the lack of imagination, the lack of generosity, and the lack of diplomacy shown by the elite'.[19] This hardly seems an adequate explanation for centuries of similar outcomes. Why, with such an abundance of resource is there such grinding poverty for the many and such unimaginable wealth for the few? Why is there such stultification and oppression across so many fronts?

What is it that has produced such an enduring hatred toward God's original people, the Jews and Christians? What is it that motivates such fear, bloodshed, division, or an overarching total control of whatever environment with which Islam comes into contact? The Kingdom of God according to the biblical model, is a kingdom characterised by freedom, love and acceptance. The Christian community may not have always exhibited such, but the teaching of Jesus and the example of the original Apostles are very clear, along with countless examples of God's compassion within the pages of the Bible. What Islam historically and consistently exhibits is certainly not the pattern of the Biblical Kingdom of God on earth. Its origins therefore, are elsewhere. Clues to this are found within common (Folk) Islam's personal tendencies of the '...darker practices of amulets, burning chickens, grinding bones, drinking blood, fasting, trances...'.[20]

The Quran condemns witchcraft (Surah 113:4) but, unlike the Bible (Deuteronomy 18:10–12), it makes no categorical condemnation of occult practices. Therefore from an Islamic perspective it was understandable that Palestinian President Yassar Arafat could consult a fortuneteller, Moussa el-Moghrabi, who was also known as the 'Palestinian Rasputin'. It was thought that about half of Mr Arafat's Cabinet members also carried Moussa's charms in their pockets.[21] In 2002 Indonesia's Minister of Religion, Munawar publicly revealed that he consulted soothsayers.[22]

Malika Oufkir writing on life as a child in the royal palaces of Morocco reported that on the feast of Mawlid, the Prophet's birthday, all the sick slaves of the household came to dance before the royal audience swaying to the rhythm of the aamara's religious chants. They would go into a trance to rid themselves of evil spirits that they believed were the cause of their illnesses. Some rubbed prickley pear skins over their bodies while others drank boiling water, all without any indication of the slightest pain. When King Hassan II noticed Princess Latifa and Malika Oufkir, her playmate begin to dance to try to enter the trance as well he was furious. He snapped 'Your rank does not permit you to behave like them. You are impervious to the devil and possession.'[23]

At a slightly different level, what sort of religion seeking a dramatic break with a patently pagan past, incorporates elements

...we certainly 'don't do evangelism simply by trying to win the minds of Muslims'.

of paganism which it purports to replace? Running between the two hills of Safa and Marwa and kissing the black stone are but two such examples. The pre-Islamic shrine at Mecca was the holiest and most sacred site of paganism's visible form in Arabia.[24] Kissing the black stone set in the eastern corner of the Kaba was also adopted from paganism.

At a different level again, what sort of belief system despises the cross and so vigorously denies the death of Christ thereby excising the critical pivotal point of the Christian message? Without the death of Jesus there is no shed blood, no atonement, no redemption, no forgiveness of sins, no salvation and no hope for the future. Reza Safa concludes that such could only originate from the anti-Christ appearing as an angel of light (2 Corinthians 11:14).[25]

The picture emerges that we certainly 'don't do evangelism simply by trying to win the minds of Muslims'.[26] It is a spiritual conflict first and foremost in which we are engaged. Dudley Woodberry of Fuller School of World Missions recounted an incident in Nigeria where a Muslim paid a local shaman to curse a group of Christians who were engaging in evangelistic activities in his area. His hope was that they would be killed. Instead the Muslim got sick and the shaman was rendered powerless. In desperation the Muslim in turn asked the Christians to pray for him. They did and he was delivered. He bowed to the superior power of Christ and became his follower.[27]

Only gradually are Christians learning that few conversions if any result merely from winning theological debates. Spiritual conflict is undertaken with spiritual weapons.

In Tajikistan two evangelists were confronted by a group of Muslim militia personnel. 'You're converting our people!' they said to the two men. 'You must die!'

The two Christians were taken to an empty field, lined up and had machine guns trained on them. The workers closed their eyes and prayed asking Jesus to receive their spirits as he did with the first martyr, Stephen. Nothing happened. When they opened their eyes they saw that their tormentors had run away in terror even though no one else was there.[28] When Christians employ spiritual means, spiritual outcomes are the result even in the toughest situations.

In Saudi Arabia, when Christian guest workers decided to hold an open air rally in a sports stadium they didn't bother to ask for permission. Knowing that it would be denied they went ahead without it. As the speaker finished his message and invited those who wished to receive Jesus Christ to come forward, from among the 5000 people who were present, about 500 responded.

Right at that time the *Mutawa* (religious police) arrived and verbally assaulted the respondees. Not surprisingly the officer in charge yelled, 'Who has given you permission to do this? Do you not know that we hate your Jesus? Do you not know that this is a Muslim country where we only preach Allah? This is against our culture…against our laws, and we will arrest all of you!'

But in response to a prompting of the Holy Spirit all 4500 of those in the stands got up, walked down and surrounded the new enquirers. The religious police became even angrier. Suddenly all 5000 people of the crowd lifted their hands toward heaven and their faces toward their accusers and said, 'God, we love you and we bless those who are against us'. The police were both so stunned and disarmed that they hastily departed and left the stadium.[29] Spiritual means yields spiritual results.

The means to our removing the barricades of spiritual opposition are being variously postulated. Peter Wagner, leader of the AD2000 and Beyond Movement's prayer track, claims that a major power behind Islam is that of the moon goddess, 'one of the Queen of Heaven's most flexible and adaptable identities. That is why we see her symbol, the waxing half moon, on all mosques and on the flags of many Islamic nations.'[30] For this reason, Wagner organised to gather 8000 intercessors in the great amphitheatre of Ephesus in Turkey in October 1999 to pray against this spiritual principality which he identified as that which the apostle Paul encountered as recorded in Acts 19:23–40.

Reinhard Bonnke who has conducted many large evangelistic meetings in sub-Saharan Africa where Muslims have often been involved, has a slightly different emphasis. He says:

In different countries where police are very careful to make statistics, we are told that crime rates have dropped 75%, even to 100% sometimes, during our campaigns. *Why? Because the gospel attacks these cancerous growths of sin in human society.*[31]

His model of operation is primarily as Jesus instructed. Those that know the truth will be set free by it (John 8:32). He preaches Truth and Muslims and many others are 'set free'. But it is not truth as a mere cerebral exercise or cognitive activity as may be the case in many Western gatherings. 'The Kingdom of God is not a matter of talk but of power' (1 Corinthians 4:20). Bonnke expresses it thus:

Preaching the gospel does not mean delivering a three-point homily. A sermon may be neatly turned and precision engineered, like the casing of an armour piercing shell, but it needs to be filled with high explosive. Otherwise it will bounce off the hardened minds of unbelievers. Prejudice may be reinforced with argument, but the message filled with the Holy Spirit can and will penetrate it.[32]

> Wagner and Bonnke would see Islam as not just an ancient religion but a contemporary spiritual principality, a ruler in this world, an invisible power to be confronted.

Bonnke's understanding of spiritual realities causes him to operate as a ground level commander in the conflict of the heavenlies. Wagner and Bonnke would see Islam as not just an ancient religion but a contemporary spiritual principality, a ruler in this world, an invisible power to be confronted.

Regardless of the history of the development of Islam or its current practice, it matters little how difficult the future may seem. Although Christians are warned to guard against being led astray by counterfeits of God's work (Matthew 7:15–16; 1 Timothy 4:1, 7; 2 Timothy 3–4:5; 2 Thessalonians 2:9–10) we are also freed from the power of any spirits or occultic practice (Galatians 4:3–7). Additionally we are assured that the Spirit that is within us is greater than that which is in the world (1 John 4:4).

In 1949 American President Dwight Eisenhower asked Afghanistan's King Muhammed Zahir Shah to permit a church to be built in Kabul for Christian diplomats. A mosque had previously been built in Washington. The king agreed. On

May 17 1970 the building was completed and dedicated as a 'House of Prayer for all Nations'. But in 1973 the Muslim government worried that Afghans were becoming Christians, sent in troops and machinery to destroy the church. A German business man warned the mayor of Kabul, 'If your government touches the House of God, God will overthrow your government'. The mayor ignored him. The workmen completed their demolition and withdrew from the site on July 17 1973. That very night the 227 year old monarchy was overthrown. For the next 28 years there was violence, famine and destruction. One refugee summed it up: 'Ever since the government destroyed that Christian church God has been judging our country'. Toward the end of that time during the oppressive rule of the Taliban no rain fell for several years within the country. Subsequent to their removal the country was once more flooded with rain. Could this be a replay of the events of I Kings 17-18?[33]

In terms of ultimate outcomes therefore, it is inconsequential how grim the future may seem or how strong the opposition may be. The most that should be admitted regarding the spiritual force of Islam is that it may be growling or even roaring throughout the world. But there is a counterforce that can block and defeat this spirit; that is the Holy Spirit operating through believing Christians, empowering the Church and propelling it toward ultimate victory. And not even the very gates of Hades can overcome it! (Matthew 16:18).

CHAPTER 20

MEANWHILE BACK ON EARTH

'Muslims are real people'. How about that? What a revelation!

The above statement was made to newspaper reporters by a hostage who had been released after an airline hijacking in Beirut. He went on to explain, 'To my surprise I found that these people had all of the emotions that ordinary people had – fear, love, the desire to succeed'.[1]

What a contrast compared to the attitude expressed by Palestinian Authority representative, Dr Ahmad Halabiya. In a sermon delivered in a Gaza mosque in October 2000 he is reported as preaching:

Oh brother believers, the criminals, the terrorists, are the Jews – they are the ones who must be butchered and killed. As Allah the Almighty said, fight them: Allah will torture them at your hands. Have no mercy on the Jews, no matter where they are in any country. Fight them wherever you are. Whenever you meet them, kill them and those Americans who are like them.[2]

Because of reports like the above, media sound bytes or vision clips, many have been conditioned to think all Muslims are the same, that they are only filled with hate, wave guns in the air, shout slogans against the Western world and treat women atrociously. Cartoonists continue the caricature by drawing Middle East Muslims as money-grubbing, wealthy sheikhs growing ever richer by the sale of oil which the rest of us are obliged to buy. If we are not careful we develop attitudes like that of Ovadia Yossef, a former chief rabbi of Israel and founder of the Shas party, which became the third largest party in the Israeli parliament after the 2001 elections. In one of his sermons he was reported as preaching:

It is forbidden to be merciful to (Arabs). You must send missiles to them and annihilate them. They are evil and damnable.[3]

We need frequent reminders that, at a personal level, the vast majority of Muslims around the world are exactly the same as the rest of us. They have the same desires

> Muslims are as hungry for God as anyone else might be. As one Muslim woman enquirer put it, 'I don't want money; I don't want healing; I want Jesus. I want peace with God.'

to be married, to raise a family and to live in peace. They hope to raise their children who in turn will find meaningful and fulfilling jobs. They want to have orderly transition of governments. They want to be understood and accepted by others. Above all they also want a personal encounter with God.

When a Sufi Muslim leader was asked, 'If you could ask Allah for one thing what would it be?'. His reply was instantaneous. 'That I might know Allah.' That is the heart of the matter. In Pakistan a couple of Afghan enquirers put it this way:

'We haven't come for money – we own a shop. And we haven't come for visas – we have close family in the States. We have come for one reason only – we want to know about Jesus.'[4]

Muslims are as hungry for God as anyone else might be. As one Muslim woman enquirer put it, 'I don't want money; I don't want healing; I want Jesus. I want peace with God.'

Even the words *Muslim* and *Islam* suggest that these are people who are serious seekers after God. They want to find him and submit to him. Toward that end Islam has its fundamental pillars and practices of faith, prayer, fasting, alms giving and pilgrimage to Mecca. These are people who, in their search, are dedicated, zealous and who hold religious convictions dearly.

From childhood Omar went to the mosque to pray and meticulously follow all the rituals. But he often cried, 'God, I would like to know you. Talk to me'. A foreigner told him to kneel in his room and call out to God in the name of Buddha, some Hindu gods, Muhammad and Jesus, to see which God might answer. Later when Omar was alone he did just that.

'God, I have prayed to you all these years. You know my heart. I want to know you. Speak to me.'

As was suggested he prayed in all the names and waited. From each there was no response. Finally he prayed in the name of Jesus. He later reported '...it was as if someone walked into the room. All my hair stood on end. From my head to my feet, I felt as if someone was touching me. I heard a voice saying, "Omar, I am Jesus your Lord. I love you. Do you want to know more?"

"No, my Lord. I trust You. From now on, you are my Lord. Today, you have answered me."'

Omar has since been baptised and serves Jesus.[5]

> One of the reasons for the popularity of what is commonly called Folk Islam is that it speaks to the heart. It is tangible. It stirs the feelings.

Adhering to legal prescriptions seldom satisfies the human heart. Because Subhan was dissatisfied with purely legalistic Islam, he turned to the study of Islamic mysticism. He wanted more than book knowledge. He wanted a spiritual experience. He found it eventually in the New Testament. There were words that spoke to his inmost being as nothing else had done before. He found in the *Injil* the central figure of his heart's secret search – Jesus Christ.[6]

One of the reasons for the popularity of what is commonly called Folk Islam is that it speaks to the heart. It is tangible. It stirs the feelings. 'It places hope in wise and pious deceased sages to help people meet the everyday challenge of life.'[7]

A Muslim Iranian doctor expressed his hunger and search as follows:

...From very early on, I had a desire to know God. I remember once when I was about four years old asking my father where God lived, but he couldn't give me an answer. He said that when I started school, my teachers might be able to tell me more about God.

I started school and was taught about Islam, but nobody was able to answer my questions. I started praying five times a day as Islam told me I was supposed to in order to please God. I lived in Iran for 14 years but during all this time I didn't meet or hear of anybody who truly knew God. Lots of people mentioned him and talked about him but even at my age I could clearly see that God was not a reality in their lives.

...Then at age 21, I was confronted with Christianity. The Bible told me that God had a deep desire to have a relationship with me! It also said that only my sins stood in the way, but that through believing in Jesus Christ all of my sins would be completely forgiven so that I could enter into a relationship with God.[8]

Christians who have heard the story of Jesus from earliest times may forget how amazing that story is for people who have never known of it. We also overlook the tremendously powerful tool that God has provided for us in the Bible itself. An Iranian woman always shared taxis whenever she travelled so that she could give Gospels to others. Once when she gave a Gospel of Luke to her taxi driver he was so excited he wanted to kiss her hand. He said, ' I really needed such a book and I didn't know where to get it from'.[9]

Middle East Media reports that the New Testament continues to be a best seller at book fairs.[10] At a bookstand at the Industrial Fair in Gaziantep, a gateway city to Turkey's southeast, Mujde Yayancilik sold 800 New Testaments in one week. Then his bookstand was bombed.[11] A small advertisement placed in a regional Middle Eastern newspaper offering Bible Study help generated over 20 000 responses in a very brief time. The written Word usually accomplishes that which God intends (Isaiah 55:11).

When two followers of Jesus visited Abdul they gave him some Christian literature to read. Upon realising what it was, Abdul rebuked the believers for distributing such items in his community. After they left he decided he would destroy the Christian material immediately. He used it as kindling for a small fire in the back yard of his family residence. Before Abdul's fiery mission was complete, his father returned home and inquired as to what was happening. When it was explained to him he complimented Abdul and blessed him for his wisdom.

However later that night, Abdul still remained anxious and disturbed by what had transpired. Sleep eluded him. He could not rid his mind of the message of the Christian literature he had destroyed. Eventually he remembered that his father had a store of some Muslim literature. He hoped that by reading it his peace of mind would return. But when he found what he was looking for, to his amazement, the literature he expected to find regarding the Muslim faith had been replaced by that which he had destroyed earlier that same afternoon. Bewildered, he took it to his room and spent the remainder of the night reading about sin and Jesus' power to forgive it. This Word set Abdul on a spiritual pilgrimage that resulted in his personally encountering Jesus as his Lord and Saviour.[12]

Within Muslims there is a deep unfulfilled spiritual hunger which can never be satisfied merely by laws, traditions or rigorous religious practice. Hass Hirji-Wilji had a great desire to learn the Quran and be regarded as a devout Muslim. From the earliest age he was taught Arabic. By the time he was five he began to fast during the month of Ramadan. He prayed towards Mecca five times a day. By the time he was ten, he was competing in Quranic competitions. When he was 12, he started to study Urdu to gain an even wider knowledge of what Muslim scholars had written in other major languages. The Quran was his favourite book. But still he was dissatisfied. It wasn't until he discovered Jesus Christ that the deepest desires of his life were satisfied.[13]

Even among the most zealous, conscientious Muslims the best that they would hope for is not to be loved by God but just to be accepted. As one put it, 'I longed to please God but with all that effort I did not experience the presence of God in my life one single time! Not even once!'

When we become aware of testimonies like this and the frequency with which one hears of them in various countries, any conditioned animosity toward these people in the midst of their deepest unfulfilled longings, melts away. The caricatures, the posturing, the media modelling, all melt away to reveal a people, as needy as ourselves, who are searching and longing for the love of God.

The hunger in the Muslim heart may arise from the huge lack of love often experienced within society and compounded by its absence within its religion. Muhammad Karoui wrote of this fundamental issue:

Who among us Arabs can claim that he was acknowledged, loved, wanted and accepted by the family or atmosphere in which he grew up? None, I am sure. Can anyone be loved who is no more than a useful object, produced to continue the family line, or for the troublesome old age of parents, or for the male chauvinist glory of the father who proves what a real man he is by the number of his offspring?[14]

When Raed, a Muslim-Palestinian, refugee camp inhabitant, first learned the religious background of his benefactor of many years, he was stunned. Silently he staggered for several minutes. The careful conditioning of his worldview was shattered. 'I just don't understand', he said, 'Why would you a Jew (!) help me…All my life, the synonyms for "Jewish" are bad things…Hate is planted into our hearts since we were children.'[15]

Where love is in such short supply and reasons for hatred seem so plentiful in society as well as in religion, is it any wonder that some of the outcomes of life and interaction with others seem to be so heartlessly violent? The basis for this predicament is that nowhere in the Quran or in the Traditions of Islam is there any demonstration of Allah's love for his creature – mankind. 'God's love in the Quran is like a businessman's love. He will love those who meet his conditions, but those who are at enmity with him, he will not love.'[16]

How different is the basis for Christianity where there is the supreme revelation that the very inmost essence of God is love! As the apostle John succinctly expresses it, 'Whoever does not love does not know God; because God is love.' (1 John 4:8). If a people are bereft of love and of being loved, how can we demand that they act up to our expectations? The deficiency in their behaviour and ignorance is directly attributed to our failure in responsibility.

If we believe that Jesus Christ is our most treasured possession then we ought to be doing everything to get that news out so that Muslims also might come to understand 'that this priceless treasure has been given by God to them also.'.[17] Followers of Jesus therefore need to be 'moulded in their attitudes towards Muslims by Jesus' attitudes and actions toward (us) – compassion, acceptance, deeds of kindness and an invitation to enjoy the life that Jesus gives'.[18]

We must remember that they also are created in the image of God. Therefore they must have 'the same needs, desires, pains, hurts, disappointments, weaknesses, failures, frustrations and emptiness that can only be met and dealt with in Christ.'.[19] Even if they are categorised as confirmed, identifiable, extremist Islamic terrorists we need to remember that they were first created in the image of God. They only became whatever they may now be because of social or political frustration, economic deprivation, religious indoctrination, or cultural conditioning. If we consider even these as unreachable it is only because we have not tried sufficiently hard to access them. 'Whoever is reachable is winable.'[20]

When Muslims' spiritual hunger is met by acts of real love and humility, the result is often surprising. Lynn Green was the director of the Reconciliation Walk that followed the journeys of the Crusaders nine centuries ago. However, instead of going with sword in hand, murdering, raping and looting in the name of Christ as did those other Crusaders, he and those with him went to offer a long overdue apology to those Muslims who live on the Crusader path today. He went in 'the opposite spirit'. He went with those walking with him believing that 'truth prospers in an open environment...'.[21]

In Istanbul, as Green was reading out the 'apology' to the deputy mufti, the official became agitated. Interrupting the meeting he suddenly stood and said, 'I cannot receive such a message from behind my desk, Mr Green. May I sit next to you?' The deputy mayor of Istanbul hosted a reception for the walkers. All major television stations and newspapers reported the walk positively.[22]

On July 15 1999, exactly 900 years to the day when the Crusaders first invaded Jerusalem, 400 members of the Reconciliation Walk stood on top of the Old City walls and prayed: 'Lord where others were motivated by hatred and prejudice we offer love and brotherhood.'.[23]

Love melts most ancient rivalries and even draws combatants closer. A pop song of some years ago in the West sounded a familiar refrain, 'All you need is love'. The words of poets and songwriters have echoed this longing in every nation from time immemorial. Why should we ever imagine that Muslims should be the exception? Unfortunately we have not always been that reflective of the deep longing and love which our Heavenly Father has for these his people, descendants from his people of Ishmael.

> Our Father in Heaven has irrevocably demonstrated his unconditional love for us in that 'while we were yet sinners, Christ died for us' (Romans 5:8). We need to demonstrate the same love God has for us to our other, yet to be found, brothers and sisters of the house of Islam.

When Hassan left his father's home in the holy city of Qom, Iran's second most sacred city, and went to study in the West, on his first Sunday with his new hosts he was taken to their Christian Church. Needless to say, it was a confusing experience for him. After the service a zealous young pastor borrowed Hassan's English/Farsi dictionary to look up specific words in Hassan's own language. The message which the pastor got across was, 'You-are-going-to-Hell.'[24] What a travesty of divine love was exhibited in that unfortunate attempt at witnessing. Fortunately, Hassan went on to make other friends who walked with him and, above all, who loved him and introduced him to hope, forgiveness and a Saviour.

Our Father in Heaven has irrevocably demonstrated his unconditional love for us in that 'while we were yet sinners, Christ died for us' (Romans 5:8). We need to demonstrate the same love God has for us to our other, yet to be found, brothers and sisters of the house of Islam. That love of God for his people on earth always satisfies a hunger that God, himself, has placed there.

Slowly, a truck made its way over the mountains of Iran between Mashad and Tehran. The driver was so emotionally depressed he decided that the only way out was to commit suicide. The method he would use would simply be to drive his truck over a cliff and plunge to a certain death. As he slipped the truck into an appropriate gear for the last minutes of his life, his hand accidentally brushed the radio controls. Suddenly, someone was talking to him.

My dear one, you might now be travelling all alone, you might be feeling nobody loves you, you might even be so depressed you want to end your life. Jesus Christ has promised to never leave you nor forsake you. Jesus Christ is with you right now. Call out to him and he will surely comfort you.

The driver was shocked. He stopped his truck and got out. Trembling he started to walk. Then he fell on his knees, sobbed and cried out to Jesus to come and comfort him. Immediately his heart was filled with peace. He knew he was not alone.[25] The driver had 'accidentally' tuned in to a Christian radio program and God had met him just in time. His hunger, his need for love was satisfied at last. But for how many and for how long will there be no such 'accident'? How many others will run out of time? Regardless of cost, both the initiative and the opportunity rest with us who have already experienced such love and obtained such knowledge imparted to us also at great cost.

On a hot afternoon in a city in northern Iran a family had spent some time looking at goods in a carpet shop. Before leaving they gave the shop owner a Bible. The man wept with tears of joy as he repeatedly kissed that book. He then shared with his surprised customers how he had given a lot of his profits to charity to try to gain favour with God. But always there was the same emptiness inside. Finally just a few days previously he had cried out to God. 'I know there must be some truth out there. Please help me to find it...' When he received the Bible he felt 'something deep inside' say, 'This is the answer.'[26]

Indeed we already have the answers. So how can we refrain from also responding in love to the opportunities that God is giving to at last meet the deepest longings within many Muslim hearts?

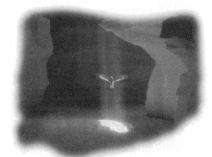

CHAPTER 21

HERE COMES THAT DREAMER

When Dudley Woodberry and Shubin conducted a survey among 600 Muslim background believers to find out why they chose to follow Jesus, their major reasons included:

- Supernatural Encounters – miracles, healings, deliverances
- A Sure Salvation – certainty of salvation
- Jesus the person – the attraction of his life and ministry
- A Holy Book – the powerful Word of God
- Relationship with God – intimacy with the Father
- Love – through God and caring believers.

But heading the list of most commonly occurring events was that of Dreams and Visions where Jesus appeared and invited each to follow.[1] Mark Robinson confirmed a similar trend occurring in Indonesia.[2] Dreams and visions have always been two of the media for God's message to mankind. In our time they have become the major means used by God for those on their way into his kingdom. This is especially so for Muslims.

One of the more widely reported events of this nature was God speaking through dreams and visions to 24 Bulgarian Muslim *mullahs* who were scattered to the north of their border with Turkey. According to these men, Jesus, himself, appeared to each unbeknown to the others. He is reported to have said, 'I am Jesus, the Messiah. You must repent of your sins and put your faith in me to be forgiven. Allah sent me to turn you from error to the truth. You must go to the mosque and proclaim this to the people.'.

Each independently obeyed and witnessed his congregation's decision to begin to seek God through Jesus. As was the case at Pentecost, immediately many gave evidences of being filled with the Spirit through speaking in tongues with interpretations, prophecies and the sick being healed.

As the leaders gradually learned of what was happening in other mosques, they realised their need for teaching beyond what they had received in visionary form. So in February 1992 two of their number travelled to Sofia, the capital of Bulgaria to seek help. The two seekers knew only to inquire about people who might worship Jesus the Messiah, speak in unknown languages and who see people healed of various diseases when they prayed. They were referred to the Bulgarian Pentecostal Church. Arriving at the Pentecostal headquarters they requested Bibles and teachers. Subsequently on each of the minarets of the first 24 mosques, crosses were erected. Since that time many thousands of former Muslims are now truly submitted to the one true God.[3]

Equally noteworthy was what had previously happened in an Algerian township in 1983, from where a similar event was reported. In the place where, in June 1315, Raymond Lull, a Spanish missionary from Majorca, was stoned to death because of his preaching, God suddenly visited the inhabitants during the night in the form of angelic visitations, visions and dreams. He did not cease until 400–450 Muslims in that location became followers of Jesus. Their transformation and enthusiasm reportedly led to thousands more throughout the countryside coming to faith.[4] Contemporary Christians have often been at a loss to know how to respond when confronted by such reports from Muslim enquirers.

Abdur testified to a vision of Jesus who came to him during a bout of serious illness. He reported that he had been almost blinded by a brilliant light that identified itself as Jesus. The being of light instructed Abdur that if he followed the path of Jesus he would be healed. Abdur complied immediately and was cured. But as sometimes happens Abdur reverted to Islam and once more fell sick. Again Jesus appeared in a vision. Again Abdur abjured his recalcitrance and was healed. To cement his decision he approached a Christian missionary with a request to be baptised.

As all Muslim converts appreciate, many may claim to believe but baptism is the ultimate sign of death to the old life and the beginning of the new. Unfortunately in many cases, that death may be physically so before much of the new has begun. In Abdur's case the missionary was suspicious of the inquirer's story and motive.

As proof of sincerity he demanded that Abdur obtain a document signed by the village magistrate testifying of his change of religion, name etc. After several attempts, Abdur finally persuaded a magistrate to comply with his request. Returning to the missionary, Abdur was referred on to someone else for baptism. A national pastor, less fearful or worried about loss of residency status believed Abdur and baptised him.[5]

Dreams and visions that draw Muslims to Christ are not new phenomena. Neither is the Church's unsympathetic response toward them.

In 1868 a group of Muslim mystics known as Shazlis met for two years in Damascus. An inner circle of leaders met at the home of Abd el Kadir to meditate and pray. On one occasion they all fell asleep and later awoke simultaneously. Each reported that they had dreamed of Jesus. Convinced of his reality and truth as recorded in the New Testament they were filled with joy.

Through a second similar supernatural event they became aware of an old white bearded man who wore a coarse brown garment and held a lighted candle. After a three month search throughout Damascus they found the person of their dreams. He was a Spanish Franciscan monk, Fray Forner.

Within a comparatively short time 25 000 Shazlis were reportedly ready and willing to be baptised. The British consul in Damascus, Sir Richard Burton, proposed having all of them resettled in a purpose built, new community outside of the city. He sought the help of Archbishop Valerga of Jerusalem whom he assumed would organise a mass baptism. Instead Valerga reported developments to the Muslim Ottoman authorities. Twelve enquirers were killed. Fray Forner died mysteriously. Sir Richard Burton was sacked.[6]

> When true believers in the supernatural impacted by God's methodology, come into contact with missionaries and others who more highly value regularity, discipline and natural explanations, the results are often disappointing especially to the enquirers

When true believers in the supernatural impacted by God's methodology, come into contact with missionaries and others who more highly value regularity, discipline and natural explanations, the results are often disappointing especially to the enquirers. This outcome is not exclusively the province of Muslim enquirers.

In Australia, aboriginal people often became Christians through their dreams. But missionaries warned them against placing any importance on their dreams. By adopting such attitudes, missionaries were denying the prime method by which aborigines both received and transmitted truth – their dreaming. What the missionaries neither knew nor appreciated was that Aborigines had assumed that what they were being taught had come to the missionaries themselves through dreams.[7]

Western Christians often explain dreams away as the mind trashing extraneous data. Some might jokingly attribute them to late night snacks. Others interpret them in terms of Freudian psychology. But in other cultures and especially that of Islam, people believe that this is still one of God's primary means of communicating with mankind. That belief often leads to life-changing decisions and discoveries of the reality of Jesus Christ.

When Abdu was 30 years of age, he heard a Christian pastor preach about Jesus. As a devout Muslim he sought more information from the pastor about what salvation and Jesus really meant. Although he did nothing in response to the pastor's message, some years later when he attended a church service, he found another pastor preaching an identical message. At the end of this service also, he questioned the pastor more closely about Jesus. Still he remained undecided. He well knew that if he decided in favour of Jesus, he would at least, sustain significant loss within his own community. This was a deterrent. Then within a few days there came a dream.

In his dream Abdu was walking through bush country during the rainy season. He eventually met four people standing in an urban clearing. Rain had caused a pool of water to form in the clearing and a fire burned in the middle of that pool. As he tried to get closer to the pool to see better what was happening the fire turned into a grave with the four people standing around it. When Abdu inquired as to who the people were, they only pointed to the grave. The grave then became an open door in which several people lay half in and half out. Abdu noticed that they were on fire. He also recognised that one of these was his Quranic teacher who had died several years earlier.

Then one of the four by the door turned and told Abdu this was his (future) condition. When Abdu pleaded to be saved from such a fate, the four responded by taking hold of him and pulling him toward the fire. The heat began to burn Abdu's skin. He cried out and promised to change for a better life. When he suddenly awoke, the lasting impression was that the four people had told him that his only hope was in Jesus. No longer would he be indecisive. He publicly confessed his faith in Jesus

Christ and consequently lost his home, his family and his cattle. Yet not even this loss could stop him from sharing his new-found faith. Abdu's dream and his belief that God had spoken to him through it, led him to become an evangelist to his own people.[8] Similarly Ahmad (an Algerian terrorist) had a dream in which he faced four doors. Through the first he viewed a dark room which he dared not enter. Through the second he saw a Muslim Sheikh preaching Islam and jihad. Into this he did not want to go. Through the third he saw people drinking and dancing. When he opened the fourth door he saw someone dressed in shining white clothes holding a known friend of his by the hand calling to him saying, 'Come unto me, all you who are heavy laden, and I will give you rest.' Ahmed remembered reading these words spoken by Jesus in the Bible. He woke up, went to this Christian brother to seek an explanation for the dream and as a result decided to follow Jesus.[9]

Muslims themselves believe that during sleep a person's soul is active and is able to rise from the body resulting in dreams. They believe that there are two souls in a person. One is the *ruhul-hayah* (life soul) and the other is *ruhul-tamayiz* (the soul that gives awareness to a Muslim of his responsibility to perform the commands of Allah).[10] That which rises from the body and causes dreams is *ruhul-tamayiz*. If *ruhul-hayah* rises from a person's body the result is death.

In Islamic cultures, dreams are not just for religious purposes. Aman, a Somali woman, told of how two beautiful tall women dressed in white spoke to her grieving mother during a dream. These apparitions asked her why she was continuously crying and thereby preventing them from resting. Aman's mother told them she was crying because she wanted a baby that had not happened yet. The ladies in white advised her to rest, remain quiet and trust in Allah. They placed hands on Aman's forehead and stomach and promised her 'lots of babies'! The mother was unsure whether she had dreamed the experience or may have even been awake. She certainly believed it because it was a normal expectation of Muslim religion within her culture.[11] Appeals to the supernatural authority of dreams to authenticate subsequent actions taken is common within Islam. When former President of Uganda, Idi Amin, expelled Asians from that country, he was not criticised by Muslim scholars. This was not only because he was a co-religionist but also because he claimed that Muhammad had told him in a dream that Asians were bad for his country.

When Amin proclaimed himself President for Life he promised to make Uganda an Islamic country regardless of its Christian majority. He justified his purge of the country of all of those he suspected of being a threat to his program by claiming visions from God.[12] To further legitimise his presidency he retrospectively claimed that back in 1952, via the medium of a prophetic dream he had been told that he would one day lead the army and the country.[13]

Whether or not Amin was speaking truth, certainly other Muslim leaders believed him and responded in kind. Libya's President Gaddafi said to Amin, 'You are a prophet. Be brave and we will support you.'[14] Similarly when Saudi Arabia's King Faisal visited he accepted Amin's claims. Among the king's gifts to Amin was a gold sword by which the king encouraged Amin saying, 'With this sword Muslimise your country.'[15]

Saddam Hussein of Iraq also claimed that in a dream Muhammad had told him where to position his missiles. Because of his reference to his dream, he was greatly respected in Pakistan and elsewhere.[16] It would seem that the uncontested claim of the Prophet appearing in a dream is of greater significance than the outcomes from the dream. Outcomes from the battle of words may outrank those from the battle with bombs in winning the hearts and minds of ordinary people.

While dreams of Jesus seem to attract people from Islam to Chrisianity those of Prophet Muhammad may have the opposite effect. Ziwar Muhammad Isma'il had converted to Christianity seven years previously when on the morning of February 17 2003 he was approached by Abd al-Karim Abd al-Salam at his taxi rank in the Kurdish authority area of northern Iraq. Abd al-Salam challenged Ziwar to return to Islam. When Ziwar declined Abd al-Salam shot him with an automatic rifle. When he was later handed over to the police he claimed that the Prophet Muhammad had appeared to him in a dream and told him to kill Ziwar.[17]

Dreams and their influential effects are not unknown in Judeo–Christian contexts. In the Bible, Genesis 37 is the record of Joseph's prophetic dreams. It also records the hostility such dreams provoked when communicated to others. 'Here comes that dreamer,' Joseph's brothers said to one another. 'Come now, let's kill him and throw him into one of these cisterns…' (Genesis 37:19–20). These days we tend to handle such matters a little more discreetly while, at the same time, trying to neutralise or ignore the dreamer's message.

In the founding and spread of Christianity, dreams and visions played significant roles. In the Old Testament, Joel had prophesied that young men would see visions and old men would dream dreams when the Spirit was poured out on all flesh (Joel 2:28–32).

Peter claimed this fulfilment at Pentecost (Acts 2:16–17). Then there was that of Saul (Paul) on the Damascus road (Acts 9: 1–5). Similarly there was that of Cornelius (Acts 10).

The Book of Job attributes both dreams and visions to divine activity as well as attempting to give some explanation of the process:

For God does speak – now one way, now another – though man may not perceive it. In a dream, in a vision of the night, when deep sleep falls on men as they slumber in their beds, he may speak in their ears and terrify them with warnings, to turn man from wrong doing and keep him from pride, to preserve his soul from the pit, his life from perishing from the sword (Job 33:14–18).

A further possible explanation of the means and the results of dreams and visions among Muslims may be found in Isaiah, 'For what they were not told, they will see and what they had not heard, they will understand.' (Isaiah 52:15).

Just as the Apostle Peter spoke directly to people from Libya, Egypt and Arabia on the Day of Pentecost, repeating the ancient promise which was for them, their children and for all who were far off – for all whom the Lord would call (Acts 2:39), so the promise and the process seem to remain operative till this day.

After graduating with honours in Islamic law from the famous Islamic University Al Azhar in Cairo, a Lebanese Muslim was appointed as a teaching sheik in mosques in Beirut, Tripoli and Sidon. He had some knowledge of the teaching of Jesus and the demonstration of his love. The love of Christ that changed people was attractive to him. He also enjoyed reading the Psalms of David. In the midst of his multifarious dutiful serving of Allah and the people of Islam, he encountered difficulties and problems. These caused him to question the will of God for his life. Eventually he asked God to show him a right way forward. Then things started to happen. He explained it thus:

...I kept having a dream in which I was walking along a path that always ended at a church. Every time I had this dream I asked God if it had come from him. And another thing–I kept thinking of Christ. The picture of him on the cross, with blood flowing from his wounds, kept imposing itself upon my mind. This was even against my will because I had been taught that Christ was not crucified. In spite of my continued rejection of Christ this picture came to my mind more and more and every time it happened I felt a great happiness. It seemed that Christ was ordering me to follow him.

After a long time I finally decided that I wanted to accept Christ. But then I feared that he would not accept me because I had rejected him for so long...

There was still a struggle. I fought long against reason with all its arguments and defences and logic. But finally the heart drew the sword of love and the battle ended with complete surrender to Christ.[18]

The instruments of God, love, his Word and a recurrent supernatural dream seldom fail to achieve the purpose God intended. Elements of this formula are effective even on the most hardened, embittered and initially antagonistic foes of the Gospel.

Hassan hated Christians. He had been erroneously taught that Christians prayed to a picture. Along with his fellow Muslims, he also wrongly believed that Christians worshipped three Gods: God the Father, God the Mother – Mary and God the Son – Jesus. Again, similarly to some of his fellow Muslims, he was infuriated by the sight of Christians wearing crosses around their necks. As a tradition testifies about his religion's founder, so it was for this twentieth century follower. He hated the sight of the Cross and this caused him to hate Christians irrationally. As an outlet for his hatred he would do anything and go anywhere to disturb and break up gatherings of Christians. But one night God started to intervene. Hassan had a dream that greatly disturbed him. In his dream, he became confusingly interlinked with the object of his hatred. He was now wearing a cross and people were asking him why.

That dream penetrated his prejudice, deflated his hatred and set him on a new search. With the dream vividly in mind, he understood at last that unlike what his religion had taught him, Jesus did, in fact, die on a cross. That death was not something just far removed in time. He realised that Jesus died for him personally as well. A follower of Jesus introduced Hassan to truth such as is found only in the Bible. From there it was a short step of faith to personal introduction to the one who had died for him. The cross that Hassan had so despised now hangs voluntarily around his own neck as a badge of honour of the one who lives in his heart – Jesus.[19]

While Western analysts might disregard dreams as being nothing more than the mind's attempts to reconcile tensions, to discard unnecessary information or as the result of discomfort caused by an over rich supper before retiring, it is not so easy to explain in natural terms how so many people can have the same dream at the same time. A whole village had the same dream of someone coming with a big book, the night before a converted villager returned home with the same book tucked under his arm. All were later baptised on the same day.[20] At a Central Asian Women's Conference in 1996 one third of the attendees had come to faith in Jesus Christ specifically through dreams.

But the ancient promise is not just of dreams. It also relates to visions.

Mustapha was an extremely religious Muslim. Every day he unrolled his prayer mat and prayed five times toward Mecca. It never brought him any peace but he resolutely persisted. One day as he assumed his prayer posture he saw a wooden post standing in the ground to which another beam was affixed horizontally near the top. To his horror this represented to Mustapha, the cross of Jesus Christ. Although he tried hard to ignore it and to get on with his prayers he could not excise the reality of this vision of that terrible cross. Exasperated he finally jumped up, put his Quran aside and said to his family, 'This book does me no good. I'm going to become a follower of Jesus'.[21]

Similarly, in a Sudanese mosque, worshippers became silent as they gazed and saw a vision of Christ on the cross. Many became convicted and gave their lives to Jesus.

> At a Central Asian Women's Conference in 1996, one third of the attendees had come to faith in Jesus Christ specifically through dreams.

An almost identical event occurred in Ethiopia where 300–400 Muslims in one community came to Christ after seeing a vision of the cross while they were praying in their mosque. They also were convicted of their sin and became followers of Jesus.[22]

A Pakistani studying overseas had a vision of Jesus walking across the waters which separated him from his home country. In this vision Jesus called out, 'Follow me!' as he walked toward the western part of Pakistan. But at the same time, this person could 'see' his uncle standing on the mountains in the north in his own home area calling out, 'Don't come here! Don't come here! The Truth is not here! The Truth is not here!' As a result of that encounter, shortly after this person became a follower of Jesus and subsequently returned to his own country to work in the area indicated by Jesus in the vision.[23]

In Lebanon, a young Muslim man who knew nothing about Christianity and who also did not personally know any Christians, nevertheless had developing within him an increasing conviction that he had to come to terms with their religion. One morning as he awoke he was startled to see a radiant figure at the end of his bed. From the brightness a voice said, 'I am Jesus Christ. Get in your car and go to Beirut and you will be told how to become a Christian.' The young man drove to Beirut but aimlessly toured the city not knowing where to go. At midday he happened to stop outside a college to seek directions as to where he might buy some food. The person he spoke to was a believer in Jesus who invited him to have lunch with him. That night he accompanied his new found host to a meeting where the Gospel was clearly explained. The enquirer believed and was baptised.[24]

In Nigeria, Kawuri had been tortured so badly he was almost dead. In his distress he nevertheless prayed aloud for his torturers who unbeknown to him were nearby. Kawuri asked God to forgive them. Two mullahs heard his prayer. The following day each independently had a vision of the Lord. In one vision the Lord revealed to one of them, three of their greatest and most secret sins. As a result of their visions these men shared what had happened with their followers, dedicated their lives to the Lord Jesus and more than 80 people followed them into discipleship of Jesus.[25]

In the same country, at three o'clock one morning, a black spitting cobra entered the compound where a missionary family was living. It spat in the eyes of the Muslim night guard. While he was blinded by the venom, a figure appeared to him in a vision and said, 'If you accept the Messiah he can easily heal your eyes'. A couple of days later the night guard's sight was suddenly restored. He shared his experience with a second Muslim. God spoke to this one also through a vision and he then came requesting to receive Jesus as his Saviour.[26]

In a northern African Middle Eastern country, a Muslim tore up a tract which had been offered to him. So incensed was he that he threatened to kill the evangelist. But the next morning to the evangelist's surprise, this same man turned up at his door. When the evangelist inquired as to how the man found his address he was told, 'The voice in the night told me your address.'. That voice had told him he had just torn up the Truth. He repented and received Jesus Christ.[27]

A thread common to most of these supernatural events is that the enquirer is confronted by a person dressed in brilliant white who often identifies himself as Jesus. Instructions are given and as a result, the enquirer searches and finds one of Jesus' disciples who explains clearly, often for the first time in the hearers' lives, the real truth about Jesus. Inevitably, after the experience of the encounter and an explanation of the Gospel, they give their lives to Jesus.

People are often wary of statistics because truth may be perverted into propaganda.[28] But nevertheless if our motivation is right, statistics can give us a valuable guideline as to what God might be doing on earth.

Wendell Evans, a former Director of the Institute of Muslim Studies at the Billy Graham Center in Wheaton, USA, concluded 'that the frequency of dreams and visions of Christ amongst Muslims has risen dramatically' in recent years.[29] It is estimated that of Muslims turning to Christ in Africa, 42% of new believers come through the experience of dreams, visions, angelic appearances or audibly hearing God's voice.[30]

In Iran, 'greater than half the recent Muslim converts…have had visions relating to Jesus'.[31] Researchers of the southern Asian scene claim that 80% of new Christians are the direct result of supernatural encounters.[32]

One possible reason for this sudden upsurge of supernatural intervention and increased harvest is, as researcher David Barrett estimated, that as many as 170 million Christians worldwide are praying daily for world evangelisation. He also estimated that approximately 20 million of these people saw their primary ministry as prayer intercession, much of which is strategically focused on the toughest spiritual strongholds of the world, particularly the areas of Islam.[33]

Whatever the reason one thing is sure. 'One word from heaven is more powerful than the most difficult circumstances and resistance.'[34] In what have hitherto been evangelistically the toughest most unresponsive fields of work, miraculous interventions by God through various visitations are no longer the exception.[35] Whenever God intervenes this way there is an inevitable ripple effect.

In Kazakhstan, twin 16 year old girls attended a showing of the Jesus film. Afterwards they discussed the content of the powerful story in that movie. Shortly after when their father fell gravely ill, they prayed for him in terms of the short prayer printed on a piece of Christian literature they had received. To their delight, their father improved. At school they met teachers who believed in Jesus. But still they were reluctant to commit. One night as the girls slept, one of them had a dream of angels coming to their window assuring her that Jesus really was who he said he was. When she awoke she shared her experience with her sister. Both invited Christ into their lives.

They started to pray for their parents. Shortly thereafter their mother had a dream in which she saw Jesus and heard him speak to her. When she awoke she realised that this was the one about whom her daughters had been speaking. Soon the whole family became followers of Jesus. This family began spreading the good news throughout their village. Others responded. Even relatives from Tajikistan accepted Jesus.[36] Experiences such as these provide an impact of such magnitude that those to whom it happens are unlikely to turn away even when under extreme pressure.

As 'Abdul' lay on his bed, he sweated profusely not knowing whether what he was seeing was a dream or a nightmare. He recognised the person suffering violently on the cross as Jesus. It was so vivid that he felt that he was a part of Jesus' struggles. He was shaken to the very core of his innermost being. As he tried to understand what all of this meant he walked into a church and heard an evangelist outline the theme of his dream. He needed no more explanations. He was ready to leave Islam to follow Jesus even if that meant a cross. He also talked to his brother about what was happening in his life. But his brother informed him that their older brother threatened to kill him as well as dynamite the church if anyone (else) in the family followed the path of Jesus. But this Muslim enquirer answered, 'Nobody will stop me from doing what I want. I want to know the power that has so obviously changed my brother's life. I want it in my own life'.[37]

God changed the course of an entire nation through one man and his dreams. That man was Joseph (Genesis 37). The nation became Israel. Many centuries later the course of history once more changed by Jesus appearing to the young zealous Jew, Saul (Acts:1-22) who went on to become the Christian apostle, Paul. It would seem that contemporary terms such as 'closed peoples' or 'restricted access countries' while missiologically useful in no way inhibit what God does through dreams and visions.[38]

Here come the dreamers again. This time it is hoped that we will be more receptive than were Joseph's brothers as God lays another foundation for changes in the history of other nations.

CHAPTER 22

NEITHER BIG MAC NOR FISH AND CHIPS

It is said that the legendary British detective, Sherlock Holmes and his associate, Dr Watson once went on a camping trip. After a good meal and a bottle of wine they lay down for the night and went to sleep. Some hours later Holmes awoke and nudged his faithful friend.

'Watson, look up and tell me what you see!'

Watson replied, 'I see millions of stars.'

'What does that tell you?' asked Holmes.

Watson pondered for a minute and then replied, 'Astronomically, it tells me that there are millions of galaxies and potentially billions of planets. Astrologically, I observe that Saturn is in Leo. Horologically, I deduce that the time is approximately quarter past three. Theologically, I can see that God is all powerful and that we are small and insignificant. Meteorologically, I suspect that we will have a beautiful day tomorrow. What does it tell you?'

Holmes was silent for a minute and then said, 'Watson, you idiot, you have overlooked the obvious. Someone has stolen our tent!'

In the search and research to understand Islam and how Muslims might be approached effectively with the Christian Gospel, there probably is in existence more Ph.D. theses than there are converts. In our efforts to understand, we may well have overlooked the most obvious.

If it is true as the Bible says that God so loved the world that he sent Jesus…(John 3:16) surely this love is meant to encompass the 20% of the world's population who may be Muslim. The Bible says that God is not willing that any should perish (2 Peter 3:9). That cannot exclude a billion Muslims. The Bible declares that the fields are ripe for harvest (John 4:35). That must include Islamic populations. Furthermore the Bible says that the Spirit which is within us is greater than the one who is in the world (1 John 4:4) and that the Gospel is the power of God for salvation (Romans 1:16).

If God is unchanged, the field is unchanged, the Spirit and the Word are unchanged, then where is the fault that precludes the circuit of power and effective witness from being completed. Within this equation the only option is to examine the harvesters and their activities. There must be something we are doing, omitting or overlooking which is preventing what God wants to effect – namely a mighty harvest of Muslims coming to Jesus. For surely he does not send us out to fail!

So what has the messenger overlooked? Just as Dr Watson failed to notice the most obvious thing, so we consistently have overlooked the most obvious, namely that of the culture and the context of those to whom we would go purportedly as living messages ourselves.

In 432 AD, compelled by a prophetic dream, a Romano-Briton, Patrick returned to Ireland where he had previously been held as a prisoner. Through his amazingly successful efforts at establishing the Christian Church throughout that country he became known as the 'Apostle of Ireland'. How did he make such an impact? 'A key element…was that he abandoned his roots and identified himself completely with the people he was reaching. He "became" Irish.'[1]

In the seventeenth century Roberto De Nobili, an Italian missionary, arrived in India where he remained till his death 50 years later (1605–1656). After carefully observing the environment in which he was to live and work, he abandoned anything that could offend eg. eating meat or wearing leather shoes. He exchanged his European clothes for that of the Sanyasi guru and ochre (kavi) robe. He mastered classical Tamil, Telegu and Sanskrit languages. He cut himself off from every attachment to the world including all contact with the local Christian Church.

By 1609 he had 63 converts including some Brahmin priests. None of these were required to break the external practices of their (previous) Hindu culture. But because others complained to Rome, papal legate Tournon banned much of de Nobili's methodology in 1704. Forty years later, Pope Benedict XIV issued the Bull, Omnium Sollicitudinum upholding Tournon's decision. The bold Jesuit experiment was over. So was the flow of conversions.[2]

Although Italian Jesuit, Matteo Ricci, made similar exploratory attempts in China, unfortunately as developments subsequently showed, these attempts were all too infrequent. Even today at the highest levels, cultural insensitivities are all too common.

In March 1999 the President of Iran, Muhammad Khatami, a Shiite Muslim cleric, held private talks with Pope John Paul II in Rome. In a public exchange of gifts President Khatami with rare sensitivity gave to the Pope an exquisite Persian rug in which was woven a design of Saint Mark's Basilica in Venice.

The Pope in return gave to the President a painting of Saints Peter and Paul.[3]

It would appear on the surface that neither the Pontiff nor his council of undoubtedly expert advisers had even considered that mostly, the theology and practice of Islam discourages if not prohibits the reproduction of human forms let alone those of the early fathers of a non-Muslim religion. This oversight is even more unfortunate when it is remembered that Iranians because of their more recent experiences, view that most Christian of nations, the United States as the 'Great Satan'.

The first Protestant missionary to India was Bartholomew Ziegenbalg (1706–1719). After some years of labour at Tranquebar he wrote polite letters to leading members of the Hindu society in his area asking them their opinion of the Gospel he preached. He received equally polite replies. Their objections were not so much about Ziegenbalg's doctrines or principles within the Gospel. Their complaint was about the messenger's social practices which they naturally believed were inseparably associated with the message he preached. What a pity Ziegenbalg was unaware of the lessons of history.

In 1730 Count Zinzendorf alerted the Moravians to the urgent need to evangelise slaves on the Virgin Islands. Leonard Dober was only 18 years of age at the time. Nevertheless he was excited as he wrestled with the challenge of how one might reach such people far off in every sense of the word. Noting what Jesus had done, he concluded that no sacrifice on his part was too great to reach these people. As the first Moravian missionary he sailed to the Virgin Islands and the sugar plantations. He initially became a servant in the Governor's house. But, at the end of three months he resigned and relocated to a small mud hut where he was able to work more closely one-on-one with the slave community. His identification with their lives was as remarkable as the results it in part produced. Within three years there were 13 000 new converts![4]

When a young and enthusiastic missionary wishing to work among Muslims in southern Asia, commenced his work in the latter half of the twentieth century, an astute observer wisely advised him, 'You will be just as big a failure as all those who have gone before you. The reason they failed was that they were not Biblical.' The observer went on to point out that in his opinion the reason for 'failure' was that missionaries had mostly failed to take into account the principles of identification as outlined in 1 Corinthians 9: 21–23. Missionaries to Muslims are often well trained but their training comes to them by way of the pursuit of intellectual study. Unless that is complemented by subjective knowledge arising out of the intimacy of personal relationships that feel pain and struggle based on love, then even the most zealous attempts usually founder in frustration and are reduced to little more than memories of wishful thinking.[5]

Missionaries to Muslims whether from Western countries or from any non-Muslim culture, have frequently failed to distinguish their message from their own culture. Unfortunately, the two were seen to be of the same order. Therefore Muslim converts were required to leave behind most of what was precious to them in the society that had birthed them. In short they were extracted and cut off from most of their culture and the context of life.

A newer Christian summarily lamented the nub of process as follows: 'I went down into the waters of baptism as a black African Muslim and came out as a white European Christian.' He went on to explain that to 'prove' his faith and become acceptable to his new community, he had to accept changes to all his relationships, his clothing and even his name.[6] Extracted from all that he previously cherished, he was 'churchianised' into a type of unnatural social hybrid human.

Muslims regard the whole of life as a seamless garment which cannot be cut into separate pieces such as religion, work, or recreation. Another new Christian summed it up this way: 'Islam is more a way of life than a religion. Our traditions are like a snail shell. If you find a snail outside its shell it's dead.'[7]

Yet Christian missionaries wonder why, after extracting converts from culture, they 'die'. To be alienated from family, social and cultural contexts is considered by Muslims to be an adverse act of the worst kind. The term applied for this activity is *irtidad*. While its primary meaning is apostasy, it is almost equivalent to treason or dis-identity. According to Islamic law apostasy is punishable by death through decapitation.[8]

When converts from Islam are stripped of kinship, social security, home, property, business, employment, even wives or husbands and children – in short, they are *in toto* extracted from their *ummah* – and then often not accepted and bonded into a new Christian community, the cultural demands made upon them by the receiving community might aptly be called a process of 'churchianisation' rather than Christianisation.

Islam is the only non-Christian religion claiming to be on a world mission of universal relevance. It is younger than Christianity and remains the only religion, which in certain parts of the world, has overwhelmed Christianity. In those places, Christianity has never regained its former position. Islam remains the most resistant of all non-Christian religions and is therefore the least penetrated with the Gospel.[9]

One of the reasons this remains so is that churches planted within Islam were all too frequently modelled on their Western counterparts. They became cultural and religious clones of the countries from where the missionaries came. Because of this, they remained largely isolated, disconnected and irrelevant to the local peoples. This was unfortunate but not terminal.

> To be alienated from family, social and cultural contexts is considered by Muslims to be an adverse act of the worst kind.

Professor Jehu J. Hanciles of Zimbabwe notes that:

During the great age of Western missionary enterprise, African thought-forms, traditional values and beliefs were wholly bypassed...The early growth of the church in Africa was more or less single-handedly achieved by foreign agencies...(yet, today) African independent churches exist and grow exclusively of, and in antithetical contrast to, those churches with links to missionary endeavour.[10]

Where religion and culture harmonise, positive results accelerate exponentially. Of course there are risks between the extremes of syncretism and exclusivism. But the risk must be taken. In Africa, it was not until Christianity was 'drummed and danced' with 'its message filtered through a prism of local custom, art and ceremony' that it truly took hold.[11]

Approaches between religions of all shades are starting to recognise the value of sensitive contextualisation. Those who work among Jews understand that Jewish believers in Jesus want to maintain their distinctive identity and to celebrate their Jewish heritage. The gospel has to be shared with them in ways that are culturally relevant without compromising the claims of Jesus.[12]

Christian mission in Korea has been exceptionally successful in the twentieth century. More recently Shamanism, Buddhism and Confucianism are attempting to reverse the trend by contextualising their rituals, worship and ceremonies based largely on Christian methodologies.[13]

In some parts of the world, Islam itself has seen the potential value of altering its approaches. Their missionary conventions now encourage outreach through educational sessions in mosques. Islam is presented as a theological continuity of Christianity. Introductory courses are held on issues such as Evolution, The Meaning of Life, The Way to Happiness and Contentment, How to be Pure of Heart, How to be Saved, The Importance of Family, Ethical Behaviour and The Compassion of God.

Jesus is even upheld as the means of salvation. Sketches, songs, testimonies of miracles, indoor sporting events of soccer, badminton, martial arts displays, bouncing castles for younger children etc. are all means used to reach non-Muslims within a Western context.[14]

As Muslims look at Christians there is no doubt their 'seamless' interpretation of life is overlaid onto their interpretation of Christian activity. Egyptian Muslims told Christian workers to 'go home. Otherwise we will kill you. We will have nothing to do with you. You are Christian, we don't want your religion. We see on television what Christianity is like'.[15] As expected Muslims assume that whatever they see of Western culture is essentially Christian. Western 'Christians' make the same mistake whenever they interpret all that they see or hear emanating from a predominantly Muslim country as being authentically Islamic. Things happen in every country which are not only distorted by media processes but are also embarrassingly destructive to the morals, values and beliefs held by sincerely religious people of each country.

Behind this interpretation lies a major reason for their resistance. They may not actually be rejecting the Christian faith[16] but the culture through which it is communicated. When it was claimed that a young woman in Algeria, on her wedding night was 'found' not to be a virgin, her in-laws placed her backwards on a donkey, shaved her head, tied her arms and sent her back home. Her elder brother did the 'honourable' thing and stabbed her to death because she had dishonoured the family.[17] In Jordan in 2000, 35 women reportedly chose to remain in jail after serving prison sentences rather than be released to return home because of their fear of possible retribution, violence or even death at the hands of male family members desirous of preserving 'honour'.[18]

Jordanian law permits a male to kill a female relative without penalty of incarceration if he discovers her committing adultery. If he kills her after finding out she was in an 'adulterous situation' he may be liable to receive a reduced penalty.[19] Between 1995 and 2002 the United Nations reportedly estimated more than 45 000 women in Jordan, the West Bank and the Gaza strip died as a result of honour killings.[20] The Iranian Islamic Criminal Code declares some people unworthy of the blood that runs in their veins. Therefore if a murderer can prove that the victim was a 'waste of blood' then no charges are brought.[21]

These sorts of happenings, while perfectly understandable and acceptable within some Muslim contexts, appear altogether otherwise from the Christian viewpoint. The only control an outsider can have, is not over the events but one's reaction to them. While no culture is completely Christian, that which might be the antithesis of essential Christianity can only be changed gradually after Christ is introduced into that culture. The requirement for change however can only come after his introduction and acceptance and not before. Had Gentiles in the New Testament era been required to accept the traditions and regulations of their Jewish counterparts, probably few of them would ever have received Jesus Christ and subsequently undergone change.[22]

> Western Christian messengers to Islam need to understand that for Muslims it is more important to belong than to believe.

Western Christian messengers to Islam need to understand that for Muslims it is more important to belong than to believe. This was the summation of a Muslim who considered himself an atheist but went occasionally to the community prayer ground to participate in public prayer lest it be suspected that he was no longer an honourable member of the community. This gives weight to the adage that it may be that what keeps a Muslim as a Muslim is 90% cultural/social and only 10% theological. Evidence of this is often seen on flights leaving more restrictive Middle Eastern countries. Once the flight is underway conservative dress codes and food habits demanded within some Islamic countries are quickly dispensed with until just prior to landing on a return flight.

The word *culture* was originally associated with an explanation of soil science. Then it became more aligned with education. More recently it has been applied to matters of manners, customs and habits as these interact and change with environments.[23]

The culture of any people is usually a product of their history and is established over an extended period of time. Its practitioners are usually unaware of its existence.[24] For those who approach a cultural unit, understanding it and acceptance by those who are part of that culture take considerable time.

A group of foreign health and agricultural specialists went to the town of Shahwa with its 2000 people in Pakistan and even though they were fluent in the language, it still took 18 months for them to be no longer regarded as intrusive novelties to the point where people actually listened to what they might want to say.[25] Similarly, when a young couple went to live among the nomadic northern African Tuaregs, it took five years to learn their language, lifestyle and music to the point where credible friendships were established.[26]

Unless we take the time to observe, learn, adapt and adopt the necessary forms to make our message and ourselves communicable, the possibility of success is diminished. In the meantime, probably the most common mistake is to apply our hierarchy of values as a measure instead of understanding what the adopted group's scale is. For example in Arab Islamic cultures honour and respect are the two most desirable values to be maintained. Honourable behaviour may be reflected in manifestations of manliness, sexual conduct and virility as evidenced by fathering many sons.[27] 'Any injury done to a man's honour must be revenged...The honour concept is easily extended from the individual, the family and the tribe to the nation as a whole.'[28]

The opposite of honour is shame. 'Shame has been defined as a matter between a person and society. Compared with Western culture, in Arab culture shame is more pronounced than guilt. What pressures the Arab to behave in an honourable manner is not guilt but shame...the drive to escape or prevent negative judgment by others.'[29] What people might say becomes the main criterion for behavioural choice.[30]

A man therefore may kill his wife or daughter for her alleged unfaithfulness to restore honour and remove shame and dishonour. From a Western Christian perspective, murder is the worst of crimes. From a Muslim Arab perspective a loss of honour is the issue. To mystified Western observers, it is this difference in values that can explain, for example, media reports of Pakistani Muslim males killing female relatives without fear of retribution or prosecution by the law. The Human Rights Commission of Pakistan estimates that in 1999 alone 'more than 1000 women were killed by their husbands or other male relatives for allegedly committing adultery or other acts considered to impinge on family honour'.[31] Martial Law Administrator General Pervaiz Musharraf promised legislation to ban the practice but in recent times the Pakistan Parliament has voted against even raising the issue as a possible legislative matter.

On April 21–22 2000, Serb police and army units marched into a remote Kosovar Albanian Muslim village. Human rights investigators later discovered that at least ten of the village's women were raped. The women were terrified that they would be blamed for what happened and therefore would be expelled from their husbands' families and denied all access to their own children. Such is the priority of 'honour' that 'a "good" woman would rather kill herself than continue to live after having been raped' concludes an investigative report of the Organisation for Security and Cooperation in Europe (OSCE).[32]

When one understands these axes of values it is easier to see why, what a Western Christian might describe as lying and cheating, in the Arab world and to a Muslim may not be a moral matter at all. To the latter, it is only a method of safeguarding honour and status and avoiding shame.[33] Similarly, corruption from a Euro-centric perspective is seen as a social evil but the same actions are interpreted quite differently within Middle Eastern countries. What the Westerner might call corruption to the Middle Easterner is simply a means of achieving power and honour. Public examinations, university appointments, government employment or positions within the armed services, the law or other institutions are not matters of meritocratic efficiency but rather they are indicators of one's ability to manipulate a situation for place and influence.[34]

The same honour and shame distinctives equally apply when one considers leaving Islam to become a Christian. Initially, the biggest inhibitor to such a move may not be a lack of understanding or perception of truth but simply the desire to avoid bringing shame and discredit to one's extended family.[35]

In Indonesian (and other) Islamic cultures, group considerations far outweigh the importance of the individual. The matter of belonging is paramount.[36] Western Christian missionaries need to understand that a concept of personalised, privatised, individualised faith is foreign to their Muslim counterparts. Therefore, how and to whom should they present their message? Even the culturally bound confessions of Nicea and Chalcedon may prove to be inadequate presuppositions to explain aspects of Christianity within a Muslim context. But if Christ is who he says he is then his witness must penetrate. Wherever his beauty or the crisis of the cross is obscured by culture, a way must be found to reveal it more clearly.

The Christian messenger must present Christ for no less a reason than that he deserves to be presented, stripped of the messenger's cultural understanding and

> Western Christian missionaries need to understand that a concept of personalised, privatised, individualised faith is foreign to their Muslim counterparts. Therefore, how and to whom should they present their message?

reclothed within that of the Muslim enquirer. If Jesus went to all the trouble to assume a body like ours and could sit down with a dishonoured woman of Samaria to relate to her personally and intimately where she was (John 4) and if Paul could communicate to the Athenians in words and phrases so that they could understand even though they might have rejected him (Acts 17:22–34), then our methods of presenting the Christian message to Muslims need to 'lead us to a radical rethinking of our whole Christian enterprise'.[37] But that is hardly a new experience for the Christian messenger.

What has happened in recent centuries is that Christian missionaries have assumed their culture was superior and authentically Christian because they have come from the economically, politically and militarily dominant countries of the West. Therefore when the remnants of their efforts are examined, outposts of isolated Christians in form and structure almost exactly the same as those of the missionaries and their culture of origin are found. But it was not always so. In the beginning from a minority position of weakness, Christians learned that it was more important to adjust their cultural forms to the groups to which they were going.

The greatest exemplar of course, was Jesus himself 'who, being in very nature God, did not consider equality with God something to be grasped, but made himself nothing, taking the very nature of a servant, being made in human likeness' (Philippians 2: 6–7). Having made such an enormous transition he was hardly likely to confine himself to the strictures of the accepted religious culture of his day. In fact, a most common criticism of him was that he refused to do so (Matthew 9:10–13). So that his audience could more clearly understand his message he was quite ready to leave behind his own native, contemporary Jewish culture to do whatever he could to get his message across (Mark 3:1–6).

At Pentecost the process continued. Each observer was at least able to hear God's message in their own language even though they were from different ethnic and linguistic groups (Acts 2:1–13).

The interplay of culture and context is quite clearly defined in the attempts of the earliest church to present its message. In preaching to Jews, the content of the message emphasised the fulfilment of promises made through patriarchs and prophets. Peter reminded them of their religious and cultural heritage, which was to climax in the Messiah (Acts 2:14–36). It was similar in Stephen's preaching (Acts 7). Paul did likewise in his synagogue preaching to 'God fearers' (Acts 13:16–41; 17:11–12). Their methodologies were appropriate for Jewish audiences.

However when non-Jews, that is Gentiles, were the congregation, the content of the messages preached changed (Acts 14:11–18; 17:18–34). There was a significant difference between Jewish, Hebrew and Greek thought patterns. But the Gospel was always presented with a priority on the culture and understanding of the listeners to facilitate their acceptance of it.

The apostles understood that salvation came through faith in Jesus Christ. This was independent of the finer points of ancient law and Jewish customs. The Council of Jerusalem was charged with deciding and separating what was appropriate for Jewish and non-Jewish believers. Even though the majority was of Jewish origin nevertheless they understood that the customs of one society should not be imposed upon another (Acts 15:19–21).

Paul specifically stated the principal methodological practice of context and culture when he affirmed that to win Jews and Gentiles he became as much as possible like each one respectively (1 Corinthians 9:19–23). At heart he was able to distinguish the core essentials of his message from the context of his culture. This enabled him to remain conservative in his theology but radical in his methodology.

Paul continued when he was with Jewish believers to follow customs appropriate to their culture. He visited the temple (Acts 21:26–27). He celebrated the Jewish festivals (Acts 20:16). He maintained his Nazarite vow (Acts 18:18; 21:23–27). He bore the expenses of four other people who maintained the Nazarite vow (Acts 21: 23–24). He acknowledged that male circumcision, the sign of the Covenant for the sons of Abraham was a very important aspect of Jewish religion and culture. Therefore in order for his disciple, Timothy, to be accepted and beyond criticism among minority Jewish communities, Paul had him circumcised (Acts 16: 1–3). But he did not compel the non-Jew, Titus, to undergo the same practice (Galatians 2:3). Because early church leaders respected appropriate cultural norms of their day, this attracted the respect of the people that they were working among (Acts 5:12).

In hostile environments, the essential elements of their message were never compromised (Acts 5:29–32). But they became quite flexible in their response to such hardships (Acts 8:1; 9:30). Changes were also made by electing different teams to make different approaches to different target groups. Paul and Barnabas were commissioned to work among non-Jews while James, Peter and John were to work among Jews (Galatians 2:7–9). This division of task and flexibility of response according to religio-cultural backgrounds was a major factor in the success and growth of the early church. There was no pressure placed upon non-Jewish believers to adapt or adopt Jewish social or religious customs. But when their numbers grew and the Jews started to become the minority group of the new movement, the reaction of jealousy did have to be worked through (Acts 17:4–5). That the Jewish groups maintained their cultural Jewishness also facilitated their continued existence within their own people group.

The constant stress was on the fundamental principle of salvation through faith alone with the believer being freed from the authority of different laws, traditions and customs (Acts 13:38–39; Galatians 5:1–6; Philippians 3:3; Colossians 2:8, 16). This liberty did not mean licence. They were not totally free to please themselves (Galatians 5:13–14). They were encouraged to limit voluntarily their own customs for the sake of others. If Jesus himself came not to be served but to serve (Mark 10:45) then we ought to be generous toward others as well (2 Corinthians 8:9) placing their needs above our own.

It was only where culture and religious practice were absolutely opposed within the core of Christian theology that such practice was to be rejected. For example magic (Acts 19:17–20), occultic practice (Acts 8:9–24; 13:6–12) or idolatry (Acts 14:11–16; 15:20; 19:26; 1 Thessalonians 1:9–10). When believers remain culturally and geographically within any society then God is able to work more easily through them to reach unbelievers (Matthew 5:13–16; John 17:14–16; 1 Corinthians 5:10). Implementing such principles is never easy. Different messengers by dint of personality or training will be able to go further than others can. But each should be encouraged to go as far as possible into the culture of the target community without compromising the essentials of Christian theology.

Ethno-centric attitudes are to be opposed. Support is to be given to the freedom of relevant cultural expression. Within the New Testament Church desirable unity never meant uniformity and neither should we expect it among emergent communities of relevant Muslim convert new believers.

When one considers what Biblical practices might be appropriate for adaptation within a Muslim community many possibilities come to mind.

For example:

- a greeting of peace (Luke 10:5)
- ablutions of washing hands and feet before worship (Exodus 40:31–32)
- removal of shoes prior to entering a worship area (Exodus 3:5)
- bowing prostrate in prayer (Psalm 95:6)
- women modestly covering their heads (1 Corinthians 11:5–6)
- circumcision (Luke 2:21)
- making an offering for a new born child (Luke 2:24)
- prolonged fasting (Exodus 34:28, 1 Kings 19:8; Matthew 4:2)
- women maintaining modesty (1 Corinthians 14:34)
- abstinence from pork and other banned foods or beverages (Leviticus 11:7; 1 Corinthians 8:8–13).

> Within the New Testament Church, desirable unity never meant uniformity and neither should we expect it among emergent communities of relevant Muslim convert new believers.

To minimise further unnecessary cultural gaps, churches or new communities in western Africa adopt praise chants. Some members wash the feet of others before entering the place of worship. Men and women separate and sit barefooted on mats with heads covered. In southern Asia, new communities have changed meeting structures for worship, teaching and fellowship using models with which former Muslims are more familiar. Leaders are chosen not necessarily on the basis of intellectual knowledge or their ability to define doctrine but according to spiritual experience.

To enhance local integrity, foreign money, which inevitably corrupts, is excluded along with publicity and other unnecessary forms of insensitivity. People are encouraged to respond to faith in ways that do not extract them from their social context thereby minimising cultural dislocation without compromising fundamentals of the Gospel.

An Egyptian woman summed the matter up succinctly when she said, 'My people do this and so I must do like they do.'[38] As much as possible such principles are to be respected.

Liberty, equality and fraternity were noble slogans of revolutionary France. We forget that in Islam there is no such equivalent. Unrestrained application of power is more admired on the politico-military scene than any other value. Self-sacrifice is akin to lunacy or martyrdom within such cultures.[39] A Muslim public servant once said, 'If it's a question of your interest and the empire's – yours comes first'.[40] In Islamic societies while the universality and culpability of sin is acknowledged, personal conviction of it, as such, does not exist. From a Christian standpoint what seems to be adultery and fornication might seem to be conveniently relabelled as temporary marriage (Surah 4:24).[41]

Wherever cultural distinctives are minimised so that the message can be contextualised, amazing results may follow. In Malawi where mosques are constructed every half kilometre, a Muslim leader decided to follow Jesus and was released to preach and interpret the message for the benefit of local hearers. Within two months there were over 300 Muslims converted to Christ and six churches had been planted.[42]

Those best able to articulate the Christian faith in ways to which Muslims will relate are the converts themselves.[43] This is especially so when the norms of local culture are followed.

Western missionaries are influenced by the power that the youth subculture of their own societies wields. Against this background they often attempt to work with university students and other potential influence makers on the youth scene. What they fail to appreciate is that beyond campus activities, youth in Muslim societies have little independence and even less lasting influence. That resides with more senior people who are leaders of their families, villages and other sub-sets of society.

So when a 105 year old village elder and his 95 year old wife were converted in Indonesia this had a profound impact. This man had been a teacher of Islam in his village for 50 years and was a person of significant presence and influence. He would certainly be listened to. Within four months this couple had helped lead an additional 40 people to Christ and had formed an active and effective church.[44] How different was this person's influence compared to a similar aged person in the West.

Because 'God is...beyond and outside of any culture, neither endorsing nor condemning any cultural system in its totality...'[45], cross-cultural missionaries to Islam feel an increasing freedom to break away from the traditions of their predecessors and establish new forms that are more culturally attuned to the people among whom they live and work. In so doing they are rediscovering principles experimented with by Matteo Ricci, a Jesuit missionary to China (1581–1610),[46] de Nobili, Francis Xavier and others who long ago made similar attempts which were subsequently buried under the unstoppable weight of precedent and tradition.

Because Muslims sometimes define Christianity as 'a foreign religion of infidels', to remove that blockage of misunderstanding more innovative workers refer to themselves as *Muslims* which literally means *those who submit to God*. They do this on the basis of James 4:7 which calls for the necessity of submission to God and that according to the Quran some of Jesus' disciples called themselves *Muslims* (Surah 5:111).[47] They would argue that to refer to oneself as a Christian is neither a core value nor a theological imperative. To delete such a title also avoids unfortunate and unnecessary historical baggage that Muslims often associate with the Crusades.

The process being adopted is known as contextualisation, a word first introduced by Taiwanese theological educator, Shoki Koh.[48] Traditional culture by its nature is more fixed. Contextualisation is dynamic, taking into account that life as it is lived within any context is always changing.[49] It affects how messengers to the Muslim world will live, dress, eat and act. It will influence whether men wear beards or not to honour local tradition. It will determine whether women, in order to reach those to whom they have come to serve and witness, will curb their own freedoms by voluntarily covering themselves in ways appropriate to the local situation. They may also choose to limit their freedom of movement beyond the home.

Whether such is inconvenient, uncomfortable or even oppressive, the choice to limit liberty is always at the discretion of the messenger.[50] By adopting such practices, at least the problem of accretions of Western culture as is represented in Churchianity is diminished to where Muslim enquirers may see more clearly the Christ who is the cornerstone of the Church. Unfortunately, longer established minority communities of Christians in some predominantly Muslim countries have not appreciated such initiatives or the response it has brought, as Phil Bourne discovered:

The Church's response to Islam has been woefully inadequate from the beginning until now. It has been more concerned with its own survival and with church politics than winning Muslims to Christ...Some even contend that it is undesirable. A neighbour's priest told her that devout Muslims would go to heaven without knowledge of Christ, so best leave them alone. Others have answered... 'Do not give what is holy to dogs; do not cast your pearls before swine'.[51]

Additionally, because of the interplay between colonisation and the religion of the imperialists, the feelings between some Christians and Muslims are equally antagonistic. As one Indonesian Muslim leader said, 'We'd rather go to hell than follow Dutch white religion'. Interestingly, when the overlay of colonial Churchianity was separated from essential Christianity so that he could see its founder more clearly he gladly accepted the teachings of Jesus Christ. Methodologies of presenting the truth have had to change. The Truth itself remains changeless. The listener could not hear the message because of the messenger.

Muslim governments have not been unaware of the effectiveness of new approaches of more recent decades. In 1988 some Malaysian state governments enacted legislation against the use of anything that could be construed as influencing a Muslim to give up his religion. Even the use by non-Muslims of certain words and phrases in common use was banned.[52] In 1989 the Malaysian federal government's Ministry of Home Affairs banned the use of the word *Allah* in Malay Bibles even though Syrian Bibles used that term before Islam was even born.[53]

In 1969 the federal government of Malaysia granted the Muslim section of its population privileges for government scholarships, purchase of property, business incentives, tax exemptions, preservation of senior political appointments and civil service executive positions, senior positions in the military, police force and education department. In 1993 government education officials instructed principals of Christian schools to remove all crosses from their classrooms. The following year the ban on non-Islamic faiths using certain words of the national Bahasa Malaysian language was extended further. As long as any of these words were used in the Bahasa Malaysian Bible it remained banned in public bookstores.[54]

But notice was being taken of new found effectiveness in Muslim evangelism not just in Malaysia. By 1997 Amir Abdullah writing in the Muslim magazine *Nida'ul Islam* was noting:

If you go to a missionary church in a typical African country you'll find that it resembles a mosque more than an archetypal church. The worshippers stand in rows during prayer and sit on the ground in circles during classes. The traditional pulpit of the preacher has given way to the minbar. When reciting the Bible they even use a style of recitation exactly the same as the Quar'nic Tajweed...They hold their services on Fridays (Jumu'ah)...You will also find the missionaries use Islamic expressions such as 'Bismillah', 'Jesus Alaihi Salam' and 'Allah Subhanah'.[55]

In Africa, as Muslims are increasingly beginning to follow Jesus, 'they call him by his Arabic name, Isa, and worship him in Messianic mosques...'[56]

How did such a change come about? Back in the 1970s missionaries to Muslims were asking a key question, 'To what extent may we incorporate Muslim forms and vocabulary without compromising our message?' In Bangladesh at that time, Phil Parshall and others believed that the change to a simple lifestyle, wearing of local clothing, adoption of dietary restrictions, worship forms and appropriate religious vocabulary, along with the writing of more appropriate literature could have been a turning point for a new beginning.[57] Parshall later provided a detailed rationale for such an approach.[58]

Although foreign workers of that era have long since departed from Bangladesh, the theories they espoused and practices they attempted may, with time, have proved to be amazingly effective. In February 1990, the Islamic Research Centre in Bangladesh claimed that in an area known as Chapainababgang, 300–400 Muslims were being converted to Christianity each year. Their article also referred to an earlier survey report of a non-government concern (Daily Sangram 14 September 1989) which had stated that 30 000 people had been converted to Christianity in that year alone.[59] By 1994 the Al-Muslimoon Weekly in Bangladesh was claiming that in the Chittagong area thousands of Muslims had 'declared their new Christian faith'. Sheikh Muhammad Akhtar Husain, Dean of the Arabic language college at Kashif University, went on to say that these new converts were different from those in the past:

The conversions taking place are not external appearances only, as have been noted in some previous group conversions, but now reflect sincere experience. The new Christians...lifted their Injils (New Testaments) high over their heads...

> ## In February 1990 the Islamic Research Centre in Bangladesh claimed that in an area known as Chapainababgang, 300–400 Muslims were being converted to Christianity each year.

This can be considered a new phenomenon in Bangladesh. If one convert incident had happened in the past, huge numbers of Muslims attacked the house of the one convert. When they do not find the convert they kill his father.

The article concluded that 'preliminary statistics are really amazing as the number of converts are reaching almost 100 000.'[60]

Even more recently, a report of the Islamic Missionary Council of Bangladesh regarding the alleged growth as a result of more contextualised approaches concluded, 'They are preaching *Isa-I* (Jesus) faith very tactfully staying under the shadow of Islam. It is spreading very fast and contagiously like AIDS virus and destroying Islam.'[61]

If these unsubstantiated reports are correct, who could have guessed that once the most obvious – culture and context – were no longer overlooked, the Spirit could be released through his messengers to achieve what God has desired for all of these long lost centuries?

CHAPTER 23

REMOVING BLOCKAGES

He was very well educated. He had successfully completed a doctoral degree at a world-famous university in the Middle East and had then gone on to do a second doctoral degree at a university of international standing in the West. He had obviously lived and travelled extensively in various countries of the world. For two years this highly intelligent Muslim enquirer was absolutely convinced of the truth of the Gospel of Jesus Christ but he could not bring himself to surrender to Jesus as Lord. Eventually he stated his reasons.

First, he could not bring himself to become a 'Christian' because he did not want to become 'dirty'. His second reason was that he loved his wife too much ever to give her up. What did this mean?

On further questioning he said the cleanliness problem related to his observation of how 'Christians', whenever they had something in their noses, took out small pieces of cloth from trouser pockets and blew the contents of their noses into the cloths. They then carefully preserved the contents in their pockets. He further observed that from time to time, these cloths were taken out, carefully re-examined and frequently more nasal discharge was added. He considered this to be a dirty habit compared to the more common practice of his country of origin, of simply holding one nostril at a time and clearing each by blowing its contents onto the side of the road or the room.

Regarding the matter of his wife, he had seen a Hollywood movie in which there was a folk dance sequence. In this particular scene the men and women danced in concentric circles and, at set intervals, changed partners. He assumed that this was a normal 'Christian' practice and that he would therefore have to give his wife into the arms of another unknown male when they became Christian.

If these sorts of cultural confusions could cause significant anxiety for such an internationally experienced, highly intelligent and well educated person, and therefore delay acceptance of truth, what hope may there be for people of less experience and education?

Cultural and theological blockages to the reception of truth are common. Unless they are known and dealt with effectively, then messengers of Jesus might go their way imagining that they have communicated truth, but remain frustrated because of the continual lack of response. The first message the Muslim receives is usually the life of the messenger. That's why it is so important that the messengers contextualise their patterns of living with those among whom they live or to whom they go. They must also live a life absolutely consistent with the Gospel they preach.

In seeking to remove blockages preparatory to the presentation of truth, many have found a favourable hearing by also judiciously using selections from the Quran. In so doing one must be careful never to say anything negative regarding that book which is holy to so many. Nor should messengers of Jesus Christ ever say anything negative about Islam's Prophet or the cultures into which they might go.

However the use of the Quran needs to be done carefully lest it is assumed that the messenger is granting to it a status of authority equal to that of the Bible. The Quran is often used as a means with which to open dialogue only.[1] In witnessing to Muslims debate and argument should be avoided at all costs. The confrontationist approach that was followed over so many centuries has proven to be singularly ineffective in results achieved. We do well to heed the well learned lesson of Paul's instruction to Timothy when he said,

Don't have anything to do with foolish and stupid arguments because you know they produce quarrels. And the Lord's servant must not quarrel; instead, he must be kind to everyone, able to teach not resentful. Those who oppose him he must gently instruct in the hope that God will grant them repentance leading them to a knowledge of the truth (2 Timothy 2:23–25).

Representatives of Jesus are '*...to slander no one, to be peaceable and considerate and to show true humility toward all men (Titus 3:2)*'.

The most common and widespread blockages that need to be addressed are:

1. The Holy Books of Jews and Christians have been corrupted.

While Muslims accuse the People of the Book (ie. Jews and Christians) of changing their own sacred writings, it is important to note that the Quran nowhere states that Christians or Jews have changed the written words of their texts. The Quran does accuse followers of such religions of changing the meaning of words with their tongues and of keeping some portions of Scripture hidden. But even if that charge was true, it is still a long way from deliberately tampering with the written sacred texts.

If there is any truth to the assumption that Christians and Jews have changed their books, then other unanswerable questions automatically follow which need to be addressed.

a. Who changed the texts?

The Quran attests that Jews and Christians were hardly the best of friends (Surah 2:113). So it would be highly unlikely that they would have colluded in such an exercise. Furthermore, whenever their books deal with common material they are in exact and total agreement still to this day.

The Quran also attests that among Christians there were sincere men who devoted themselves to learning (Surah 5:82). It would be nigh on impossible to believe that such unrelated scholars would willingly impugn their personal integrity by deliberately tampering with the sacred texts to manipulate collusively such an outcome, especially when they also knew that this was expressly forbidden with dire consequences should such ever be attempted (Revelation 22:18–19).

Also both Bible and Quran attest that once God's word is uttered it is impossible for anyone else ever to alter it (Psalms 119:89; Isaiah 40:8; Mark 13:31; Surah 6:34; 10:64).

b. When were they changed?

Given that Muhammad himself admits to the existence of the Holy Books and always speaks of them with the utmost respect, it would appear as unlikely that it could be conjectured that such books were changed before his time. If it is postulated that the Jewish and Christian texts had been grossly corrupted prior to or during Muhammad's time, then why would he have been 'instructed' to praise and declare his belief in and make appeals to the Holy Books which preceded him (Surah 2:136; 5:46, 68)? Why would their contents be so uniformly confirmed (Surah 10:94; 42:15)?

The Quran declares that it was sent to confirm the preceding Holy Books (Surah 2:89, 91, 101) in like manner as the Gospel confirms the Law (Surah 5: 46). If that was the case up to the time of Muhammad, then the question arises: Were the Holy Books changed after his time? There is certainly no historical evidence for such an unthinkable phenomenon before or after the time of Muhammad. Still today the fourth and fifth century Codecies Sinaiticus, Alexandrinus and Vaticanus may be viewed by scholars in the British Museum and the Vatican Library respectively. These quite early manuscripts demonstrate that the text of the Bible isn't changed. 'The theory of the falsification of the Bible appears to have been designed to vindicate the Quranic claim that Muhammad's coming was foretold in the Scriptures.' [2]

c. How were they changed?

By the time of Muhammad, Christianity was already established across three continents. How could all copies of all translations have been changed simultaneously and then that which previously existed also have been simultaneously destroyed so completely as to leave absolutely no trace? Surely in some of the study centres, synagogues, monasteries, libraries or even homes there would be some evidence of previously unchanged versions in existence. But this is never alluded to nor conceived within the history of either Judaism or Christianity. Collusion to commit such an act could certainly not have so totally escaped the attention of all the participants and all the adherents. Some evidence must remain somewhere. The undertaking of such a procedure at any time would be impossible to arrange and expect such an equally impossible outcome.

d. Why would the Holy Books be changed?

There is no answer as to why either Jews or Christians would even consider changing any of their texts. Even more so is the case when one reads that the Quran itself declares that it was sent to confirm previous revelations (Surah 5:48; 6:91–92; 46:12).

The reason the Quran gives for being a means of confirming the preceding Holy Books is that those previous revelations contain God's guidance to mankind (Surah 3:3), light (Surah 5:44, 46) and admonition (Surah 28:43). Furthermore the Quran states that those who reject such 'signs' of God will suffer the severest penalties (Surah 3:4; 4:56; 5:10). In all of this there is no suggestion that the Quran was given to modify, annul or replace any of the previous books. According to Islam's own teaching the Quran's role is one of confirmation. Therefore why would one ever want to destroy the original source material upon which everything else presumably depended?

Occasionally Muslims will claim that there are copies of the original, unchanged, unexpurgated editions of the Holy Books in existence which were pre-existent to the 'change'. Presumably these do agree with the testimony of the Quran. When asked for the location of such texts, usually a sacred mosque in some far off place may be named. Occasionally it is even agreed that such copies can be viewed. None of course has ever been produced even at the named sacred sites.

The battle of the Books is of fundamental importance to the revelation of truth. Usually it is not solved by asking the above questions in response to the claims of corruption, but at least the questions are lodged in the mind of the enquirer. That step is often the beginning of a journey of adventure.

2. Christians worship three gods

One of the strongest objections Muslims make against Christian belief is their understanding that Christians worship three gods. This assumption is based on a false understanding of what Christian theology means when it refers to the Trinity. When Muslims use the word *trinity* they have been taught that what Christians mean by *trinity* is God the Father who had relationships with God the Mother (Mary) to produce God the Son (Jesus). It is this *trinity* against which the Quran speaks (Surah 5:73, 116). It is thought that this mistaken understanding may have come about because at the time of Muhammad 'pagan deities were male and female and had children'.[3]

Trinitarianism as understood by Muslims cuts across their doctrine of the unity of God – *tawhid* (Surah 4:171). Those who ascribe partners to God commit the sin of *shirk* (Surah 5:73). Fortunately the doctrine of the trinity does not contradict the concept of *tawhid*.

The Quran affirms that God does have a Will which is expressed through his Word – Jesus (Surah 4:171) *kalimatuhu* (cf. John 1:1–2, 14) and implemented by his Spirit (Surah 4:171; 16:40; 36:82; 58:22). Therefore at creation when God spoke through his Word and by his Spirit he created a universe which came into being (cf. Genesis 1:1–3; Psalms 33:6; 104:24, 30). God, the Creator, his Word and his Spirit are uncreated, eternal and of divine essence. The concepts are common both to the Quran and the Bible.

Christians also believe that God is one. Moses taught it (Deuteronomy 6:4). Jesus confirmed it (Mark 12:29). Paul adhered to it (Galatians 3:20). Ask any Christian how many gods they worship. The answer is always 'one' – even from children.

The Bible reveals the tri-unity of God.[4] Because of the theological complexity of the concepts behind the word it is probably best not to introduce it into any conversation other than to note that although Christians and Muslims use the same word they attach significantly different meanings to it. The relationship between God, Word and Spirit is a mystery and probably ought to remain so in spite of the best attempts at description and definition by mere mortals.

3. Jesus cannot be the Son of God

Here again, is another example of usage of the same words by different religions that for the unwary represents a misunderstanding unless the meanings ascribed by each to these words are clearly understood. As noted earlier, Muslims are taught that the usage of this term relates to a physical relationship between God the Father and God the 'Mother'(Mary) which resulted in God the Son (Jesus). The concept is repulsive to Muslims and justifiably so. Unknown to Muslims that concept is equally repugnant to Christians.

There is a need to explain that the term 'Son of God' is not used in the normal, literal, physical, biological sense. The use of 'son' is pregnant with a plethora of meanings according to context variations.

Followers of Jesus are called 'sons of God'(John 1:12). The term 'son' in this context is used of those who are representative of God's power and authority. In certain Middle East contexts, travellers are called 'sons of the road'. But this does not mean that they are made of bitumen, concrete or stones. Bedouin nomads are referred to as 'sons of the desert'. But this does not mean they are made of sand. A common insult within Muslim culture is to call someone the 'son of a pig'. But that does not imply the one insulted is a piglet. In an African context a merchant is called a 'son of a table' because he sits in one place all day in the market. A policeman is called 'a son of a stick' because he wields a rod of authority. None of these terms convey concepts of biological descent.[5]

In the Bible this term in relating to Jesus is used by God himself to describe a most intimate relationship between himself and his Word – Jesus (Matthew 3:17).

4. Christianity is a Western religion and is therefore weak and immoral

During a plane journey, a Saudi Arabian was once asked what he knew about Christianity. He replied, 'Everything. I watch a Christian movie on my VCR every night.'[6] The misunderstanding that Christianity is 'Western' arises from the fact that through most of the twentieth century, Western nations have been economically, militarily and culturally dominant.

Muslim enquirers need to be reminded that Christianity was actually founded in the Middle East and still has many followers in that area as well as having the majority of its followers in non-Western countries. Just as Western Christians assume that anything that they see in their media originating in Muslim countries is the activity of sincere Muslims which is a mistake, so Muslims think that anything they view on their VCRs or television is a product of Christianity. They cannot conceive of atheism or people without religious belief. Because Islam is a seamless garment across Islamic society it is assumed that Christianity operates likewise. If atheism is an impossible concept for Muslims to grasp, the modern Western division of secular and sacred is equally difficult for them to understand. Therefore whatever is on display is assumed to be the product of Christianity. A Muslim who later became a Christian recorded how he was grossly offended on his visit to America when he first saw 'sexually lewd billboards and the tremendous number of liquor ads. We had never seen such corruption and immorality.'[7]

Regarding society in Great Britain another Muslim observed:

...the great majority of the Christian people in the UK would accept the philosophy of safe sex...This is a country that encourages promiscuity. The great majority of those who speak on behalf of Christianity today have gone back to paganism in their religious life, their morality and their lifestyle.[8]

Speaking on the situation in the West in general yet another Muslim commented:

I am now convinced that they have literally transformed themselves into animals...(They) have transformed their society into a Satanic and animal like culture...Their laws that permit a lifestyle that suits their lust is a major cause...they indulge in free sex, nudity, homosexuality, lesbianism and the like.[9]

What can be said regarding such observations? We can only point out that people who do these things are not the true followers of Jesus Christ. This is what makes it vitally important that messengers remember that they are the message that is being watched.

The charge of immorality comes even from those who are unaware of secularised Western culture and its effects. In many Muslim countries the majority of women may live in purdah or if they go out, are well covered. But Western tourists or even indigenous Christians in those countries, by comparison are relatively uncovered, giving rise to the charge of flaunting immorality. This once more raises the significant question of contextualisation. Will the Christian messenger so limit his or her freedom to dress appropriately to avoid such an offence?

Regarding the charge of weakness one Muslim commentator put it thus:

Christianity has failed to challenge the onrush of secular civilisation. It hasn't challenged human reason or the ideas of enlightenment, humanism, liberalism, free sexuality of the so-called morality of conscience. The Church has allowed standards to fall to a point where they have virtually ceased to exist. It supports the secular state...Christianity has basically surrendered to secular civilisation.[10]

It is difficult to deny the charge especially with the Western division of State and Church. Again the Muslim finds it difficult to understand how religion is not interwoven with politics and the rest of society. Perhaps the best defence against the charge of 'weakness' is to personalise it, pointing out that many have willingly died for their faith in Jesus. Such is only possible because of a true believer's close relationship with God and the strength he gives. And that may very well be tested in the witnessing situation to hand.

The charge against Western culture, its immorality and the perceived weakness of Christianity is a major evangelising point for Muslim preachers. They hold that 'humanity' has become tired of purely materialistic conditions and desires some spiritual comfort. But the materialistic life of the West can only offer him as reassurance a new materialism of sin, passion, alcohol, promiscuity, noisy gatherings and showy attractions which people have come to enjoy.[11]

Christians need to confess there is truth in some of this and resolve to live in the opposite spirit. We need to remind ourselves that nothing will offend a Muslim more than someone who 'talks the talk' while not 'walking the walk'.[12]

Muslims may be reminded that in the Holy Quran, it is written that among the followers of Jesus there are many holy men and that there is no pride or envy in them (Surah 5:82). It is hoped that the one who now bears witness might be counted as one such regardless of the culture of his country of origin.

5. A new believer will be obliged to eat pork and drink wine

Unfortunately in some countries where Christianity has been a pressured minority, the above practice may have been used by the Christian community by way of a test of the sincerity of the almost feared Muslim enquirer. Enquirers need to be relieved of such a strain. They need to be reminded that Jesus never makes such demands as to cause us to change eating habits, clothing or other customs when we become his follower (Mark 7:14–23).

CHAPTER TWENTY THREE

6. A new believer must place his feet on the Holy Quran and speak against it

From the beginning it is important that the greatest respect is shown to the Quran and certainly it should never be placed anywhere below waist level. The same practice should apply to the Bible. It should be placed in a position of honour in the highest possible location in any room and when taken down very carefully handled, always held above the waist or placed on an appropriate support base. It should never be placed on the ground and never near the feet.

7. A new believer will be given money, a car, a house, a wife, employment, an overseas trip, etc.

A common charge is that Christians 'buy' Muslims. The introduction of any (foreign) funds into a primary witnessing situation is fraught with the possibilities of misunderstanding and charges of bribery and corruption. From the very beginning the enquirer needs to know that true religion cannot be bought or sold. If it could, there would be many more followers. Every believer has to stand on his own feet. It might seem a hard thing for messengers from more affluent countries to say to someone from a less affluent background but nevertheless the statement needs to be put within the religious and cultural context of the enquirer. He needs to be reminded that the question is not what will an enquirer be given, but rather what will he give to show his appreciation for and show his support of his new teacher in these crucial life matters. As hard as it seems, that principle ought to be followed lest compassion be misconstrued as corruption.

> The charge against Western culture, its immorality and the perceived weakness of Christianity is a major evangelising point for Muslim preachers. They hold that 'humanity' has become tired of purely materialistic conditions and desires some spiritual comfort.

Having hopefully and effectively dealt with some of the blockages which are surely in the mind of the enquirer, even if unspoken, it is only then time to proceed with the introduction of Truth. Evangelism is more than a knowledge of apologetics. Apologetics is simply an aid in communicating the Gospel. There can be no substitute for presenting the gospel itself (Rom 1:15–16; 1 Cor 9:16; 1 Cor 15:3– 4).

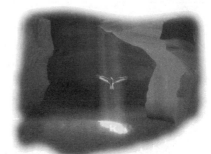

CHAPTER 24

THE ENTRANCE OF TRUTH

As Bishop Warne of the North India Methodist Church preached, his congregation sat on the ground before him. They listened attentively as once more he told them the story of Jesus. Using all of his narrative skills he came to the climax of events. He vividly described the last hours of Jesus' life. He told how the very people whom Jesus came to help seized him, mocked him, tortured him, led him away to crucifixion, indescribable suffering, desertion by his friends and finally death.

When the Bishop reached this point, an old Hindu priest could contain himself no longer. He rushed forward, threw himself at the Bishop's feet and shouted repeatedly, 'We want you to leave India!' The Bishop quietly asked why. The priest replied, 'Because we have no story like this. We have no saviour who lived a sinless life, who died for his enemies and prayed for the forgiveness of those who took his life. We have no story like this in any of our religions. If you keep on telling this story to our people, they will leave our temples and follow your saviour!'[1]

Storytelling has always been the most powerful and effective means of communication. Still today in Wales people gather for annual summer storytelling festivals. Stories always affect the listeners. Jesus demonstrated their power by teaching in parables as a means to attract and hold audience attention. 'To be successful in capturing people's attention, we (also) must find the stories of God working in the lives of people.'[2]

As President Mengistu Haile Mariam's communist government in Ethiopia was staggering toward its end in 1990, five young men found a book which they had never seen before. It was a Bible. Fascinated by its contents, during their daily factory lunch break they went off to read it to one another. It changed their lives. As they continued to read they felt compelled to tell others the story of Jesus. In the town of Nazaret, they asked the local Bishop if they could tell Bible stories in the church courtyard on Sunday afternoons. He agreed. So a weekly Bible story time was commenced.

As these young men told their stories from the Bible more and more people started to turn up. From the larger group, smaller Bible study clusters were developed.

Inevitably from these eager listeners many came to accept Jesus Christ. These new converts were encouraged to share their story with others. The small groups multiplied. By the end of the first year there were 800 new believers. After two years there were 2000.

At this point it became a bit too much for the local church officials and the storytellers were obliged to move on. As they continued to tell their stories now in an open field, new people kept coming. As members of the group found work in other towns the process was repeated. Eventually small groups of believers were established throughout the region. The movement continued to grow. By the end of 1998 more than 200 000 people had responded to the story of Jesus Christ.[3]

The hunger for stories about real life is not confined to developing countries or religion. A leading Australian journalist, Martin Flanagan, wrote:

Dinner parties usually bore me, people swapping opinions acquired at little or no cost to themselves and worn externally like fashion accessories. I want to know what people really think – what makes them laugh and what makes them cry, what gets them through the long dark night of their souls, what is the wisdom of their days? I want their testimony.[4]

As Western societies become more technologically sophisticated resulting in human exchanges being more fleetingly brief if not illusory, not surprisingly, we also crave real interaction through human stories. Every nation, every civilisation has them and needs to repeat them. Storytelling is a means of secular salvation or destruction.

When Russia wanted to incorporate the Ukrainian peoples, it is said that the Czar's troops rounded up all the village storytellers and killed the men. They believed that if a people's stories could be destroyed then the people themselves would be subjugated more easily.[5]

In contemporary Western society, cinema centres have replaced the Cathedral, the medieval storytelling centre. Western sociologists think they have made a significant discovery by finding that Generation X people prefer storytelling as a means of information transmission. But storytelling has always been with us. It is the universal form of communication. Furthermore, with a half of the world's population still illiterate or semiliterate it is likely to remain so. Propositional thinking as a means of defining the abstract concepts of philosophy and theology with its dogmas and creeds will seldom grip the soul of any people. Stories stir our imaginations and touch our emotions.

When one analyses the Bible, it is not surprising that only 10% of its writings (the Pauline Greek influenced sections) follow logical, linear outlines. Poetry comprises 15% of the sacred text. A full 75% of the Bible is narrative.[6] The stories of heroes and antiheroes in the Bible are not ends in themselves. They are there to reveal the activities of God in his ongoing relationship with humanity. Jesus followed a similar methodology. His stories were drawn from the life of the common person but were packed with theological application. Often it was left to the stirred imagination of the listeners to reach their own conclusions.

In teaching truth to Muslim enquirers, the same methodologies need to be emphasised. 'It is not difficult to retell the Biblical parables in modern and Islamic dress.'[7] Wherever possible we need not only to communicate by logic but supremely by story, using all possible descriptive and narrative skills to stir the imagination of the listener. There are undoubtedly many ways in which to approach an authentic Bible centred witness to Muslims. The Appendix in this book contains one outline that has proven effective.

Having first addressed the misconceptions in the mind of the hearer (Appendix – Lesson 1), the 'story' starts with the second coming of Jesus (Appendix – Lesson 2). This is an appropriate starting point because it is a common meeting ground of Islam and Christianity. The signs of that coming referred to by Jesus in Matthew 24 read like headlines in the daily newspapers of many countries in which Islam predominates. Wars, famine, earthquakes, persecution, social indiscipline etc may not be frequent experiences for Western Christians, if at all. But it is the daily stuff of life in many other countries.

...storytelling has always been with us. It is the universal form of communication. Furthermore, with a half of the world's population still illiterate or semiliterate it is likely to remain so.

In many places Muslims have never been visited in their villages by a follower of Jesus. The very presence of one of these messengers is a dramatic fulfilment of what Jesus said must happen before his return (Matthew 24:14). The listeners become highly aware of this and are intrigued and riveted by its implications.

In that it is accepted that Jesus is coming a second time, curiosity is aroused to understand why he came the first time. This takes us back to the beginning and the next lesson on the creation of the world (Appendix – Lesson 3).

This presentation is a storyteller's dream. The Quran makes brief reference to the event but as in the case with Jesus and many other Biblical references in the Quran the Bible gives a much fuller account which always fascinates the listener.

The first conflict with a Muslim's traditional worldview is found when the storyteller arrives at Genesis 2:17. That mankind should be given freedom to choose good or evil is a concept foreign to Islamic theology. The implications of their thought form become clear when the story moves on to Genesis 3.

In checking for application and comprehension, whenever a Muslim enquirer is asked who was responsible for Adam and Eve's downfall, almost without exception the answer given is that Allah deceived them. While Islamic teaching acknowledges the universality of sin, its deterministic outlook on the world makes little allowance for the human attribute of freedom of choice. That we ourselves are responsible for our own sin has to be emphasised by repeating the original story again and again. Fortunately repetition is usually greatly appreciated.

Because we chose to disobey God, the next major unfolding in the story is of God's giving us Law by which we could live and re-establish relations with him (Appendix – Lesson 4). In speaking on the lesson of Law we are on familiar ground to Muslim listeners. But as they well know it is impossible for us to keep God's Law. Therefore the next lesson in the unfolding drama moves on to the introduction of the concept of sacrifice (Appendix – Lesson 5).

Many Christians may have often wondered why God caused the book of Leviticus to be written. Apart from its use as a law code by his original people, it is certainly a vital book for Muslims. They frequently express an enthusiastic appreciation for its minute attention to the detail of Law. It, of course, gives specifics for daily living which are closely parallel to the constructs and approach to life in Islam.

They laugh at the stories of the need for spotless animals to be presented and how the one who offers the sacrifice sometimes comes forth with a second rate doctored animal. They are amazed that long ago God was aware of such tendencies and practices. They are embarrassed to think that he knows of some of their occasional contemporary practices as well. But not even the system of sacrifice could be maintained by errant humanity. This leads onto the next chapter of the story, the coming of Jesus (Appendix – Lesson 6).

In presenting Jesus, it is vitally important that we allow him to stand as he is without all of our accretions of dogmatic interpretation or theological extraction. Again the story in itself is of sufficient strength and drama to grip the hearer and achieve what is intended. Just as it is important that the Old Testament preceded the New Testament in telling the story, so it is best that some chronological construct be outlined for the listener.

Western witnesses find it difficult not to jump ahead of where the listener might be at and move straight to the climax of the story, the death and resurrection of Jesus.[8] With this 'the greatest story ever told' we need to allow truth to unfold slowly just as Jesus did with his own potential disciples.[9]

We should not seek to do what only the Holy Spirit should do. We need to trust him in exactly the same way Jesus did. For example in the first lesson about Jesus the point may be reached where his divinity is encountered. But this should not be done through proof texting. It can be done more powerfully by understanding a Muslim's outline of the characteristics of divinity then simply telling stories of Jesus demonstrating his performance of these same things. Of course the temptation for the messenger is to draw the conclusions to reach another level. That would be a mistake.

The Muslim enquirer needs the more personal self-revelation of the nature of Jesus just as much as did the Apostle Peter

> While Islamic teaching acknowledges the universality of sin, its deterministic outlook on the world makes little allowance for the human attribute of freedom of choice.

(Matthew 16:13–20). It is the privilege of the storyteller not to race ahead to beat a theological drum and batter the listener's understanding both insensitively and prematurely. The storyteller tells the story and then prays. It is the role of the Holy Spirit to give revelation to bring understanding, conviction and response. The question for the enquirer always is who is Jesus? Only he can make that decision for himself.

In the following lessons on the death and resurrection of Jesus we are now on familiar troubled territory in Muslim–Christian dialogue (Appendix – Lessons 7–8). Again the storyteller can only tell the story. He is not to get into conflict with his Muslim enquirer over which Book is truthful. References in this lesson are designed to aid toward reaching a Biblical conclusion, but response is always the prerogative of the enquirer.

That any enquirer ultimately agrees that Jesus died is absolutely pivotal. If there was no death then there was no atonement. If there is no atonement then there is no forgiveness. If there is no forgiveness there is no salvation. The whole of the Christian message and God's approach to humankind pivots on the events of the Cross and our response to them. This is why extra time needs to be spent on discussing Jesus' death and resurrection.

Whether the telling of the story takes six hours, six weeks or six months, the question inevitably has to be put to the enquirer as to the nature of his response. It is never enough to engage in dialogue or to build bridges. The purpose of dialogue is to reach a conclusion. A bridge is meant to be walked over. That invitation must be given. It cannot be avoided (Appendix – Lesson 9).

If the response is in the affirmative, then a minimum of simple teaching must be given on two of Christianity's most basic practices, Baptism and the Lord's Supper (Appendix – Lessons 10 – 11). These are complex matters, again fraught with theological controversy over the centuries. Such has little place in introducing these practices to a new enquirer. Although it might irk the highly trained messenger, even these issues preliminarily have to be reduced to their simplest elements.

Having seen the Holy Spirit bring conviction and conversion of yet another enquirer that is merely the end of the beginning. To birth a baby is a pleasure of nine months' gestation. To bring the newborn to full reproductive maturity is a far more challenging prospect. But at least the end of the beginning has at last successfully arrived.

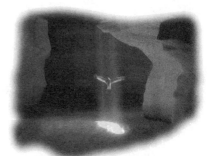

CHAPTER 25

THE TWENTY-FIRST CENTURY?

As we gaze out from the sheltered islands of our homes or churches through the reedy swamps of television antennae and satellite dishes via the media snowstorm of magazines and newspapers, the news reaches us that, in our time there has been unleashed upon the world spiritual forces of tremendous magnitude and power. These are already affecting our daily lives. The most powerful of these on the international scene is Islam.

For many years Christian missionaries have gone out to witness to the Muslims. But in these days, the tide of missionary endeavour is reversed. In England, the home of the father of Protestant missionaries of the modern era, William Carey, more missionaries are received from Islam than are sent out to Islam. Muslim universities and missionary training colleges are now established in Western countries. Islam is on the march.

Almost 14 centuries ago under the guidance of its Prophet Muhammad, it swept out from the sands of what is today known as Saudi Arabia. Its conquest of other peoples began with the defeat of Heraclius on the Yarmuk in 636 AD by the forces of Omar.[1]

Within the century, its armies had conquered the richest most populous parts of the formerly Christian countries from Afghanistan in the east to Spain in the west. From time to time in its history, Islam has seemed to lull into recession. But in our time, especially since the days of the first major oil crisis in 1973, Islam is once more expanding rapidly. This movement is strong, self-confident and in some forms, is aggressive, stern, unyielding and hostile to everything outside of itself. This previously underestimated movement with the perspective of history will probably be judged as one of the most profound, widespread and influential of our era.

In politics, by 2003 there were 56 acknowledged Islamic nations. Twenty-five percent of the delegates to the United Nations are from those countries.

The most recent Islamic resurgence came to international attention in 1981 when Ayatollah Rohollah Mussavi Khomeini urged all Muslims to commit themselves to

> In politics, by 2003 there were 56 acknowledged Islamic nations. Twenty-five percent of the delegates to the United Nations are from those countries.

the holy war of *jihad* against all infidel (ie. non-Muslim) governments. He said, 'Muslims have no alternative if they wish to enforce those in power to conform to the laws and principles of Islam. Holy war means the conquest of all non-Muslim territories, and this war is the duty of all Muslims.'

Since September 11 2001 most people have a much better understanding of exactly what he meant. Iranian Christians themselves say that:

Khomeini has been the biggest blessing (their) country has ever had, because he has revealed Islam for what it really is. Before he came Islam was a pretty package all wrapped up on the mantlepiece. Khomeini took the parcel, undid the wrapping and showed the world what is really inside.[2]

In 2001 Osama bin Laden did a similar thing as did the Indonesian Bali bombers in 2002. The Quran is Islam's holy book. Once more the principles of that book are being used to chart a course of world conquest. Joseph Farah believes that "Islam has been at war...with the entire non-Muslim world ever since the days of Muhammad. This struggle, more than any other, has defined history for the last 1200 years'.[3]

Ziauddin Sardar, a Pakistani research scholar, wrote that division of time in the West is on a work–play basis. In a Muslim country it is on a fight–pray basis so that the external limits of Islam can be expanded and that the people of Islam can be strengthened from within.[4]

Sukri al-Quwatli, a former President of Syria, said, 'Our frontiers are not our limits but our wounds'. Abd-al Qader as Sufi Ad Darqawi expressed it thus, 'All Muslims are at war and our battle has only just begun...Islam is moving across the earth...and nothing can stop it.'

In international finance it is widely recognised that Middle Eastern Islamic nations certainly wield significant power. We are reminded of the linkage every time we refuel our vehicles. In spite of developments elsewhere, for many years to come, oil from the Middle East will remain an economic jugular for the Western world. If it is closed there would be massive disruption to Western economies. Saudi Arabia has 25% of the world's known oil reserves. America uses 25% of the world's production. In 1973 Middle Eastern authorities may have thought that 'they have (the West) over a barrel with gasoline.'[5] Samuel Huntington believes that 'The actions of the oil-rich Muslim states if placed in their historical, religious, racial and cultural setting, amount to nothing less than a bold attempt to lay the Christian West under tribute to the Muslim East. The Saudi, Libyan, and other governments have used their oil riches to stimulate and finance the Muslim revival.'[6]

With OPEC's inability to control the international price of oil the contest for economic supremacy is now waged on other fronts. Waseem Shehzad reports that Muslims have mounted boycotts against United States products. American giants such as McDonald's, Burger King, Kentucky Fried Chicken and Pepsi have all been affected. The boycott campaign started unofficially on university and college campuses in Egypt. It spread to mosques and from there to many countries from Morocco to Indonesia. Islamic replacement products such as Zam Zam Cola and Mecca Cola have been spectacularly successful in the Middle East and France. With an estimated US$1.2 trillion invested by Muslims in the USA, calls are made for them to redirect their investments within the Islamic sphere.[7] Malaysia is attempting to become a global hub for Islamic finance and is promoting itself as a banking place for the Muslim world for corporate debt to be processed in compliance with Islamic rules.[8]

Malaysia was also responsible for introducing the Islamic gold dinar in 2003 as a first step to replace the US dollar in a 'move toward unifying the currency used in commercial dealings between Islamic countries'.[9]

But it is in the area of religious evangelism that a most startling change has occurred around the world in recent decades. Back in the 1970s the secular organisation of the United Nations estimated that Islam was making up to 10 million new converts a year among animist Africans alone. As mosques have been multiplying from Cairo to the Cape conversions to Islam are accelerating even more rapidly. Throughout much of the twentieth century Islam grew at a rate 11 times faster than that of Christianity.

Islam offers certainty of belief through its simple creed. From millions of mosques around the world there echoes the daily cry *La illaha illa Allah. Muhammad rasullah* (There is no God but Allah. Muhammad is his Prophet).

In the United States of America during the decade of the 70s, the number of Muslims quadrupled. Islamic centres and mission bases within America are producing a generation of Muslim missionaries who anticipate that within a short time America will no longer be a Judeo – Christian country. Islam is set to overtake Judaism as the second religion of America. From then on it will be an Islamic – Christian country.

In the United Kingdom, for some years, new Islamic centres were opening at the rate of approximately one every two weeks. Empty churches have been converted into fast filling mosques. Islamic law is slowly becoming accepted as valid in British courts. Already 5% of Muslims in England are former English Christians.

As mentioned earlier, British officialdom seemed to demonstrate amazing ignorance when in 1976 they allowed the Head of their State Church, Queen Elizabeth II, to open an amazing festival, the principal aim of which was to de-Christianise Britain and to convert it to Islam. Precisely that is happening. But decades later on it still seemed as if no lessons had been learned.

On June 18 1998, President Maumoon Abdul Gayoom of the Maldives imprisoned every Christian national within the republic and expelled all known foreign Christian workers.[10] Those in prison remained there for almost a year.[11] The government claimed that all Christians had reverted to Islam.[12] But during the time Christian believers were under such pressure, the President was warmly received in Britain where again Queen Elizabeth II, still 'Defender of the Faith', invested him with the Grand Cross of St Michael and St George at Edinburgh during a Commonwealth Heads of Government conference![13]

In the 1940s the English Channel stopped the invasion of Adolf Hitler and his armies but it has been powerless against that of Islam. The land of John Wesley now boasts more Muslims than either Methodists or Baptists. Islam has already become its second religion.

In Italy a massive mosque rivals St Peter's Basilica in Rome, the heartland for many of the world's Christians. In Australia Muslim prayer times are printed in newspapers. Special arrangements are made for the slaughter of animals for Muslims. The Federal Government granted land to establish an Islamic centre in Darwin. In Australia also, the claim is made that Islam is now that nation's second religion.

Wherever one goes in the Western world one may hear Muslim evangelists preaching that where Christianity has failed, Islam will rescue that nation from the mire of its drunkenness, sexual permissiveness, political corruption, violence, blasphemy and all the other sicknesses of the ailing, isolated, technocratic Christian West. Their evangelists say that while the West boozes its way to destruction, Islam offers a better and more wholesome way of life. They insist that the life of a true Muslim is a better source of propagation than a hundred missionary societies.

They believe that a day is coming when all will turn towards Mecca, the holy city in Saudi Arabia, bow down and confess that 'There is no God but Allah. Muhammad is his Prophet.' They declare that in pursuit of this objective a holy war is to be unremittingly pursued against all unbelievers and that this war shall not be revoked until all submit or until the Day of Judgment at the end of the world.

Islam is on the march and it has reached well within the borders of all Western nations.

In the light of this, the question must be asked, 'What is to be done?'

> The land of John Wesley now boasts more Muslims than either Methodists or Baptists. Islam has already become its second religion.

For those who are aware of the situation the spiritual battle has already been joined. 'All evangelism is a spiritual battle and Muslim evangelism is no exception.'[14] The only battle ever lost is when one surrenders.

In 1948 the infant State of Israel was surrounded by hostile armies. It teetered on the brink of annihilation. At that time Prime Minister David Ben Gurion sent a young woman, Golda Meier to the American Jewish community to appeal for help. To them she said, 'You cannot decide whether we will fight or not. We will. You can only decide one thing: whether or not we will be victorious.' Within weeks the American Jewish community raised 50 million dollars that Ben Gurion used to buy weapons for his underground army, the Hagganah. This secured the infant Israel's existence.

'You cannot decide whether we will fight or not. We will. You can only decide one thing: whether or not we will be victorious.' The question is how can a victory for Christ be more fully assured than it may appear to be at present? As stated earlier, there are a couple of things we need to do.

Change Attitudes

First, if followers of Jesus are to rise to the challenge of this day rather than to collapse in a whimper of night, we must change our attitude toward this challenge.

Down through the centuries of the Islamic era, Christians have believed that it is impossible to win Muslims. If we speak and think defeat usually that is what we get.

Christians have so allowed themselves to be deceived by a lying spirit, to where we have become like the Children of Israel who, when they came to the Promised Land (Numbers 13–14), sent out twelve spies to see what it was like. Those spies agreed that it was indeed a rich land of much milk and honey, that the crops were magnificent. But ten of them said, 'Oh, the cities, the armaments, the weapons, the people – they are like giants and we are like grasshoppers before them. We cannot go into that place.'

Their evaluation was based only on the physical situation as it appeared to be, rather than on the realities of the spiritual dimension. God had said, 'Go in, possess the land. I have already given it to you.'

But they chose to limit his greatness, might and power by the circumstances as they understood them. And so a faithless, deceiving report was released within their camp that was believed by all the tribes. This in turn brought death upon all as they returned to wander helplessly in the wilderness for the next 40 years. Similarly today, Satan wants to seduce us into believing that Muslims are unreachable. He wants to discourage us with a spirit of defeat.[9]

We need to know again the greatness of our God. We need to have our eyes opened as did that fearful young man who was with Elisha, to see again that 'the mountains are (still) filled with the horses and chariots of fire of our God' (2 Kings 6:17). Know you not that, 'The angel of the Lord encamps around those who fear him and that he (still) delivers them?' (Psalm 34:7).

We need to experience that the power that is within us is greater than that which is within the world (1 John 4:4). We need to remember that 'God (has) raised us up with Christ and (has) seated us with him in the heavenly realms in Christ Jesus' (Ephesians 2:6). Our place therefore is far above all the powers of any spiritual enemy. We have a position of authority and dominion over them. We are more than conquerors in Christ Jesus '…Thanks be to God! He gives us the victory through our Lord Jesus Christ' (1 Corinthians 15:57). Therefore we do not live under but over the circumstances.

Jesus is Lord of Lords and King of Kings. He does not send us forth to frustration and defeat but to victory. He is the all conquering, lion-lamb of God. It is only at his name that every knee shall bow and every tongue shall confess that he is Lord (Philippians 2:10–11).

There is no need to fear. Fear takes us out of the realm of the supernatural and into the natural. But faith takes us out of the natural and returns us to the supernatural. Later in their history, the Israelites looked at the size of the man, Goliath. But David, full of faith, gazed at the greatness of God (1 Samuel 17).[16] Fear seeks to control faith, to cause compromise, to decrease strength. But fear is overcome by faith. When faith enters then we can truly say we love Muslims.

Andrew Van de Bijl (Brother Andrew) once said, 'We need to begin by saying, "**I Sincerely Love All Muslims (I.S.L.A.M.)**". Then we should prove that statement by our presence…putting our arms around them and saying to them, "God loves you; therefore I love you".'[17]

During World War II an old drinking house favoured by American news correspondents in London was the Yorkshire Grey. There was a sign on the door that quoted Queen Victoria. It said, 'Please understand there is no pessimism in this house and we are not interested in the possibilities of defeat. They simply do not exist'.

At the beginning of the twentieth century when a small group of missionaries was first trying to enter Korea, their Board in New York informed them that they could send no senior missionaries nor could they give them much information about the country that they sought to enter. The Korean government of the day decided that in order to preserve the honour and dignity of the Orient, they would destroy the 'trespassing foreigners'. Yet those young missionaries were convinced that they were called by God to do what everyone else said was impossible. Gripped with a sense of urgency they declared, 'We are going to take Korea for Christ…We will be satisfied with nothing less'.[18]

Within a century almost 35% of the nation of South Korea had been won for Jesus Christ. These were people who by faith understood that when Jesus said, 'I have placed before you an open door that no one can shut' (Revelation 3:8), that was exactly the case. If from a human perspective the door seemed closed then they would crawl through a window, dig under the foundation or do whatever it took. But they would certainly settle for nothing less.[19]

Believe and Expect

Not only do we need to change our attitudes but secondly we need to believe and expect greater things from God.

Faith is that key which unlocks and releases the Spirit's resources that are placed within us. The Bible says that 'all things are possible to him who believes:' (Mark

> Not only do we need to change our attitudes, but secondly we need to believe and expect greater things from God.

9:23). Faith helps us to reach the unreachable, touch the untouchable and see the invisible. Our problem is that down through the ages we have not believed that it is even possible for our Lord to win Muslims and to overcome the world. This shows not just in our words but in our actions.

When a Muslim enquirer was first told of the Good News of Jesus Christ he asked, 'How long has this message been around?'

'About two thousand years,' replied the messenger.

'If that is so why haven't I heard of it before? There must be no Christians in my country.'

'Yes, there are,' said his informant.

'Well then, there are certainly none in this city.'

'Yes, there are,' was the reply.

'How is this possible? The only reason I can think of is that you Christians do not believe your own Gospel.'

What an indictment!

It is a fact that while many of us await the second coming of the Lord Jesus many know nothing yet of his first coming. People know more about Coca-Cola than about Jesus.[20] What an indictment!

In northern Africa the average ratio has been one cross cultural Christian worker per one million people.[21] The ratio of those involved directly in evangelism may be little better across the Muslim world. What an indictment!

Only one tenth of one percent of the Christian church's total income is spent on direct ministry outside the Christianised world. And only one hundredth of one percent is spent on the toughest unevangelised areas of the world that include Islam.[22] What an indictment!

We are to be lifeboats not tourist cruising ships. We need to reconsider our laid back, easy going, fun loving Christian culture which prefers our attendance at exciting Christian conventions to hear famous speakers, singers and musicians rather than the discipline of battle.

The Church has often turned its back on the evangelisation of the Muslim claiming it is too difficult, too dangerous or even impossible. We forget that our God is the God of the impossible (Matthew 19:26). In this situation the problem is not in the world but in the Church; not in the target people but in the mission, among the people of God. Jesus has called us to radical commitment, but we haven't lived it in our mission to Muslims. 'Until we do, Islam will continue to be the world's fastest growing religion – not because of its strength, but because of our weakness.'[24] It is we who need to change our attitudes and repent of our unbelief.

> Wherever people choose to believe God and push forward in faith, he is doing amazing things even amongst Muslims.

Is it possible that where the Bible says, 'Whosoever shall call upon the name of the Lord shall be saved' (Acts 2:21) that the 'whosoever' excludes a fifth of the world's population? Can it be that where the Apostle Paul says that 'the Gospel is the power of God unto salvation to everyone who believes' (Romans 1:16) that that 'every one' does not include the Muslim? The Bible says that God wants all people to be saved (1 Timothy 2:4). He does not want any to perish (2 Peter 3:9). The blood of Jesus Christ has purchased people from every tribe, language, people and nation (Revelation 5:9).

Wherever people choose to believe God and push forward in faith, he is doing amazing things even amongst Muslims. But as long as we continue to think or act defeat, then the tragic situation which confronts many who work in difficult access countries will continue to exist. People may live and die without ever hearing once the truth about that which we may hear of every day of our lives – the Gospel of Jesus Christ. In Islamic Bangladesh in November 1970 during one night alone as a result of a tidal wave an estimated 500 000 people died. In the same country from March 25 to December 10 1971 as a result of a war of independence from former West Pakistan, 3 million people were killed. The overwhelming majority of these were Muslims who had never heard once a meaningful presentation of the gospel of

Jesus Christ. Confronted with the challenge and opportunity of our times each needs to do at least three things.

Reaffirm and Prepare

First, we must reaffirm that we are involved in spiritual warfare and be prepared to enter into it. The Apostle Paul put it like this:

Finally, be strong in the Lord and in his mighty power. Put on the full armour of God so that you may be able to take your stand against the devil's schemes. For our struggle is not against flesh and blood but against the rulers, against the authorities, against the powers of this dark world and against the spiritual forces of evil in the heavenly realms. Therefore put on the full armour of God, so that when the day of evil comes, you may be able to stand your ground, and after you have done everything to stand. Stand firm then. (Ephesians 6:10–14a).

Elsewhere the Bible reminds us that 'the weapons of our warfare are not worldly but have divine power to destroy strongholds' (2 Corinthians 10:4). We need to use those spiritual weapons so that the 'strong man' (Matthew 12:29) will be bound so that we might plunder hell to populate heaven. A spiritual war is being waged as it has been since the beginning of time. It may not be seen but its casualties have been very high. It is the war between good and evil, darkness and light, God and his adversaries...This is the mother of all wars. War is not being fought over one country or one issue but for the hopes and fears of all humanity.[25]

Pray

Second, we need to pray. We are to lift our faces confidently toward heaven rather than lowering them in submission toward Mecca. In World War II the 'Battle of Britain' was won in the skies over England. In this battle too, the powers of the air may decide the outcome.

In 1924 a well-known missionary to the Muslim world, Samuel Zwemer wrote:

We are convinced that the present apparent inability of the Christian Church to deal effectively with the great problem of the evangelisation of Muslims is due above all else to the weakness of the prayer-life alike in the home churches and in the branches of the church in foreign lands.[26]

His call applies to our time as well.

But in addition to general prayer we are to pray specifically to the Lord of the harvest. Jesus said, '...the harvest is plentiful but the workers are few. Ask the Lord of the harvest, therefore, to send out workers into his harvest field' (Matthew 9:37–38).

Ask — Lord, What do you want of me?

Third, in the light of the situation which we face, each must ask himself before God, 'Lord, what do you want me to do? What do you want me to become? Where do you want me to go right now?'

In 1271 Mogul Emperor Kublai Khan ruled from the China Sea in the east to the Danube River in the west, from the Ural Mountains in the north to the Himalayas in the south. He sent a petition to the centre of world Christianity at that time, Rome. He asked them to send him missionaries who could explain the Christian faith. According to the custom of that time if the Emperor became Christian his whole court and his empire would follow him. However, as has often been the case, the Church was so preoccupied with internal housekeeping matters that it ignored his request for 18 years. Then they responded by sending too few too late. The door had closed. Buddhist lamas from Tibet had responded to a similar invitation much sooner. 'The night is far gone, the day is at hand, let us cast off the works of darkness and put on the armour of light' (Romans 13:12).

In Acts 9 there is the story of a young man called Saul. He was making his way to the city of Damascus in Syria breathing out his murderous threats against the Lord's disciples. He had set his direction. He had established his plans and purposes. He thought he knew where he was going. Then suddenly in a flash he was surrounded by light and struck to the ground. As he grovelled confusedly in the dust at the side of the road he called out, 'Who are you, Lord?' Back came the answer, 'I am Jesus. Now get up and go and you will be told what you must do.'

Today, just as was the case with Paul, we need to choose whether we will hide our eyes from the need and close our ears to the call or whether we will tackle with new decisiveness mixed with humility and devotion the unchanging command of our faithful God.[27] Upon our choice may very well depend the outcomes for this next century and beyond.

EPILOGUE

In answer to a telephoned order, a courier home delivered a copy of a video about Jesus. He was surprised when a Muslim sheikh opened the door at the designated address. The householder reassured the delivery person he had come to the right place. When the sheikh received his video, he turned to the room full of other Muslim leaders inside and joyfully shouted, 'Jesus is here! Jesus is here!'[1]

Indeed he was. He is. He will be.

But the question remains – where are we?

In July 1999 a correspondent of the New York Times sent a dispatch from Teheran. In it he wrote about his experience of going to see what was considered the most popular film in Iran at that time. It was called Two Women. The film concluded with the liberation of an Iranian woman from her cruel father and loveless husband. In the final scenes, the woman declared that in her newly found freedom she would start life all over again by going to computer classes and also learning how to drive. 'With that,' the correspondent wrote, 'the Iranian theatre erupted in cheers and applause.'[2]

Whether or not ruling authorities recognise it, there is a great yearning by many within Muslim societies for freedom? The question is what sort of freedom? Jesus said it is only as we know truth that we will be really free (John 8:32). Later he identified himself as that 'Truth' (John 14:6).

In the city of Damascus in Syria stands what was once the Cathedral of St John the Baptist. At huge cost it was converted into Islam's first great mosque. Within that building there still remains a single inscription written in ancient Greek. It is a reminder of former greatness and future hope. The inscription translates: 'Your kingdom come, Christ, is the kingdom of eons and your rule (is) in all generations.'

This book has been written in the hope that the declaration in the great mosque in Damascus might be fulfilled as God's people humbly and lovingly go forth, removing veils of misunderstanding, pointing toward the Way by which as many as choose may flow from the House of Islam into the Kingdom of God, free at last, forever in Jesus. Toward that end Christian responsibility and privilege is to persuade compassionately, wait patiently and pray earnestly.[3]

APPENDIX

🔲 *LESSON 1*

REMOVING BLOCKAGES

1. *Have the Holy Books of Jews and Christians been corrupted? Who? When? How? Where? Why?* (See pp 294–297).

2. *Do Christians really worship three Gods?* (see pp 297–298).

3. *How can Jesus be the Son of God?* (See p 298).

4. *Is Christianity a Western religion and therefore weak and immoral?* (See pp 298–300)

5. *Will a new believer be obliged to eat pork and to drink wine?* (See p 300).

6. *Will a new believer be required to place his feet on the Quran and speak against it?* (See p 301).

7. *Will a new believer be given money, a car, a house, a wife, employment or an overseas trip?* (See p 301).

🔲 *LESSON 2*

THE SECOND COMING OF JESUS

Followers of Jesus believe that Jesus will return to the world (John 14:3). Our Muslim brothers and sisters also believe that Jesus will return to judge the world (Surah 43:61). There is mention of this also in the Traditions (Hadith).

Before the second coming, what will we see?

1. Wars . . . . .Matthew 24:4 –7

2. Famines . . . . .Matthew 24:7

3. Earthquakes . . . . .Matthew 24:7

4. Persecution of followers of Jesus . . . . .Matthew 24:9 –10

5. False prophets . . . . .Matthew 24:11

6. Social indiscipline . . . . .Matthew 24:12; 2 Timothy 3:1–3

7. The Gospel preached in the whole world . . . . .Matthew 24:14

8. Times like the days of Noah . . . . .Matthew 24:37–39

When we look at the condition of the world today, we observe that many of these things have already been fulfilled.

When will he return? . . . . .Matthew 24:36, 44

We don't know. Therefore we must be ready.

How will he return? . . . . .Acts 1:9–11

The same way that he went. The archangel's call will be heard and the trumpet of God will be sounded (1 Thessalonians 4:16).

Why will he return?

To judge the earth . . . . .Acts 10:42; 2 Corinthians 5:10

What will be the results of this judgment? . . . . .Matthew 25:31–34, 41, 46; John 3:36, 5:24

The Holy Word is unchanging. Seven hundred years before the birth of Jesus, God through his prophets made known that Jesus was coming:

His birth . . . . .Isaiah 7:14

His birth place . . . . .Micah 5:2

The aim of his life . . . . Isaiah 53:5–6

Just as God kept the promise of Jesus' first coming, so we can be sure that the promise of his second coming will be kept. He will come to take his followers, the true believers, to be with him (John 14:3).

If Jesus is coming a second time, it is important to know why he came the first time. To understand that we need to go back to the beginning.

■ *LESSON 3*

CREATION OF THE WORLD

The Quran mentions this event (Surah 4:1; 6:2; 10:15; 11:7)

Day 1 The day and night ....Genesis 1:1–5

Day 2 The firmament ....Genesis 1:6–8

Day 3 The earth, the seas, the trees, etc. ....Genesis 1:9–13

Day 4 The sun, moon and stars, etc. ....Genesis 1:14–19

Day 5 Fish and birds, etc. ....Genesis 1:20–23

Day 6 Animals and man ....Genesis 1:24–31, 2:1–3

God is almighty (Psalm 115:3) (Surah 42:1–5).

He is the Creator ....Hebrews 11:3

Creation of the First Man and Woman

The creation of Adam ....Genesis 2:4–7

The life God gave to man is not the same as he gave to animals .....Genesis 2:7

God's first law *(shariah)* for man and the gift of free will ....Genesis 2:17

Creation of the first woman ....Genesis 2:23–25

The first marriage ....Genesis 2:23–25

How did sin first enter the world? ....Genesis 3:1–7

The nature of sin:

    1. Hidden ....Genesis 3:8

    2. Fear ....Genesis 3:10

    3. Blaming others ....Genesis 3:12–13

Note: We ourselves are responsible for sin.

Judgment ....Genesis 3:14–19, 24

A special word:

Many Muslims think that Adam's and Eve's sin was eating a forbidden (unclean, prohibited) thing, but that is not so. It was because they broke a law of God. Although mankind disobeyed God once, to help us, God gave other laws to live by.

■ *LESSON 4*

THE LAW *(SHARIAH)*

When Adam and Eve disobeyed God they sinned. Because of their sin they were separated from God. Since then, every one of the descendants of Adam has been ruled over by sin. Every single person has sinned (Romans 3:23).

What is sin?

1. Breaking the law . . . . .1 John 3:4

2. Wrongdoing . . . . .1 John 5:17

3. Knowing what we should do but not doing it . . . . .James 4:17

4. Evil thoughts and desires . . . . .Mark 7:20–23

In that God still wanted to establish a special relationship with mankind, after many years, he revealed his commands and laws through the prophet Moses (Exodus 20:1–21).

But humanity chose and was too weak to obey the law. The law made us even more aware of our sins (Romans 3:20). No one can stand before God. But because he loves mankind, he does not want his precious creation to be destroyed.

Therefore he provided another way of saving his highest creation - us. He introduced a system of sacrifice.

■ *LESSON 5*

SACRIFICE (KURBAN)

How did the system of sacrifice commence?

The personal test of prophet Abraham (Genesis 22:1–14).

God established special days for sacrificing (Leviticus 23).

There were also different sacrifices for different types of sin (Leviticus 4:1– 4, 27, 29; 5:1, 4, 6 –9; 6:2, 6 –7).

The most important thing in the sacrifice was the blood (Hebrews 9:22).

Why was blood necessary (Leviticus 17:11)?

Conditions of acceptable sacrifice:

1. Confession of one's own sins (Leviticus 5:5).
2. Repentance (Leviticus 6:5).
3. Perfect spotless animal (Leviticus 1:3; 22:21).
4. Belief (Leviticus 1:4).
5. Sacrificing in the place specially appointed by God (Leviticus 1:3, 11; 6:1–7).

If these conditions were not met, then the sacrifice was unacceptable to God. Mankind also broke the rules of acceptable sacrifice.

But more than sacrifice, God desires:

1. Obedience . . . . .1 Samuel 15:22

2. Mercy . . . . .Hosea 6:6

3. Repentance and contrition . . . . .Psalm 51:16 –17

Mankind broke the conditions of sacrifice and therefore the sacrificial system became unacceptable to God (Isaiah 1:10 –17). Because we could not keep the Law or the sacrificial system, finally, Jesus came.

◼ *LESSON 6*

JESUS

Is Jesus a prophet? Is he the Messiah? Is he an ordinary man? Who is he (John 7:40–43)?

How are we able to learn about a person?

1. From his birth.

Before Jesus' birth, God made special announcements (Matthew 1:18–23) (Surah 3:45–46). He was born of a virgin (Surah 3:47; 19:20–21) as a holy son (Surah 19:19)

2. From his life.

Other prophets asked for forgiveness of sins: Adam (Surah 7:23), Abraham (Surah 26:82), Moses (Surah 28:16), David (Surah 38:24), Solomon (Surah 38:35), Jonah (Surah 37:142–144), Muhammad (Surah 48:1–2). But Jesus never had to ask for forgiveness.

3. From his work.

Jesus performed many mighty miracles (Surah 3:49) (John 21:25).

4. From his words.

Jesus' own declarations about himself:

1. The light of the world .... John 8:12

2. The resurrection and the life .... John 11:25–26

3. The way, the truth and the life .... John 14:6

4. The good shepherd .... John 10:11

5. Power to forgive sin .... Luke 5:18–24

6. The Saviour .... John 10:9–10

7. Before Abraham .... John 8:58

8. I and the Father are one .... John 10:30

The witness of others concerning Jesus:

1. John the Baptist. . . . . .John 1:32, 34

2. The disciples . . . . .John 20:30–31

3. The soldier . . . . .Matthew 27:54

4. God . . . . .Matthew 3:16; Mark 9:7

Jesus is placed nearest to God (Quran 3:45).

Note: Our Muslim brothers and sisters believe that **there are four things that only God can do:**

1. Give life

2. Cause death

3. Provide daily needs

4. Answer prayers.

These four characteristics were all seen in Jesus:

1. Giving life (John 11:38– 44).

2. Causing death (Matthew 21:18 –20).

3. Providing daily needs (Mark 8:1– 9).

4. Answering prayers (John 15:7, 16; 16:23–24).

So who is He?

Luke 8:22–25; Mark 9:2–7.

In various ways we have learnt about him. What do you think? Who is He?

■ *LESSON 7*

THE DEATH AND RESURRECTION OF JESUS

In the Quran it says '(the Jews) did not kill Jesus' (Surah 4:157). True. It was the Roman soldiers. Elsewhere the Quran refers to the death and resurrection of Jesus (Surah 19: 33–34).

It is necessary to read the Holy Injil to learn about these events. The Holy Injil was revealed through Jesus (Surah 19:30).

His Death

His death is recorded in various places in the Holy Injil.

1. He died on the cross . . . . .John 19:33–34

2. Joseph of Arimathea took his corpse . . . . .John 19:38– 42

3. His enemies put out a false story . . . . .Matthew 28:11–15

These prove that Jesus died on the cross.

His Resurrection

Other prophets returned to dust but Jesus returned to heaven (Surah 3:55; 4:158). In the Holy Injil these events prove without doubt that he is alive. For example:

1. The empty tomb . . . . .John 20:1–10

2. After he rose from the grave, he was seen with people:

   Mary Magdalene . . . . .John 20:11–18

   The disciples . . . . .John 20:19–25; 21:1–14

   More than five hundred . . . . .1 Corinthians 15:1– 8

Because of that day, a tradition was established that followers of Jesus worship together on Sundays.

■ *LESSON 8*

WHY DID JESUS DIE AND RISE AGAIN?

To answer this we must understand what sin is.

What is sin?

1. Disobedience to God's law (1 John 3:4; Matthew 5:28; Galatians 5:19–21).

2. The nature of sin. The effects of sin are extremely bad, eg. Adam and Eve (Genesis 3:4–19). Their relationship with God was destroyed and death came.

All have sinned (Surah 16:61) (Romans 3:23; John 1:8).

Note: One sin destroys all righteousness (James 2:10). No amount of prayer, sacrifice and good works can alter this!

Punishment is the result of sin.

1. Death . . . . .Romans 6:23

2. Judgment . . . . .Hebrews 9:27

3. Hell . . . . .2 Thessalonians 1:8–9

Jesus willingly submitted to God and died for the sins of mankind so that we might receive salvation:

(Philippians 2:8–10; Romans 3:25; 5:8; Hebrews 10:10–12; 1 John 2:2)

Why did Jesus rise from the dead?

1. To lift the burden of our sin . . . . .1 Corinthians 15:20–23

2. To secure our faith. . . . . .1 Corinthians 15:17

3. To make us blameless . . . . .Romans 4:25

Only if we believe in the death and resurrection of Jesus is it possible to be reconciled with God (Romans 5:8–11; 10:9–10).

■ *LESSON 9*

WHAT WILL YOU DO?

There are two paths before you (Matthew 7:13–14).

What is the wide path? ....Galatians 5:19–21

What are the consequences? ....Galatians 5:21

Where will it lead?

1. Eternal death ....Romans 6:23

2. Hell ....Revelation 21:8

What is the narrow path?

Jesus ....John 14:6

What are the consequences?

In one's personal life ....Galatians 5:22–23

Where will it lead?

1. Eternal life ....John 5:24

2. Heaven ....John 14:1–3

How do we start on the narrow path?

1. Agree with the word of God:

That we have all sinned ....Romans 3:23

That the result of sin is death ....Romans 6:23

That after death is judgment ....Hebrews 9:27

That we cannot save ourselves ....Ephesians 2:8–9

2. Recognise that God still so loved us that he took action .....John 3:16

In view of what God has done, he now expects four responses:

1. Repentance toward God ....Acts 2:37–38

Repentance means to turn from sin and self and turn toward God. It involves:

Renunciation...............................Isaiah 55:6–7

Reconciliation ....Matthew 5:23–24

Restitution ....Luke 19:8–9

■ *LESSON 10*

BAPTISM

Baptism is a practice of the followers of Jesus. By this practice we show that we have repented of our sin, we have put our faith in Jesus, and we have accepted him as Saviour.

How is it administered?

A follower of Jesus immerses a new follower in water (Acts 8:26 – 40).

Why is it necessary?

1. Jesus himself set the example for his followers (Matthew 3:13; 1 Peter 2:21, 24).

2. Jesus commanded it (Matthew 28:19 – 20).

Who can be baptised?

Anyone who has become Jesus' disciple (Acts 2:3– 41; 18:7– 8; Matthew 28:19 –20).

Baptism has spiritual significance:

In baptism we identify with the death and resurrection of Jesus (Romans 6:3–4; Colossians 2:12).

If we in faith accept baptism, then the mercy of God is shown to us (John 14:23).

Beware! . . . . . .After baptism, Satan may tempt us to sin (Matthew 3:16 – 4:11).

■ *LESSON 11*

THE LORD'S SUPPER

What is the Lord's Supper?

It is a special practice or function for followers of Jesus by which:

1. We remember the death of Jesus . . . . .1 Corinthians 11:23–25

2. We proclaim the death of Jesus . . . . .1 Corinthians 11:26

3. We remember the second coming of Jesus . . . . .1 Corinthians 11:26

4. We show the unity of believers . . . . .1 Corinthians 10:16 –17

Why is it necessary?

1. Jesus established it . . . . .Mark 14:17–26

2. It is a command of Jesus . . . . .1 Corinthians 11:23–26

3. The first followers of Jesus followed this practice . . . . . .Acts 2:41– 42

Who can participate?

1. One who has become a disciple of Jesus . . . . .Acts 2:41– 42

2. If a believer has sinned and not repented,
that one should not partake . . . . .1 Corinthians 11:27–31

How does one partake?

By faith (Romans 1:16; 1 Corinthians 5:7).

Without faith the Lord's Supper becomes an ordinary meal

(and baptism becomes an ordinary bath).

By faith we realise the presence of Jesus (Matthew 18:20; John 14:21–23).

GLOSSARY OF TERMS

AH	After hijrah.
Al-Amin	The Faithful or Trusted One.
Allah	The title or name given to the Supreme Being.
Allahu akbar	Allah is greatest.
Al-taqiuua	Religious dissimulation denying religious belief to avoid persecution.
Amma	To proceed towards a given objective.
Ansar	Assistant, helper. A term first used for the earliest converts at al Medina.
Arab ul-Ariba	True or pure Arab Semites.
Arab ul-Baidah	The lost Arabs.
Arab ul-Mustaribah	Mixed or naturalised Arabs.
Arkanu'd-din	The five duties of all Muslims commonly known as Pillars.
Ashab	The Companions or Associates of Muhammad.
Asr	Midafternoon prayer.
Ayat	A sign or verse.
Baqt	A peace pact.
Bismillah	In the name of Allah. Spoken frequently at the commencement of any undertaking.
Allah Dadjdjal	A monster like type of anti-Christ.
Dar Al-Harb	The house or territory of warfare. A country predominantly of non-Muslims ie. Infidels, not yet subdued by Islam.

Dar Al-Islam	A Muslim country.
Dar Al-Kufr	A non-Muslim country.
Dawa	Islamic mission.
Dawah	The invitation or call to conversion in Islamic evangelism.
Dhimma	Originally a protection pact or treaty granted by the Prophet Muhammad to Jewish and Christian populations whom he had subjected.
Dhimmi	Monotheists who are non-Muslims living in Islamic countries against whom is levied an annual capitation tax which in return is meant to afford a degree of protection for their person and property.
Dhimmitude	Being in the state of dhimmi.
Din	Right religion.
Du'a	Supplication of spontaneous prayer.
Eid Al-Adhar	The great festival of sacrifice held on the tenth day of the twelfth month.
Eid Al-Fitr	The minor festival of the breaking of the fast held at the end of Ramadan which is the month of daylight fasting.
Fajr	Daybreak or dawn but before sunrise.
Al Fath	The victory.
Fatwa	A religious or judicial sentence pronounced by an appropriate religious authority.
Furqan	Separation, distinction, proof (between good and evil) revelation, salvation. Also a term applied to the Quran.
Ghusl	A complete washing of the entire body after legal or religious impurity.
Hadith	The Traditions, that is sayings or actions attributed to the Prophet Muhammad.

Halal	That which is lawful or permitted.
Hajj	Pilgrimage to Mecca and its environs; one of the pillars (required practices) of Islam.
Hanifs	Those inclined toward seeking truth.
Haran	That which is unlawful or prohibited.
Harbis	Those who inhabit *dar al-harb*.
Hijaz	Barrier or that which separates.
Hijjatu l, Wada	The valedictory or farewell pilgrimage.
Hijrah	Flight, migration or breaking of old ties, fleeing from sin. Usually applied to Muhammad's departure from Mecca.
Hilf ul Fuzul	Federation of the Fuzul.
Huris	The perpetually virgin, beautiful maidens who welcome righteous men into Paradise.
Iftar	The meal shared immediately after sunset during the month of Ramadan.
Ihya	Renewal.
Imam	Religious leader of a mosque.
Iman	Faith. Belief of the heart and confession with the mouth that Islam is the true religion.
Injil	The Gospels of Jesus.
Irtidad	Apostasy punishable by death for males. Females may be kept in confinement until they recant.
Isha	Prayers said well after nightfall.
Islah	Reformation.
Islam	The Submission to the will of Allah.
Jahiliyah	The time of ignorance or barbarism in pre-Islamic Arabia.

Jibril	Gabriel. The angelic being who is supposed to have been the medium of revelation of the Quran to Muhammad.
Jihad	An internal struggle or striving for personal purity. An incumbent religious duty to wage holy war continuously against all non-Muslims to advance Islam.
Jinn	Invisible good or evil spirits constituting an entire race similar to humankind.
Jizya	An extra tax levied on all those living wherever Islam rules but who have not (yet) submitted to that which Islam enforces. This levy is meant to afford a degree of protection.
Kaba	The cube like building in the centre of the great mosque in Mecca. In the eastern corner is built into its wall the *al-hadjar al-aswad* or black stone. The whole is covered by a black curtain replaced annually.
Kafir	An unbeliever in the ministry of Muhammad and the message of the Quran.
Kafir Harbi	An Arabic term for non-Muslims who can be legally killed.
Kahin	Soothsayer.
Kalima	The Word. The confessional creed of all Muslims.
Kalamu'llah	The Word of Allah. A title given to the Quran.
Kalimatuhu	The fiat of God.
Kara (Hebrew)	To read or to recite.
Khadijah	Muhammad's first wife.
Khalifah	The concept of a centralised world-wide Muslim government which administers totally through Islamic law.
Khalwas	Strict religious schools.

Khutbah	Sermon preached in the mosque at Friday noon prayer.
Al Kitab	The Book. A term used to refer to the Quran and the Scriptures of Jews and Christians.
Al Lat	An idol goddess associated with the moon and the sun, worshipped by ancient Arabians.
Laylat al Qadr	The Night of Power or Destiny in the month of Ramadan during which Allah sent down revelation to Muhammad.
Madjinun	One possessed by a jinn.
Magrib	Soon after sunset.
Mahdi	A long awaited divinely guided Islamic ruler who is to appear on earth.
Allah Majid	The Glorious One. One of the ninety-nine names or attributes of Allah. Also used to describe the Quran.
Malik	One in authority. A king or chief.
Al Manat	A goddess of fate or death worshipped by ancient Arabians.
Mansukh	A term used for a verse or sentence of the Quran which has been abrogated by a later revelation.
Masjid	Mosque. A place of public and corporate prayer.
Mihrab	A niche in the end wall in a mosque indicating the direction of Mecca.
Minaret	A tower attached to mosques from where the summons to prayer is called.
Minbar	The pulpit in a mosque from which the *khutbah* (sermon) is spoken.
Mola	A committee of prominent merchants.
Muezzin	The one who summons the faithful to prayer.

Muhajirun	Emigrants or refugees from Mecca, who fled from there to Medina with the Prophet Muhammad.
Mujahuddin	One who strives, soldiers of Allah, warriors of the faith.
Mullah	Islamic leader, a teacher or interpreter of religious law within a mosque.
Munafiqun	The hypocrites. A term applied to those Medinans whom Muhammad could not trust.
Musab	Teacher.
Muslim	One who is an adherent of Islam.
Mutah	Temporary "marriage" contracted for a sum of money.
Mutawa	Religious police.
Nadha	Renaissance.
Namus al akbar	Messenger and message, an angel or spirit being.
Nasikh	A term used for a verse or sentence of the Quran which abrogates a previous one.
Niya	A declaration of intention to perform prayers.
Nobi	Prophet. Any person directly inspired by Allah.
Quibla	The direction in which all Muslims must pray ie. facing towards Mecca.
Quran	The holy book of Islam. It is also known as Furqan, Distinguisher, Kalamu'llah, Word of Allah and al Kitab, the Book.
Rabita-al-alam al-Islam	Muslim World League.
Al Rahman	The Merciful. One of the ninety-nine names or attributes of Allah.
Ramadan	The ninth month of the Islamic calender during which Muslims fast daily from dawn to dusk.
Rasul	Messenger or apostle, the sent one.

Razzia	A raid.
Rehel	An ornately decorated or carved book stand on which the Quran is often rested.
Ruhul-hayah	Life soul.
Ruhul-tamayiz	The soul that gives awareness to a Muslim of his responsibility to perform the commands of Allah.
Sadaqa	Free will offerings or charitable gifts.
Sahur	A meal which is shared before dawn during the month of fasting.
Salat	The obligatory liturgical prayers which must be said five times every day; one of the pillars of Islam.
Saum	Fasting; one of the pillars of Islam.
Shahadah	The confession of faith; the first pillar of Islam.
Shair	Knower or poet.
Shariah	Sacred Islamic law including both the teaching of the Quran and the traditional sayings of Muhammad.
Sharif	Noble, exalted. Also used to describe the Quran.
Shaytan	Satan. The wicked one who opposes.
Shirk	Ascribing partners to God or associating anything with God.
Shur	A wall of fortification.
Subha	A rosary of ninety-nine beads in accordance with the ninety-nine names of Allah.
Subhana	Holiness.
Surah	A step, row or series. Used exclusively for a chapter of the Quran of which there are 114.
Tajdid	Renewal.
Tanzil	Revelation, sent down to Muhammad.

Tarawith	Special prayers recited at night during the month of Ramadan.
Tawhid	The doctrine of the unity of Allah, a fundamental of Islamic doctrine.
Torah	The law books of Moses.
Ummah	A people or nation. Used particularly to describe inclusively the entire international Muslim community.
Umrah	The lesser pilgrimage to Mecca.
Al Uzza	An idol goddess worshipped by ancient Arabians, associated with the morning star.
Wadu	The lesser ablution.
Zabur	The Psalms of David.
Zakat	Almsgiving; an obligatory pillar of Islam by which a portion of wealth is given to the poor at the commencement of each year.
Zuhr	Between sunrise and noon.
Zul Fiqar	The Lord of the backbone. The name given to a well-known sword chosen as war booty by Muhammad.

ME&M

ENDNOTES

Introduction

1   Ron Peck, The Shadow of the Crescent. Springfield: Centre of Ministry to Muslims, n.d., 1.

2   Intercede, May/June 1999, 3.

3   Akbar S. Ahmed, Living Islam. London: BBC Books, 1993.

4   Islamic Affairs Analyst, Intelligence International, n.d., 3.

5   The State Department's Terror List, Terrorism & Security Monitor, November 1999, 4 – 5.

6   David B.Barnett and Todd M.Johnson, 'Annual Statistical Table on Global Mission: 2000'. International Bulletin of Missionary Research, January 2000, 25.

7   Ibid, 25.

8   Global Christianity Figures Static, The Queensland Baptist, October 1996, 1.

9   Patrick Sookhdeo, 'Cry Justice', Barnabas Magazine, October-November 2002, 2.

10 The Victorian Baptist Witness, September 1996, 9.

11 Douglas Layton, 'Islam Could Become Predominant Religion in US by 2020', Mission Network News quoted in HCJB News Update, 22 June 2000.

12 Fareed Zakaria, 'Look East for the Answer', Newsweek, November 5 2002, 73.

13 Newsweek, July 1 1997, 87.

14 Muslim World Prayer Update. Seaforth, New South Wales: Open Doors Inc., January 1998.

15 Robin Wright, Sacred Rage. New York: Simon and Schuster, 1985, 99.

16 Brother Andrew, For the Love of my Brothers. Minneapolis, Minnesota: Bethany House Publishers, 1998, 212.

17 Ustaz Ashaari Muhammed, The West on the Brink of Death. London: Asoib Publishing Limited, 1988, xii.

18 Ibid, 93.

19 Bulletin, 21 March 2000, 18.

20 Go, Third Quarter, 1997, 8.

21 Reaching Out in Love. Springfield, Missouri: Assemblies of God.

22 Dudley Woodberry, 'New Hope for Muslim Evangelism'. Fuller Focus, Summer 1996, 10.

23 Christianity's Supreme Opportunity. Toronto: Fellowship of Faith for Muslims, n.d., 3.

24 Wesley Richards, 'The Challenge of Islam', Restoration. Markfield, Leicester: March/April 1991, 5.

25 'Islam in Britain: Part 2'. ISIC Bulletin, February/March 1997, 8.

26 Muhammad Khan, The Muslim News. 28 June 1996.

27 Samuel P. Huntington, 'The Clash of Civilizations', New York: Simon & Schuster, 1996, 110.

28 Hassan Al-Turabi, 'The Islamic Awakening's Second Wave', New Perspectives Quarterly, 8 (Summer 1992), 50.

29 'Modern Day Martyrs', ISIC Bulletin, April/ May 1997, 6.

30 Dean Gilliland, 'New Hope for Muslim Evangelism', Fuller Focus, Summer 1996, 11.

31 Ibn Warraq, 'Why I Am Not a Muslim'. New York: Prometheus Books, 1995, 1.

32 'A Time to Pray', New Day, March 1993, 7.

33 Bryant Myers, 'The Water Suite'. MARC Newsletter, December 1997, 3.

34 Reza F. Safa, Inside Islam. Orlando, Florida: Creation House, 1996, 81.

35 Muhammad Marmaduke Pickthall, The Meaning of the Glorious Koran. New York: Mentor, n.d., 300.

36 Abdallah Al – Naggar, Al – Gumhurya (Cairo), 7 October 2001.

37 Sheikh Muhammad Al – Gamei'a, www.lilatalqadr.com, 4 October 2001.

38 Matthew Moore, 'Indonesia moves on prime suspect for Bali bombing', Age (Melbourne), October 18 2002, 2

39 Ibn Warraq, 'Why I Am Not a Muslim', New York: Prometheus Books, 1995, 26.

40 Peter E. Makari, 'Kenneth Cragg on Mission', MECC News Report, Summer/Autumn 1999, 41.

41 Keith Suter, 'Cold War Returns, starring Islam', Age, 1 June 2000, 17.

42 Diana Bagnall, 'Muslims with attitude', The Bulletin, March 25 2003, 16.

43 David Brickner, 'The Mosque, the Synagogue and the Church', Jews for Jesus, January 2002, 2.

44 Thirty Days of Focussed Prayer for the Muslim World. Ashgrove, Queensland: Youth With a Mission, February 20 – March 23, 1993.

45 Hass Hirji – Walji and Jaryl Strong, Escape from Islam. Wheaton: Tyndale House, 1981, 92.

46 Samuel Huntington, 'The Clash of Civilizations', New York: Simon & Schuster, 1995, 209-217

47 Jane Cadzow, 'The Secret of Suzuki', Good Weekend, April 8, 2000, 21.

48 Zainon Ahmad, 'Turabi's Approach to a Better Sudan', New Straits Times (Kuala Lumpur), January 22, 1994, 10.

49 Ibn Warraq, 'Why I Am Not a Muslim', New York: Prometheus Books, 1995, 11.

50 Anisa Buckley in 'Through Islamic eyes', Good Weekend, 1 December 2001, 23.

51 Khaldoun Hajaj in 'Through Islamic eyes', Good Weekend, 1 December 2001, 23.

52 Ibn Warraq, Statement by Ibn Warraq on the World Trade Centre Atrocity, Institute for the Secularisation of Islamic Society, www.secularislam.org/wtc.htm.

53 Tony Parkinson, 'We will fight until we runout of blood', Age (Melbourne), October 15 2002, 13.

54 Diana Bagnall, 'Call of Islam', The Bulletin, November 5 2002, 37.

55 Khalid Duran, Age (Melbourne), 18 December 2001, 9.

56 Paul McGeough, 'Iraq pays suicide bonus to entice new bombers', Age, 26 March 2002, 11.

57 Matt Spetalnick, 'Poverty, rage fire terrorism martyrs', Age (Melbourne), 4 December 2001, 12.

58 Danielle Haas, 'Suicide blast rocks Jerusalem', Age (Melbourne), 28 January 2002, 6.

59 Fareed Zakaria, 'The Roots of Rage', Newsweek, 16 October 2001, 62.

60 David Hirst, 'Egypt's love – hate affair with bin Laden', Age (Melbourne), 6 December 2001, 15.

61 Tim Colebatch, 'Malaysia's call to condemn attacks on civilians as terrorism finds no support', Age (Mebourne), 4 April 2002, 9.

62 Hawa Ayra in 'Through Islamic eyes', Good Weekend, 1 December 2001, 28.

63 Eric Campbell in Tora Bora for Australian Broadcasting Commission TV 7.30 Report, 19 December 2001.

64 Ibn Warraq, 'Why I Am Not a Muslim', New York: Prometheus Books, 1995, 326.

65 Jeff M.Sellers, 'How to Confront a Theocracy', Christianity Today, July 2002, 34

66 Reza F. Safa, in 'Secrets of the Koran' by Don Richardson, Ventura, California: Regal, 2003, 10.

Chapter 1

1 Ziauddin Saddar, The Future of Muslim Civilisation. London: Croom Helm, 1979, 204–205.

2 Massoud Ansari, 'Junior School Jihad', HQ, December/January 2001–2002, 47–53.

3 Marian Wilkinson, 'Extremist's history leaves experts suspicious', Age (Melbourne), 9.

4 Ziauddin Saddar, The Future of Muslim Civilisation. London: Croom Helm, 1979, 2–5.

5 Ian Brown, The Impact of Islam. South Auckland: Baptist Promotions, n.d., 8,9.

6 Kerry Lovering, Islam on the March. Singapore: Sudan Interior Mission, 10.

7 Peter Coleman, 'Export or Die', The Australian Weekend, March 8–9 2003.

8 Kerry Lovering, Islam on the March. Singapore: Sudan Interior Mission, 9.

9 Anthony Paul, 'Settle in for a long conflict', Melbourne Courier, November 3 2002, 7.

10 Miles Clemans, Flashback to Intolerance, The Australian, May 22 1998, 15.

11 Ustaz Ashaari Muhammad, The West on the Brink of Death. London: Asoib International Limited, 1992, 147, 155.

12 Bryn Jones, God's Radical Church, Restoration, March/April 1991, 10.

13 Christopher Dickey, 'In the name of God', Newsweek, May 21, 2002, 65.

14 Ashaari, The West on the Brink of Death, 155–160.

15 ISIC Bulletin, October/November, 1997, 2.

Chapter 2

1 ISIC Bulletin, October/ November 1996, 4.

2 Steve Addison, Sharing the Vision, August 1998, 1.

3 Thomas, George. "Hyde Park Preacher Debate - Witnesses to Radical Muslims". CBN News, March 19 2003, 3.

4 On Being, March 1997,13.

5 'Britain, Bengali but British', Go, Interserve, 2nd Quarter 1997, 10.

6 'Islam in Britain', ISIC Bulletin, June /July 1996, 8.

7 ISIC Bulletin, October/ November 1996, 1.

8 Ibid.

9   'British Muslims Could Soon Outnumber Anglicans', Today (South Africa), February 2002, 63.

10 Manilla Chronicle, July 12 1989.

11 Patrick Johnstone and Jason Mandayk. Operation World. Lifestyle, Cumbria, U.K.: Paternoster, 2001, 649.

12 Intercede, March/April 2003, 7.

13 'Islam in Britain,' Religious Freedom Today Digest, December 1998, 13.

14 ISIC Bulletin, August / September 1995, 9.

15 ISIC Bulletin, December 1996/January 1997, 10.

16 ISIC Bulletin, April/ May 1998, 9.

17 Ibid.

18 Ibid.

19 Muslim World Prayer Update, April 1998, 2.

20 ISIC Briefing, September 10 2002, 2.

21 ISIC Briefing, December 23, 2002.

22 Age (Melbourne), January 6, 1992.

23 'Black Islam in the UK', ISIC Bulletin, October/ November, 1995, 6.

24 Alan Scotland, 'Kingdoms in Conflict', Restoration, March/April 1991, 20.

25 The Australian Baptist, August 28, 1988.

26 Rippin, Andrew. Muslims: Their Religious Beliefs and Practices. Vol. 1. London, 1991, 47.

27 'Muslim World Briefs', Intercede, 1989, 3.

28 'Major Opening', Middle East Media, memo No.68 1995/3.

29 ISIC Bulletin, February/ March 1998, 5.

30 'British Christianity in Crisis', The Good News, March/April 2000, 20.

31 Ibid

32 Roger Day, 'Christians Fail to Challenge Society', Restoration, March/April 1991,16.

33 'Jesus Can be Lampooned unless it Upsets Islam', The Victorian Baptist Witness, March 1993, 8.

34 "Are Easter eggs next?", Sydney Morning Herald, April 2003.

35 Jenkins, Roy. Churchill. London: Tan Books, 2002, 360.

Chapter 3

1   Patrick Johnstone and Jason Mandryk. Operation World. Cumbria U.K.: Paternoster Lifestyle, 2001, 225.

2   Emily Mitchell, 'All God's Children', Time, April 17, 1989, 58.

3   James Graff, 'One Faith Divided', Time, May 5 2003, 42.

4. Nassim Majidi and Christina Passariello, "France Gives Its Muslims a Voice", BusinessWeek online, March 27 2003, 2.

5   Emily Mitchell, 'All God's Children', Time, April 17, 1989, 59

6   Maurice Antonelli, Go Global, n.d., 2.

7   'Europe's Largest Mosque', Memo No. 68, Middle East Media, 1995, 3.

8   'Sweden', Intercede, May/June 1999, 3.

9   Daniel Pipes and Lars Hedegaard, 'Muslim extremism: Denmark's had enough', www.nationalpost.com, August 2002.

10 Bat Ye'or, "European Fears of the Gathering Jihad", FrontPageMagazine.com, February 21 2003, 2.

11 'Spain Recognises Islam', Manilla Chronicle, July 16, 1989.

12 'The Objectives of Islamic Mission', Islam, 1987, 7.

13 Mitchell, 'All God's Children', Time, 59.

14 'Muslims in Western Europe', The Economist, August 10 2002, 21.

15 'Protestants Collect Money for Mosque', New Life, April 16, 1992.

16 Jordan Bonfante Duisberg, 'No Rest in the Ruhr', Time, February 24, 1997, 41.

17 'Islam Finds New Home in Western Europe', Christianity Today, March 1990, 40.

18 Massimo Calabresi and Alexandra Stiglmayer, 'Under the Influence', Time, September 30 1996, 57.

Chapter 4

1   'Iraqis won't Budge in Document Dispute', Pensacola News Journal, 25 November 1998, 2A.

2   Sania El-Badry, 'Understanding Islam in America', American Demographics (vol.16 no.1), January 16 1994, 10–11.

3   Ron Peck, The Shadow of the Crescent. Springfield, MO: Center for Ministry for Muslims, 1997, 1.

4   Understanding Islam and the Muslims. Washington: The Embassy of Saudi Arabia, 1989, 30.

5   'Muslim "Mission" to America', The Australian Baptist, May 1990, 27.

6   1997 Year of Prayer for the World of Islam, September/October, no.5, 1997, 2.

7   Time, May 23, 1988, 58.

8   Timothy George, 'Is the God of Muhammad the Father of Jesus', Christianity Today, 4 February 2002.

9   Reza F. Safa, Inside Islam. Orlando, Florida: Creation House, 1996, 52.

10 Religious Strife Growing, Victorian Baptist Witness, June 1997.

11 George W. Braswell Jr., Islam, Its Prophet, Peoples, Politics and Power. Nashville, Tennessee: Broadman and Holman, 1996, 242.

12 Daniel Pipes, 'American Muslims vs. American Jews', www.danielpipes.org, December 24 2002, 3.

13 Beverley Pegues, 'I Took a Prayer Journey', The 10/40 Window Reporter, Winter 1998, 2.

14 Peck, 1.

15 Charisma, 1997 quoted in 'The Voice of the Martyrs', The 10/40 Window Reporter, Winter 1998, 12.

16 Peck, 13.

17 The Australian Baptist, 27.

18 Peck, 13–16.

19 'American Muslim Council', Intercede, May/June 1997, 3.

20 'The Americans New Pilgrims', Asiaweek, February 23 1990, 34.

21 Understanding Islam and the Muslims, 30.

22 Asiaweek, February 23 1990, 4.

23 Ibid.

24 'North American Muslims Rise to Prominence', Religious Freedom Today Digest, January 1999, 11.

25 Khalid Duran and Daniel Pipes, 'Faces of American Islam', www.danielpipes.org, August / September 2002, 3–6

26 Safa, 55.

27 Leonard Lovett, 'Who does God Say We Are', Ministries Today, November/December 1991, 36.

28 Timothy Larsen, 'Success for Black Muslims', Restoration, March/April 1991, 26.

29 Julia Duin, 'Daring Leaps of Faith', The Washington Times, New York, October 13 2002.

30 'A Wave of Conversion to Islam in the US Following September 11', thetruereligion.org, March 22 2003, 1.

31 Daniel Pipes, 'PBS, Recruiting for Islam', New York Post, December 17 2002.

32 'US Public Schools Embrace Islam', www.assist-ministries.com, February 2002.

33 Paul M. Weyrich, "Wake Up! Islam is About More Than Hate Crimes". CNSNews.com Commentary, January 29 2003.

34 Charles Colson, "Radical Islam in American Prisons", BreakPointonline, March 3 2003, 1.

35 Yvonne Yazbeck Haddad and Jane Idleman Smith, Muslim Communities in North America. Albany: State University of New York, 1994, xix–xx.

36 Jim Downing, 'Kuwait's Plan Blows Up', Mission Frontiers Bulletin, September–December 1992, 21.

37 Arthur Clark, 'The New Push for Middle East Studies', Saudi Aramco World, January 2003, 13.

38 Richard N. Ostling, 'Americans Facing Towards Mecca', Time, May 23 1998, 59.

39 'California's New Mosque', Religious Freedom Today Digest, December 1998, 11.

40 Kent Hart, 'Muslims Target United States', Moody, July/August 1987, 81.

41 Larsen, 26.

42 'Black Islam in the West. Theology and Background of Black Islam', ISIC Bulletin, October/November, 1995, 5.

43 Braswell, 228.

44 Braswell, 239

45 Christopher Farley, 'Muslim Faithful in USA Tackle Misconceptions', USA Today, 1989.

46 Stan Guthrie, 'A Crescent or a Cross: Islam Prospers in America', Christianity Today, October 28 1991, 40.

47 Timothy George, 'Is the Father of Jesus the God of Muhammad?' Grand Rapids, Michigan: Zondervan, 2002, 25.

48 Frank J. Gaffney, "The fifth column syndrome", www.townhall.com, March 25 2003, 1.

49 'North American Muslims', 11.

50 www.isnacanada.com, April 26 2003, 2.

51 Timothy George, Is the Father of Jesus the God of Muhammad? Grand Rapids, Michigan: Zondervan, 2002, 25.

52 Alice Reid, 'Mosque's Children Await Playground', Washington Post, November 22, B4.

53 Julian Bonger, 'Arabs in US Vent Fury at Film about Islamist Terror', Guardian, November 7, 18.

54 ISIC Bulletin, October/November, 1996, 5.

55 Peck, 15.

56 David Pryce-Jones, The Closed Circle: An Interpretation of the Arabs. London: Paladin, 1990, 226.

57 Ian Stewart, 'GDP Fall puts Heat on Mahatir', Australian, June 1 1998, 7.

58 'Shooting or Voting for Islam', The Economist (London), August 21 1993.

59 'Notebook', Time, 21 June 1999, 17.

60 Amos Permutter, 'Islam and Democracy Simply Aren't Compatible', Manilla Bulletin, January 1992, 23.

61 Robin Wright, 'The Darling Son of Iran', The Age News Extra (Melbourne), May 30 1998, 12.

62 Reuters, Vatican City, 'Blunt Attack on Islam at Vatican Synod', Canberra Times, October 15 1999, 9.

63 A. M. Abdulmohaymen, 'Down with the Satanic Bush Order', Hong Kong Muslim Herald, April 1992, 2.

64 Daniel Pipes, 'It Matters What Kind of Islam Prevails', Times (Los Angeles), 22 July 1999.

65 Andres Tapia, 'Churches Wary of Inner City Islamic Inroads', Christianity Today, January 10 1998.

66 Pipes, 'It Matters What Kind of Islam'.

Chapter 5

1 'Libyan Leader's "Holy War" Against Christianity in Africa', The Australian Evangel, May 1986, 16.

2 'Ugly Algeria', The Economist, July 16 1994, 18.

3 'Algeria Country Update', Middle East Council of Churches News Report, Summer/Autumn 1999, 8.

4 'A Blow to Algerian Peace Hopes', Islamic Affairs Analyst, December 1999, 6.

5 'Something New out of Africa', The Economist, July 16 1994, 41.

6 'An Islamic Africa?', Memo No.72 (Quarterly Newsletter of Middle East Media), 1996/3.

7 Mozammel Haque, 'Christian Missionaries in African Continent', The Muslim World League Journal, February 1992, 8.

8 Ibid, 33.

9 Bryant Myers, 'Africa', MARC Newsletter No. 94/4, December 1994, 4.

10 Elizabeth Kendal, 'Facing Giants', Working Together, 2002,8.

11 Haque, 31.

12 Patrick Johnstone and Jason Mandryk. Operation World. Harrisburg, Virginia: R.R.Donnelley and Sons, 2001, 21.

13 Ibid, 28.

14 'The Presence of Islam in Africa and the Challenges it Poses to Religious Liberty (Part 1)', ISIC Bulletin, December 1995/January 1996, 7.

15 Josiah Fearon, , 'Islamic Fundamentalism in Africa', The Unknown Faces of Islam, 16.

16 'Have Your Pastors Alerted You', Voice of the Martyrs, December 1990.

17 Dan Wooding, 'Islam Declares 'Holy War' on Africa', New Life, September 1990.

Chapter 6

1 Source withheld.

2 Letter from E. Bakhi Muluzi of Malawi to Col. Muammar Gaddafi, President of Libya, F/SNJ 32/135, 4 May 1999.

3 'The Presence of Islam in Africa and the Challenges it Poses to Religious Liberty (Part 2)', ISIIC Bulletin, February/ March 1996, 7.

4 Odhiambo Okite, 'Muslim–Christian Riots Rock Nairobi', Christianity Today, January 8 2001, 33.

5 'Jihad Threatened if Muslim Demands Are Not Met', info@barnabasfund.org, April 30 2003.

6 'Ethiopian Protestants Persecuted by Muslims and Orthodox Christians', New Life, August 26, 1993.

7 'The Danger of Fat Hearts', The Voice of the Martyrs, October 1994, 12.

8 Name withheld, May 27 2003.

9 ISIC Bulletin, April/ May 1998.

10 'South Africa: Islamic Groups Promise Upheaval as Muslim Protester Dies of Injury', Religious Freedom Today Digest, February 1999, 3.

11 Fellowship of Faith Prayer News Bulletin, April/July 1994, 9.

12 Elizabeth Kendall, 'Ivory Coast - Serious Situation', www.christiansincrisis.net, December 4 2002.

13 Patrick Johnstone, Operation World. Rydalmere: OM Publishing, 1993, 421.

14 Ibid, 422.

15 'The Call of Islam', The Economist, August 21 1993.

16 Patrick Johnstone and Jason Mandryk. Operation World. Harrisburg, Virginia: R.R.Donnelly and Sons, 2001, 488.

17 'Crescent versus Cross in Troubled Nigeria', Time, June 1 1992, 15.

18 'Downturn in Nigeria', ISIC Bulletin, December 1997/January 1998, 5.

19 'Early Test of Nigerian Democracy', Islamic Affairs Analyst, December 1999, 4.

20 The Church in the Muslim World Update, Nigeria, January 1999.

21 Dan_Kelly@wvi, 6 March 2002.

22 James Rupert, 'Nigerian Military Gives Power to the People', Washington Post quoted in Age (Melbourne), 31 May 1999, 12.

23 Mark Kelly, International Missions Board News Stories, SBC, 22 February 2000.

24 Nigerian Churches Face Shariah', Voice of the Martyrs, Special Edition 1998.

25 'Will Shari'a Law Curb Christianity?' Christianity Today, October 23 2000, 24.

26 Tim Sullivan, 'Nigeria Backs Away From Islamic Law', Associated Press (Abuja), February 29 2000.

27 'Nigerian States Split over Islamic Code', Age (Melbourne), 4 March 2000, 25.

28 Tim Butcher, 'Despite legal setback, fundamentalists march on', Age (Melbourne), 27 March 2002, 13.

29 'Shariah Law Spreading to South West Nigeria', BFS Overseas, 4 May 2002, 1.

30 'Religious War Possible in Nigeria', Victorian Baptist Witness, April 2000, 6.

31 'Nigerian Baptists Celebrate 150 Years', Victorian Baptist Witness, June 2000, 9.

32 Josiah Fearon, Shariah in Nigeria', Barnabas Magazine, May–June 2003, 5.

33 'Kaduna Riots', March 2003, 8.

34 'Twelve Killed in Student Riot.' info@barnabasfund.org, October 15 2002, 1.

35 'Truth and Innocence are not Enough', ISIC Bulletin, August / September 1997, 2.

Chapter 7

1   Peter Hammond, 'The Growth of the Church in Sudan', Frontline Fellowship, 1995/3, 4.

2   'Soldiers Butcher Christians in Sudan', The Victorian Baptist Witness, May 1998, 9.

3   'Sudan: Annihilation of the Nuba', IISIC Bulletin, October/November 1995, 8.

4   'Islamic Oppression Worsens', Alpha News, April 1993.

5   'Millions of Christians Killed in Sudan', Memo Brief No.72, Quarterly Newsletter of Middle East Media, 1996/3.

6   'Sudan Bombs a Hospital Again', Victorian Baptist Witness, April 2000, 2.

7   Brian Eads, 'Slavery's Shameful Return to Africa', Readers Digest, March 1996.

8   Patrick Johnstone, Operation World. Rydalmere: OM Publishing, 1993, 511.

9   'Sudan Nightmare Continues', Prayer Link, May 1997, 7.

10 Kevin Turner, 'Sudan: Hope in the Midst of Tragedy', Voice of the Martyrs, 1997, 3.

11 Karin Davies, The Price of Freedom in Sudan: $1.48', Age (Melbourne), February 21 1998, World, 21.

12 Simon Denyer, '2,035 Slaves Freed for A$ 75 Each', Age (Melbourne), 10 July 1999, 27.

13 'Christians Redeem Slaves', Victorian Baptist Witness, September 2000, 25.

14 Jim Wackett, 'Sudan on the Brink', World Vision News, May 1998, 7.

15 Greg and Judy Blaxland, Operation Abba Inc. Newsletter, May 2000, 1.

16 Eads.

17 Ibid.

18 Ibid.

19 Alpha News, 1993.

20 James Reat Gorny, 'Help Sudan's Christians,' Victorian Baptist Witness, June 2001, 10.

21 'Persecution in 10 Countries,' Victorian Baptist Witness, June 2001, 13.

22 'Why Won't We Help the Sudan', The Victorian Baptist Witness, June 1995, 4.

23 Ibid.

24 George Bezuidenhout

Chapter 8

1   James Hunt, Hussein of Jordan: A Political Biography, London: Macmillan, 1989, 212.

2   'Islam's Solemn March West', Asia Week, February 23 1990, 33.

3   Alan Cipress, The Arab Connection', Age (Melbourne), January 11 2003.

4   H.A.R. Gibb and J.H. Kramers, 'al Dadjdhjal' in Shorter Encyclopedia of Islam. Leiden: E.J.Brill, 1974, 67.

5   C.M.H.Clark. A History of Australia, Vol.1, Melbourne: Melbourne University Press, 1979, 14–15.

6   C. Markham, The Voyages of Pedro de Quiros, Vol.1, London: Hakluyt Society, 1904, 512–13.

7   'Love a Muslim Whom Christ Loves', Operation Abba, Lithgow.

8   John Stevens, 'More Prayers from Followers of Islam', Hume Observer, October 8 1997, 5.

9   Wafia Omar and Kirsty Allen, The Muslims in Australia. Canberra: The Australian Government Publishing Service, 1996, 24.

10 'Splendour and Magnificence,' Sydney Gazette, 23 March 1806.

11 Les Hiddins, Bush Tucker Man Stories of Exploration and Survival, Sydney: Australian Broadcasting Corporation, 1996, 79–80.

12 Hanifa Deen, Caravanserai: Journey amongst Australian Muslims. St Leonards, New South Wales: Allen and Unwin, 1995, 15.

13 Gary D. Bouma, Mosques and Muslim Settlement in Australia. Canberra: The Australian Government Publishing Service, 1994, 42.

14 Omar and Allen, 22.

15 Stevens, 5.

16 Omar and Allen, 25.

17 Christine Stevens, 'Afghan Camel Drivers: Founders of Islam in Australia', in An Australian Pilgrimage; Muslims in Australia from the Seventeenth Century to the Present, ed. Mary L. Jones, Melbourne: Victoria Press, 1993, 60.

18 'Islamic Bodies in Australia', www.islam-australia.linet.au.

19 Georgie Allen, 'Muslim Life Flourishes Down Under', Momtage, April 1995, 11.

20 Abdur Rauf, 'Islam Enlightens Australia', www.renaissance.com.pk, 2.

21 Edmund Campion, 'Devotion to Duty', The Bulletin, 30 December 1997/6 January 1998, 79.

22 Barney Zwartz, 'Koran added to VCE Studies for First Time', Age (Melbourne), February 13 2003, 3.

23 John Masanauskas, 'Council to Consider Islamic Centre', Age (Melbourne), May 23 1990.

24 Chris Griffith, 'Brunei injects $10m into UQ College', Courier Mail, September 7 2000, 6.

25 Omar and Allen, 46.

26 Lucinda Schmidt, 'Bankers trust', Money Manager, Age (Melbourne), November 18 2002, 8.

27 George Lekakis, 'Islamic Super Fund Pioneered', The Australian Financial Review, August 15 2002.

28 Muslim Business Register, www.icv.org.au November 23 2002, 1.

29 The Victorian Baptist Witness, July 2002, 18.

30 Abdur Rauf, 'Islam Enlightens Australia', www.renaissance.com.pk.

31 'Terror "frontman" expelled', Age (Melbourne), October 28 2002, 1.

32 Fiona Carruthers, 'Alice's Afghans at Loss on Preacher's Visit', Australian, February 13 1998, 2.

33 Geoff Strong, 'Putting God in Check', Sunday Age (Melbourne), May 18 1997.

34 Diana Bagnall, 'Peace and the Prophet'. Bulletin, February 11 2003, 13.

35 'Forces Dimming The Light of the Crescent', www.islamicsydney.com, March 22 2003, 1.

36 John Masanauskas, 'Victorian Muslims to Launch Political Campaign', Age (Melbourne) December 10 1990.

37 Martin Daly, 'Minister in Row over Wine, Religion and Song', Age (Melbourne) February 17 1993.

38 Greg Callaghan, 'The Man behind the Mosque', Weekend Australia Magazine, September 14–15 2002, 18.

39 Abdur Rauf, 'Islam Enlightens Australia', www.renaissance.com.pk

40 'Goals, Principles and Strategy', Nida'ul Islam Magazine, September 2 2002, 2.

41 Linda Morris, 'Cleric "sowed seeds of Australian state"', Sydney Morning Herald, December 10 2002, 1.

42 Sources withheld.

43 'Religious Liberty and the Islamic Fundamentalists', The National Alliance Magazine, October 1996, 17.

44 Amir Abdullah, 'Preserving the Islamic Identity in the West, Threats & Solutions', Nida'ul Islam, April–May 1997.

45 John Stapleton, 'Zealots' quest for purity', The Australia, November 19, 2002, 13.

46 Amir Abdullah, 'Christians Missionaries in the Muslim World Manufacturing Kufr', Nida'ul Islam Magazine, September–October 1997.

47 Rowan Callick, 'Bearing the Backlash'. Time, October 15 1990, 51.

48 Gary D. Bouma, 103,104.

49 Sally Finlay, 'Violent Home Raid in Quest for Kosovo Recruits, Court Told', Age (Melbourne), 30 April 1999.

50 Source withheld.

51 'Laksar Jihad alive and well in Papua', info@barnabasfund.org, March 5 2003.

52 Nisid Hajari, 'Days of the Long Knives', Time, 5 April 1999, 51–52.

53 Louise Williams, 'When Blood is War', Age (Melbourne), 27 March 1999, 7.

54 'Muslims in Latin America', ISIC Bulletin, August/September 1996, 11.

55 The Victorian Baptist Witness, April 2000, 18.

56 'Islam in Big Business', ISIC Bulletin, October/November 1996, 10.

57 Ibid..

58 Loren Cunningham, 'A Speck on the Globe', Ministries Today, January/February 1994, 24, 25.

59 'From Russia with Love', The Bulletin of Fuller Theological Seminary, 1989/2, 2.

60 Christopher Ogden, 'Central Asia: The Next Crisis', Time, December 16 1991, 18.

61 Dilip Hiro, Between Marx and Mohammad. London: Harper Collins, 1994, 358.

62 'Islamic Offensive in the USSR', The Voice of the Martyrs, December 1991.

63 'Worries about Islam', The Economist, February 21 1998, 28.

64 'Christians and Jews Flee', Victorian Baptist Witness, December 1991, 17.

65 New Life (Melbourne), 1994.

66 PrayerLink (Brisbane), Vol.4/1, January 1997.

67 'Out of Ruins – the New Nations', ISIC Bulletin, April/ May 1998, 7.

68 'Islamic Law Adopted', Barnabas, Summer 1999, 11.

69 'Rebels Threaten Russians', Australian, 13 August 1999, 8.

70 'Russians Enter Chechen Capital', Age (Melbourne) 19 October 1999, 14.

71 'Doors Team Helps Chechen Refugees', Open Doors, April 2000, 8.

72 William Dalrymple, 'Demolition of an Ancient Culture', Age Extra (Melbourne), April 22 1989, 3.

73 The Voice of the Martyrs, July 1994, 4.

74 Source withheld.

75 'More Turkish Trouble', Victorian Baptist Witness, July 2000, 19.

76 'Putting Down Roots', Barnabas, Summer 1999, 6.

77 New Day, September 1996, 32.

78 Bertil Lintner, 'A Cocoon of Terror', Far Eastern Economic Review, April 4 2002, 15–16,

79 Victorian Baptist Witness, December 1992.

80 'Bible Bashing in Bangladesh', Open Doors/Newsbrief, July 1996.

81 Source withheld.

82 WEF Religious Liberty E-mail Conference, May 26 1998.

83 The Voice of the Martyrs, Special Edition 1998, 19.

84 'Pakistan – Cascade of Intolerance', ISIC Bulletin, June /July 1998, 11.

85 'Judge Assassinated in Pakistan', Go, First Quarter 1998, 7.

86 Brig (Rtd) M. Abdul Hafiz, 'The Self-defeating Politics of Religion', Daily Star (Dhaka), 26 October 1998, 4.

87 'Pakistan: A Nation Wide Movement Against Senators Opposing Shari'ah', Religious Freedom Today Digest, February 1999, 9–10.

88 'Islamist Politicians and Church Attacks', info@barnabasfund.org, February 4 2003, 1.

89 Maggie O'Kane, 'The Invisible Martyr', Good Weekend, 15 August 1998, 33.

90 'Pakistani Christians Angry', The Victorian Baptist Witness, June 1998,21.

91 Mark Baker, 'The Zealots who Crushed Kabul', Age (Melbourne), September 1996, A24.

92 Maggie O'Kane, 'The Terror of the Warriors of Taliban', Age (Melbourne), September 28 1996, A25.

93 'Afghanistan: a Smuggler's Haven', Intelligence Digest, 26 November 1999, 3.

94 Barry Bearak, 'The Taliban just says no in heroin's heartland,' The New York Times, quoted in Age (Melbourne), 12 June 2001, 17.

95 Craig Neilson, 'Deadly fields set to bloom', Age (Melbourne), 26 December 2001, 10.

96 Source withheld.

97 Fellowship of Faith Prayer News Bulletin, December 1994–March 1995, 13.

98 Source withheld, 4 August 2000.

99 'Taliban will kill new converts', World Evangelical Fellowship's Religious Liberty E-mail; quoted in Victorian Baptist Witness, March 2001, 21.

100 Teymour Shaheeni, 'The Church in Iran: Her Past, Her Present, Her Future', Elam Review, 26–37.

101 'Iran: Persecution of Protestants', ISIC Bulletin, December 1996/January 1997, 2.

102 'Muslims Banned from Churches', Fellowship of Faith, 1994, 25.

103 Col Stringer, 'Persecution Iraq', May 22 2003, 1.

104 The Voice of the Martyrs, Special Edition 1998.

105 'Bethlehem: There's Still not Enough Room', ISIC Bulletin, February/ March 1998, 3.

106 'Exodus Now – It Still Goes On', ISIC Bulletin, December 1997/January 1998, 9.

107 'Arsonists Torch Christian Bookstore in Jordan', ISIC Bulletin, April/ May 1998, 11.

108 'The Middle East or the Heart of Islam', The Lausanne Letter, No.2 October 1990, 2.

109 'Australia', ISIC Bulletin, June /July 1997, 10.

110 David Pryce-Jones, The Closed Circle. London: Paladin,1990, 384.

Chapter 9

1 Tony Walker, 'Saddam: Most Dangerous Man in World,' Age (Melbourne), 25 June 1990, 11.

2 Raphael Patai, The Arab Mind, New York: Hatherleigh Press, 2002, 12.

3 Peter Mansfield, The Arabs. Great Britain: Allen Lane, 1976; reprint, London: Penguin Books, 1985, 13.

4 Alfred Guillaume, Islam. Ringwood, Australia: Penguin Books, 1956, 2.

5 Thomas Patrick Hughes, Dictionary of Islam. New Delhi: Cosmo Publications, 1977, 17–20.

6 Louis Bahjat Hamada, Understanding the Arab World. Nashville: Thomas Nelson, 1990, 79.

7 Clarence H. Wagner Jr., 'Between a Rock and a Holy Site,' Christianity Today, February 5 2001, 63.

8 David Hesselgrave, 'A Legacy of Enmity,' Moody Monthly, October 1987, 74.

9   David Horowitz, 'The Continuing Arab Israeli Conflict,' The Vineyard, December 1998, 3.(1–5)

10 Michael Asher, Lawrence The Uncrowned King of Arabia. London: Viking, 1998, 154–155.

11 David Pryce-Jones, The Closed Circle. London: Paladin, 1990, 6.

12 Fouad Ajami, The Arab Predicament. Cambridge: Cambridge University Press, 1985, 4.

13 Pryce-Jones, 17.

14 Ibid., 20.

15 www.news.bbc.co.uk/1/hi/world/south_asia, February 16 2002.

16 James L. Payne, Why Nations Arm. Oxford: Basil Blackwell, 1989, 138–139.

17 Samuel P. Huntington, The Clash of Civilizations and the Remaking of World Order. New York: Simon & Schuster, 1996, 256–258.

18 Ibid, 263–265

19 Reported in Sunday Age Agenda, 21 May 2000, 6.

20 Lisa Beyer, 'We Are a Tough and Small People,' Time, 23 October 2000, 37.

21 Jamil Hamad, 'I Shot an Israeli,' Time, 23 October 2000, 53.

22 Phillip K. Hitti, The Arabs. A Short History. Princeton: Macmillan, 1949, 1,2.

Chapter 10

1   Mansour Khalid, The Socio Cultural Determinants of Arab Diplomacy in George N. Attiya ed. *Arab and American Cultures*. Washington, DC: American Enterprise Institute for Public Policy Research, 1977, 128.

2   Alfred Guillaume, *Islam*. Ringwood, Australia: Penguin Books, 1956, 4.

3   Ameer Ali, *The Spirit of Islam*. Christophers, 1922; reprint, London: Methuen, 1965, lxv.

4   Peter Mansfield, *The Arabs*. Great Britain: Allen Lane, 1976: reprint, London: Penguin Books, 1985,16.

5   Guillaume, 7.

6   Ibid., 11,12.

7   Ali, 7.

8   Millard J. Erickson, *Christian Theology*. Grand Rapids, Michigan: Baker Book House, 1985, 726–728.

9   Ali, liii.

10 Ibid., liv.

11 Ibid., lv.

Chapter 11

1   Alfred Guillaume, Islam. Ringwood, Australia: Penguin 1954, 2nd ed. 1956, 23.

2   George Braswell, Islam, Its Prophet, Peoples, Politics and Power. Nashville, Tennessee: Broadman and Holman, 1996, 10.

3   Ameer Ali, The Spirit of Islam. London: Christopher's, 1922, reprint, London: Methuen, 1965, 8.

4   Guillaume, 25.

5   Abul Fida, Abulfeda trans. into Latin J. Gagnier, London: 1728, 64.

6   Louis Bahjat Hamada, Understanding the Arab World. Nashville: 1990, 117.

7   H.A.R.Gibb and J.H. Kramers, Shorter Encyclopedia of Islam. Laymen, Netherlands: E.J.Brill, 1974, 392.

8   Guillaume, 28.

9   Thomas Patrick Hughes, Dictionary of Islam. New Delhi: Cosma Publications, 1977, 372.

10 Ali, 43, quoted from Ibn Hisham, 289, Ibn al-Athir, vol II, 73–74.

Chapter 12

1   Philip K. Hitti, The Arabs. A Short History. Chicago: Macmillan, 1962, 35–36.

2   Ameer Ali, The Spirit of Islam. London: Christophers, 1922; reprint, London: Methuen, 1965, 85.

3   Muhammad Marmaduke Pickthall, The Meaning of the Glorious Koran. Mentor: New York, 406.

4   Ali, 88.

5   Pickthall, 364.

6   Ibid, 147–148.

7   The Message of the Prophet to the Omani People, www.answering-islam.org/Muhammed/oman.htm.

8   William Muir, Life of Muhammad. London: Smith Elder and Co., 1883, quoted in Thomas Patrick Hughes, Dictionary of Islam. New Delhi: Cosmo Publications, 1977, 382.

9   Ibid.

10 Ibid, 501ff.

11 Ibid.

Chapter 13

1   Wan Hamid, 'Up to God to Discern on Apostasy'. The Star. August 27, 1998.

2   J. Wansbrough, Quranic Studies: Sources and Methods of Scriptural Interpretation. Oxford: Oxford University Press, 1977, 119.

3   H.A.R.Gibb and J.H.Kramers, A Shorter Encyclopedia of Islam. Leiden: E.J.Brill, 1974, 393.

4   Philip K. Hitti, The Arabs, A Short History. Chicago: Gateway, 1962, 41.

5   Sahih Al-Bukhari, The Translation of the Meanings of Sahih Al-Bukhari, 6th rev.ed., trans. Muhammad Mushir Khan, Lahore, Pakistan: Kazi Publications, 1983, Vol.1, 29.

6   Thomas P. Hughes, Dictionary of Islam. New Delhi: Cosmo Publications, 1977, 376.

7   Muhammad Husayn Haykal, The Life of Muhammad, Indianapolis: North America Trust Publications, 1976, 298.

8   Helen Beth Davies, 'The Bible and Quran compared and contrasted in terms of Christian and Muslim claims as to their status as the Word of God', unpublished paper, 1991, 1.

9   N.L.Geisler and W.E.Nix, General Introduction to the Bible, Chicago: Moody Press, 1968, 387.

10 Muhammad Abdul Rauf, Islam: Creed and Worship, Washington, D.C.: The Islamic Centre, 1974, 5.

11 Kevin J. Conner, 'Hearing God, A Biblical Basis for Prophecy in the Present Age'. Ministries Today Magazine. January/ February, 1992, 51.

12 Barry Chant, 'The Gift of Prophecy'. Australia's New Day. October 1986, 20.

13 Kevin Giles, 'Prophecy in the Bible and the Church Today'. Interchange, papers on Biblical and current questions, Sydney, No.26, 1980, 76ff.

14 Wayne Grudem, The Gift of Prophecy in the New Testament and Today. Eastbourne: Kingsway Publications, 21.

15 Ronald H. Sunderland and Earl E Shelp, 'Prophetic Ministry: An Introduction'. The Pastor as Prophet. New York: The Pilgrim Press, 1985, 10.

16 Geoffrey Bingham, Islam Prophecy for Today. Adelaide: New Creation Publications, 1982, 2.

17 Grudem, 78.

18 Jay Smith, Muhammad, a Christian Apologetic, 99 truth Papers, unpublished, 8,9.

19 Leon Morris, Revelation. London: Tindale, 1969,228.

20 Alfred Guillaume, Islam. Ringwood (Australia): Penguin, 1956, 38.

21 George W. Braswell Jnr., Islam, Its Prophet, Peoples, Politics and Power. Nashville: Broadman and Holman, 1996, 20.

22 Kenneth Cragg, The Call of the Minaret. New York: Oxford University Press, 1964, 93.

Chapter 14

1 Syed Ashrim Ali, 'Compilation of the Holy Quran', Bangladesh Observer, February 1, 1992.

2 William Watt, Muslim–Christian Encounters. London: Routledge, 1991, 41.

3 Pipes, Daniel. The Rushdie Affair. The Novel, the Ayatollah and the West. New York: 1990, 75–76.

4 Alexander Stille, 'Radical theories offered on origins of the Quran, Star Tribune (Minneappolis), March 10 2002, A21.

5 Farrukh Dhondy, 'The Danger Within', Australian Financial Review, 14 December 2001, 2–5.

6 H.A.R.Gibb and J.H.Kramers, The Shorter Encyclopedia of Islam. Leiden: E.J.Brill, 1974, 285.

7 Chawcat Moucarry, Faith to Faith. Leicester, England: Inter-varsity Press, 2001, 26.

8 Norman Daniel, Islam and the West. The Making of an Image. Oxford: One World, 1993, 53.

9 Ibn Warraq, Why I am not a Muslim. New York: Prometheus Books, 1995, 294.

10 Norman L. Geisler & Abdul Saleeb, Answering Islam. Grand Rapids, Michigan: Baker Books, 1993, 179.

11 Toby Lester, 'What is the Quran', in The Last Great Frontier compiled by Phil Parshall. Quezon City: Open Doors With Brother Andrew, 2000, 332.

12 A friend of Muslims, 'The Muslim View of the Quran and the Bible', Intercede, May 1995, 6.

13 cf Thomas Patrick Hughes, Dictionary of Islam. New Delhi: Cosmo Publications, 1977, 484.

14 Gibb, 274.

15 Ibid., 277.

16 Ali Dashti, Twenty Three Years. London: George Allen & Unwin, 1985, 98.

17 Ibid., 280.

18 Ibid..

19 Ibn Warraq, Why I am not a Muslim. New York: Prometheus Books, 1995, 110.

20 Yusef Smith, 'The Quran (A Christian Apologetic)', Ninety-nine Truth Papers. Hyde Park Christian Fellowship, June 24, 1995, 21

21 Twenty Three Years, 50.

22 Gibb and Kramers, 276.

23 Smith, 24–34.

24 Hughes, 516.

25 L. Bevan Jones, The People of the Mosque. London: Student Christian Movement Press, 1932, 62.

26 Anne Underwood, Donna Foote, Claudia Kalb and Brad Stone, 'Islam God Listening?' Newsweek (Australian Edition), 1 April 1997, 63.

Chapter 15

1 Aubrey Whitehouse, 'Some Faiths We Encounter, Islam'. Mission Scene, n.d..

2 'Islam'. Interfaith Witness Belief Bulletin, 1996, 2.

3 'Islamic Law'. SIM Now, March–April 1984, 8.

4 Mark Durie, 'Isa, The Muslim Jesus', Unpublished manuscript, 5.

5 Thomas Patrick Hughes, Dictionary of Islam. New Delhi: Cosmo Publications, 1977, 475.

6 'Islam and the West', The Economist, 6 August 1994, 13.

7 Patricia Crone and Michael Cook, Hagarism. Cambridge: Cambridge University Press, 1977, 24.

8 'Ramadan. The Fourth Pillar of Islam'. Thirty Days Muslim Prayer Focus, 1996.

9 Bernard Lane, 'The devil is more real for Muslims', The Australian, July 8 2002, 3.

Chapter 16

1 The Persecution of Christians, Voice of the Martyrs, 1.

2 'Sudan Persecuted but not Forsaken', Christian Information Network, Fall 1997, 5.

3 Ibid.

4 ISIC Bulletin, October/November, 1997, 5.

5 'Forcing Houses for Fanatics', ISIC Bulletin, April/ May, 1998, 3.

6 'Prayer Watch for the Muslim World', S.F.I., October/November, 1996, 3.

7 ISIC Bulletin, February/ March, 1998, 8.

8 'No justice for Egyptian Copts', The Voice of the Martyrs, February 1999, 6.

9 Christopher Dickey, 'Inside Suicide, Inc.' Newsweek, April 16 2002, 65.

10 Andrew Bolt, 'Islam's deadly truth', Herald Sun, March 28 2002, 19.

11 Colleen Egan, 'The insider', Weekend Australian, November 23–24 2002, 22.

12 Arutz-7. 'Getting to Know America's Saudi Allies', May 7 2002.

13 ibriefings@isic-centre.org, October 15 2002, 1.

14 Home Pages Australia, Voice of the Martyrs, 2.

15 Muhammad Ustaz Ashaari, The West on the Brink of Death. London: Asoib International Limited, 1992, 120.

16 Greg Callaghan, 'The Man Behind the Mosque', The Weekend Australian Magazine, September 14–15 2002, 18–19.

17 Emir R. Caner and M. Ergun, 'The Doctrine of Jihad in the Islamic Hadith', Evangelical Society, Colorado Springs, Colorado, November 15 2001, 7–8.

18 Jacques Ellul, foreword to The Decline of Eastern Christianity under Islam, by Bat Ye'or (London: Associated University Presses, 1996), xvii.

19 Victorian Baptist Witness, March 2001, 18.

20 Stan Guthrie, 'Muslim Mission Breakthroughs', Christianity Today, 13 December 1993, 22.

21 Muhammad Sa-id Ramadan al-Buti, Jurisprudence in Muhammad's Biography, 7th edition, 134.

22 E. Van Donzel, Islamic Desk Reference. New York: E.J.Brill, 1994, 136.

23 'Threats to kill Australian', Herald Sun, March 20 2003, 2.

24 'Calls for Jihad widespread in Islamic world', ibrifing@isic-centre.org, April 11 2003, 2.

25 Mark Forbes, 'Australians were bombers' target'. Age (Melbourne), February 11 2003, 3.

26 Bat Ye'or, The Decline of Eastern Christianity under Islam. London: Associated University Presses, 1996, 40.

27 'One Person's Journey: Mina's Story,' Shalom-Salam, The Pursuit of Peace in the Biblical Heart of the 10/40 Window, nd., 10.

28 Charles Kranthammer, 'The Barak Paradox,' Time, 23 October 2000, 88.

29 Suzanne Gotenberg and Brian Whitaker, 'Barak turns his back on peace effort, Age (Melbourne), October 24 2000, 11.

30 Lally Weymouth, 'Barak: Die or Separate', Newsweek, 24 July 2001, 80–81.

31 Mark Raphael Baker, 'Israel and me', Age (Melbourne), 28 April 2002, Agenda 4.

32 Clarence H. Wagner Jr., 'Christianity Needs Israeli Sovereignty over Jerusalem', Dispatch From Jerusalem, 15.

33 Tony Parkinson, 'Speech last roll of the dice for PLO leader', Age (Melbourne), 16 December 2001, 1.

34 Dennis Ross, 'Why Arafat must act', Age (Melbourne), 16 December 2001, 17.

35 Tony Pearce, 'The Assault on Israel', Light for the Last Days Supplement, April 2002.

36 Uwe Siemon-Netto, 'Scholar warns West of Muslim Goals', www.upi.com/view, 22 June 2002.

37 The Jews: 'Enemies of Allah, descendants of Pigs and Apes.' ibrifings@isic-centre.org, November 5 2002, 1.

38 Alex Perry, 'Deadly Cargo', Time, October 1 2002, 45.

39 Marian Wilkinson, 'Extremist's history leaves experts suspicious', Bali News, 9.

40 Hilmy Bakar Almascaty, 'Panduan Jihad untuk Adtivis Gerakan Islam. Jakarta: Gema Insani, May 2001.

41 Massoud Ansari, 'Junior School Jihad', HQ, December/January 2001–02, 47–53.

42 M.A. Muqtedar Khan, 'An Executive Summary of Milestones by Sayyid Qutb', www.young-muslims.ca/online_library/books/milestones/freshlook.asp, April 2 2003, 1.

43 David Pryce-Jones, The Closed Circle. London: Paladin, 1990, 195.

44 SBS (Melbourne) News, February 23, 1999.

45 Iqbal Ali Abdullah, 'Yemen Kidnapper Tells of Plan to Kill', Age (Melbourne), 15 January 1999.

46 'US, UK Envoys get Warnings', Age (Melbourne), 8 March, 1999.

47 'Kill Americans and Britons: Bin Laden', Age (Melbourne), 26 December 1998.

48 Melinda Liu, 'Holy War on the Web', Newsweek, 16 October 2001, 66.

49 Robin Wright, Sacred Rage. New York: Simon and Schuster, 1985, 36.

50 John Pilger, 'Punishing the Innocent,' Good Weekend, 8 April 2000, 31.

51 John F. Burns, 'Bin Laden Stirs Struggle on Meaning of Jihad', International New York Times, 27 January 2002, 2.

52 Anton La Guardia, 'The Promise of Paradise Makes a Suicide Bomber Tick', Age (Melbourne), 2 August, 1997, A15.

53 'Weddings and Funerals for the Martyrs', ISIC Bulletin, October/November 1996, 6.

54 Pryce-Jones, The Closed Circle, 322.

55 SBS Broadcasting, 5 December 2001.

56 'Izz al-Din al-Faris, 'A False and Regrettable Issue', Hong Kong Muslim Herald, April 1992, 2.

57 R. Wright, Sacred Rage, 35.

58 Bat Ye'or, The Decline of Eastern Christianity under Islam, 108–9.

59 Ibid., 195.

60 'Memo to the West – Hands Off', ISIC Bulletin, April/May, 1998, 2.

61 ISIC Bulletin, April/May, 1998, 9.

62 Bat Ye'or, The Decline of Eastern Christianity under Islam, 197.

63 'Turkey warns France on Armenian genocide bill,' Karachi International News, 2 November 2000, 10.

64 William Dalrymple, From the Holy Mountain, Great Britain: Flamingo, Harper Collins, 1997, 33.

65 Michael Dobbs, 'The Unknown Enemy', Washington Post quoted in Sunday Age, 4 April 1999, 4.

66 'Tragedy in the Making', ISIC Bulletin, June/July 1998, 4.

67 'Muslims Attack Church in Kosovo', Newsroom quoted in Victorian Baptist Witness, June 2000, 20.

68 'Church Destroyed" Info@barnabasfund.org, November 21 2002.

69 Hugh Riminton, 'Slaves of Sudan', Good Weekend, 7 August 1999.

70 'Christian Muslim Conflict Continues', Moody, May/June 2001, 48.

71 Ibid., 219.

72 Amir Ali, 'Jihad Explained', Institute of Islamic Information & Education, www.themodern-religion.com/jihad/jihad-explained.html, November 11 2002.

73 Ibn Warraq, Why I am not a Muslim. New York: Prometheus Books, 1995, 219.

74 'Islands and Lombok Erupt in Violence,' Open Doors, April 2000, 7.

75 'Extremism Knows No Bounds', ISIC Bulletin, April/ May, 1998, 8–9.

76 Louise Williams, 'Food Scarce on Isle Racked by Violence', (Melbourne) Age, 13 March, 23.

77 Source withheld.

78 Louise Williams, 'Indonesian Ethnic Wars Hit New Low', (Melbourne) Age, 22 March 1999, 9.

79 Pakistan, SBS World Guide, 6th Edition. Melbourne: Ausfino, 1998, 572.

80 Barry Bearak, 'The Taliban just say no in heroin's heartland,' New York Times, quoted in Age (Melbourne), 12 June 2001, 17.

81 Stephen Gibbs and Matthew Moore, 'Bashir's warning to Australians: you will be dragged into war', Age (Melbourne) December 13 2002, 1.

82 John F. Burns, 'Bin Laden Stirs Struggle on Meaning of Jihad', New York Times, 29 January 2002, 5.

83 Ed O'Loughlin, "Hamas has stranglehold on Palestinian future", Age (Melbourne) June 21 2003, 16.

Chapter 17

1 'Christians in Pakistan', Barnabas Magazine, August–September 2002, 7.

2 James A. Beverley, 'Is Islam a Religion of Peace?' Christianity Today, January 7 2002, 40.

3 James A. Ferrier, HCJB World Radio E-mail, 27 April 1999.

4 Rachael Howes, 'Mosque Takes on Council', Weekend Australian, February 13–14, 1999, 11.

5 David G. Littman, 'Human Rights and Human Wrongs', www.nationalreview.com/comment/comment-littman011903.asp, January 19 2003.

6 Jacques Ellul, foreword to The Decline of Eastern Christianity under Islam, by Bat Ye'or (London: Associated University Presses, 1996), 19.

7 Bat Ye'or, The Decline of Eastern Christianity under Islam. London: Associated University Presses, 1996, 108.

8 Ibn Warraq, Why I am not a Muslim. New York: Prometheus, 1995, 230.

9 William Dalrymple, From the Holy Mountain. Hammersmith, London: Flamingo 1998, 18.

10 Munier Ahmed, 'Faithful Sees Bishop's Body', Sunday Age (Melbourne), 10 May, 1998.

11 Barbara G. Baker, Owner – Religious Liberty@xc.org. 8 May, 1998.

12 Chris Walker, 'Struggling under Oppression', On Being , October 1993, 7.

13 Muhammad Marmaduke Pickthall, The Meaning of the Glorious Koran, An explanatory translation. New York: Mentor, 147–148.

14 Abdullah Yusuf Ali, The Meaning of the Glorious Quran. Istanbul: Asir Media, 2002.

15 Hugh Riminton, 'Slaves of Sudan', Good Weekend, 7 August 1999, 52.

16 Richard Wurmbrand, 'Saudis Will have the Word of God,' Voice of the Martyrs, January 1991, 2.

17 'Just Another Sunny Day', Barnabas, Spring 1998, 7.

18 Glen P., 'Churches Devastated in Sudan', The Voice of the Martyrs, March 1998, 2.

19 'Jumaa Prayer Fellowship', Intercede, March/April 2003, 7

20 Bat Ye'or, The Decline of Eastern Christianity under Islam, 87.

21 'Taking the Blame', The Economist, February 28, 1998, 32.

22 Statistics of churches destruction in Indonesia, ISIC Bulletin, June /July 1998, 8.

23 'Church blasts rock Indonesia, Aceh introduces sharia law', Age (Melbourne), 2 January 2002, 10.

24 'Indonesian Christians Warn of Coming Chaos', Newsbrief, April 1998, 1.

25 'Militant Islam on the rise in Indonesia,' Indonesian Christians via WEF Religious Liberty E-mail Conference quoted in Victorian Baptist Witness, June 2001, 12.

26 Patrick Walters, 'West, Islam Clash on Human Rights, Democracy', Australian, 1–2 April 1995, 16.

27 'Punished for Caring,' Open Doors, April 2000, 4–5.

28 'Christian Widow's Arrest is to be Enforced', info@barnabasfund.org, April 15 2003, 1.

29 James S. Murray, 'A Prayer for Pluralising', Weekend Australian, September 18/19, 1993, 24.

30 Dr Badr El Deen Abdel Moumin, Journal of Administration of Governmental Judicial Cases, July/ September, 1979, quoted in Behind the Veil, Unmasking Islam, 139.

31 'Saudi Arabia: Fatwa for non-Muslims'. Al_Muslimoon, Vol. 8, no. 418, Riyadh, February 5 1993 in Ye'or, Bat. Islam and Dhimmitude. Lancaster UK: Fairleigh Dinkenson University Press, 2002.

32 Sarah Smiles, 'Strangers in a strange land', Sunday Age, June 8 2003, 5.

33 Russell Skelton, 'Non-Muslims "stoned, abused and degraded" at Woomera', Age (Melbourne), May 10 2002, 2.
Russell Skelton, 'No escape from persecution', Age (Melbourne), May 10. 2002, 13.

34 Two Lies Don't Make a Truth', ISIC Bulletin, June /July 1998, 2.

35 Patrick Johnstone, Operation World. Rydalmere: OM Publishing, 1993, 204.

36 Albert M. Hyasom, ed. The British Consulate in Jerusalem in Relation to the Jews of Palestine, 1938–1913 (London, 1939), 1; 171, 261, 431– 43.

37 Behind the Veil, 128–29.

38 Cathy Scott-Clark and Adrian Levy, 'Pakistan's War on Christians' Sunday Times Magazine, 24 January 1999 quoted in Readers Digest, April 2000, 117.

39 Religious Freedom Today, February 1999, 2.

40 David Pryce-Jones, The Closed Circle. London: Paladin, 1990, 185.

41 'Uproar in Malaysia', The Voice of the Martyrs, April 1998, 6.

42 ISIC Bulletin, October/ November 1997, 7.

43 Ibid., 8.

44 Voice of the Martyrs, Special edition 1988, 22.

45 ISIC Bulletin, February/ March, 1998, 3.

46 Abe Ata, 'The forgotten Christians of the Holy Land', Age (Melbourne), 25 December 2001, 8.

47 'No Church in the Middle East by 2040', Barnabas, Winter 1999–2000, 4.

48 L.R.Scudder, 'The First Conference of Catholic Patriarchs and Bishops in the Middle East,' MECC News Report, Summer/Autumn 1999, 36–37.

49 Isobel Kershner and Mark White, 'Houses of God,' HQ, June /July 2001, 90–92.

50 'World Watch, Nazareth', Time, April 19 1999,24.

51 'The Town Where Jesus Grew Up', Religious Freedom Today Digest, February 1999, 6.

52 The Holy Land, www.barnabasfund.org, 5 March 2002.

53 Delip Hero, Holy Wars; the Rise of Islamic Fundamentalism. N.Y.: Routledge, 1989, 63.

54 'Enthusiasm Knows no Bounds', ISIC Bulletin, April/ May 1998, 9.

55 Dr Elass, 'What Muslims Think of America', Moody, November/December 2001, 17.

56 Razaf Safa, Inside Islam. Orlando, Florida: Creation House, 1996, 12.

Chapter 18

1   Gerald Flurry, 'The Watchman', The Phildelphia Trumpet, November 1998, 19.

2   Martin Gilbert, Winston S. Churchill – The Prophet of Truth. 684.

3   Ibid, 731.

4   Bryant Myers, 'Africa', MARC Newsletter no.94–4, December 1994, 4.

5   Allen Webb, 'How to Share Your Faith with a Muslim', East Asia's Millions, 4th Quarter, 1998, 3.

6   'My Muslim Family', East Asia's Millions, 4th Quarter, 1998, 9.

7   Ron Peck, 'Speaking on Behalf of Muslims', Intercede, September/October 1998, 2.

8   'Islam and The West Survey', The Economist, 6 August 1994, 13.

9   'From Russia With Love', The Bulletin, Fuller Theological Seminary, Spring Quarter, 1989, 3.

10 'Reaching out to Muslims', Reaching and Teaching the Nations, Derek Prince Ministries, March 1998, 4.

11 'Muslims Coming to Christ', Dawn Fridayfax, 1997/46 via E-Mail.

12 Stan Guthrie, 'Veiled threat', World Pulse, May 16, 1997, 2.

13 Revival World Report, May–June 1999, 6.

14 Michelle O'Donoghoe, 'Kazakhstan: Changed Lives', Missions Update, October/December, 1997,2.

15 'Ethiopia', Brigada-Orgs Missionmobilizers, 27/11/97 via E-Mail.

16 Del Kingsriter, 'Ethiopia Holds the Key', Intercede, September/October, 1996, 6.

17 Greg Livingstone, The Challenge of Planting Churches in Muslim Cities. Grand Rapids: Baker, 1993, 60.

18 'Israel', Brigada-Orgs Missionmobilizers, 27/11/97 via E-Mail.

19 'The Challenge of Islam', Compass Direct, 23 April 1996.

20 'Arab Leads Kuwaiti Church', The Voice of the Martyrs, March 1999.

21 Ed Larby, 'Will the Gulf Crisis Become a Crisis of Faith for Muslims?' New Life, December 5, 1990.

22 '24 Baptised,' Elam News, 1st Quarter 2001, 1.

23 'Iraq Church Growth', OM Headlines, February 1998, 3.

24 'Pastor Daniel', 'Be Brave and Go', Missions Update, April/June 1998, 8–9.

25 Stuart Robinson, Praying the Price. Tonbridge, Kent: Sovereign World, 1994, 24.

26 'Converts and Enquirers', Fellowship of Faith Prayer News Bulletin, December 94–March 95, 19.

27 'Prayer the Greatest Thing', Australia's New Day, April 1983, 40.

28 Name Withheld, 'Hope for Christians in War-torn Sudan', April 2000.

Chapter 19

1 Thirty Days Muslim Prayer Focus. Buderim, Australia, 1993, 5.

2 Paul Hiebert, 'Power Encounter and Folk Islam', Muslim's and Christians on the Emmaus Road, Ed. by J. Dudley Woodbury, MARC Publication, 1989, 47.

3 Michael Asher, Lawrence The Uncrowned King of Arabia. London: Viking, 1998, 155.

4 Janice Morgan Strength, 'Lessons from Russia Regarding Spirituality', Theology News and Notes, Fuller Theological Seminary, 1999, 19.

5 Ibid, 20.

6 Vivienne Stacey, 'The Practice of Exorcism and Healing', Muslims and Christians on the Emmaus Road, Ed. By J.Dudley Woodbury, MARC, 1989, 292.

7 L. Bevan Jones, The People of the Mosque. YMCA Publishing, Calcutta, 1939, 33–42.

8 David Pryce-Jones, The Closed Circle. Paladin: London, 1990, 15.

9 Fouad Ajami, The Arab Predicament. Cambridge University Press, 1985, 4.

10 Hashem Hassan, Al-Quds Al-Arabi (London), 7 October 2001.

11 Tony Pearce, 'The Struggle for the Soul of Islam', Light for the Last Days, January 2002, 10–11.

12 The Closed Circle, 17.

13 Ibid, 17.

14 Ibid, 73.

15 Ibid, 160.

16 Boutros Boutros-Ghali, 'The Socio Cultural Determinants of Arab Diplomacy' in George N. Atiyeh, ed.Arab and American Cultures. Washington, D.C.: American Enterprise Institute for Public Policy Research, 1977, 236.

17 Chloe Saltau, 'One man's road from Damascus but where to from here?' Age (Melbourne), 16 June 2001, 1.

18 Barbara Crossette, 'Arab Nations repressed, says report', New York Times in Age (Melbourne), 3 July 2002, 7.

19 Ibid

20 Ministry in Islamic Contexts, Lausanne Committee for World Evangelisation, Occasional Paper No.28, 1996, 14.

21 'Wonder Boy Impresses Muslim and Jew Alike', The Age (Melbourne), 19.1.98.

22 'Incense, silk and jihad', The Ecomist, May 29 2003, 4.

23 Oufkir, Malika and Fitoussi, Michele. Stolen Years, Twenty Years in a Desert Jail. New York: Hyperion, 2000, 45–45.

24 Syed Ameer Ali, The Spirit of Islam, Methuen, London, 1922, LXIV.

25 Reza F. Safa, Inside Islam. Orlando, Florida: Creation House, 1996, 17.

26 Stan Guthrie, 'Muslim Mission Breakthrough', Christianity Today, December 13, 1993, 26.

27 Ibid, 26.

28 'Tajikistan Miracle', Victorian Baptist Witness, March 1998, 19.

29 Brother Andrew, 'Campaign for the Church in the Middle East', Open Doors, September 14 1992, 1 and 2.

30 'United Prayer Track', Friday fax, Volume 98, No. 5, February 13, 1998.

31 Colin Whittaker, Reinhard Bonnke. Eastbourne: Kingsway, 1998, 183.

32 Reinhard Bonnke, Revival Report Telegram, 1 November 1995, 4.

33 'Why did this monarchy cease?' Wisness, June 2002, 3.

Chapter 20

1 Del Kingsriter, Sharing Your Faith With Muslims. Minneapolis: Center for Ministry to Muslims, , 3.

2 Tzvi Fleescher, 'How Arafat chose war over peace', Age (Melbourne), October 24 2000.

3 Ross Dunn, 'New plots for Jews spark outrage', Age (Melbourne), April 11 2001.

4 'Mission to Afghanis', Elam News, Third Quarter, 1998, 4.

5 'If only My People will Pray', Revival World Report, September–October 2000, 18.

6 L. Bevan-Jones, From Islam to Christ, Focus on Islam Series No. 6. Birmingham: Warwickshire Publishing, n.d., 3–4.

7 G.W. Braswell. Islam It's Prophet, Peoples, Politics and Power. Nashville,Tennesee: Broadman and Holmann Publishers, 1996, 77.

8 Reza F Safa, Inside Islam. Orlando:Creation House, 1996, 182.

9 'Queen Esther Walks the Streets of Tehran', Elam News, Winter 1998,1.

10 Memo, The Quarterly Newsletter of Middle East Media, Number 75, 1997/2, 1.

11 'Explosive Hunger for New Testaments in Turkey', The Voice of the Martyrs, November 1997, 6.

12 Ron Peck, 'Speaking on Behalf of Muslims', Intercede, November/December 1998, 2.

13 Hass Hirji-Wilji and Jaryl Strong, Escape from Islam. Wheaton: Tyndale House, 1981, 8.

14 Muhammad Karoui, Les Temps Modernes, September–October 1972, Quoted in The Closed Circle by David Price-Jones, 396.

15 Geraldine Brooks, 'One Boy's Story', Good Weekend, 19 June 1999, 51.

16 Hass Hirji-Wilji and Jaryl Strong, Escape from Islam, Wheaton: Tyndale House, 1981, 136.

17 William Miller, A Christian's response to Islam,…… 160.

18 Ian Hawley, 'Are Muslims the Enemy?' Alive Magazine, May 1999, 21.

19 Vicki Mustafa, 'Muslims; Can they be reached?', New Day, June 1996, 28.

20 Tim Luke, 'For the Love of my Brothers,' In Touch Ministries, n.d., 10.

21 'Reconciliation Walk Softens Muslim Memories of Crusades', PULSE, May 16, 1997, 4.

22 Ibid, 21.

23 Sofia Javed, 'After 900 years it's not too late to say sorry', Age, 17 July 1999, 20.

24 'Hassan Finds Jesus through the Word', Intercede, March/April, 1996, 5.

25 'Suicide Saved', Elam News Third Quarter, 1998, 1.

26 'There Must be Truth Somewhere,' Elam News, 1st Quarter 2000, 1.

Chapter 21

1 Mark Robinson, 'Ministering to Muslims', Leadership NOW! January 2002, 18.

2 Mark Robinson, 'Pentecostal power among Pancasila People', unpublished paper, 2001.

3 Raymond Perkins Jr., Prayer for Israel, New Zealand, No. 71 July–August 1993, 1.

4 George Otis Jr., The Last of the Giants. Tarrytown, New York: Fleming H. Revell, 1991, 157–158.

5 'Testimony of a Martyr?', Intercede, May/April 1998, 6.

6 'The Shazlis of Damascus', ISIC Bulletin, February/ March 1996, 12.

7 Stewart Gill, 'Conquerors or saviour? The Aboriginals and the United Aborigines Mission', Kategoria, Spring 1997, 14–17.

8 'Fulani, Dreams Wake the Soul', Intercede, 6.

9 'From Terror to Christ', July–August 2002.

10 Muhammad Ustaz Ashaari, The West on the Brink of Death. London: Asoib International Limited, 1992, 56.

11 Aman, Aman, The Story of a Somali Girl. London: Bloomsbury Publishing Place, 1994, 11.

12 Hass Hirji Walji and Jaryl Strong, Escape from Islam. Wheaton: Tyndale House, 1981, 7.

13 Ibid, 23.

14 Festo Kivengere, I Love Idi Amin. Old Tappin, N.J.: Revell, 1977, 30.

15 Ibid, 30.

16 Lausanne Committee for World Evangelisation, Ministry in Islamic Contexts, International Institute for the Study of Islam and Christianity, Occasional Paper no. 28, 1996, 14.

17 'Christian Shot Dead', info@barnabasfund.org, February 25 2003.

18 'The Sword of Love', SIM.Now, September/October 1989, 11.

19 'Captured by the Power of the Cross', Intercede, November/December 1998, 6.

20 'Dreams and Visions', Prayerlink, No. 3, August 1997, 2.

21 'Captured by the Power of the Cross', Intercede, November/December 1998, 6.

22 'Ethiopia and Eritrea', Servants Fellowship International, February/ March 1997, 1.

23 Robert Smith, 'Pakistan, Land of Opportunity', Red Sea Team International, September 1997, 2,3.

24 'Appointment in West Beirut', Crossroads, January/ March 1998, 2.

25 'Prayer and Visions', Open Doors/ Newsbrief, April 1996, 4.

26 Newsletter, Good Shepherd Ministries International, June 1992, 1.

27 'Increase of Miracles', Prayerlink No.4, December 1997, 9.

28 Patrick Johnstone, The Church is Bigger than you Think. Bulstrode, Gerrads Cross, Bucks.: Christian Focus Publications/WEC, 1998, 87–88.

29 'Jesus Dreaming', On Being, June 1995, 13.

30 'Africa: Muslims See Visions, and House Churches are Started', Fridayfax, February 13 1998, 1.

31 'Jesus Dreaming', On Being, June 1995, 13.

32 'The Night of Power', Thirty Days Muslim Prayer Focus, 1996.

33 'The Reason', Prayerlink, No.3, August 1997, 2.

34 Ulf Ekman, 'Go to the Mountain People', Newsletter, No.1, 1997, 2.

35 'A Christian Arab Reports from Israel', The 10/40 Window Reporter, Winter 1998, 4.

36 'Kazakhstan', The 10/40 Window Reporter, Fall 1997, 1.

37 Mark Robinson, 'Ministering to Muslims', Leadership Now, January 2002, 18.

38 'Lebanon. Jesus on the Cross', Muslim World Prayer Update, October 1997, 1.

Chapter 22

1   Clive Price, 'How the Irish Saved our Souls', Compass, May 1998, 22.

2   Patrick Sookhdeo, 'Issues in Contextualisation', World Evangelisation, September/October 1997, 5–6.

3   Richard Boudreax, 'Khatami's Exit Terminates Dialogue', Age, Friday 12 March 1999, 9.

4   'Christian Martyrs, Leonard Dober, a Slave for Christ', The Voice of the Martyrs, October 1998, 5.

5   'Basic Issues in a Muslim's Understanding of the Christian Faith', July 1997.

6   Source withheld.

7   'Christian 'Mosque' in Benin', Victorian Baptist Witness, October 1997, 20.

8   Zafhar Ismail, 'What about the Muslim Convert?', World Evangelisation, 20.

9   Len Bartloiti, 'Why Islam is Christianity's Greatest Opportunity', Prayer Pilgrimage Through the Muslim World, Center for Ministry to Muslims, 8.

10 Professor Jehu J. Hanciles, 'What Needs to be Done?', Fuller Focus, Fall 1998, 18.

11 Todd Crowell, 'In Search of an Asian Path', Asia Week, December 1997, 33.

12 Lawrence Hirsch, 'Celebrate Messiah Australia', 3.

13 Dr Ho Jin Jun, 'The Challenge of the Korean Church Missions', Korean Torch, Winter 1998, 7.

14 'Western Converts to Islam', ISIC Bulletin, December 1996/January 1997, 10.

15 Marcel Rebiai, 'Muslim Evangelism and Jew-Arab Reconciliation – Jerusalem', Prayer for Israel – New Zealand, January/February 1994, 3.

16 Greg Livingstone, Planting Churches in Muslim Cities. Michigan: Baker Book House, 1993, 154.

17 Lallia Djanet Lachmet, Manchester: Carcenet Press, 1987, 40.

18 Source withheld.

19 BBC News, 2000.

20 Bidinost, Marcella. 'A debt of love', Sunday Age (Melbourne), February 9 2003, 10.

21 Maziar Bahan and Christopher Dickey, 'And Along Came a Spider', Newsweek, August 21 2001, 81.

22 'A Culturally Relevant Church', Missions Update, April/June 1998, 17.

23 Charles Taylor, 'Cultural Relativity', New Day, November 1996, 29.

24 Kalervo Oberg, 'Culture Shock: Adjustment to New Cultural Environments', July–August 1960, 3.

25 Briar Whitehead, 'Tools you Can Trust', Go, Third quarter 1997, 2–4.

26 'Unreached Peoples Profile', Intercede, March 1990, 7.

27 Mansour Khalid, 'The Sociological Determinants of Arab Diplomacy' in George N. Atiyeh, ed. Arab and American Cultures. Washington D.C.: American Enterprise Institute for Public Policy Research, 1977, 128.

28 Raphael Patai, The Arab Mind. New York: Hatherleigh Press, 2002, 96.

29 Ibid, 113.

30 Sania Hamady. Temperament and Character of the Arabs. New York: Tawyne Publishers, 1960, 35.

31 Age (Melbourne) Today Life and Times, 26 April 2000, 7.

32 Donatella Lorch and Preston Meridenhall, 'A War's Hidden Tragedy', Newsweek, August 18 2000, 83–84.

33 David Pryce-Jones, The Closed Circle. London: Paladin 1990, 41.

34 Ibid, 92, 93.

35 Hass Hirji-Waljii and Jaryl Strong, Escape from Islam. Wheaton: Tyndale House, 1981, 81.

36 Elizabeth Bennett, 'Understanding Muslims', New Day, June 1996, 30

37 David Penman, 'A Continuing Surprise', On Being, November 1979, 11.

38 The Closed Circle, 131.

39 Ibid, 99.

40 Megel J. Mandel, The Arabs and Zionism before World War I. Berkeley and Los Angeles: University of California, 1980, 19.

41 Reza F Safa, Inside Islam. Orlando, Florida: Creation House, 1996, 81.

42 Cedric Whayo, 'Supporting Ministry to the Muslims', Sovereign World Trust Annual Report, December 1994.

43 Stan Guthrie, 'A Crescent for a Cross: Islam Prospers in America', Christianity Today, October 28 1991, 40.

44 Suzanne Martin, 'Dreams May Seem Impossible but God is Alive', Queensland Baptist, August 1992, 1.

45 Charles H. Kraft and Marguerite G. Kraft, 'Understanding and Valuing Multi-ethnic Diversity', Theology News and Notes, Fuller Seminary, December 1993, 7.

46 Bong Rin Ro, 'Communicating the Concept of God to the Korean Culture', Korean Torch, 7.

47 Shah Ali, 'South Asia: Vegetables, Fish and Messianic Mosques', Theology News and Notes, Fuller Seminary, March 1992, 12.

48 Shoki Koh, Ministry in Context. London:London Theological Fund, 1972, 209.

49 John Olley, 'God Speaks our Language – A Look at Contextualisation', Vision, August 1997, 13.

50 Bruce Bradshaw, 'Communicating Christ to Muslims Requires Attitude Adjustments', MARC Newsletter, April 1990, 1.

51 Phil Bourne, 'Learning to Listen', Crossroads, April–June 1996, 6.

52 Suhaini Azman, 'Mum's the Word', Far Eastern Economic Review, 5 May 1988, 35.

53 'Malaysia Ban', The Victorian Baptist Witness, June 1989, 6.

54 Andrew Wark, 'Islam the Future of the Malaysian Church at Risk?', New Life, 21 January 1993, 11.

55 Amir Abdullah, 'Christian Missionaries in the Muslim World: Manufacturing Kufr', Nida'ul Islam, September–October 1997.

56 Charles Edward White, 'Teaching Mark's Gospel to Muslims', Christianity Today, February 8 1993, 39.

57 Stan Guthrie, 'Muslim Mission Breakthrough', Christianity Today, December 13 1993, 26.

58 Phil Parshall, New Paths in Muslim Evangelism, Evangelical Approaches to Contextualisation. Grand Rapids, Michigan, Baker Book House, 1980.

59 Shakil Arsalan, 'Masihee Jamat Under Moslem Veil', Pritibi, February 1990.

60 'Faith Tragedy in Bangladesh', Al-muslimoon Weekly, January 9 1994.

61 Religious Survey-7, 90–96AD Narsingdi Zone-9, Islamic Missionary Counsel of Bangladesh, 2.

Chapter 23

1 Del Kingsriter, Answers to Muslim Objections. Minneapolis: Center for Ministry to Muslims, n.d., 55.

2 Chawcat Moucarry, Faith to Faith. Leicester, England: Inter-varsity Press, 2001, 45.

3 Geoffrey Parrinder, Jesus in the Quran. New York: Oxford University Press, 1977, 58.

4 Hass Hirji-Walji and Jaryl Strong, Escape from Islam. Wheaton: Tyndale House, 1981, 128.

5 Charles Edward White, 'Teaching Mark's Gospel to Muslims', Christianity Today, February 8 1983, 40.

6 Greg Livingstone, Planting Churches in Muslim Cities. Grand Rapids, Michigan: Baker Book House, 1993, 44.

7 Hass Hirji-Walji, 50.

8 'Christians Fail to Challenge Society', Restoration, March/April 1991, 16,17.

9   Ustaz Ashaari Muhammad, The West on the brink of Death. London: Asoib International Ltd., 1992, x–xi.

10 Restoration, 18.

11 John J. Donohue and John L. Esposito, eds. Islam in Transition. New York: Oxford University Press, 1982, 79.

12 Waleed Nassar, 'Ten Hindrances to Reaching Muslims', Ministries Today, July/August 1994, 80.

Chapter 24

1   Walter Anderson, *Against All Odds.* Ringwood, Australia: LMS International, 1998, 201.

2   Terry Paulson, 'God Is in Charge of Operations…but We Are All in Sales,' *Fuller Focus*, Fall 1999, 4.

3   'A Manual Mahaber (The Jesus Association) and the Orthodox Church, The Horn of Africa Challenge and Opportunity, *AD 2000 and Beyond Movement*, n.d., 7,8.

4   Martin Flanagan, 'Careful, You Might Hear Us', *Age* (Melbourne), 18 April 1998, E6.

5   Michael Frost, 'The Power of Stories', *On Being*, November 1997, 46.

6   Tom Stettan, 'Story Telling Why Do It?', *Mission Frontiers Bulletin*, March–April 1997, 11.

7   Vivienne Stacey, 'Practical Lessons for Evangelism among Muslims', *Interserve*, 1998, 10.

8   Craig Bird, 'Telling Gospel as Story Opens Muslim Ears', Pulse, July 21 1995, 5.

9   Terry Muck, 'The Mosque Next Door', *Christianity Today*, February 1988, 19.

Chapter 25

1   Thomas Arnold and Alfred Guillaume, eds. The Legacy of Islam. London: Oxford University Press, 1931, 41.

2   Brother Andrew, For the Love of My Brothers. Minneapolis, Minnesota: Bethany House Publishers, 1998, 203.

3   Joseph Farah, 'Are we at war with Islam?' WorldNetDaily.com, June 25 2002.

4   Ziauddin Sardar, The Future of Muslim Civilisation. London: Croonhelm, 114.

5   Stephen Schwartz, 'The Real Islam', Atlantic Unbound, March 20 2003, 7.

6   Samuel P. Huntington, The Clash of Civilisations and the Remaking of World Order. New York: Touchstone, Sime & Schuster, 1996, 116.

7   Waseem Shehzad, 'American companies feeling the impact of Muslim boycotts', Crescent International, Toronto, February 1 2003.

8   Khaled Hanafi, 'Islamic Gold Dinar Will Minimize Dependency on U.S. Dollar', www.islamonline.net, March 4 2003.

9   'Face to face with Brother Andrew', Open Doors, October 2002, 3.

10 'Foreign Christians Expelled from Maldives', The Voice of the Martyrs, September 1998, 5.

11 'Believers Released in Maldives', The Voice of the Martyrs, May 1999, 6.

12 'Maldives', Intercede, July–August 2000, 3.

13 'Persecuting President Gets British Honour', Barnabas, Winter 1998, 4.

14 Greg Livingstone, 'The Challenge', Frontiers, n.d.

15 'New Evidence', September/October, 1994.

16 Reza F. Safa, Inside Islam. Orlando, Florida: Creation House, 1996, 153.

17 Dan Wooding, 'Opening Doors to the Islamic World', Assist Communications, March 19 1999, 2.

18 Everett Hunt, Protestant Pioneers in Korea. Maryknoll, New York: Orbis, 1980, 34, 48, 90.

19 'From the Breech', Umma, January 1996, 1.

20 Maurice Antonelli, 'Coke and the Great Commission', Global News, June /July 1988, 1.

21 'Waiting for a Friend Like You', Report Operation Mobilisation, June 1994, 1.

22 Barrett and Johnson, Our Globe and How to Reach it. Birmingham, Alabama: Global Diagram 12, 25.

23 David Brickner, "Just War?" Jews for Jesus, 2001.

24 Brother Andrew, For the Love of My Brothers, 208.

25 David Brickner, "Just War?" Jews for Jesus, 2001.

26 'Fundamentalist Islam: A Christian Response', Southern Cross, November 1989, 32.

27 Ralph D. Winter, 'Unreached Peoples Update Where Are We Now?' World Evangelisation, March/April 1988, 12.

Epilogue

1 Source withheld.

2 Thomas L. Friedman, 'Why Iran needs Ayatollah Deng', New York Times quoted in Age (Melbourne), Friday 23 July 1999, 15.

3 Ergun Mehmet Caner & Emir Fethi Caner, Unveiling Islam, An Insiders Look At Muslim Life and Beliefs. Grand Rapids Michigan: Kregel Publications, 2002, 80.

SELECTED BIBLIOGRAPHY

Books

Ahmed, Akbar S. *Living Islam.* London: BBC Books, 1993.

Ajami, Fouad. *The Arab Predicament.* Cambridge: Cambridge University Press, 1985.

Al-Bukhari, Sahih. *The Translation of the Meanings of Sahih Al-Bukhari.* 6ᵗʰ rev.ed., trans. Muhammad Mushir Khan. Lahore, Pakistan: Kazi Publications, 1983, Vol.1.

Ali, Abdulluh Yusuf. *The Meaning of the Glorious Quran.* Istanbul: Asir Media, 2002.

Ali, Ameer. *The Spirit of Islam.* London: Christophers, 1922; reprint, London: Methuen, 1965.

Almascaty, Hilmy Bakar, *Panduan Jihad untuk Adtivis Gerakan Islam.* Jakarta: Gema Insani, May 2001.

Aman. *Aman, The Story of a Somali Girl.* London: Bloomsbury Publishing Place, 1994.

Anderson, Walter. *Against All Odds.* Ringwood, Australia: LMS International, 1998.

Arnold, Jose`. *Golden Swords and Pots and Pans.* London: Gollancz, 1964.

Arnold, Thomas and Alfred Guillaume, eds. *The Legacy of Islam.* London: Oxford University Press, 1931.

Asher, Michael. *Lawrence The Uncrowned King of Arabia.* London: Viking, 1998.

Barrett and Johnson. *Our Globe and How to Reach it.* Birmingham, Alabama: Global Diagram 12.

Behind the Veil, n.a., n.d.

Bevan-Jones, L. *From Islam to Christ, Focus on Islam Series No. 6.* Birmingham: Warwickshire Publishing, n.d.

_____. *The People of the Mosque.* YMCA Publishing, Calcutta, 1939.

Bouma, Gary D. *Mosques and Muslim Settlement in Australia.* Canberra: The Australian Government Publishing Service, 1994.

Boutros-Ghali, Boutros. The Socio-Cultural Determinants of Arab Diplomacy in George N. Attiya ed. *Arab and American Cultures.* Washington, DC: American Enterprise Institute for Public Policy Research, 1977.

Braswell, George W. Jr. *Islam, Its Prophet, Peoples, Politics and Power.* Nashville, Tennessee: Broadman and Holman, 1996.

Brother Andrew. *For the Love of my Brothers.* Minneapolis, Minnesota: Bethany House Publishers, 1998.

Brown, Ian. *The Impact of Islam.* South Auckland: Baptist Promotions, n.d.

Caner, Ergun Mehmet & Caner, Emir Fethi. *Unveiling Islam, An Insiders Look At Muslim Life and Beliefs.* Grand Rapids Michigan: Kregel Publications, 2002.

Christianity's Supreme Opportunity. Toronto: Fellowship of Faith for Muslims 1993.

Clark, C.M.H. *A History of Australia*. Vol.1, Melbourne: Melbourne University Press, 1979.

Critchfield, Richard. *Shahat*. Cairo: American University in Cairo Press, 1982.

Crone, Patricia and Michael Cook. *Hagarism*. Cambridge: Cambridge University Press, 1977.

Dalrymple, William. *From the Holy Mountain*. Great Britain: Flamingo, Harper Collins, 1997.

Daniel, Norman. *Islam and the West. The Making of an Image*. Oxford: One World,

Dashti, Ali. *Twenty Three Years*. London: George Allen and Unwin, 1985.

Deen, Hanifa. *Caravanserai: Journey amongst Australian Muslims*. St Leonards, New South Wales: Allen and Unwin, 1995.

Donohue, John J. and John L. Esposito. eds. *Islam in Transition*. New York: Oxford University Press, 1982.

Erickson, Millard J., *Christian Theology*. Grand Rapids, Michigan: Baker Book House, 1985.

Fida, Abul. *Abulfeda* trans. into Latin J. Gagnier, London: 1728.

Gibb, H.A.R. and J.H. Kramers. 'al Dadjdhjal' in *Shorter Encyclopedia of Islam*. Leiden: E.J.Brill, 1974.

Geisler, Norman L. and Abdul Saleeb. *Answering Islam*. Grand Rapids, Michigan: Baker Books, 1993.

Geisler, N.L. and W.E.Nix. *General Introduction to the Bible*. Chicago: Moody Press, 1968.

Gilbert, Martin. *Winston S. Churchill-The Prophet of Truth*.

Guillaume, Alfred. *Islam*. Ringwood, Australia: Penguin Books, 1956.

Haykal, Muhammad Husayn. *The Life of Muhammad*. Indianapolis: North America Trust Publications, 1976.

Hirji-Walji, Hass and Jaryl Strong. *Escape from Islam*. Wheaton: Tyndale House, 1981.

Hunt, Everett. *Protestant Pioneers in Korea*. Maryknoll, New York: Orbis, 1980.

Hamada, Louis Bahjat. *Understanding the Arab World*. Nashville: Thomas Nelson, 1990.

Huntington, Samuel P. *The Clash of Civilizations*. New York: Simon & Schuster, 1996

Hero, Delip. *Holy Wars; the Rise of Islamic Fundamentalism*. N.Y.: Routledge, 1989.

_____. *Between Marx and Mohammad*. London: Harper Collins, 1994.

Hiddins, Les. *Bush Tucker Man Stories of Exploration and Survival*. Sydney: Australian Broadcasting Corporation, 1996.

Hitti, Phillip K. *The Arabs. A Short History*. Princeton: Macmillan, 1949.

Hughes, Thomas Patrick. *Dictionary of Islam*. New Delhi: Cosmo Publications, 1977.

Hunt, James. *Hussein of Jordan: A Political Biography*. London: Macmillan, 1989.

Huntington, Samuel P. *The Clash of Civilisations and the Remaking of World Order*. New York: Touchstone, Simon & Schuster, 1998.

Jenkins, Roy. *Churchill*. London: Tan Books, 2002, 360.

Johnstone, Patrick. *Operation World*. Rydalmere: OM Publishing, 1993.

_____. *The Church is Bigger than you Think*. Bulstrode, Gerrads Cross, Bucks.: Christian Focus Publications/WEC, 1998.

Johnstone, Patrick and Mandryk, Jason. *Operation World*. Cumbria U.K.: Paternoster Lifestyle, 2001.

Karoui, Mohammed. *Les Temps Modernes*, September–October 1972, Quoted in The Closed Circle by David Price-Jones.

Khalid, Mansour. 'The Sociological Determinants of Arab Diplomacy' in George N. Atiyeh, ed. *Arab and American Cultures*. Washington D.C.: American Enterprise Institute for Public Policy Research, 1977.

_____. The Socio Cultural Determinants of Arab Diplomacy in George N. Attiya ed. *Arab and American Cultures*. Washington, DC: American Enterprise Institute for Public Policy Research, 1977.

Kingsriter, Del. *Answers to Muslim Objections*. Minneapolis: Center for Ministry to Muslims.

_____. *Sharing Your Faith With Muslims*. Minneapolis: Center for Ministry to Muslims.

Kivengere, Festo. *I Love Idi Amin*. Old Tappin, N.J.: Revell, 1977.

Koh, Shoki. *Ministry in Context*. London:London Theological Fund, 1972.

Lachmet, Djanet. *Lallia*. Manchester: Carcenet Press, 1987.

Lester, Toby. 'What is the Quran' in *The Last Great Frontier* compiled by Phil Parshall. Quezon City: Open Doors With Brother Andrew, 2000, 332.

Livingstone, Greg. *The Challenge of Planting Churches in Muslim Cities*. Grand Rapids: Baker, 1993.

Mandel, Megel J. *The Arabs and Zionism before World War I*. Berkeley and Los Angeles: University of California, 1980.

Mansfield, Peter. *The Arabs*. Great Britain: Allen Lane, 1976; reprint, London: Penguin Books, 1985.

Markham, C. *The Voyages of Pedro Fernandez de Quiros*. Vol.1. London: Hakluyt Society, 1904.

Miller, William. *A Christian's response to Islam,.....*.

Moucarry, Chawcat. *Faith to Faith*. Leicester, England: Inter-varsity Press, 2001.

Moumin, Badr El Deen Abdel, Dr. Journal of Administration of Governmental Judicial Cases, July/September, 1979, quoted in *Behind the Veil, Unmasking Islam*.

Muhammed, Ustaz Ashaari. *The West on the Brink of Death*. London: Asoib Publishing Limited, 1988.

Muir, William. *Life of Mohammed*. London: Smith Elder and Co., 1883.

Muslim World Prayer Update. Seaforth, New South Wales: Open Doors Inc., January 1998.

Omar, Wafia and Kirsty Allen. *The Muslims in Australia*. Canberra: The Australian Government Publishing Service, 1996.

Otis, George, Jr. *The Last of the Giants*. Tarrytown, New York: Fleming H. Revell, 1991.

Oufkir, Malika and Fitoussi, Michele. *Stolen Years, Twenty Years in a Desert Jail*. New York: Hyperion, 2000, 44–45.

Pakistan, SBS World Guide, 6th Edition. Melbourne: Ausfino, 1998.

Parrinder, Geoffrey. *Jesus in the Quran*. New York: Oxford University Press, 1977.

Parshall, Phil. *New Paths in Muslim Evangelism, Evangelical Approaches to Contextualisation*. Grand Rapids, Michigan, Baker Book House, 1980.

Patai, Raphael, *The Arab Mind*. New York: Hatherleigh Press, 2002, 12.

Peck, Ron. *The Shadow of the Crescent*. Springfield: Centre of Ministry to Muslims, n.d.

Pickthall, Mohammed Marmaduke. *The Meaning of the Glorious Koran*. New York: Mentor, n.d.

Pipes, Daniel. *The Rushdie Affair. The Novel, the Ayatollah and the West*. New York: 1990, 75–76.

Pryce-Jones, David. *The Closed Circle: An Interpretation of the Arabs*. London: Paladin, 1990.

Rauf, Muhammad Abdul. *Islam: Creed and Worship*. Washington, D.C.: The Islamic Centre, 1974.

Rippin, Andrew, *Muslims: Their Religious Beliefs and Practices*. Vol.1. London 1991, 47.

Robinson, Stuart. *Praying the Price*. Tonbridge, Kent: Sovereign World, 1994.

Saddar, Ziauddin. *The Future of Muslim Civilisation*. London: Croom Helm, 1979.

Safa, Reza F. *Inside Islam*. Orlando, Florida: Creation House, 1996.

Sania Hamady. *Temperament and Character of the Arabs*. New York: Twayne Publishers, 1960, 35.

Stevens, Christine. 'Afghan Camel Drivers: Founders of Islam in Australia.' In *An Australian Pilgrimage; Muslims in Australia from the Seventeenth Century to the Present*, ed. Mary L. Jones. Melbourne: Victoria Press, 1993.

George, Timothy. *Is the Father of Jesus the God of Muhammad?* Grand Rapids, Michigan: Zondervan, 2002, 25.

Understanding Islam and the Muslims. Washington: The Embassy of Saudi Arabia, 1989.

Van Donzel, E. *Islamic Desk Reference*. New York: E.J.Brill, 1994.

Warraq, Ibn. *Why I Am Not a Muslim*. New York: Prometheus Books, 1995.

Watt, William. *Muslim-Christian Encounters*. London: Routledge, 1991.

Whittaker, Colin. *Reinhard Bonnke*. Eastbourne: Kingsway, 1998.

Woodbury, J. Dudley (ed). *Muslims and Christians on the Emmaus Road*. MARC Publication, 1989.

Wright, Robin. *Sacred Rage*. New York: Simon and Schuster, 1985.

Yazbeck Haddad, Yvonne and Idleman Smith, Jane. *Muslim Communities in North America*. Albany: State University of New York, 1994.

Ye'or, Bat. *The Decline of Eastern Christianity under Islam*. London: Associated University Presses, 1996.

_____. Islam and Dhimmitude. Lancaster UK: Fairleigh Dinkenson University Press, 2002.

Magazines

1997 Year of Prayer for the World of Islam. September/October, No.5, 1997, 2.

'A Blow to Algerian Peace Hopes.' *Islamic Affairs Analyst*, December 1999, 6.

'A Christian Arab Reports from Israel.' *The 10/40 Window Reporter*, Winter 1998, 4.

'A Culturally Relevant Church.' *Missions Update*, April/June 1998, 17.

'A friend of Muslims, The Muslim View of the Quran and the Bible.' *Intercede*, May

'A Time to Pray.' *New Day*, March 1993, 7.

Abdullah, Amir. 'Christian Missionaries in the Muslim World: Manufacturing Kufr.' *Nida'ul Islam*, September–October 1997.

_____. 'Preserving the Islamic Identity in the West, Threats & Solutions', *Nida'ul Islam*, April–May 1997.

Addison, Steve. *Sharing the Vision.* August 1998, 1.

'Afghanistan: a Smuggler's Haven.' *Intelligence Digest*, 26 November 1999, 3.

Al-Faris, 'Izz al-Din, 'A False and Regrettable Issue.' *Hong Kong Muslim Herald*, April 1992.

'Algeria Country Update', *Middle East Council of Churches News Report*, Summer/Autumn 1999, 8.

Ali, Shah .'South Asia: Vegetables, Fish and Messianic Mosques.' *Theology News and Notes,* Fuller Seminary, March 1992, 12.

Ali, Syed Ashrim. 'Compilation of the Holy Quran.' *Bangladesh Observer*, 1 February 1992.

Allen, Georgie. 'Muslim Life Flourishes Down Under.' *Momtage*, April 1995, 11.

'American Muslim Council.' *Intercede*, May/June 1997, 3.

'An Islamic Africa?' *Memo No.72 (Quarterly Newsletter of Middle East Media)*, 1996/3.

Ansari, Massoud. 'Junior School Jihad', *HQ*, December/Janaury 2001–02, 47–53.

Antonelli, Maurice. 'Coke and the Great Commission.' *Global News*, June/July 1988.

'Appointment in West Beirut.' Crossroads, January/March 1998, 2.

'Arab Leads Kuwaiti Church.' *The Voice of the Martyrs*, March 1999.

Arsalan, Shakil. 'Masihee Jamat Under Moslem Veil.' *Pritibi*, February 1990.

'Arsonists Torch Christian Bookstore in Jordan.' *ISIC Bulletin*, April/May 1998, 11.

'Australia.' *ISIC Bulletin*, June/July 1997, 10.

Ayra, Hawa in 'Through Islamic eyes', *Good Weekend*, 1 December 2001, 28.

Azman, Suhaini. 'Mum's the Word.' *Far Eastern Economic Review*, 5 May 1988, 35.

Bagnall, Diana. 'Muslims with attitude'. *The Bulletin*, March 25 2003, 16.

_____. 'Call of Islam', *The Bulletin*, November 5 2002, 37.

_____. 'Peace and the Prophet', *Bulletin*, February 11 2003, 13.

Bahari, Maziar and Dickey, Christopher. 'And Along Came a Spider', *Newsweek*, August 21 2001, 81.

Barnett, David B. and Todd M.Johnson. 'Annual Statistical Table on Global Mission: 2000'. *International Bulletin of Missionary Research*, January 2000, 25.

Bartloiti, Len. 'Why Islam is Christianity's Greatest Opportunity.' *Prayer Pilgrimage Through the Muslim World,* Center for Ministry to Muslims, 8.

'Basic Issues in a Muslim's Understanding of the Christian Faith.' July 1997.

'Believers Released in Maldives.' *The Voice of the Mart*yrs, May 1999, 6.

Bennett, Elizabeth. 'Understanding Muslims.' *New Day*, June 1996, 30

'Bethlehem: There's Still not Enough Room.' *ISIC Bulletin*, February/ March 1998, 3.

Beverley, James A. 'Is Islam a Religion of Peace?' Christianity Today, January 7 2002, 40.

Beyer Lisa. 'We Are a Tough and Small People.' *Time*, 23 October 2000, 37.

Bezuidenhout, George. 'Before the Bombing.' *Frontline Fellowship News*, 1995/3, 8.

'Bible Bashing in Bangladesh.' *Open Doors/Newsbrief*, July 1996.

Bird, Craig. 'Telling Gospel as Story Opens Muslim Ears.' *Pulse*, July 21 1995, 5.

'Black Islam in the UK.' *ISIC Bulletin*, October/November, 1995, 6.

'Black Islam in the West. Theology and Background of Black Islam.' *ISIC Bulletin*, October/November, 1995, 5.

Bonnke, Reinhard. *Revival Report Telegram*, 1 November 1995, 4.

Bourne, Phil. 'Learning to Listen.' *Crossroads*, April–June 1996, 6.

Bradshaw, Bruce. 'Communicating Christ to Muslims Requires Attitude Adjustments.' *MARC Newsletter*, April 1990,1.

Brickner, David. 'The Mosque, the Synagogue and the Church', *Jews for Jesus*, January 2002, 2.

'Britain, Bengali but British.' *Go,* Interserve, 2nd Quarter 1997, 10.

'British Christianity in Crisis.' *The Good News*, March/April 2000, 20.

'British Muslims Could Soon Outnumber Anglicans', *Today* (South Africa), February 2002, 63.

Brooks, Geraldine. 'One Boy's Story.' *Good Weekend*, 19 June 1999, 51.

Brother Andrew. 'Campaign for the Church in the Middle East.' *Open Doors,* 14 September 1992, 1 and 2.

Buckley, Anisa in 'Through Islamic eyes.' *Good Weekend*, 1 December 2001, 23. *Bulletin*, 21 March 2000, 18.

Cadzow, Jane. 'The Secret of Suzuki.' *Good Weekend*, April 8, 2000, 21.

Calabresi, Massimo and Alexandra Stiglmayer. 'Under the Influence.' *Time*, September 30 1996, 57.

'California's New Mosque.' *Religious Freedom Today Digest*, December 1998, 11.

Callaghan, Greg. 'The Man Behind the Mosque', *The Weekend Australian Magazine*, September 14–15 2002, 18–19.

Callick, Rowan. 'Bearing the Backlash.' *Time*, 15 October 1990, 51.

'Captured by the Power of the Cross.' *Intercede*, November/December 1998, 6.

Campion, Edmund. 'Devotion to Duty.' *The Bulletin*, 30 December 1997/6 January 1998, 79.

Carruthers, Fiona. 'Alice's Afghans at Loss on Preacher's Visit.' *Australian*, 13 February 1998, 2.

Charisma 1997 quoted in 'The Voice of the Martyrs.' *The 10/40 Window Reporter*, Winter 1998, 12.

'Christian Martyrs, Leonard Dober, a Slave for Christ.' *The Voice of the Martyrs*, October 1998, 5.

'Christian "Mosque" in Benin.' Victorian Baptist Witness, October 1997, 20.

'Christian Muslim Conflict Continues', *Moody*, May/June 2001, 48.

'Christians and Jews Flee.' *Victorian Baptist Witness*, December 1991, 17.

'Christians Fail to Challenge Society.' *Restoration*, March/April 1991, 16,17.

'Christians in Pakistan', Barnabas Magazine, August–Septenmber 2002, 7.

'Christians Redeem Slaves', *Victorian Baptist Witness*, September 2000, 25.

Clark, Arthur. 'The New Push for Middle East Studies', *Saudi Aramco World*, January 2003, 13.

'Converts and Enquirers.' *Fellowship of Faith Prayer News Bulletin*, December 94–March 95, 9.

'Crescent versus Cross in Troubled Nigeria.' *Time*, 1 June 1992, 15.

Crowell, Todd. 'In Search of an Asian Path.' *Asia Week*, December 1997, 33.

Cunningham, Loren. 'A Speck on the Globe.' *Ministries Today*, January/February 1994, 24,25.

Day, Roger. 'Christians Fail to Challenge Society.' *Restoration*, March/April 1991, 16.

Dhondy, Farrukh. 'The Danger Within.' *Australian Financial Review*, 14 December 2001, 2–5.

Dickey, Christopher. 'In the name of God', *Newsweek*, May 21, 2002, 65.

_____. 'Inside Suicide Inc.' *Newsweek*, April 16 2002, 65.

'Doors Team Helps Chechen Refugees.' *Open Doors*, April 2000, 8.

Downing, Jim. 'Kuwait's Plan Blows Up.' *Mission Frontiers Bulletin*, September–December 1992, 21.

'Downturn in Nigeria.' ISIC Bulletin, December 1997/January 1998, 5.

'Dreams and Visions.' *Prayerlink*, No. 3, August 1997, 2.

Duisberg , Jordan Bonfante. 'No Rest in the Ruhr.' *Time*, 24 February, 1997, 41.

Eads, Brian. 'Slavery's Shameful Return to Africa.' *Readers Digest*, March 1996.

'Early Test of Nigerian Democracy.' *Islamic Affairs Analyst*, December 1999, 4.

Ekman, Ulf. 'Go to the Mountain People.' *Newsletter*, No.1, 1997, 2.

Elass, Dr. 'What Muslims Think of America.' Moody, November/December 2001, 17.

El-Badry, Sania. 'Understanding Islam in America.' *American Demographics* (vol.16 no.1), 16 January 1994, 10–11.

'Enthusiasm Knows no Bounds.' *ISIC Bulletin*, April/May 1998.

'Ethiopian Protestants Persecuted by Muslims and Orthodox Christians.' *New Life*, August 26, 1993.

'Europe's Largest Mosque.' Memo No. 68, *Middle East Media*, 1995, 3.

'Exodus Now – It Still Goes On.' *ISIC Bulletin*, December 1997/January 1998, 9.

'Explosive Hunger for New Testaments in Turkey.' *The Voice of the Martyrs*, November 1997, 6.

'Face to face with Brother Andrew', *Open Doors*, October 2002, 3.

'Faith Tragedy in Bangladesh.' *Al-muslimoon Weekly*, January 9 1994.

Farley, Christopher. 'Muslim Faithful in USA Tackle Misconceptions.' *USA Today*, 1989.

Fearon, Josiah. 'Islamic Fundamentalism in Africa.' *The Unknown Faces of Islam*, 16.

_____. 'Shariah in Nigeria', *Barnabas Magazine*, May–June 2003, 5.

Fellowship of Faith Prayer News Bulletin, April/July 1994, 9.

Fellowship of Faith Prayer News Bulletin, December 1994–March 1995, 13.

'Foreign Christians Expelled from Maldives.' *The Voice of the Martyrs*, September 1998, 5.

'From Russia with Love.' *The Bulletin of Fuller Theological Seminary*, 1989/2, 2.

'From Terror to Christ', July–August, 2002

'From the Breech', *Umma*, January 1996, 1.

Frost, Michael. 'The Power of Stories.' *On Being*, November 1997, 46.

Fulani, 'Dreams Wake the Soul.' *Intercede*, 6.

'Fundamentalist Islam: A Christian Response.' *Southern Cross*, November 1989, 32.

George, Timothy. 'Is the God of Muhammad the Father of Jesus.' *Christianity Today*, 4 February 2002.

Gerald Flurry. 'The Watchman.' *The Phildelphia Trumpet*, November 1998, 19.

Gill, Stewart. 'Conquerors or saviour? The Aboriginals and the United Aborigines Mission.' *Kategoria*, Spring 1997, 14–17.

Gilliland, Dean. 'New Hope for Muslim Evangelism.' *Fuller Focus*, Summer 1996, 11.

Glen, P. 'Churches Devastated in Sudan.' *The Voice of the Martyrs*, March 1998.

'Global Christianity Figures Static.' *The Queensland Baptist*, October 1996.

Go, Third Quarter, 1997, 8.

Gorny, James Reat. 'Help Sudan's Christians.' *Victorian Baptist Witness*, June 2001, 10.

Graff, James. 'One Faith Divided', *Time*, May 5 2003, 42.

Guthrie, Stan. 'A Crescent or a Cross: Islam Prospers in America.' *Christianity Today*, 28 October 1991, 40.

_____. 'Muslim Mission Breakthrough.' *Christianity Today*, December 13 1993.

Hajaj, Khaldoun in 'Through Islamic eyes', *Good Weekend*, 1 December 2001, 23.

Hajari, Nisid. 'Days of the Long Knives.' *Time*, 5 April 1999, 51–52.

Jamil Hamad. 'I Shot an Israeli.' *Time*, 23 October 2000, 53.

Hammond, Peter. 'The Growth of the Church in Sudan.' *Frontline Fellowship*, 1995/3, 4.

Hanciles, Jehu J., Professor. 'What Needs to be Done?' *Fuller Focus*, Fall 1998, 18.

Haque, Mozammel. 'Christian Missionaries in African Continent.' *The Muslim World League Journal*, February 1992, 8.

Hart, Kent. 'Muslims Target United States.' *Moody*, July/August 1987, 81.

'Hassan Finds Jesus through the Word.' *Intercede*, March/April, 1996, 5.

Hassan Al-Turabi, 'The Islamic Awakensing's Second Wave'. *New Perspectives Quarterly*, 9 (Summer 1992), 50.

'Have Your Pastors Alerted You.' *Voice of the Martyrs*, December 1990.

Hawley, Ian. 'Are Muslims the Enemy?' *Alive Magazine*, May 1999, 21.

Hesselgrave, David. 'A Legacy of Enmity.' *Moody Monthly*, October 1987, 74.

Hiebert, Paul .'Power Encounter and Folk Islam.' *Muslim's and Christians on the Emmaus Road*, Ed. by J. Dudley Woodbury, MARC Publication, 1989, 47.

Hirsch, Lawrence. 'Celebrate Messiah Australia', 3.

Horowitz, David. 'The Continuing Arab Israeli Conflict.' *The Vineyard*, December 1998.

Huntington, Samuel P. *The Clash of Civilizations and the Remaking of World Order*. New York: Simon & Schuster, 1996 256–258, 263–265.

'If only My People will Pray', *Revival World Report*, September–October 2000, 18. 'Indonesian Christians Warn of Coming Chaos.' *Newsbrief*, April 1998.

'Incense, silk and jihad'. The Economist, May 29 2003, 4.

'Iran: Persecution of Protestants.' *ISIC Bulletin*, December 1996/January 1997.

'Iraqis won't Budge in Document Dispute.' *Pensacola News Journal*, 25 November 1998, 2A.

Intercede, May/June 1999, 3.

Intercede, March/April 2003, 7.

ISIC Bulletin, August / September 1995, 9.

ISIC Bulletin, October/November 1996, 1.

ISIC Bulletin, October/November 1996, 4.

ISIC Bulletin, October/November, 1996, 5.

ISIC Bulletin, December 1996/January 1997.

ISIC Bulletin, October/November 1997.

ISIC Bulletin, February/ March 1998, 5.

ISIC Bulletin, April/ May 1998, 9.

'Islam.' *Interfaith Witness Belief Bulletin*, 1996.

'Islam and the West.' *The Economist*, 6 August 1994, 13.

'Islam Finds New Home in Western Europe.' Christianity Today, March 1990.

'Islamic Law Adopted.' *Barnabas*, Summer 1999, 11.

'Islam in Big Business.' ISIC Bulletin, October/November 1996, 10.

'Islam in Britain.' *ISIC Bulletin*, June /July 1996, 8.

'Islam in Britain: Part 2.' *ISIC Bulletin*, February/March 1997, 8.

'Islam in Britain.' *Religious Freedom Today Digest*, December 1998, 13.

'Islam's Solemn March West.' *Asia Week*, 23 February 1990, 33.

'Islamic Law.' *SIM Now*, March/April 1984.

'Islamic Offensive in the USSR.' *The Voice of the Martyrs*, December 1991.

'Islamic Oppression Worsens.' *Alpha News*, April 1993.

'Islands and Lombok Erupt in Violence,' *Open Doors*, April 2000, 7.

Ismail, Zafhar. 'What about the Muslim Convert?' *World Evangelisation*, 20.

'Jesus Can be Lampooned unless it Upsets Islam.' *The Victorian Baptist Witness*, March 1993.

'Jesus Dreaming.' *On Being*, June 1995, 13.

Jones, Bryn. 'God's Radical Church.' *Restoration,* March/April 1991.

'Judge Assassinated in Pakistan.' *Go*, First Quarter 1998, 7.

Jun, Ho Jin, Dr. 'The Challenge of the Korean Church Missions.' *Korean Torch*, Winter 1998, 7.

'Jumaa Prayer Fellowship', *Intercede*, March/April 2003, 7.

'Just Another Sunny Day.' *Barnabas*, Spring 1998.

'Kaduna Riots', March 2003, 8.

'Kazakhstan.' *The 10/40 Window Reporter*, Fall 1997, 1.

Kelly, Mark. *International Missions Board News Stories*, SBC, 22 February 2000.

Kendal, Elizabeth. 'Facing Giants', *Working Together*, 2002, 8.

Kershner, Isobel and White, Mark. 'Houses of God.' *HQ*, June /July 2001, 90–92

Kingsriter, Del. 'Ethiopia Holds the Key.' *Intercede,* September/October, 1996, 6.

————————. 'Miracles in the Muslim World.' Intercede 1992, 12.

Kraft ,Charles H. and Marguerite G. Kraft. 'Understanding and Valuing Multi-ethnic Diversity.' *Theology News and Notes, Fuller Seminary*, December 1993, 7.

Kranthammer Charles. 'The Barak Paradox.' *Time*, 23 October 2000, 88.

Larby, Ed. 'Will the Gulf Crisis Become a Crisis of Faith for Muslims?' *New Life*, December 5 1990.

Lintner, Bertil. 'A Cocoon of Terror', *Far Eastern Economic Review*, April 4 2002, 15–16.

Liu, Melinda. 'Holy War on the Web.' *Newsweek*, 16 October 2001, 66.

Lorch, Donatella and Meridenhall, Preston. 'A War's Hidden Tragedy', *Newsweek*, August 18 2000, 83–84.

Larsen, Timothy. 'Success for Black Muslims.' *Restoration*, March/April 1991.

Layton, Douglas. 'Islam Could Become Predominant Religion in US by 2020',

Mission Network News quoted in HCJB News Update, 22 June 2000.

'Lebanon. Jesus on the Cross.' *Muslim World Prayer Update*, October 1997, 1.

'Libyan Leader's "Holy War" Against Christianity in Africa.' *The Australian Evangel*, May 1986.

Livingstone, Greg. 'The Challenge.' *Frontiers*, n.d.

'Love a Muslim Whom Christ Loves.' *Operation Abba*, Lithgow.

Lovering, Kerry. *Islam on the March.* Singapore: Sudan Interior Mission.

Lovett, Leonard. 'Who does God Say We Are.' *Ministries Today*, November/December 1991.

Luke, Tim. 'For the Love of my Brothers.' *In Touch Ministries*, n.d., 10.

'Major Opening.' *Middle East Media*, memo No.68 1995/3.

Makari, Peter E. 'Kenneth Cragg on Mission.' *MECC News Report*, Summer/Autumn 1999, 41.

'Maldives', *Intercede*, July–August 2000, 3.

'Malaysia Ban.' *The Victorian Baptist Witness*, June 1989, 6.

Martin, Suzanne. 'Dreams May Seem Impossible but God is Alive.' *Queensland Baptist,* August 1992, 1.

Massoud Ansari. 'Junior School Jihad', *HQ*, December/January 2001–2002, 47–53.

'Militant Islam on the rise in Indonesia,' Indonesian Christians via WEF Religious

Liberty E-mail Conference quoted in *Victorian Baptist Witness*, June 2001, 12.

'Millions of Christians Killed in Sudan.' Memo Brief No.72. *Quarterly Newsletter of Middle East Media,* 1996/3.

Ministry in Islamic Contexts, Lausanne Committee for World Evangelisation, Occasional Paper No.28, 1996,14.

'Mission to Afghanis', *Elam News*, Third Quarter, 1998, 4.

Mitchell, Emily. 'All God's Children.' *Time*, 17April, 1989, 58.

'Modern Day Martyrs.' *ISIC Bulletin,* April/ May 1997, 6.

'More Turkish Trouble', *Victorian Baptist Witness*, July 2000, 19.

Morgan Strength, Janice. 'Lessons from Russia Regarding Spirituality.' *Theology News and Notes*, Fuller Theological Seminary, 1999, 19.

Muck, Terry. 'The Mosque Next Door.' *Christianity Today*, February 1988, 19.

'Muslim "Mission" to America.' *The Australian Baptist*, May 1990, 27.

'Muslims Attack Church in Kosovo', Newsroom quoted in *Victorian Baptist Witness*, June 2000, 20.

'Muslim World Briefs.' *Intercede*, 1989, 3.

Muslim World Prayer Update, April 1998, 2.

'Muslims Banned from Churches.' *Fellowship of Faith*, 1994, 25.

'Muslims in Latin America.' *ISIC Bulletin*, August / September 1996, 11.

'Muslims in Western Europe', *The Economist*, August 10 2002, 21.

Mustafa, Vicki. 'Muslims; Can they be reached?', *New Day*, June 1996, 28.

Myers, Bryant. 'Africa.' *MARC Newsletter* no.94–4, December 1994, 4.

_____. 'The Water Suite.' *MARC Newsletter,* December 1997, 3.

Nassar, Waleed. 'Ten Hindrances to Reaching Muslims.' *Ministries Today*, July/August 1994, 80.

Nelson, Craig. 'Deadly fields set to bloom.' *Age* (Melbourne), 26 December 2001, 10.

New Day, September 1996, 32.

'New Evidence.' September/October, 1994.

New Life (Melbourne), 1994.

Newsweek, 1 July 1997, 87.

'Nigerian Baptists Celebrate 150 Years', *Victorian Baptist Witness*, June 2000, 9.

'Nigerian Churches Face Shariah.' *Voice of the Martyrs*, Special Edition 1998.

'No Church in the Middle East by 2040.' *Barnabas*, Winter 1999-2000, 4.

'No justice for Egyptian Copts.' *The Voice of the Martyrs*, February 1999, 6.

'Notebook.' *Time*, 21 June 1999, 17.

'North American Muslims Rise to Prominence.' *Religious Freedom Today Digest*, January 1999, 11.

Oberg, Kalervo. 'Culture Shock: Adjustment to New Cultural Environments.' July – Occasional Paper No.28, 1996, 14.

O'Donoghoe, Michelle. 'Kazakhstan: Changed Lives,' *Missions Update*, October/December 1997.

Ogden, Christopher. 'Central Asia: The Next Crisis.' *Time*, 16 December 1991, 18.

O'Kane, Maggie. 'The Invisible Martyr.' *Good Weekend*, 15 August 1998, 33.

Okite, Odhiambo. 'Muslim-Christian Riots Rock Nairobi.' *Christianity Today*, 8 January 2001, 33.

Olley, John. 'God Speaks our Language – A Look at Contextualisation.' *Vision*, August 1997, 13.

'One Person's Journey: Mina's Story,' *Shalom-Salam, The Pursuit of Peace in the Biblical Heart of the 10/40 Window*, nd., 10.

Ostling, Richard N. 'Americans Facing Towards Mecca.' *Time*, 23 May 1998, 59.

'Out of Ruins – the New Nations.' *ISIC Bulletin*, April/ May 1998, 7.

'Pakistan: A Nation Wide Movement Against Senators Opposing Shari'ah.' *Religious Freedom Today Digest*, February 1999, 9 –10.

'Pakistan – Cascade of Intolerance.' *ISIC Bulletin*, June/July 1998, 11.

'Pakistani Christians Angry.' The Victorian Baptist Witness, June 1998.

Paulson, Terry. 'God Is in Charge of Operations…but We Are All in Sales.' *Fuller Focus*, Fall 1999, 4.

'Pastor Daniel'. 'Be Brave and Go.' *Missions Update*, April/June 1998, 8–9.

Payne, James L. *Why Nations Arm*. Oxford: Basil Blackwell, 1989, 138–139.

Pearce, Tony. 'The Struggle for the Soul of Islam', *Light for the Last Days*, January 2002, 10 –11.

_____. 'The Assault on Israel', *Light for the Last Days Supplement*, April 2002.

Peck, Ron. 'Speaking on Behalf of Muslims.' *Intercede*, September/October 1998, 2.

Pegues, Beverley. 'I Took a Prayer Journey.' *The 10/40 Window Reporter*, Winter 1998, 2.

Penman, David. 'A Continuing Surprise.' *On Being*, November 1979, 11.

Permutter, Amos. 'Islam and Democracy Simply Aren't Compatible.' *Manila Bulletin,* January 1992.

Perry, Alex. 'Deadly Cargo', *Time*, October 1 2002, 45.

'Persecuting President Gets British Honour.' *Barnabas*, Winter 1998, 4.

'Persecution in 10 Countries,' *Victorian Baptist Witness*, June 2001, 13.

Pilger, John. 'Punishing the Innocent'. *Good Weekend*, 8 April 2000, 31.

'Prayer and Visions.' *Open Doors/Newsbrief,* April 1996, 4.

Prayer Link (Brisbane), Vol.4/1, January 1997.

'Prayer the Greatest Thing.' *Australia's New Day*, April 1983, 40.

'Pray for Nazareth Christians', *Victorian Baptist Witness*, June 1999, 20.

Price, Clive. 'How the Irish Saved our Souls.' *Compass*, May 1998, 22.

'Protestants Collect Money for Mosque.' *New Life*, 16 April, 1992.

'Punished for Caring'. *Open Doors*, April 2000, 4–5.

'Putting Down Roots.' *Barnabas*, Summer 1999, 6.

'Queen Esther Walks the Streets of Tehran.' *Elam News*, Winter 1998,1.

'Ramadan. The Fourth Pillar of Islam,' *Thirty Days Muslim Prayer Focus*, 1996.

Reaching Out in Love. Springfield, Missouri: Assemblies of God.

Rebiai, Marcel. 'Muslim Evangelism and Jew-Arab Reconciliation – Jerusalem.' *Prayer for Israel-New Zealand,* January/ February 1994, 3.

'Reconciliation Walk Softens Muslim Memories of Crusades.' *PULSE*, May 16, 1997, 4

Religious Freedom Today, February 1999, 2.

'Religious Liberty and the Islamic Fundamentalists.' *The National Alliance Magazine*, October 1996.

'Religious Strife Growing.' *Victorian Baptist Witness*, June 1997.

'Religious War Possible in Nigeria.' *Victorian Baptist Witness*, April 2000, 6.

Revival World Report, May-June 1999, 6.

Richards, Wesley. 'The Challenge of Islam.' *Restoration,* March/April 1991.

Riminton, Hugh. 'Slaves of Sudan.' *Good Weekend*, 7 August 1999, 52.

Ro, Bong Rin. 'Communicating the Concept of God to the Korean Culture.' *Korean Torch*, 7.

Robinson, Mark. 'Ministering to Muslims', *Leadership NOW!* January 2002, 18.

Ron Peck. 'Speaking on Behalf of Muslims.' *Intercede*, November/December 1998, 2.

Scotland, Alan. 'Kingdoms in Conflict.' *Restoration*, March/April 1991.

Scott-Clark, Cathy and Adrian Levy, 'Pakistan's War on Christians' Sunday Times

Magazine, 24 January 1999 quoted in *Readers Digest*, April 2000, 117.

'Shooting or Voting for Islam.' *The Economist* (London), 21 August 1993.

Scudder, L.R. 'The First Conference of Catholic Patriarchs and Bishops in the Middle East'. *MECC News Report*, Summer/Autumn 1999, 36–37.

Sellers, Jeff M. 'How to Confront a Theocracy', *Christianity Today*, July 2002, 34.

'Shariah Law Spreading to South West Nigeria', *BFS Overseas*, 4 May 2002, 1.

Shaheeni, Teymour. 'The Church in Iraq: Her Past, Her Present, Her Future', Elam Review, 26–37.

Smith, Robert. 'Pakistan, Land of Opportunity.' Red Sea Team International, September 1997, 2,3.

Smith, Yusef. 'The Quran (A Christian Apologetic).' *Ninety-nine Truth Papers*.

Hyde Park Christian Fellowship, June 24, 1995.

'Soldiers Butcher Christians in Sudan.' *The Victorian Baptist Witness*, May 1998.

'Something New out of Africa.' *The Economist*, 16 July 1994, 41.

Sookhdeo, Patrick. 'Issues in Contextualisation.' *World Evangelisation*, September/October 1997, 5–6.

_____. 'Cry Justice' *Barnabas Magazine*, October-November 2002, 2.

'South Africa: Islamic Groups Promise Upheaval as Muslim Protester Dies of Injury.' *Religious Freedom Today Digest*, February 1999, 3.

Stacey, Vivienne 'Practical Lessons for Evangelism among Muslims.' *Interserve*, 1998, 10.

_____. 'The Practice of Exorcism and Healing.' Muslims and Christians on the Emmaus Road, Ed. By J.Dudley Woodbury, MARC, 1989, 292.

'Statistics of churches destruction in Indonesia.' *ISIC Bulletin*, June /July 1998, 8.

Stettan, Tom. 'Story Telling Why Do It?' *Mission Frontiers Bulletin*, March–April 1997, 11.

Stevens, John. 'More Prayers from Followers of Islam.' *Hume Observer*, October 8 1997.

Strength, Janice Morgan. 'Lessons from Russia Regarding Spirituality,' *Theology News and Notes*, Fuller Theological Seminary, 1999.

'Sudan: Annihilation of the Nuba.' *IISIC Bulletin*, October/ November 1995.

'Sudan Bombs a Hospital Again.' *Victorian Baptist Witness*, April 2000, 2.

'Sudan Nightmare Continues.' *Prayer Link*, May 1997, 7.

'Suicide Saved.' *Elam News* Third Quarter, 1998, 1.

'Sweden.' *Intercede*, May/June 1999, 3.

'Tajikistan Miracle.' *Victorian Baptist Witness*, March 1998, 19.

'Taking the Blame.' *The Economist*, February 28, 1998.

'Taliban will kill new converts.' World Evangelical Fellowship's Religious Liberty E-mail; quoted in *Victorian Baptist Witness*, March 2001, 21.

Tapia, Andres. 'Churches Wary of Inner City Islamic Inroads.' *Christianity Today*, 10 January 1998.

Taylor, Charles. 'Cultural Relativity.' *New Day*, November 1996, 29.

'Testimony of a Martyr?' *Intercede*, May/April 1998, 6.

'The Americans New Pilgrims.' *Asiaweek*, 23 February 1990, 34.

The Australian Baptist, 28 August 1988.

'The Call of Islam.' *The Economist*, 21 August 1993.

'The Challenge of Islam.' *Compass Direct*, 23 April 1996.

The Church in the Muslim World Update, Nigeria, January 1999.

'The Danger of Fat Hearts.' *The Voice of the Martyrs*, October 1994, 12.

'The Middle East or the Heart of Islam.' *The Lausanne Letter*, No.2 October 1990, 2.

'The Night of Power.' *Thirty Days Muslim Prayer Focus*, 1996.

'The Objectives of Islamic Mission.' *Islam*, 1987, 7.

'The Presence of Islam in Africa and the Challenges it Poses to Religious Liberty (Part 1).' *IISIC Bulletin*, December 1995/January 1996.

'The Presence of Islam in Africa and the Challenges it Poses to Religious Liberty (Part 2).' *IISIC Bulletin*, February/March 1996.

'The Reason.' *Prayerlink*, No.3, August 1997, 2.

'The State Department's Terror List.' *Terrorism & Security Monitor*, November 1999, 4–5.

'The Sword of Love.' *SIM. Now*, September/October 1989, 11.

'The Town Where Jesus Grew Up.' *Religious Freedom Today Digest*, February 1999, 6.

The Victorian Baptist Witness, September 1996, 9.

The Victorian Baptist Witness, April 2000, 18.

The Voice of the Martyrs, July 1994, 4.

The Voice of the Martyrs, Special Edition 1998, 19.

Thirty Days of Focussed Prayer for the Muslim World, Ashgrove, Queensland: Youth With a Mission, February 20–March 23, 1993.

'Tragedy in the Making.' *ISIC Bulletin*, June /July 1998, 4.

'Truth and Innocence are not Enough.' *ISIC Bulletin*, August / September 1997.

Turner, Kevin. 'Sudan: Hope in the Midst of Tragedy.' *Voice of the Martyrs*, 1997.

'24 Baptised.' *Elam News*, 1st Quarter 2001, 1.

'Two Lies Don't Make a Truth', *ISIC Bulletin*, June /July 1998, 2.

'Ugly Algeria.' *The Economist*, 16 July 1994, 18.

Underwood, Anne, Donna Foote, Claudia Kalb and Brad Stone, 'Islam God Listening?' Newsweek (Australian Edition), 1 April 1997, 63.

'Unreached Peoples Profile.' *Intercede*, March 1990, 7.

'Uproar in Malaysia', *The Voice of the Martyrs*, April 1998.

Victorian Baptist Witness, December 1992.

Victorian Baptist Witness, July 1996.

Victorian Baptist Witness, March 2001, 18.

Wackett, Jim. 'Sudan on the Brink.' *World Vision News*, May 1998, 7.

Wagner Jr., Clarence H. 'Between a Rock and a Holy Site.' *Christianity Today*, February 5 2001, 63.

'Waiting for a Friend Like You.' *Report Operation Mobilisation*, June 1994, 1.

Walker, Chris. 'Struggling under Oppression.' *On Being* , October 1993.

Wark, Andrew. 'Islam the Future of the Malaysian Church at Risk?' *New Life*, 21

Webb, Allen. 'How to Share Your Faith with a Muslim.' *East Asia's Millions*, 4ᵗʰ Quarter, 1998, 3.

'Weddings and Funerals for the Martyrs.' *ISIC Bulletin*, October/November 1996, 6.

'Western Converts to Islam.' *ISIC Bulletin*, December 1996/January 1997, 10.

Weymouth, Lally. 'Barak: Die or Separate.' *Newsweek*, 24 July 2001, 80–81.

Whayo, Cedric. 'Supporting Ministry to the Muslims.' Sovereign World Trust Annual Report, December 1994.

White, Charles Edward. 'Teaching Mark's Gospel to Muslims.' *Christianity Today*, February 8 1993, 39.

Whitehead, Briar. 'Tools you Can Trust.' *Go*, Third quarter 1997, 2–4.

Whitehouse, Aubrey. 'Some Faiths We Encounter, Islam,' *Mission Scene*, n.d.

'Will Shari'a Law Curb Christianity?' *Christianity Today*, October 23 2000, 24.

'Why did his monarchy cease?' *Witness*, June 2002, 3.

'Why Won't We Help the Sudan.' *The Victorian Baptist Witness,* June 1995.

Winter, Ralph D. 'Unreached Peoples Update Where Are We Now?' *World Evangelisation*, March/April 1988, 12.

Woodberry, Dudley. 'New Hope for Muslim Evangelism.' *Fuller Focus*, Summer 1996.

Wooding, Dan. 'Islam Declares 'Holy War' on Africa.' *New Life*, September 1990.

_____. 'Opening Doors to the Islamic World.' *Assist Communications*, March 19 1999, 2.

'World Watch, Nazareth.' *Time*, April 19 1999,24.

'Worries about Islam.' *The Economist*, 21 February 1998, 28.

Wurmbrand, Richard. 'Saudis Will have the Word of God.' *Voice of the Martyrs*, January 1991, 2.

Zakaria, Fareed. 'The Roots of Rage.' *Newsweek*, 16 October 2001, 62.

_____.'Look East for the Answer', *Newsweek*, 5 November 2002, 73.

Newspapers

Abdullah, Iqbal Ali. 'Yemen Kidnapper Tells of Plan to Kill', *Age* (Melbourne), 15 January 1999.

Adulmohaymen, A. M. 'Down with the Satanic Bush Order.' *Hong Kong Muslim Herald*, April 1992, 2.

Age (Melbourne), 6 January 1992.

Age (Melbourne) Today Life and Times, 26 April 2000, 7.

Ahmad, Zainon. 'Turabi's approach to a Better Sudan.' *New Straits Times* (Kuala Lumpur), 22 January 1994, 10.

Ahmed, Munier. 'Faithful Sees Bishop's Body.' *Sunday Age* (Melbourne), 10 May 1998.

Al-Naggar, Abdallah. *Al-Gumhurya* (Cairo), 7 October 2001.

'Are Easter eggs next?', *Sydney Morning Herald*, April 2003

Ata, Abe. 'The forgotten Christians of the Holy Land.' *Age* (Melbourne), 25 December 2001, 8.

Baker, Mark. 'The Zealots who Crushed Kabul.' *Age* (Melbourne), September 1996, A24.

_____. 'Israel and me', *Age Agenda* (Melbourne), 28 April 2002, 4

Bearak, Barry. 'The Taliban just says no in heroin's heartland,' The New York Times, quoted in *Age* (Melbourne), 12 June 2001, 17.

Bidinost, Marcella. 'A debt of love', *Sunday Age* (Melbourne), February 9 2003, 10.

Bolt, Andrew, 'Islam's deadly truth', *Herald Sun*, March 28 2002, 19.

Bonger, Julian. 'Arabs in US Vent Fury at Film about Islamist Terror.' *Guardian*, November 7, 18.

Boudreax, Richard. 'Khatami's Exit Terminates Dialogue.' *Age* (Melbourne),12 March 1999, 9.

Burns, John F. 'Bin Laden Stirs Struggle on Meaning of Jihad.' *International New York Times*, 27 January 2002, 2.

Butcher, Tim. 'Despite legal setback, fundamentalists march on.' *Age* (Melbourne), 27 March 2002, 13.

Callaghan, Greg. 'The Man behind the Mosque', *Weekend Australia Magazine*, September 14–15 2002, 18.

'Church blasts rock Indonesia, Aceh introduces sharia law', *Age* (Melbourne), 2 January 2002, 10.

Cipress, Alan. 'The Arab Connection', *Age* (Melbourne), January 11 2003.

Clemans, Miles. 'Flashback to Intolerance.' *Australian*, 22 May 1998.

Colebatch, Tim. 'Malaysia's call to condemn attacks on civilians as terrorism finds no support.' *Age* (Melbourne), 4 April 2002, 9.

Coleman, Peter. 'Export or Die', *The Australian Weekend*, March 8–9 2003.

Crossette, Barbara. 'Arab Nations repressed, says report'. New York Times in *Age* (Melbourne), 3 July 2002, 7.

Dalrymple, William. 'Demolition of an Ancient Culture.' *Age Extra* (Melbourne), 22 April 1989, 3.

Daly, Martin. 'Minister in Row over Wine, Religion and Song.' *Age* (Melbourne), 17 February 1993.

Davies, Karin. 'The Price of Freedom in Sudan: $1.48.' *Age* (Melbourne), 21 February 1998, World, 21.

Day, Phillip. 'Bankers have faith in Islam', *The Australian Financial Review*, March 13 2003.

Denyer, Simon. '2,035 Slaves Freed for A$ 75 Each.' *Age* (Melbourne), 10 July 1999, 27.

Dobbs, Michael. 'The Unknown Enemy.' Washington Post quoted in *Sunday Age*, 4 April 1999, 4.

Duin, Julia. 'Daring Leaps of Faith', *The Washington Times*, New York, October 12 2002.

Dunn, Ross 'New plots for Jews spark outrage', *Age* (Melbourne), April 11 2001.

Duran, Khalid. *Age* (Melbourne), 18 December 2001, 9.

Egan, Colleen. 'The Insider', *Weekend Australian*, November 23–24 2002, 22.

Finlay, Sally. 'Violent Home Raid in Quest for Kosovo Recruits, Court Told.' *Age* (Melbourne), 30 April 1999.

Flanagan, Martin. 'Careful, You Might Hear Us.' *Age* (Melbourne), 18 April 1998, E6.

Fleescher, Tzvi. 'How Arafat chose war over peace.' *Age* (Melbourne), October 24 2000.

Forbes, Mark. 'Australians were bombers' target'. *Age* (Melbourne), February 11 2003, 3.

Friedman, Thomas L. 'Why Iran needs Ayatollah Deng.' New York Times quoted in *Age* (Melbourne), 23 July 1999, 15.

Gibbs, Stephen and Moore, Matthew. 'Bashir's warning to Australians: you will be dragged into war', *Age* (Melbourne) December 13 2002, 1.

Gorman, Edward. 'Britain's Radical Muslims tell Gays to Mend their Ways.' *Australian*, 15 August 1995.

Gotenberg, Suzanne and Whitaker,Brian. 'Barak turns his back on peace effort, *Age* (Melbourne), October 24 2000, 11.

Griffith, Chris. 'Brunei injects $10m into UQ College.' *Courier Mail*, September 7 2000, 6.

Hafiz, M. Abdul, Brig (Rtd). 'The Self-defeating Politics of Religion.' *Daily Star* (Dhaka), 26 October 1998, 4.

Haas, Danielle. 'Suicide blast rocks Jerusalem.' *Age* (Melbourne), 28 January 2002, 6.

Hassan, Hashem. *Al-Quds Al-Arabi* (London), 7 October 2001.

Hirst, David .'Egypt's love-hate affair with bin Laden.' *Age* (Melbourne), 6 December 2001, 15.

Howes, Rachel. 'Mosque Takes on Council.' *Weekend Australian*, 13–14 February 1999.

Javed, Sofia. 'After 900 years it's not too late to say sorry.' *Age*, 17 July 1999, 20.

Khan, Mohammed. *Muslim News*. 28 June 1996.

'Kill Americans and Britons: Bin Laden.' *Age* (Melbourne), 26 December 1998.

La Guardia, Anton. 'The Promise of Paradise Makes a Suicide Bomber Tick.' *Age* (Melbourne), 2 August 1997.

Lane, Bernard. 'The devil is more real for Muslims', *The Australian*, July 8 2002, 3.

Lekakis, George. 'Islamic Super Fund Pioneered', The Australian Financial Review, August 15 2002..

Manilla Chronicle, 12 July 1989.

Masanauskas, John. 'Victorian Muslims to Launch Political Campaign.' *Age* (Melbourne), 10 December 1990.

_____. 'Council to Consider Islamic Centre.' *Age* (Melbourne), 23 May 1990.

McGeough, Paul. 'Iraq pays suicide bonus to entice new bombers.' *Age*, 26 March 2002, 11.

Moore, Matthew. 'Indonesia moves on prime suspect for Bali Bombing', *Age* (Melbourne), October 18 2002, 2.

Morris, Linda. 'Cleric "sowed seeds of Australian state"', *Sydney Morning Herald,* December 10 2002, 1.

Murray, James S. 'A Prayer for Pluralising.' *Weekend Australian*, 18/19 September 1993.

'Nigerian States Split over Islamic Code.' Age (Melbourne), 4 March 2000, 25.

O'Kane, Maggie. 'The Terror of the Warriors of Taliban.' *Age* (Melbourne), 28 September 1996, A25.

O'Loughlin, Ed. 'Hamas has stranglehold on Palestinian future', Age (Melbourne) 21 June 2003, 16.

Parkinson, Tony. 'Speech last roll of the dice for PLO leader.' *Age* (Melbourne), 16 December 2001, 1.

_____. 'We will fight until we run out of blood'. *Age* (Melbourne), October 15 2002, 13.

Paul, Anthony. 'Settle in for a long conflict', *Melbourne Courier*, November 3 2002, 7.

Pipes, Daniel. 'It Matters What Kind of Islam Prevails.' *Times* (Los Angeles), 22 July 1999.

Reid Alice. 'Mosque's Children Await Playground.' *Washington Post*, November 22, B4.

'Rebels Threaten Russians', *Australian*, 13 August 1999, 8.

Reuters, Vatican City, 'Blunt Attack on Islam at Vatican Synod', *Canberra Times*, October 15 1999, 9.

Ross, Dennis. 'Why Arafat must act.' *Age* (Melbourne), 16 December 2001, 17.

Rupert, James. 'Nigerian Military Gives Power to the People.' Washington Post quoted in *Age* (Melbourne), 31 May 1999, 12.

'Russians Enter Chechen Capital.' *Age* (Melbourne) 19 October 1999, 14.

Saltan, Chloe. 'One man's road from Damascus but where to from here?' *Age* (Melbourne), 16 June 2001, 1.

'Saudi Arabia: Fatwa for non-Mulsims'. *Al_Muslimoon*, Vol. 8, no 418, Riyadh, February 5 1993.

Schmidt, Lucinda. 'Bankers trust,' Money Manager, *Age* (Melbourne), November 18 2002, 8.

Skelton, Russell. 'Non-Muslims "stoned, abused and degraded" at Woomera', *Age* (Melbourne) , May 10 2002, 2.

_____. 'No escape from persecution', *Age* (Melbourne), May 10 2002, 13

Smiles, Sarah, 'Strangers in a strange land', *Sunday Age*, June 8 2003, 5.

'Spain Recognises Islam.' *Manilla Chronicle,* 16 July 1989.

Spetalnick, Matt. 'Poverty, rage fire terrorism martyrs', *Age* (Melbourne), 4 December 2001, 12.

'Splendour and Magnificence.' *Sydney Gazette,* 23 March 1806.

Stapleton, John. 'Zealots' quest for purity'. *The Australian,* November 19 2002, 13.

Stewart, Ian. 'GDP Fall puts Heat on Mahatir.' *Australian,* 1 June 1998, 7.

Stille, Alexander. 'Radical theories offered on origins of the Quran, *Star Tribune* (Minneappolis), March 10 2002, A21.

Strong, Geoff . 'Putting God in Check.' *Sunday Age* (Melbourne), 18 May 1997.

Suter, Keith. 'Cold War Returns, starring Islam', *Age,* 1 June 2000.

'Sudan Persecuted but not Forsaken.' *Christian Information Network,* Fall 1997.

Sullivan, Tim. 'Nigeria Backs Away From Islamic Law.' *Associated Press* (Abuja), February 29 2000.

'Terror "fontman" expelled', *Age* (Melbourne), October 29 2002, 1.

The Victorion Baptist Witness, July 2002, 18.

'Threats to kill Australians', *Herald Sun,* March 20 2003, 2.

'Turkey warns France on Armenian genocide bill,' *Karachi International News,* 2 November 2000.

'US, UK Envoys get Warnings.' *Age* (Melbourne), 8 March 1999.

Wagner Jr., Clarence H. 'Christianity Needs Israeli Sovereignty over Jerusalem', *Dispatch From Jerusalem,* 15.

Walker, Tony. 'Saddam: Most Dangerous Man in World.' *Age* Melbourne)*,* 25 June 1990, 11.

Walters, Patrick. 'West, Islam Clash on Human Rights, Democracy.' *Australian,* 1–2 April 1995, 16.

Wilkinson, Marian. 'Extremist's history leaves experts suspicious', *Age* (Melbourne), 9.

Wilkinson, Marian. 'Extremist's history leaves experts suspicious', *Bali News,* 9.

Williams, Louise. 'Food Scarce on Isle Racked by Violence.' *Age* (Melbourne), 13 March 1999, 23.

_____. 'Indonesian Ethnic Wars Hit New Low.' *Age* (Melbourne), 22 March 1999, 9.

_____. 'When Blood is War.' *Age* (Melbourne), 27 March 1999, 7.

'Wonder Boy Impresses Muslim and Jew Alike.' *Age* (Melbourne), 19 January 1998.

Wright, Robin. 'The Darling Son of Iran.' *Age News Extra* (Melbourne)*,* 30 May 1998, 12.

Zwartz, Barney, 'Koran added to VCE Studies for First Time', *Age* (Melbourne), February 13 2003, 3.

Electronic Documents

'Africa: Muslims See Visions, and House Churches are Started.' Fridayfax, 13 February 1998, 1.

Al-Gamei'a, Sheikh Muhammad. www.lilatalqadr.com, 4 October 2001.

Ali, Amir. 'Jihad Explained', Institute of Islamic Information & Education, www.themodernreligion.com/jihad/jihad-explained.html, November 11 2002.

Arutz-7. 'Getting to Know America's Saudi Allies', May 7 2002.

'A Wave of Conversion to Islam in the US Following September 11', thetruereligion.org, March 22 2003, 1.

Baker, Barbara G. Owner-Religious Liberty@xc.org. 8 May 1998.

'Calls for Jihad widespread in Islamic world', ibriefings@isic-centre.org, April 11 2003, 2.

'Church Destroyed' info@barnabasfund.org, November 21 2002.

'Christian Shot Dead', info@barnabasfund.org, February 25 2003.

'Christian Widow's Arrest is to be Enforced'.info@barnabasfund.org, April 15 2003, 1.

Colson, Charles. 'Radical Islam in American Prisons', BreakPointonline, March 3 2003, 1.

Duran, Khalid and Pipes, Daniel, 'Faces of American Islam', www.danielpipes.org, August/September 2002, 3–6.

'Ethiopia.' *Brigada-Orgs Missionmobilizers,* 27 November 1997 via e-mail.

Farah, Joseph. 'Are we at war with Islam?' WorldNetDaily.com, June 25 2002.

Ferrier, James A. *HCJB World Radio* e-mail, 27 April 1999.

'Forces Dimming The Light of the Crescent', www.islamicsydney.com, March 22 2003, 1.

Gaffney, Frank J. 'The fifth column syndrome', www.townhall.com, March 25 2003, 1.

'Goals, Principles and Strategy', *Nida'ul Islam Magazine*, September 2 2002, 2.

Hanafi, Khaled. 'Islamic Gold Dinar Will Minimize Dependency on U.S. Dollar', www.islamonline.net, March 4 2003.

ibriefings@isic-centre.org, October 15 2002, 1.

'Islamic Bodies in Australia', www.islam-australia.linet.au.

'Islamist Politicians and Church Attacks', info@barnabasfund.org, February 4 2003, 1.

'Israel', *Brigada-Orgs Missionmobilizers*, 27 November 1997 via e-mail.

ISIC Briefing, September 10 2002, 2.

ISIC Briefing, December 23 2002.

'Jihad Threatened if Muslim Demands Are Not Met'. info@barnabasfund.org, April 30 2003.

Kendall, Elizabeth. 'Ivory Coast - Serious Situation', www.christiansincrisis.net, December 4 2002.

Khan, M.a. Muqtedar. 'An Executive Summary of Milestones by Sayyid Qutb', www.youngmuslims.ca/online_library/books/milestones/freshlook.asp, April 2 2003, 1.

'Laskar Jihad alive and will in Papua', info@barnabasfund.org, March 5 2003.

Littman, David G. 'Human Rights and Human Wrongs', www.nationalreview.com/comment/comment-littman011903.asp, January 19 2003.

Majidi, Nassim and Passariello, Christina. 'France Gives Its Muslims a Voice', *BusinessWeek online*, March 27 2003, 2.

Muslim Business Register, www.icv.org.au, November 23 2002, 1.

'Muslims Coming to Christ.' *Dawn Fridayfax*, 1997/46 via e-mail.

Pipes, Daniel and Hedegaard, Lars. 'Muslim extremism: Denmark's had enough', www.nationalpost.com, August 2002.

Pipes, Daniel. 'American Muslims vs. American Jews', www.danielpipes.org, December 24 2002, 3.

Pipes, Daniel. 'PBS, Recruiting for Islam', *New York Post*, December 17 2002.

Rauf, Abdur. 'Islam Enlightens Australia', www.renaissance.com.pk

The Holy Land, www.barnabasfund.org, 5 March 2002.

The Jews: 'Enemies of Allah, descendants of Pigs and Apes.' ibriefings@isic-centre.org, November 5 2002, 1.

The Message of the Prophet to the Omani People. www.answering-islam.org/Muhammed/oman.htm.

Thomas, George. 'Hyde Park Preacher Debate - Witnesses to Radical Muslims', *CBN News*, March 19 2003, 3.

'Twelve Killed in Student Riot', info@barnabasfund.org, October 15 2002, 1.

Siemon-Netto, Uwe. 'Scholar warns West of Muslim Goals.' www.upi.com/view, 22 June 2002.

Shehzad, Waseem. 'American companies feeling the impact of Muslim boycotts', Crescent International, Toronto, February 1 2003.

Stringer, Col. 'Persecution Iraq', May 22 2003, 1.

'United Prayer Track.' *Fridayfax*, Volume 98, No. 5 13 February, 1998.

'US Public Schools Embrace Islam', www.assist-ministries.com, February 2002.

Warraq, Ibn. Statement by Ibn Warraq on the World Trade Centre Atrocity, Institute for the Secularisation of Islamic Society, www.secularislam.org/wtc.htm.

WEF Religious Liberty e-mail Conference, 26 May 1998.

Weyrich, Paul M. 'Wake Up! Islam is About More Than Hate Crimes'. CNSNews.com Commentary, January 29 2003.

www.isnacanada.com, April 26 2003, 2.

www.news.bbc.co.uk/1/hi/world/south_asia, February 16 2002.

Ye'or, Bat. 'European Fears of the Gathering Jihad', FrontPageMagazine.com, February 21 2003, 2.

Documents

A Manual Mahaber (The Jesus Association) and the Orthodox Church, The Horn of Africa Challenge and Opportunity. *AD 2000 and Beyond Movement*, n.d., 7, 8.

Antonelli, Maurice. *Go Global*, n.d., 2.

Blaxland, Greg and Judy. *Operation Abba Inc. Newsletter*, May 2000, 1.

Brickner, David. 'Just War?' Jews for Jesus, 2001.

Caner, Emir R and Ergun M. 'The Doctrine of Jihad in the Islamic Hadith', Evangelical Society, Colorado Springs, Colorado, November 15 2001, 7–8.

Davies, Helen Beth. *The Bible and Quran compared and contrasted in terms of Christian and Muslim claims as to their status as the Word of God*, unpublished paper 1991.

Durie, Mark. *'Isa, the Muslim Jesus*. Unpublished manuscript, 5.

Hyasom, Albert M. ed. *The British Consulate in Jerusalem in Relation to the Jews of Palestine*, 1938–1913 (London, 1939).

Islamic Affairs Analyst, *Intelligence International*, n.d., 3.

Lausanne Committee for World Evangelisation, Ministry in Islamic Contexts,

International Institute for the Study of Islam and Christianity, *Occasional Pap*er no. 28, 1996, 14.

Memo, *The Quarterly Newsletter of Middle East Media*, Number 75. 1997/2, 1.

Muluzi, E. Bakhi of Malawi. Letter to Col. Muammar Gadaffi, President of Libya, F/SNJ 32/135, 4 May 1999.

Name Withheld. 'Hope for Christians in War-torn Sudan', April 2000.

Newsletter, *Good Shepherd Ministries International*, June 1992, 1.

Perkins Jr., Raymond. *Prayer for Israel,* New Zealand, No. 71 July–August 1993, 1.

Religious Survey-7, 90-96AD Narsingdi Zone-9, Islamic Missionary Counsel of Bangladesh, 2.

Robinson, Mark. 'Pentecostal power among Pancasila People', unpublished paper, 2001.

Schwartz, Stephen. 'The Real Islam', Atlantic Unbound, March 20 2003, 7.

Television/Radio

Campbell, Eric in Tora Bora for Australian Broadcasting Commission TV 7.30 Report, 19 December 2001.

SBS Broadcasting, 5 December 2001.

INDEX